D1242303

Social History of Africa

MAKING THE TOWN

MAKING THE TOWN

GA STATE AND SOCIETY
IN EARLY COLONIAL ACCRA

John Parker

HEINEMANN
Portsmouth, NH

JAMES CURREY
Oxford

DAVID PHILIP
Cape Town

Heinemann
A division of Reed Elsevier Inc.
361 Hanover Street
Portsmouth, NH 03801-3912
USA
www.heinemann.com

James Currey Ltd.
73 Botley Road
Oxford OX2 0BS
United Kingdom

David Philip Publishers (Pty) Ltd.
208 Werdmuller Centre
Claremont 7708
Cape Town, South Africa

Offices and agents throughout the world

ISBN 0-325-00191-X (Heinemann cloth)
ISBN 0-325-00190-1 (Heinemann paper)
ISBN 0-85255-693-4 (James Currey cloth)
ISBN 0-85255-643-8 (James Currey paper)

British Library Cataloguing in Publication Data is available

Library of Congress Cataloging-in-Publication Data

Parker, John, 1960–
     Making the town : Ga state and society in early Colonial Accra / John Parker.
        p.   cm.—(Social history of Africa, ISSN 1099-8098)
     Includes bibliographical references and index.
     ISBN 0-325-00191-X (alk. paper)—ISBN 0-325-00190-1 (pbk. : alk. paper)
        1. Accra (Ghana)—Politics and government—19th century. 2. Gä (African people)—Ghana—Accra—Politics and government—19th century. I. Title. II. Series.

     DT512.9.A3 P37 2000
     966.7—dc21   00-025969

Printed in the United States of America on acid-free paper.

04 03 02 01 00 SB 1 2 3 4 5 6 7 8 9

CONTENTS

ILLUSTRATIONS

PREFACE

The Ga people of Accra have an old saying: *Ga se gbe ji gbe*. Literally, it means "The way of the Ga, that is the way." It was first written down in the 1850s by a missionary of the Basel Mission, who noted that it alluded to the fact that the Ga townsfolk considered themselves a "leading people." *Ga se gbe ji gbe* can also be translated as "All roads lead to Accra," and it is likely that it was in this sense that it was adopted by the Accra Town Council during the colonial period as the official motto of the city. In common with other Ghanaian proverbs that reflect on the meanings of culture, this maxim neatly encapsulates a range of theoretical ideas that have long been of concern to Western-trained social scientists and historians. In this case, the ideas are about the nature of "the urban" and the function of the city as a site of exchange, transaction, and power. The notion that "all roads lead to Accra" also captures the essence of my own relationship with the city and with this study over much of the past decade.

This book is a revised version of my Ph.D. thesis, "Ga State and Society in early colonial Accra, 1860s–1920s," submitted to the School of Oriental and African Studies in London in 1995. The thesis was completed under the supervision of Richard Rathbone, and it is to him that I owe the greatest of intellectual and personal debts. As a teacher, a friend, and a colleague, he has been a constant source of inspiration since I embarked on the study of Ghanaian history in 1991. It was during our long walks through the old quarters of Accra in the summer of that year that this project began to take shape. I would also like to acknowledge the help and support of David Anderson, Gareth Austin, Gail Beuschel, Alistair Chisolm, William Gervase Clarence-Smith, David Killingray, Tom McCaskie, John Peel, Andrew Roberts, and Larry Yarak. In Basel, Paul Jenkins has been an enormous help in guiding me through the superb collection of photographs at the Basel Mission Archive. Thanks also to Michael Chollet for his assistance in the preparation of many of the images that illustrate these pages.

In Ghana, my deepest gratitude goes to Eric Twum Barimah and Akua Karikari, the most generous of hosts during my long stay in Accra in 1992–1993. I am equally indebted to Mrs. Emily Asiedu for the kind hospitality she has offered on subsequent research visits. Of the many other Ghanaians to whom I owe so much, Kofi and Olivia Baku, A. S. Hamidu, Sydney Heward-Mills, and Samuel S. Quarcoopome deserve special mention. So too does my good friend Seth Ansah Kwapong of "The People's Choice." I would also like to thank the many Ga people of James Town, Ussher Town, and Osu who have given me their time, help, friendship, and assistance. I owe a particular debt to those who so generously invited me into their midst to celebrate the annual *Homowo* festival: in 1991, the Golightly family of Palladium Down; in 1992, Sydney Heward-Mills and the Ankra family of Otublohum; and in 1996, the Akanmaji *mantse* Nii Ayikai and his household. Thank you also to members of the Kpakpatsewe family in both London and Accra. I would also like to acknowledge the Nleshi Alata *mantse* Kojo Ababio V and his councillors, who invited me to observe the James Town *odwira* celebrations during the *Homowo* of 1996. A huge debt is also owed to the staff of the National Archives of Ghana, many of whom have assisted me over the years with great patience and courtesy. I would especially like to mention Edith Wood, Frank Ablorh, Joseph Anim-Asante, Felix Ampong, and Thelma Ewusie.

Jean Allman and Peter Haenger have provided friendship, inspiration, and enthusiasm for all things Ghanaian that transcend the scope of this work. Thanks too to Sonia Abun-Nasr. I am also hugely indebted to David Henderson-Quartey, from whom I have obtained innumerable insights in the course of our long discussions on the Ga past in both London and Accra. Finally, a special thank you to Berit Vinegrad and Rosalind Vinegrad, whose initial generosity got me started and made all this possible.

ABBREVIATIONS

ARPS	Gold Coast Aborigines' Rights Protection Society
ATC	Accra Town Council
BMA	Basel Mission Archive, Basel, Switzerland
CC	Civil Commandant, Accra
CEP	Commissioner for the Eastern Province
CJ	Chief Justice
CLO	Compulsory Labour Ordinance, 1895
CS	Colonial Secretary
DC	District Commissioner, Accra
Div. Court	Accra Divisional Court Civil Record Book
FC	Furley Collection of translations, Balme Library, University of Ghana, Legon
GCC	Gold Coast Correspondence, WMMS
GS	General Secretaries, WMMS
IAS	Institute of African Studies, University of Ghana, Legon
JAH	*Journal of African History*
JAS	*Journal of the African Society*
LTR	Land Title Registry, Accra
MCO	Municipal Corporations Ordinance, 1924
NAG	National Archives of Ghana, Accra

NAO	Native Administration Ordinance, 1927
NCBWA	National Congress of British West Africa
NJO	Native Jurisdiction Ordinance, 1883
PP	Great Britain Parliamentary Papers
PRO	Public Record Office, London
QA	Queen's Advocate
RCS	Royal Commonwealth Society Library, London
SNA	Secretary for Native Affairs
THSG	*Transactions of the Historical Society of Ghana*
WMMS	Wesleyan Methodist Missionary Society Archive, London

GLOSSARY OF GA WORDS

abeboo shia   ancestral house

agbamei   body of religious functionaries or cult members

agbonaa   traditional compound house

aklabatsa   sacred tree grove, fence around a shrine

aklowa (pl. *aklowai*)   village

akon (Twi *akom*)   religious cult of Akan origin

akpakai   palanquin

akutso (pl. *akutsei*)   town quarter

akwashon   court comprising representative from each *akutso*

akwashon onukpa   member of *akwashon* court

akwashontse   head of *akwashon* court and Ga military commander

anobulo (pl. *anobua*)   councillor

asafo (pl. *asafoi*)   military company

asafoatse (pl. *asafoatsemei*)   captain of an *asafo*

asafobii   members of an *asafo*

asayere   ritual dances performed by women during wartime

blohun   street, urban neighborhood

caboceer (Portuguese *cabeceiro*)   headman

dadefoi   musicians who play for *woyei*

fa (pl. *fajii*)   lagoon

Ga mashi   original Ga settlers, Ga of Kinka and Nleshi

Ganyo kron   "pure" or "true" Ga person

gbatsu (pl. *gbatsui*)   shrine

gbo (pl. *gboi*)   stranger, guest

hewale   strength, power, authority

Homowo   the great annual Ga festival

jase (Twi *gyase*)   household of an officeholder

jemawon (*jemawojii*)   "god of the world," tutelary deity

kose   country, bush

kosenyo (pl. *kosebii*)   country person, farmer, rustic

kpabu (pl. *kpabui*)   prison

kpakpa   good, brave, virtuous

kple   indigenous Ga religious cult

man (pl. *majii*)   town, state

manbii   townspeople, citizens

mankralo   office in towns from Osu to Tema subordinate to *mantse*

manso   town strife, civil war

mantse (pl. *mantsemei*)   "father of the town": leading officeholder in each town and in each *akutso* of Kinka and Nleshi

me   religious cult of Dangme origin

mo din sane   "black man's palaver," "African affairs"

Mojawe   *Ga mantse*'s court of appeal, lit. "house of blood"

niiatse (pl. *niiatsemei*)   richman, q.v. *sikatse*

nmo (pl. *nmojii*)   farm

no-he ke won   to attach oneself to a shrine as a *wonwebi*

nshonaman (pl. *nshonamajii*)   seaside town

nyon (pl. *nyojii*)   slave

oblahii   youngmen, nontitled "commoners"

oblempon (Twi *obirempon*)   richman, honorary stool holder

odonko (pl. *odonkofo*; Twi *nnonkofoo*)   slave of northern origin

omanhene (pl. *amanhene*) [Twi]   Akan chief

onukpa (pl. *onukpai*)   elder, senior, headman

oshi   dance performed during *Homowo*

otsiami (Twi *okyeame*)   "linguist," spokesman

owula (pl. *owulai*) [Twi *wura*]   honorific title, master, gentleman

sei   stool

shia   house

shiabii   household members, domestic slaves

shiatse   household head

shipi   military commander

sika (Twi)   money, gold

sikatse (pl. *sikatsemei*)   richman, q.v. *niiatse*

sobii   country people who come into Accra on "*Homowo* Thursday"

tabilo (pl. *tabiloi*)   warrior

tsofatse   healer or doctor, lit. "father of tree roots"

tsulo (pl. *tsuloi*)   servant, slave

we (pl. *wei*)   lineage, family, house

webii   members of a lineage or house

wonbi (pl. *wonbii*)   person dedicated as a child to a deity

wonwebii   slaves attached to a shrine, q.v. *no-he ke won*

wontse   healer, "medicine man"

woyo (pl. *woyei*)   medium—usually female

wulomo (pl. *wulomei*)   ritual specialist, "priest"

INTRODUCTION:
MAKING THE TOWN

"God made the country, and man made the town."[1]

Mokome efee man.
(One person does not make a town).[2]

This book is the history of an African urban community, the Ga people
of Accra, Ghana. Its focus is town politics from the 1860s to the 1920s,
and in particular the ways in which Ga political action shaped Accra's
transition from precolonial city-state to colonial city. The Ga have a long
history of urbanism, so this period of transition is not about the creation
of new urban identities and institutions but the reconfiguration of old
ones. Accra emerged in the seventeenth century as one of the many trading entrepôts on the Gold Coast of West Africa that served as links between the expanding Atlantic economy and the African interior. By the
beginning of the eighteenth century, the three townships that together
constituted Accra were the political, economic, and sacral epicenter of
Ga state and society. For the next two hundred years, local leaders competed with powerful African neighbors, with European trading forts, and
with each other for jurisdiction over the town and for a share of its mercantile wealth. A new phase in this contest opened in the mid-nineteenth
century, as the British consolidated their position as the dominant coastal
power. In 1877, Accra became the headquarters of the newly created
Crown Colony of the Gold Coast. Eighty years later, in 1957, it emerged
from colonial rule as the capital of tropical Africa's first independent
nation-state, the symbolic urban headquarters of the African liberation
struggle. In Ghana's last census, in 1984, the population of Accra was
recorded as 859,600. At the beginning of the twenty-first century, Accra
remains the most important site of exchange, transaction, and power in

Ghana. With a current population perhaps approaching two million, it is one of West Africa's largest cities.

The early colonial period forms a crucial hinge in this long urban history. The detailed arguments of this book rest on two fundamental observations about Ga state and society in the late-nineteenth and early-twentieth centuries. First, despite the dominance of chronologies of change, the transformation of Accra was characterized by a striking continuity of precolonial forms. Second, Ga townsmen and women played an active role in (re)making the colonial city. It has often been assumed that colonial cities were built largely in spite of, rather than in active dialogue with, any vestiges of indigenous urbanism. This was not the case in Accra. Far from being marginalized by colonial power and the processes of urbanization, Ga townspeople struggled with outside forces and with each other to retain control over the center of their urban civilization. Their story contributes to a better understanding of Africa's urban past, and in particular to the history of the reconfiguration of established precolonial African cities under colonial rule.

Throughout its history, Accra has been a quintessential "middleman" state, its inhabitants mediating a variety of transactions across geographical, political, and cultural frontiers.[3] Like the city and the people with which it is concerned, this is a study that straddles established boundaries. The most obvious of these boundaries is temporal: the well-entrenched scholarly borderline between precolonial and colonial African history. By bridging the era of informal imperialism of the mid-nineteenth century and the heyday of direct colonial control in the interwar years, this book attempts to move away from the tendency to consider the transition to colonialism in Africa as a sudden leap from one structural state to another.[4] As such it contributes to the renegotiation of conventional chronological divisions in colonial history, and in particular the history of the hybrid coastal enclaves of nineteenth-century West Africa.[5] The point at which the Ga themselves began to perceive their long encounter with Europeans as having become a situation of colonial subjugation is difficult to discern, the rise of British rule on the Gold Coast being characterized by subtle continuities and discontinuities rather than abrupt rupture. To define the six decades from the late 1860s to the 1920s as Accra's "early colonial period" is therefore not to privilege colonialism as the only force shaping the lives of its inhabitants. While the chronological framework of this study is defined by shifts in the nature of colonial control, the aim is to reconstruct the inner workings of an indigenous core community for which colonial rule was but one—albeit important—thread in the fabric of urban life.

This leads to a second duality in the study of the African past, which is challenged by a closer examination of Accra's historical evolution: the lingering tendency to draw a distinction between indigenous and European forms of urbanism. This binary formulation, which contrasts new, rapidly growing cities with established, precolonial urban centers, first appeared in Southall's pioneering schema of 1961.[6] Although typologies have subsequently became more refined, the divide between the essentially "African" city on the one hand and the essentially "colonial" city on the other continues to recur.[7] Between the 1860s and the 1920s, Accra certainly acquired the attributes of a typical colonial port city, its built environment fashioned by the requirements of imperial control and the capitalist world economy. Yet it was also an established African town, the site of Ga social, political, military, and religious institutions. Since the seventeenth century, layer upon layer of historical accretions had fused into the distinctive urban culture of the Ga quarters. Accra was at once the headquarters of the new colonial order and the epicenter of an older Ga world. The tension between these two contrasting urban identities underlies the transformations of the early colonial period.

THE "URBAN PROBLEMATIQUE" AND AFRICAN HISTORY

One of the defining features of twentieth-century Africa has been the growth of cities and the accompanying transformations in urban life. Yet the study of the continent's towns and cities has barely begun to approach a thematically integrated view of the past. Historians have made only a limited impact on the interdisciplinary field of African urban studies. Rather than being concerned with the interaction of social, political, economic, and cultural forms in particular localities over time, research has been dominated by the social sciences and their emphasis on general process-models of urbanization.[8] Although archaeology has played an important role in revealing the diversity of Africa's urban past stretching back to ancient times, research overviews continue to make little mention of the historical antecedents of contemporary urbanism.[9] In a recent essay, pioneering urban geographer and theorist Akin Mabogunje stresses that the "urban problematique" in Africa "revolves around the issue of who shapes the city, in what image, by what means and against what resistance."[10] This issue arises from the interaction of a complex variety of forces, from global capitalism on the one hand to shifting domestic relationships within individual urban households on the other. Mabogunje's research agenda remains firmly focused on the contemporary city, yet his "problematique" can usefully be extrapolated back in time to provide an entry into the social and political history of African towns and cities. Indeed, the contested process of shaping the city emerges from the historical record as a central concern of the people of Accra in the early colonial period. Drawing on an indigenous Ga construction, I have termed this process "making the town." The use of the verb "to make" (Ga: *feê*) is deliberately ambiguous. It is meant to refer both to the essence or quality of a town and to the historical processes by which a town is constructed.

What does make a town? In common with the broader trajectory of urban history and urban sociology, the study of African cities has been dogged by problems of definition and generalization.[11] The need to define the essence of "the city" and "the urban" and to construct a broad model of change appeared especially acute in sub-Saharan Africa, where the development of scholarly research coincided with dramatic transformations in urban life and in the economic relationship between town and country. From the terminal phase of colonial rule onward, a succession of research paradigms have struggled to get to grips with the meanings and dynamics of African urbanism.

The identification of the African city as a distinct sociological entity and field of inquiry has its origins in the growing alarm among colonial officials with the rapidly changing urban environment in the interwar period. With the onset of the Depression of the 1930s, the most pressing problem in many territories was seen as one of asserting control over labor migration, which was beginning to swell urban populations and to challenge the colonial stereotype of a traditional Africa fixed in rural stasis. In burgeoning towns and cities across the continent, officials confronted what they perceived to be the disintegrative impact of "detribalization."[12] Scholarly research into the linked concerns of towns and workers was spearheaded by the Rhodes-Livingstone Institute in Northern Rhodesia, where migration to the mines of the Copperbelt had resulted in the rapid growth of new urban centers. The principal unit of analysis of the Rhodes-Livingstone anthropologists was ethnicity. The reinvention of identities—"retribalization" rather than an inexorable detribalization—was seen as emerging in a variety of new adaptive organizations: mutual-aid societies, voluntary associations, dance groups, religious movements.[13] Similar findings followed for cities elsewhere on the continent, as the scope of research widened to the dynamics of urban politics. Banton's classic study of Freetown and Cohen's of the Hausa *sabo* of Ibadan both portrayed a politicized ethnicity characterized by the manipulation of established custom in a new urban context.[14]

If colonial rulers tended to regard the urban environment as the locus of new social and political problems, then the rise of nationalism in the 1950s also influenced an alternative perception of the African city as a crucible of modernity. The question of modernization lay at the heart of an issue that preoccupied much of the early social science literature: the transformative nature of the urban. In this formulation, the "modern" city was seen as a potential motor of development for the "traditional" countryside. Although the idea of the dualism of town and country was being abandoned elsewhere, it proved remarkably persistent in the African and Asian context, where colonial cities were seen as foreign implants distinct from the wider indigenous environment. What has subsequently been crititiqued as a misplaced "urban essentialism" was not limited to colonial creations. The location of precolonial Yoruba towns on a "folk-urban continuum" derived from the Chicago school of urban studies also became the focus of an inconclusive debate over the essence of traditional African urbanism.[15] As Marshall has convincingly demonstrated with regard to Calcutta, even urban centers created as outposts of European rule had an important indigenous context. The values of the countryside had as great an impact on the nature of the colonial city as vice versa.[16]

Both the ethnic and the modernization paradigms in African urban studies were countered by the appearance in the 1970s of marxist-orientated analyses offering class as an alternative theoretical framework. The colonial era was portrayed as one in which the creation of a capitalist mode of production led to the formation of incipient working classes living in cities organized to facilitate surplus extraction.[17] The conceptual rigidities of the "underdevelopment" thesis was in turn succeeded by a more nuanced materialist approach to the history of the urban workplace, which argued that the struggle not to become a class was often more important than proletarianization.[18] These insights signaled a new concern with the social history of African cities. With the notable exception of van Onselen's exploration of the underbelly of turn-of-the-century Johannesburg, the best of this work focused on the threat to colonial control posed by the changing urban environment of the 1930s and 1940s.[19] The precolonial and early colonial periods continued to receive little attention. Moreover, it remained unclear how far the extent to which these insights into the contest over urban space drawn from East, Central, and Southern African case studies could be applied to the older cities of West Africa.[20]

Definitions and generalized models of change appear to have been at best illusive and at worst misplaced. In 1990, Mabogunje could conclude only that the "African city remains today a human agglomeration with no clear set of criteria to help its identification as a socially distinct entity."[21] Despite this theoretical pessimism, two crucial insights have emerged from recent comparative scholarship. The first is that sheer numbers alone do not constitute "the urban." As Philip Curtin notes in a recent collection of essays on Atlantic port cities, a city "is a place where people do different things, and the more different things they do, the more the place is a city."[22] As an analytical term, in other words, urban should be taken to mean the systematic linkage of specialized technologies and institutions in particular localities.[23] The recognition that size does not matter renders any distinction between "town" and "city" redundant, and in line with current practice these terms are used interchangeably to refer to Accra. Second, the city must never be analyzed as an isolate, but as a nodal point within wider societal systems. While there is widespread consensus on this count, some scholars have demanded an even more radical break with older notions of the urban. Dismissing Weber's thesis that in the end only cities are truly urban, Leeds has argued that it is entire societies—both town and country—that are "urban," not just particular places within them.[24]

Although this theoretical injunction is useful in dispensing with the outmoded dualism of town and country, it clashes somewhat with indigenous Ga readings of urban civilization. In common with other West African peoples with a long history of urbanism such as the Akan and Yoruba, the Ga possessed a finely nuanced set of cultural criteria that distinguished between urban and rural life. It is here that this study also seeks to advance our understanding of the African city, by exploring changing Ga perceptions of the urban arena. By the late colonial period, newly arrived rural migrants comprised the overwhelming majority of sub-Saharan Africa's urban population. Much more is known of their struggles, identities, and adaptations to city life than of the dynamics of long-established urban communities like the Ga.[25] From the 1920s onward, the rising tide of migrants from the Gold Coast and beyond would transform the character of Accra, and by 1948 the proportion of Ga in the total population had fallen to 51.6 percent.[26] The perception that the Ga were losing control of their own town injected a degree of tension into both local and nationalist politics in the capital, although not on the scale of other major West African cities.[27] In the early colonial period, however, Accra remained very much a Ga town. The "struggle for the city" was contested largely within its indigenous community.

This leads to the importance of politics in the urban arena, and in particular to the pivotal role of capital cities. If a city is a locus of exchange and transaction, then conflicts over who controls these exchanges and transactions—politics, in other words—further defines the nature of the urban. More than any other criteria, it was Accra's role as an arena of Ga political competition that lent the town its specifically urban character.

MEN, WOMEN, AND THE MAKING OF ACCRA

A further problem with the dominance of urbanization as an analytical framework in the study of African cities is that the overwhelming majority of rural-urban migrants in the colonial era were men. The process of urbanization and its concomitant social transformations have therefore often been portrayed as largely male affairs, and it is only recently that the rise of women's history has begun to challenge the view of colonial towns as predominantly male domains.[28] Simply in numerical terms alone, women outnumbered men in colonial Accra by a significant margin until the second decade of the twentieth century, and after that Ga women continued to predominate in the old downtown quarters. Although the prominent role of women in the exchange economies of established West African trading centers such as Accra and Lagos has long been recognized, pioneering studies tended to categorize women in terms of their relationship to men: as wives, daughters, concubines, and prostitutes.[29] The first wave of writing to relocate women at the centre stage of African history focused on the themes of economic productivity and political influence, the "market women" and "elite women" of coastal West African towns emerging as prime exemplars of female agency.[30] It is a mark of the visibility of women in Accra that the only monographic treatment of the town's history, Claire Robertson's *Sharing the Same Bowl*, takes as its theme the changing socioeconomic position of Ga women under colonial rule.[31]

Scholarship on the historical experience of African women, and in particular the experience of women in towns, has undergone a shift in emphasis since the 1970s. In 1988, Jean Hay labeled this shift as one from "queens to prostitutes," the effort to emphasize the autonomy and social agency of women having been replaced by a new concern with women as "victims": as slaves, prostitutes, and domestic servants.[32] It is an indication of just how fast the field is evolving that less than a decade later, Nancy Hunt could identify a further shift, toward what she calls the "colonialism and culture" school of writing.[33] Drawing on the lexicon of cultural studies and emphasizing the importance of representations, identities, consumption, the body, and the production of culture, this postmodernist turn extends the language of historical enquiry in a number of fruitful directions. Perhaps most importantly, it signals a move away from a separate women's history, as men and the construction of masculinity begin to join women in the broader frame of gender history.

This study draws on insights at each stage of this historiographical trajectory in an effort to locate women at the center of the process of making the town. While the emerging "colonialism and culture" nexus provides a useful entry into the making of Accra's hybrid urban culture, the central narrative of political action demands a return to the earlier concern with the political role of women. The emphasis here is neither on heroines nor on victims, but on the social and political action of ordinary townswomen. It is not simply that the relative economic and social autonomy of Ga women could at times be translated into political clout in an otherwise male-dominated public arena, although this in itself is an important aspect of Accra's urban history. Rather, the collective and individual struggles of Ga women further challenge the old distinction between a male-dominated political domain and a female-dominated domestic realm. This duality has already been subjected to considerable criticism, and it seems particularly inappropriate with regard to Ga state and society in Accra.[34] Just as both women and men made Accra, so men and women made its constituent households. The processes of resource allocation in both must be regarded as "political." It is here that recent theoretical departures in urban studies intersect with those in the study of African women. Not only did capitalism and colonialism reshape domesticity, but changes in the domestic realm interacted with wider forces in ways that defined the nature of the town as a locus of transaction and exchange.

ACCRA, THE GA, AND GHANAIAN HISTORIOGRAPHY

Ghana's capital city represents a glaring lacuna in what is one of the most developed national historiographies in tropical Africa.[35] While this is in part due to the shortcomings of African urban studies, it is also a result of the particular trajectory of historical research in Ghana. It is a neglect that has deep roots, predating the emergence of African history as an academic discipline. Indeed, a reluctance to confront the ambiguities of the Gold Coast trading towns is apparent in nineteenth- and early-twentieth-century sources. The accounts of missionaries, colonial officials, ethnographers, and early historians were concentrated on the Akan forest states, and in particular the powerful kingdom of Asante. The result is what has been described as an entrenched "hinterland bias" in Ghanaian historiography.[36] Asante exerted a powerful hold over the imaginations of Europeans on the Gold Coast, as it did over the imaginations of the Ga and other coastal peoples. Fueled by dense historical traditions and voluminous written records, the scholarly literature on Asante has subsequently developed into what is arguably the most comprehensive and sophisticated body of work on any precolonial sub-Saharan state.[37]

The hinterland bias is not simply the result of an enduring fascination with one of precolonial Africa's most renowned and well-documented states. It is also rooted in the very nature of coastal urbanism, in the eclecticism and idiosyncrasies of Accra's indigenous culture. Conflicting visions of the city will be analyzed in more detail in the following chapters. The crucial point, however, can be made quite simply: succeeding generations of observers have viewed urban Accra as not being the "real" Africa. Africa—pristine, untainted, and essentially rural—was instead to be found in the Akan forests, beyond the distant blue line of the Akuapem escarpment ris-

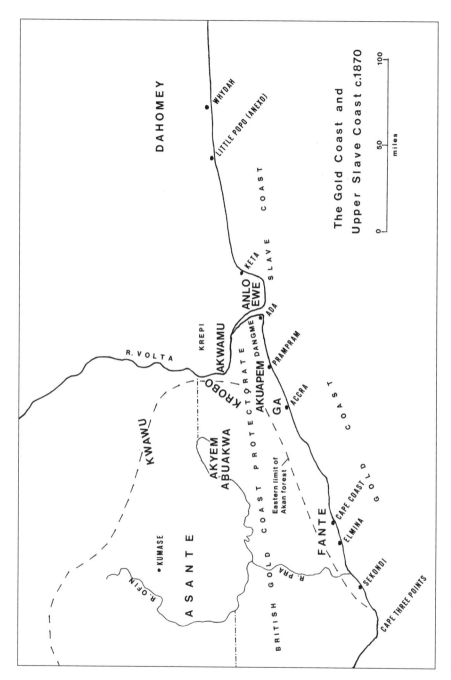

Map I.1 The Gold Coast and Upper Slave Coast, c. 1870

ing visibly to the north of Accra. The pioneering Methodist missionary T. B. Freeman (1809–1890), for example, left extensive accounts of Asante, Dahomey, and Yorubaland, yet had little or nothing to say on the Ga, among whom he lived for the last three decades of his life.[38] Growing from a nucleus of three European trading forts and overshadowed by a succession of more powerful Akan kingdoms to the north, Accra was often regarded as a confusing jumble of outside influences, its indigenous institutions corrupted by borrowings from both European and African overlords. Colonial officer and amateur ethnographer A. B. Ellis set another early precedent when he chose to omit the Accra region from his studies of the Gold and Slave Coasts, dismissing the culture of the Ga and related Dangme peoples as a pale replication of that of the Akan kingdoms.[39]

The importance of Akan culture in southern Ghana has also shaped the study of the coast itself. As part of the Akan region, the Fante states of the western Gold Coast have received more attention than those of the Ga, Dangme, and Ewe to the east, despite the fact that by the late-nineteenth century Accra had eclipsed Cape Coast and Elmina as the principal coastal urban center.[40] The notion of a hinterland bias therefore requires qualification. It is the culturally fragmented eastern Gold Coast rather than the entire littoral that remains the most stubborn geographical gap in historical understanding. If Accra's middleman identity was defined by its location between land and sea, it was also forged by the town's role as the economic and cultural hinge between the Gold Coast to the west and the Slave Coast to the east. Few scholars have paused to consider the history of the Ga-Dangme coast between Accra and the River Volta, yet it divides two of Africa's most intensively researched cultural agglomerations: the Twi-speaking Akan kingdoms to the west, and the Aja- and Yoruba-speaking kingdoms to the east.[41]

None of this is too surprising given that the Ga-Dangme formed a small ethnic enclave in what, by the turn of the century, was a British colony encapsulating Asante and the bulk of the adjoining Akan kingdoms. What is striking is that a major corrective appeared as early as 1895, in the form of Carl Reindorf's *History of the Gold Coast and Asante*.[42] Like Samuel Johnson, whose famous *History of the Yorubas* was also completed in the 1890s, Reindorf (1834–1917) was an indigenous pastor whose historical scholarship was profoundly shaped by his multiple identities as a Christian, an African, and a patriotic member of an ethnic community.[43] A catechist of the Basel Mission ordained in 1872 as the church's first Ga pastor, Reindorf began collecting oral traditions and testimonies in the 1860s, working this material into a dense historical narrative in combination with European written accounts. In contrast with Johnson, whose text was focused on a reemergent Yoruba nation,

Reindorf's work was a conscious attempt to draw the Ga into a broader political entity, that of the British-protected Gold Coast. Indeed, Reindorf was unusual among the first generation of mission-educated West African historians with regard to his treatment of ethnic communities other than his own, his incorporation of Asante into a putative national history prefiguring the subsequent shape of the enlarged Gold Coast Colony. Although its narrative ends in 1854, *History of the Gold Coast and Asante* is a reading of the past animated by the uncertainties and anxieties of the new imperial age in which it was written. Just as Johnson's *History* remains the foundation stone of Yoruba historiography, so Reindorf's neglected work represents the most richly textured source for the reconstruction of Ga state and society in Accra.

Despite the possibilities suggested by Reindorf's *History*, the first wave of modern scholarship on Accra, as elsewhere in Africa, was the preserve of social anthropology. The pioneering figure was Margaret Field, appointed to the post of Government Anthropologist in 1938 and the author of two important monographs on Ga belief and social structure.[44] Like R. S. Rattray, her counterpart in Asante and acknowledged mentor, Field conceptualized the African past in ways that have had a profound influence on the study of Accra.[45] Just as Rattray studiously avoided the Asante capital of Kumase, Field carried out much of her research in Tema, then an isolated fishing town free from what she perceived as the contaminating urban influences of colonial Accra. By peeling away the layers of "unnatural" authority accumulated by chiefs through their dealings with Europeans and Akan peoples, she hoped to reveal what she saw as the traditional form of Ga government: a democratic gerontocracy of priests and elders.[46] Seeking out elderly, nonliterate traditionalists as informants, she held a profound distrust for those Western-educated Ga who "carry in their heads only garbled and impoverished fragments of book history—mostly culled in the first place from Reindorf, whom I often wish had never existed."[47]

Field's attitude toward Ghana's first homegrown historian may appear harsh, but Reindorf's "book history" and the literate urban elite from which it emerged clearly created major conceptual problems for her protofunctionalist project. Ironically, just as Reindorf's *History* became the authorized recension of historical tradition in Accra, so Field's anthropological vision became enshrined as an alternative orthodoxy among subsequent scholars. Unlike Asante, where Rattray's huge corpus of work has been superseded by modern historical studies, the prevailing scholarly view of Accra remains embedded in Field's analysis of a consensual Ga order corrupted by its urban locality and the forces of modernity. The perception that Accra represents what one historian called "a jungle of intractable complexities" has remained remarkably persistent.[48] Despite a wealth of written sources, historical research on Accra has long remained confined to unpublished dissertations and other fugitive materials.[49] With the notable exception of Robertson's monograph, the study of Accra has remained dominated by the social sciences, new generations of anthropologists continuing to build on Field's pioneering studies.[50]

Where Accra has featured in the historical literature, it has tended to be as a setting for the emergence of Ghanaian nationalism, a process culminating in the rise to power of Kwame Nkrumah and his Convention People's Party in the 1950s.[51] This brings us back to the problem of "the city," for it is with regard to nationalism that the concern with the nature of African urbanism most obviously intersects with the historiography of Ghana. If the African city has been portrayed by a succession of research paradigms as a site of political, social, and economic transformation, then Accra was clearly a precocious exemplar of this transformative power. It was the capital city and commercial hub of what by the 1920s was tropical Africa's wealthiest colony, where economic growth and educational advance had created the region's most articulate middle-class urban elite. Twenty years later, Accra was at the center stage of the emergent anticolonial struggle in Africa, the riots of 1948 and the formation the following year of Nkrumah's radical nationalist party shattering the political quietude of tropical Africa. In short, Accra has long been recognized as a locus of nationalism and unequivocally "modern" political action. The aim of this study is to qualify and complicate this view of the pivotal role of the capital city.

METHODOLOGY AND ORGANIZATION

The methodology and organization of this study have been informed by the historiographical and theoretical concerns outlined above. In terms of methodology, research has been based overwhelmingly on documentary sources. The reason for this imbalance lies less with the weakness of oral sources than with the strengths of the documentary archive. That Accra represents such an obvious gap in the historiography of Ghana and the anglophone West African coast is especially startling in light of the voluminous, diverse, and richly detailed nature of written sources relating to the town. In common with other protocolonial British enclaves on the West African coast, locally run newspapers, missionary correspondence, transcripts of legal proceedings, and colonial records date back to at least the 1850s. The volume and quality of these sources increase dramatically in the last quarter of the nineteenth century, and it is interesting to note that for many aspects of urban life these years represent the most richly documented period in Accra's history.

As will become apparent, these sources are characterized by the clarity with which the people of Accra make themselves heard. Literacy had an early impact in the town, and by the start of our period the voice of the Western-educated elite emerges from the documentary record, both in its own right and as mediator for nonliterate townsmen and women. As lawyers, journalists, catechists, teachers, pastors, translators, traders, and politicians, many Ga have left a record of their own lives and their views on the past, present, and future of the town. Two sources stand out in this respect. The first records the voice of one man, Carl Reindorf. The leading Ga intellectual of his age, Reindorf's published and unpublished writings contain some of the most trenchant insights on state and society in Accra. The second records the voice of innumerable ordinary townspeople, often no less articulate than that of the historian Reindorf. They are the record books of the colonial courts, which despite their well-recognized analytical hazards have been crucial for the reconstruction of the social history of the town.

In terms of organization, the story that follows unfolds over six chronologically ordered chapters. The reasons for the essentially narrative structure are twofold. First, the lack of an existing chronological foundation on which to build the social history of Accra created a basic imperative to "set the story straight." More importantly, the period under consideration was a time of transformation, and that transformation was driven on not simply by underlying shifts in Accra's social and political structure, but by the force of events. Within this narrative, each chapter picks up on a particular theme in Accra's urban history. The first offers a survey of state and society in precolonial Accra, identifying the principal forces that shaped the town from the seventeenth to the mid-nineteenth centuries. Chapter 2 charts the period of military conflict between 1866 and 1874, which acted as a catalyst for the consolidation of British colonial rule. It locates Accra at the center of a variety of exchanges in the eastern Gold Coast and explores the connections in Ga political thought between warfare, wealth, and civic virtue. Chapter 3 deals with the expansion of colonial rule in the 1870s, a process examined through the dual prism of law and the abolition of slavery. Chapter 4 locates political action in the last two decades of the nineteenth century in the context of the changing urban economy. The subject of Chapter 5 is religion and belief, examining in more detail a theme that threads through the entire narrative. The final chapter examines escalating political conflict in Accra in the 1920s, and concludes that the nuances of indigenous political culture are crucial to any understanding of the expanding colonial city.

NOTES

1. William Cowper, cited in Roy Porter, *London: A social history* (London, 1996), 160.

2. Ga proverb, from Rev. J. Zimmermann, *A grammatical sketch of the Akra or Gā-language* (Stuttgart, 1858), Vol. 1, 161.

3. For a comparative West African case study, see Ralph A. Austen and Jonathan Derrick, *Middlemen of the Cameroons Rivers: The Duala and their hinterland c.1600–c.1960* (Cambridge, 1999).

4. For an attempt to rectify this tendency, see John Lonsdale, "European scramble and conquest in African history" in R. Oliver and G. N. Sanderson (eds.), *The Cambridge history of Africa*, Vol. 6 (Cambridge, 1985).

5. This renegotiation is more advanced for the American side of the Atlantic world: see Franklin W. Knight and Peggy K. Liss (eds.), *Atlantic port cities: Economy, culture, and society in the Atlantic world, 1650–1850* (Knoxville, 1991), Introduction.

6. Aiden Southall (ed.), *Social change in modern Africa* (London, 1961), 1–13.

7. See Anthony O'Conner, *The African city* (London, 1983), 28–41; Anthony D. King, *Colonial urban development: Culture, social power and environment* (London, 1976); Robert Ross and Gerald J. Telkamp (eds.), *Colonial cities: Essays on urbanism in a colonial context* (Dordrecht, 1985).

8. J.D.Y. Peel, "Urbanization and urban history in West Africa," *Journal of African History* [hereafter *JAH*], 21 (1980). For a useful survey—itself an indication of the continuing dominance of the urbanization paradigm—see Catherine Coquery-Vidrovitch, "The process of urbanization in Africa (from the origins to the beginning of independence)," *African Studies Review*, 34 (1991).

9. Graham Connor, *African civilizations: Precolonial cities and states in tropical Africa* (Cambridge, 1987); for recent surveys of urban studies, see Josef Gugler, "Urbanization in Africa south of the Sahara: New identities in conflict" in J. Gugler (ed.), *The urban transformation of the developing world* (Oxford, 1996); Akin L. Mabogunje, "Overview of research priorities in Africa" in Richard Stren (ed.), *Urban research in the developing world. Vol. 2. Africa* (Toronto, 1994).

10. Mabogunje, "Overview of research priorities." 22–23.

11. See Philip Abrams, "Towns and economic growth: Some theories and problems" in P. Abrams and E. A. Wrigley, *Towns in societies: Essays in economic history and historical sociology* (Cambridge, 1978); Anthony Leeds, *Cities, classes, and the social order*, ed. by Roger Sanjek (Ithaca, 1994).

12. See Bill Freund, "Labor and labor history in Africa: A review of the literature," *African Studies Review*, 27 (1984).

13. See, for example, J. Clyde Mitchell, *The kalela dance: Aspects of social relationships among urban Africans in Northern Rhodesia* (Manchester, 1956). For a recent reconsideration of this body of work, see idem, *Cities, society and social perception: A Central African perspective* (London, 1987); and Hilary Sapire and Jo Beall, "Introduction: Urban change and urban studies in southern Africa," special issue of *Journal of Southern African Studies*, 21 (1995).

14. Michael Banton, *West African city: A study of tribal life in Freetown* (London, 1957); Abner Cohen, *Custom and politics in urban Africa: A study of Hausa migrants in Yoruba towns* (London, 1969); see also Kenneth Little, *West African urbanization: A study of voluntary associations in social change* (Cambridge, 1965); Enid Schildkrout,

People of the zongo: The transformation of ethnic identities in Ghana (Cambridge, 1978).

15. See esp. Eva Krapf-Askari, *Yoruba towns and cities: An enquiry into the nature of urban social phenomena* (Oxford, 1969); for a critique of "urban essentialism," see Peel, "Urbanization and urban history," 271; and for a necessary corrective, idem, *Ijeshas and Nigerians: The incorporation of a Yoruba kingdom* (Cambridge, 1983).

16. P. J. Marshall, "Eighteenth-century Calcutta" in Ross and Telkamp, *Colonial cities.*

17. Richard Sandbrook and Robin Cohen (eds.), *The development of an African working class* (London, 1975); P.C.W. Gutkind, R. Cohen, and J. Copans (eds.), *African labor history* (Beverly Hills, 1979).

18. Frederick Cooper, "Urban space, industrial time and wage labor in Africa" in F. Cooper (ed.), *Struggle for the city: Migrant labor, capital and the state in urban Africa* (Beverly Hills, 1983).

19. Charles van Onselen, *New Babylon and New Ninevah: Studies in the social and economic history of the Witwatersrand, 1886–1914* (Johannesburg, 1982); on the later period, see esp. Frederick Cooper, *On the African waterfront: Urban disorder and the transformation of work in colonial Mombasa* (New Haven, 1987).

20. On this point, see Kristin Mann, *Marrying well: Marriage, status and social change among the educated elite in colonial Lagos* (Cambridge, 1985), 134; and for an important exception to the general neglect of precolonial urbanism, Ray A. Kea, *Settlements, trade, and polities in the seventeenth-century Gold Coast* (Baltimore, 1982).

21. Akin L. Mabogunje, "Urban planning and the post-colonial state in Africa: A research overview," *African Studies Review*, 33 (1990), 122.

22. Philip Curtin, Preface in Knight and Liss, *Atlantic port cities*, xi.

23. Leeds, *Cities, classes, and the social order*, 33–35.

24. Ibid., 53–54; cf. Max Weber, *The city* (New York, 1958 [1921]).

25. On this point, see Claire Robertson, "Women in the urban economy" in Margaret Jean Hay and Sharon Stichter (eds.), *African women south of the Sahara* (2nd ed., Harlow, 1995).

26. Ioné Acquah, *Accra survey* (London, 1958), 32; J. C. Caldwell, *African rural-urban migration: The movement to Ghana's towns* (London, 1969).

27. On Freetown and Lagos, see Banton, *West African city*; Barbara E. Harrell-Bond, Allen M. Howard, and David E. Skinner, *Community leadership and the transformation of Freetown (1801–1976)* (The Hague, 1978); Akintola Wyse, *H. C. Bankole-Bright and politics in colonial Sierra Leone, 1919–1935* (Cambridge, 1990); P. D. Cole, *Traditional and modern elites in the politics of Lagos* (Cambridge, 1975); Pauline H. Baker, *Urbanization and political change: The politics of Lagos, 1917–1967* (Berkeley, 1974); Sandra Barnes, *Patrons and power: Creating a political community in metropolitan Lagos* (Manchester, 1986).

28. Kathleen Sheldon (ed.), *Courtyards, markets, city streets: Urban women in Africa* (Boulder, 1996), Introduction, 3–27.

29. Kenneth Little, *African women in towns: An aspect of Africa's social revolution* (Cambridge, 1973).

30. For useful surveys, see Margaret Jean Hay, "Queens, prostitutes and peasants: Historical perspectives on African women, 1971–1986," *Canadian Journal of African*

Studies, 23 (1988); Nancy Rose Hunt, Introduction to special issue on "Gendered colonialisms in African history," *Gender and History*, 8 (1996); and for two pioneering monographs, Nina Emma Mba, *Nigerian women mobilized: Women's political activity in southern Nigeria* (Berkeley, 1982); Mann, *Marrying well*.

31. Claire C. Robertson, *Sharing the same bowl: A socioeconomic history of women and class in Accra, Ghana* (Bloomington, 1984); see too the anthropological study by Deborah Pellow, *Women in Accra: Options for autonomy* (Algonac, 1977).

32. Hay, "Queens, prostitutes and peasants," 433–436.

33. Hunt, Introduction to "Gendered colonialisms," 324.

34. See Karen Tranberg Hansen (ed.), *African encounters with domesticity* (New Brunswick, 1992), esp. "Introduction: domesticity in Africa," 15.

35. See Irene Odotei, "The Ga-Danme" in J. O. Hunwick (ed.), *Proceedings of the seminar on Ghanaian historiography and historical research, 20–22 May 1976* (Legon, 1977).

36. Ray Jenkins, "Gold Coast historians and their pursuits of the Gold Coast pasts, 1882–1917," Ph.D. thesis, University of Birmingham, 1985, 2–10.

37. See K. Hart, "The social anthropology of West Africa," *Annual Review of Anthropology*, 14 (1985); and for a more extensive review, T. C. McCaskie, *State and society in pre-colonial Asante* (Cambridge, 1995), 1–23.

38. See esp. T. B. Freeman, *Journal of various visits to the kingdoms of Ashanti, Aku, and Dahomi in Western Africa* (London, 1844).

39. A. B. Ellis, *The Ewe-speaking peoples of the Slave Coast of West Africa* (London, 1890), v–vi; idem, *The Tshi-speaking peoples of the Gold Coast of West Africa* (London, 1887).

40. On Cape Coast, see J. Hinderink and J. Sterkenburg, *Anatomy of an African town: A socio-economic study of Cape Coast, Ghana* (Utrecht, 1975); Roger Gocking, "The historic Akoto. A social history of Cape Coast 1843-1948," Ph.D. thesis, Stanford University, 1981; M. McCarthy, *Social change and the growth of British power in the Gold Coast: The Fante states, 1807–1872* (Lanham, 1983); on Elmina, Larry W. Yarak, *Asante and the Dutch 1744–1873* (Oxford, 1990).

41. On the social history of the Anlo Ewe to the immediate west of the Volta, see Sandra E. Greene, *Gender, ethnicity, and social change on the Upper Slave Coast: A history of the Anlo-Ewe* (Portsmouth, NH, 1996).

42. Rev. Carl Christian Reindorf, *History of the Gold Coast and Asante* (Basel, 1895).

43. For a comparison of the two historians, see Paul Jenkins (ed.), *The recovery of the West African past. African pastors and African history in the nineteenth century: C. C. Reindorf and Samuel Johnson* (Basel, 1998).

44. M. J. Field, *Religion and medicine of the Gã people* (London, 1937); idem, *Social organization of the Gã people* (London, 1940).

45. Cf. T. C. McCaskie, "R. S. Rattray and the construction of Asante history: An appraisal," *History in Africa*, 10 (1983).

46. Field, *Social organization*, 71–81.

47. Ibid., 196.

48. Björn M. Edsman, *Lawyers in Gold Coast politics c.1900–1945: From Mensah Sarbah to J. B. Danquah* (Uppsala, 1979), 94; see too the similar comment by Kathryn Firmin-Sellars, *The transformation of property rights in the Gold Coast: An empirical analysis applying rational choice theory* (Cambridge, 1996), 37.

49. Irene Quaye, "The Ga and their neighbours 1600–1742," Ph.D. thesis, University of Ghana, Legon, 1972; Samuel S. Quarcoopome, "The impact of urbanisation on the socio-political history of the Ga Mashie people of Accra: 1877–1957," Ph.D. thesis, University of Ghana, Legon, 1993.

50. For an excellent sociolinguistic analysis with a keen historical awareness, see too M. E. Kropp Dakubu, *Korle meets the sea: A sociolinguistic history of Accra* (New York, 1997).

51. See the monumental work by David Kimble, *A political history of Ghana: The rise of Gold Coast nationalism 1850–1928* (Oxford, 1963); and the classic work of political science by Denis Austin, *Politics in Ghana 1946–1960* (London, 1964).

1

STATE AND SOCIETY IN PRECOLONIAL ACCRA

Woman moomo, woman
Womantiase wo ye mli
Jen bo ade aye mli
Woman moomo, woman.
(It is our town from long ago, it is our town
We are in the heart of our town
We have been in it since the world was created
It is our town from long ago, it is our town.)[1]

Gbo hinmeii kpleikplei, si enaa man mlinii.
(The eyes of a stranger may be very large, but
he does not see the inner things of the town.)[2]

This first chapter charts the trajectory of Accra's urban history from the emergence of the coastal-based Ga state in the late seventeenth century to the eve of the consolidation of British colonial rule in the 1860s and 1870s. In order to locate social and political action in Accra within a set of assumptions concerning the nature of the urban, we begin with a discussion of Ga readings of landscape, space, and the moral topography of town and country. This is followed by an examination of the institutional growth of precolonial Accra, focusing on the multiple hierarchies of power in the three coastal townships that together would form the nucleus of the colonial city. Finally, these urban institutions are located in a narrative of historical change, which traces the evolution of the Ga middleman role from the era of the slave trade to the era of "legitimate" commerce. Contrary to Field's anthropological view of a consensual Ga past rooted in a closed moral community, it is argued that urban Accra was a volatile arena of cultural innovation and political competition.

TOWN AND COUNTRY, LAND AND SEA

Accra's urban history and Ga perceptions of that history have been shaped by a narrow and often precarious cultural niche between the forest and the sea. The country inhabited by the Ga people is bounded on the south by the Gulf of Guinea and on the north by the hills of the Akuapem escarpment, which begin to rise from the coastal plain some fifteen miles from the sea. A number of small rivers flow from the well-watered hills across the dry Accra plains and into a succession of lagoons that punctuate the open surf beaches of the coast. The traditional western limit of Ga settlement is the Sakumo River and the Sakumofio lagoon, a frontier marked by a hill known to the Ga as Lanma and to passing European mariners as Cook's Loaf. Thirty miles to the east, between the town of Tema and the Laloi lagoon, the Ga country merges with that of the closely related Dangme-speaking peoples, who occupy the coast down to the Volta River. The centuries-old European division of the Gold Coast into "windward" and "leeward" sections at the Sakumo River coincided with indigenous mental mapping, which drew a fundamental cultural distinction between the Akan-speaking Fante peoples to the west and the Ga-Dangme peoples to the east. By the beginning of our period in the 1860s, the river also demarcated the Western and Eastern Districts of the British Gold Coast Protectorate.[3] Since the end of the seventeenth century the Ga social formation has been centered on seven towns dotted along the coast: Nleshi, Kinka, Osu, La, Teshi, Nungwa, and Tema.[4] In the early colonial period Nleshi, Kinka, and Osu would be drawn together to form the nucleus of the city of Accra. It is the resulting social, political, economic, and cultural changes in the indigenous Ga communities of these three old townships that is the focus of this study.

The ecology of Accra's coastal hinterland is characterized above all by aridity. Ga country forms the western extremity of what geographers call the Dahomey Gap, an intrusion of open grasslands and thickets that cuts through the West African forest zone between Accra in the west and Badagry in modern-day Nigeria in the east. Two wet seasons, from April to June and in September, provide Accra with an average of between only twenty and thirty inches of rain a year, compared with over eighty inches in much of the Akan forest zone.[5] Variability is great, with annual rainfall falling to as low as ten inches. Periods of recurring drought on the Accra plains are not uncommon and have resulted, particularly in times of war and insecurity, in shortages of the staple food crops, maize and cassava.[6] The inability of the coastal savanna to sustain tree crops such as oil palm and cocoa, together with the absence of older export commodities such as gold and ivory, has meant that the Ga have tended to enter the international economy not as producers but as traders, exploiting their position as coastal "middlemen" in

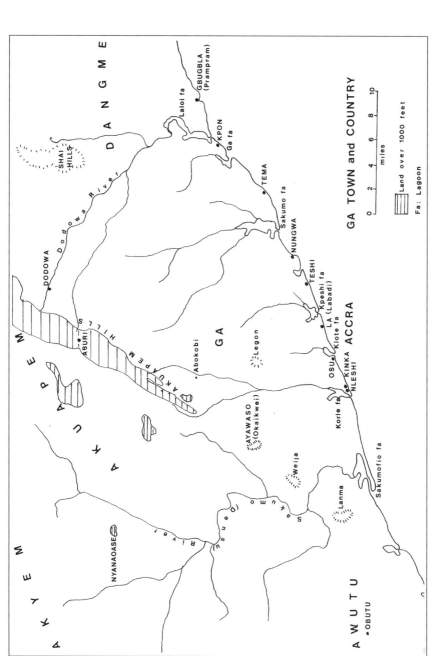

Map 1.1 Ga Town and Country

Figure 1.1 The sea front of Kinka and Nleshi, c. 1880. Ussher Fort in the center and James Fort to the left. (Courtesy of the Foreign and Commonwealth Office Library, London.)

order to alleviate the constraints of a marginal ecology. Accra's location between the open plain and the sea has facilitated intensive, long-standing contacts with other peoples: the European maritime powers, the Twi-speaking Akan kingdoms of the forests to the north and the coast to the west, and the peoples of the Slave Coast to the east.[7] The result has been the rise of a highly eclectic, heterogeneous urban culture. The ability of the Ga to prosper in this dry and often adverse environment is acknowledged annually in the *Homowo* festival. The great celebration of the Ga ritual calender, *Homowo*, from the phrase *homo yi womo*, means literally "hooting at [i.e., ridiculing] hunger."

Fishing and saltmaking are the two main productive activities that have compensated for the limited agricultural capacity of the coastal plain. European reports from the seventeenth century indicate that although the region produced little or no agricultural surplus, large numbers of merchants from the interior arrived at Accra daily to purchase salt and fish.[8] Oral tradition holds that the Ga, like the peoples of the Slave Coast, had no history of maritime navigation, and that their fishing activities were limited to the lagoons before the Twi-speaking Fante to the west introduced seagoing canoes.[9] Genealogical histories of leading fishing families indicate that this innovation may have occurred in the mid-eighteenth century; by the 1780s

Figure 1.2 Klote lagoon and Christiansborg Castle at Osu, c. 1900. The seat of British colonial power juxtaposed with Ga sacred space. (Photograph by Max Schultz, Basel Mission. Copyright Basel Mission Archive, Basel, Switzerland. Ref. No. D-30.01.018. Reproduced with permission.)

the Ga were definitely engaged in sea fishing.[10] The Gold Coast Colony's first census in 1891 recorded one in four adult African males in Accra as fishermen, who continued to form an important group in the town throughout our period.[11] Although fishermen in early colonial Accra were often relatively poor, they cultivated a robust, self-conscious occupational identity, the office of *woleiatse*, head fisherman, retaining considerable prominence in town affairs.[12] The fishing industry historically has contained a division of labor with important implications for Ga gender relations and the organization of the domestic economy: whereas men have done the fishing, women have been largely responsible for preservation, marketing, and trading.[13]

The high salinity of the coastal lagoons between Accra and the Volta also made the Ga and Dangme towns important sources of salt for the Akan forest zone and the savanna beyond, and a thriving salt trade has been reported at Accra from the seventeenth century.[14] European merchants at various times appear to have attempted to enter the productive sector of the salt industry, leading to the hostility of the Ga for whom the lagoons were powerful deities requiring careful ritual management.[15] The importance of salt as a commodity that the Ga traded for foodstuffs is captured in a song of the *kple* religious cult: *"Minyoo La ngoo; Ake mi tsake sebe ke engmoni; Mijee La ngoo"*—"I am not La salt; they do not exchange me for garden eggs and okra; I am not La salt."[16] This verse draws an analogy between salt and another commodity of great historical significance for Accra—people. "A bag of salt" was an abusive term for a slave, emphasizing his or her reduction to a chattel, and the cry "I am not La salt" a ringing affirmation of the status of a free person.[17]

The name of Accra in the Ga language is also *Ga*. The Twi-speaking peoples refer to both town and people as *Nkran* ("Accra"), clearly cognate with the Ga root.[18] Sources suggest that both names are derived from either the swarms of ants or the ubiquitous termite mounds of the Accra plains.[19] Reindorf confirms this etymology, positing a link between the martial qualities and migratory behavior of the local ants and those of the Ga, and adding a wry racial twist to his entomological observations: "Ga is gaga, . . . the big black ants which bite severely and are formidable to the white ants.... As their name designates, [the Ga] must have been a very numerous and powerful wandering tribe who very easily subdued the aborigines."[20] This dual usage conveys the close association in the minds of both the Ga and their neighbors between the whole Ga social formation and the urban center of Accra. The link between the ethnonym and ants also served to locate the Ga in their distinctive regional environment, and was explicitly reflected in the recognition of anthills as sacred places. Often ringed by sacred fences (*aklabatsa*), the tall red mounds dotting Accra's hinterland were seen as microcosms of human community and as nodal points between the known world and the world of the dead.[21]

How did the Ga conceptualize urban society in precolonial times? The term *man*, cognate with the Twi *oman*, is most commonly used to mean "town." As with *oman*, however, *man* (pl. *majii*) has wider social and political connotations and is also rendered as "people," "nation," or "state."[22] The original locus of Ga settlement and state formation was not the coast but the more fertile northwestern fringe of the Accra plains. Following the destruction by Akwamu of a powerful centralized kingdom at Ayawaso hill in 1677, the Ga state fragmented into the seven "seaside towns," *nshonamajii* (sing. *nshonaman*). It is possible only to speculate on the extent to which this violent rupture reshaped Ga epistemology, but sources point to the sea (*nshon*) as the most salient parametric feature of the physical world. Whereas in Ga thought the south connotes the sea, the great sea god Nai, civilization, and urban culture, the north represents land, lesser deities, and rustic culture located in an essentially untamed and hazardous nature.[23] Present here, in common with many African societies, is the notion that the cultural order of the *man* must be vigilantly defended against the encroachments of the anarchic and morally disorderly *kose*, "bush." Far from being a timeless, static construction, this divide was historically phrased by the political economy of urban Accra. In the forests to the north lay the threat of larger, alien, and potentially hostile kingdoms, while from the waters of the sea flowed wealth in the form of fish, salt, imported commodities, and merchant capital.

If moral topography gave shape to a perceived cleavage between the Ga world and that of their Akan neighbors to the north, then it also reinforced a divide within Ga society, that between town and country. *Ga* the town, in other words, was distinguished from *Ga* the people. Each seaside town possessed a number of outlying villages (*aklowai*, sing. *aklowa*) settled by both free and unfree farmers who belonged in a variety of ways to the central institutions of the *man*. Despite Field's characterization of the Ga in the 1930s as "neither town people nor country people," there is no doubt that the inhabitants of Kinka, Nleshi, and Osu have long nurtured a notion of their own urbanity.[24] The term *manbii* (lit. "children of the town"), with its connotations of full civic rights, is typically used as "townspeople" in contrast to *kosebii*, "country people" or "bush people."[25] *Kosenyo*, bushman or farmer, is also rendered by the Basel missionary Johannes Zimmermann as "rough person," "boor," or "clown."[26] Although kinship and political institutions straddled the rural-urban divide, socioeconomic differentiation engendered by expanding trade in the eighteenth century probably deepened the cultural cleavage between Accra and its hinterland. The perceived superiority of urban culture on the part of townspeople was further heightened by the growing numbers of slaves and other dependents settled by their masters in *aklowai* following the collapse of the Atlantic slave trade in the early nineteenth century. In 1891 only 814 people in Accra—about 5 percent of the total population of 20,000—were classified as farmers, compared to the 1,190 "mechanics" and 2,103 engaged in commerce.

This is not to argue that the existence of a nuanced terminology of Ga settlement can be translated into the outmoded theory of an essentialized dualism between town and country.[27] Social and cultural exchanges flowed in both directions, and the hegemony of Accra's urban elites was neither unambiguous nor unchallenged. The accumulation of wealth and power may have made Accra the arena of civilized order, but the *kose* remained a place of Ga tradition, rustic authenticity, and ritual power. The ambiguous nature of the rural hinterland was encapsulated in the sacred precincts of the old deserted capital at Ayawaso, a brooding reminder of an antebellum past of peace, unity, and political independence.[28] The divide between *man* and *kose* was dramatically bridged each year at *Homowo*, public festivities opening with the ceremonious entry of the rural population into the town. In an exchange during a conflict in the *nshonaman* of La in 1872, the received association of the bush with slavery was neatly turned on its head. "We are farmers," sneered a group of La *kosebii* at some of Osu's literate, Christian elite.

"When we take a single grass from the ground under that grass is five cowries. You don't like to cultivate therefore you have made yourself slaves to Europeans."[29]

By the beginning of our period in the 1860s and 1870s, social change in Accra had begun to reshape prevailing urban attitudes toward the rustic "north." As new lifestyles and notions of leisure arose, prominent members of the literate merchant elite built country bungalows on the Accra plains, where they could repair from the bustle of town to enjoy horseriding, shooting, and country walks. The political transformations of the early colonial period also began to remold perceptions of the African interior beyond the Accra plains. The removal of the Asante military menace after 1874 combined with rising European racism to create a new willingness on the part of urban elites to embrace rather than reject the idea of "traditional" Africa.

NSHONAMAN: THE GROWTH OF THE SEASIDE TOWNS

Ga Origins and State Formation

Oral traditions hold that the Ga-Dangme peoples migrated to their present homeland on the Accra plains from the east, settling among existing aboriginal populations known to the Ga as *kpeshi*.[30] There is no archaeological evidence to confirm traditions of external origin, and the "arrival" of the Ga may be interpreted not as a literal migration but as their gradual rise to demographic, linguistic, and political ascendancy over neighboring Guang-speaking peoples.[31] Migration traditions, however, remain central to Ga notions of history and identity. Those Ga who trace their descent from groups of original migrants are often referred to collectively as *Ga mashi*, a designation that serves to distinguish a "true" Ga (*Ganyo kron*) from autochthonous peoples and from later settlers. Alternatively, *Ga mashi* can mean all the Ga-speaking inhabitants of the seven quarters of Kinka and Nleshi, whatever their original origin.[32] The importance of migratory origins in Ga thought may have been reinforced by the written collections of oral tradition produced from the mid-nineteenth century by the literate Christian intelligentsia. In common with early Yoruba historiography, these recensions are characterized by an anxiety to demonstrate links between the Ga and famous civilizations: the Benin empire, pharaonic Egypt, and, most pervasively, the ancient Jews.[33] Despite their lack of historicity, such claims are striking characters for cultural tensions in early colonial Accra, when traditions of origin were mobilized and further elaborated in Ga political action.

The original locus of Ga-Dangme settlement was the hills that rise sporadically from the northern reaches of the Accra plains. Fragmentary evidence suggests that rather than being a purely internal development, state formation may have been associated with changes resulting from contact with European maritime trade. Oral tradition recounts a struggle for political supremacy involving the control of wealth in gold between migrant Ga and Guang-speaking Awutu (or Obutu) peoples, which could coincide with the rise of European trade by the 1550s.[34] The upshot of the conflict was the founding under King Ayite of the Ga state on Ayawaso hill, which archaeological evidence dates to the late sixteenth century. Great Accra, as it was known to the Europeans, was one of the most populous and wealthy commercial centers on the seventeenth-century Gold Coast, the capital of a centralized state that established a considerable degree of political and economic ascendency over the Accra plains.[35] In a trenchant comparison of the evolution of Akan and Ga government, Reindorf posits that the original Ga rulers were prophets or "foretelling priests" called *lomei* (sing. *lomo*).[36] Corrupted to *lumoi* (sing. *lumo*), this term refers generally in modern Ga to those who govern, and is also evidently linked to the word for priest, *wulomo* (pl. *wulomei*). Continuing a sequence that may betray his mission training rooted in Old Testament history, Reindorf argues that the *lomei* were succeeded by "priest-kings," who in turn delegated secular authority to kings and chiefs. The separation of sacred and secular power, he suggests, was prompted by the influence of both European commerce and the political organization of the neighboring Akan, a process accelerated by the removal of the Ga to the coast after the destruction of Great Accra by the Akwamu.[37] By the nineteenth century, secular office was dominated by the *mantsemei* (sing. *mantse*: "father of the town"), who would emerge as the historical "chiefs" of the coastal towns.

The evolution of Ga kingship, and a social structure of dominance and subordination, were clearly connected to the economic expansion of Great Accra. If the economy of the *Ga mashi* was initially based on farming, fishing, and saltmaking, by the seventeenth century Great Accra was a thriving urban center surrounded by numerous satellite settlements and inhabited by traders and artisans.[38] Salt, preserved fish, and European trade goods from the Ga coastal outposts were exchanged for gold and ivory from the north, while slaves moved in both directions.[39] The intensification of European mercantile competition on the eastern Gold Coast is an indication of this expansion. The Ga seem to have been reluctant to allow European traders to build permanent establishments following their destruction of a Portuguese fort in 1576. This reluctance was overcome by a series of agreements in the second quarter of the seventeenth century with the Dutch West India Company that culminated in the construction of Fort Crèvecoeur at Aprang, or "Little Accra," in 1649.[40] The Danes supplanted a tenuous Swedish presence in 1661, when King Okaikoi (c. 1646–1677) granted them permission to construct Fort Christiansborg at the settlement of Osu, two miles to the east of the Dutch establishment. An English fort was added in 1672–1673, when the Royal African Company built James Fort a mere half a mile to the west of Fort Crèvecoeur.[41] The forts would act as catalysts for the urban growth of the three Accra *nshonamajii*, the "seaside towns."

The overthrow of the centralized state at Ayawaso by the Akwamu in 1677 represents the first major watershed in the history of Ga state and society. The desire by the militaristic Akwamu state to control the lucrative trade routes to the coast was the likely cause of the war.[42] Reindorf, utilizing oral sources together with an account by Römer compiled in the 1740s, emphasizes internal conflict, and this may well explain the defeat of the superior Ga forces and the capture and execution of Okaikoi in 1677.[43] Many survivors of the initial Akwamu assault fled to the coast, seeking protection from the cannons of the three European forts. Resistance continued under the leadership of a son of Okaikoi, Ofori, until the final conquest of the remaining Ga territory by the Akwamu in 1680–1681. The coastal towns suffered badly and many Ga refugees, including Ofori and his mother, eventually relocated to Glidji on the Slave Coast where they founded the new kingdom of Little Popo.[44] The remaining Ga were subjected to Akwamu overrule until the latter were in turn defeated by the Akyem kingdoms and themselves pushed east of the Volta in 1730. Ga identities and perceptions of history have subsequently been rooted in the idea of a golden age of political unity and social cohesion that was brutally terminated by the Akwamu conquest. In contrast, the removal of the surviving *Ga mashi* to the coast was remembered as a time of weakness, division and civil strife.[45]

Town Quarters

The institutional reconstruction of the Ga social formation following the violent rupture of 1677–1681 was based on the formation of quarters, or *akutsei* (sing. *akutso*), within the coastal towns.[46] Although three Akan powers, Akwamu, the Akyem kingdoms, and Asante, exercised successive suzerainty over the Ga by rights of conquest between the 1680s and the 1820s, sociopolitical and spatial organization within Accra was fashioned more by its tripartite division into European zones of influence. Four *akutsei*, Asere, Abola, Gbese, and Otublohum, arose in the vicinity of Fort Crèvecoeur, at the settlement known in the seventeenth century as Aprang. The four quarters came under Dutch "protection," which, as in the other towns, gradually evolved—at least in the minds of the Europeans—into a vague jurisdiction. Collectively they became known as Dutch Accra, and after 1868 when jurisdiction over the town passed from the Dutch to the British, as Ussher Town. The Ga name for the Dutch town is Kinka, clearly cognate with the Fante term for the Dutch, *Kanka*.[47] Three *akutsei*, Alata, Sempe, and Akanmaji,

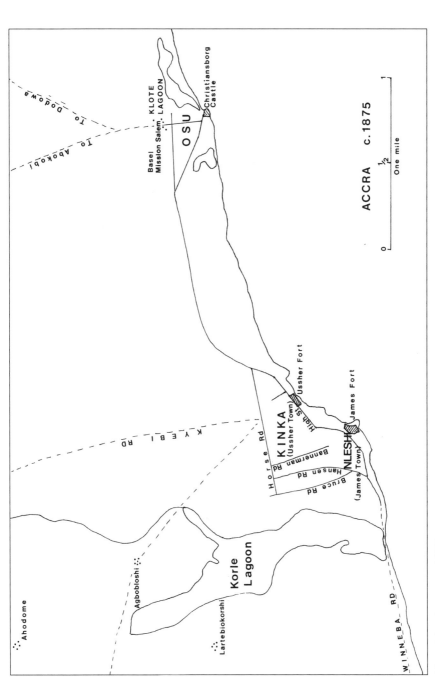

Map 1.2 Accra, c. 1875

emerged in the vicinity of James Fort on land originally associated with the village of Tsoco (modern Chorkor). These were called collectively James Town, or English Accra, which in Ga became Nleshi. Two miles to the east of these contiguous towns lay Danish Accra (Christiansborg, or Osu) which by the nineteenth century consisted of four *akutsei*: Kinkawe, Asante Blohum, Alata, and Anecho. William Smith, who visited Accra in 1726, was struck by the irony that although the Ga were "the most courteous and civil to strangers of any on the Gold Coast," the people of Nleshi and Kinka "can never well agree, each distinguishing themselves by titles of either *Englishmen* or *Dutchmen*."[48] The way in which discord between the three European forts often escalated into conflict between political factions in the towns is also evoked by the Ga maxim *Tu fee ye Abrotsiri, ni ebamomo ye Ga*—"A musket does not burst in Europe, without wounding people in Accra."[49]

The formation of the *akutsei* was a result of both conflict and accommodation: political disputes that led to the division of lineage and factional groups, and the incorporation of a diverse range of free and unfree settlers. The creation of new lineages and of Akan-style "stools" is preserved in oral traditions that serve as powerful mnemonics for the origin of collective identities.[50] The Asere and Abola peoples were *Ga mashi* who relocated to Kinka from Ayawaso. There the Asere reincorporated the Sempe, a group of migrant kinsfolk who had remained on the coast with their family god, Oyeni, and had themselves absorbed a Guang-speaking element. The Abola refugees rejoined their kinsmen the Gbese, another group of fishing people, who worshipped the sea god Nai. A distinctive Gbese *akutso* was later forged by Okaija, a dominant power broker in mid-eighteenth-century Accra politics who separated from Abola following a period of civil conflict in 1737–1739.[51] The Sempe are also said to have "quarrelled" with the Asere and to have moved across the Korle lagoon to Tsoco with the Akanmaji, who had similarly fallen out with the Gbese.[52] On their return from the western bank of the lagoon, the Sempe and Akanmaji resettled not with their *Ga mashi* kin in Kinka, but in English Accra—on the invitation of the Alata chief Wetse Kojo.

The Alata quarter of James Town was originally comprised not of Ga patrilineages but of slaves and free artisans attached to the English fort. The name Alata is evidently Allada, the Slave Coast middleman kingdom where many of these people were engaged or purchased by the English, Dutch, and Danish companies.[53] Whereas Alata communities attached to Fort Crèvecoeur were incorporated into the emerging Ga *akutsei*, those in Osu and James Town coalesced into distinct quarters. Osu Alata would remain small, but James Town or Nleshi Alata emerged as a powerful force in town affairs due to the economic and political clout of its founder, Wetse Kojo.

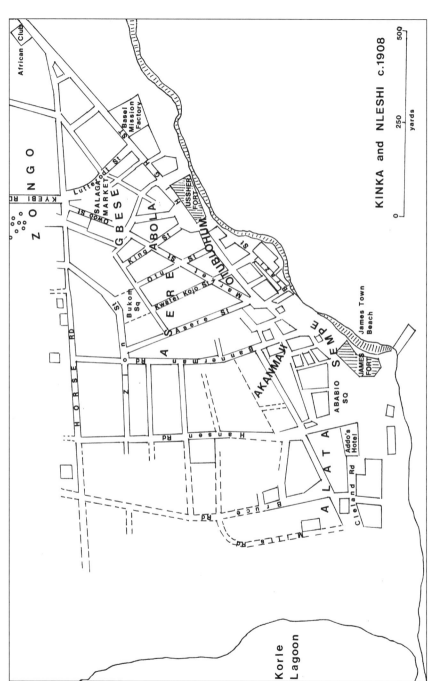

Map 1.3 Kinka and Nleshi, c. 1908

The founding of the Alata *akutso* in James Town by Wetse Kojo is an important illustration of how from the outset the institutional growth of Accra was intimately connected with changes wrought by the Atlantic economy.[54] Wetse Kojo is remembered as being brought to Accra as either a slave or a servant of the Royal African Company. Due to his commercial acumen he became its chief broker, acquiring wealth and influence and becoming a large slaveowner himself.[55] Tradition holds that with the ritual guidance of the Akwamu inhabitants of the Otublohum quarter he legitimized his economic and political power by founding an Akan-style stool and adopting the Akan *odwira* ceremony, a variation of which continued to be celebrated in the Alata *akutso* into the twentieth century. Versions of Wetse Kojo's rise to power recorded by Reindorf and Field, respectively, emphasize his control over people and his access to firearms. With both the means of coercion and the ritual paraphernalia of chiefly authority at his disposal, Wetse Kojo was acknowledged—by both Europeans and Ga— as the King of James Town, or, if we extrapolate later terminology back to the eighteenth century, the *Nleshi mantse*.[56] Although the Sempe people, as the original *Ga mashi* settlers and mediators of the Oyeni and Koole deities,[57] continued to be acknowledged as the custodians of the land around James Fort, mercantilist power enabled Wetse Kojo and his successors to establish the office of Alata *mantse* as the senior title of James Town.[58]

The Otublohum *akutso* originated as a branch of an Akwamu lineage descended from Otu, the first Akwamu governor of Accra.[59] Like Wetse Kojo, Otu began his career as a "company slave," having been pawned by his Akwamu family to the Dutch at Fort Crèvecoeur. The Dutch subsequently made him their chief broker (*makelaar*) and, following the consolidation of Akwamu power on the coast in 1681, he was also appointed as the representative of the Akwamu king in Accra. His son Amu, however, played a key role in the revolt against the *Akwamuhene* in 1730, enabling the Otublohum *akutso* to consolidate a position of influence in Kinka after the overthrow of Akwamu overrule. As in the other quarters, the balance of political power within Otublohum remained highly fluid. By the late 1820s, the Dutch *makelaar* and most powerful figure in the *akutso* was not the established *mantse*, but rather one Kwaku Ankra.[60] Accra's leading slave trader until his death in 1840, Ankra founded an *oblempon*, or "rich man's" stool, which remained a source of alternative authority within Otublohum throughout our period. His clout was demonstrated in 1836 when a party of ex-slaves deported from Bahia in Brazil landed in Accra. The returnees, most of whom were Muslims originally from the Sudanic savanna, were incorporated into Otublohum under the personal patronage of *makelaar* Ankra.[61] The insertion of the "Brazilian" or "Tabon" community represented a significant modification to Accra's increasingly diverse town quarters. Within a few years of

Table 1.1 Accra: Political Structure and *Mantsemei*, 1860s–1920s

TOWN (MAN)	KINKA (DUTCH ACCRA; AFTER 1868, USSHER TOWN)				NLESHI (ENGLISH ACCRA or JAMES TOWN)			OSU (DANISH ACCRA TO 1850, or CHRISTIANSBORG)			
Quarter (Akutso)	**Abola (Akutso of Ga Mantse)**	**Asere**	**Gbese**	**Otublohum**	**Alata**	**Sempe**	**Akanmaji**	**Kinkawe (Akutso of Osu Mantse)**	**Asante Blohum (Akutso of Osu Mankralo)**	**Alata**	**Anecho***
Mantsemei	Taki Kome c.1826-1856 Ofori Kakpo 1856-1858 Yaote 1859-1862 Taki Tawia 1862-1902 Taki Obili 1904- destooled 1919 Taki Yaoboi 1919- destooled 1929 Taki Obili reinstated 1932- destooled 1944	Teiko Ansa c.1860-c.1869 Akrama c.1869-1896 Nii Boi a.k.a. D.P. Hammond a.k.a. Teiko Akotia II 1902-1922 Ayi Ansa (stool caretaker 1922-1930; formally enstooled 1930 as Nii Teiko Ansa II)	Ayite-Ajin c.1859-c.1880 Nii Ama c.1880-c.1892 Okaija 1892-1910 Ayi Bonte 1911-?	Amu Nakwa c.1859-c.1894 Amponsa c.1902-1930	Kojo Ababio III c.1844-c.1871 Kofi Oku a.k.a. Edward Solomon 1871-1885 George Francis Cleland (regent 1882-1887) Kojo Ababio IV 1892-1938	Allotei Obuo c.1870-1876 Allotei 1891-1895 Anege Akwei 1906-1937	James Henry Badu a.k.a. Badu Ablotsrikente (stool caretaker c.1858-1894) Ayikai II (Jacob Vanderpuye) 1914- stood down 1925	Frederik Noi Dowuona 1854-1866 Naku c.1867-c.1883 Gottfried Alema Dowuona 1887-1897 Noi Ababio 1897- destooled 1914 William Notei Dowuona 1916-1931	Tete Wuruku c.1855-c.1878 Yeboa Kwamii 1880-1912 Ako Notei III 1917-c.1928		

Note: While the Alata and Anecho quarters of Osu do not appear to have had Mantsemei as leaders in the precolonial and early colonial periods, it is not being suggested that the present-day Mantsemei have not been elected in accordance with Ga custom.

their arrival a number of Tabons had emerged as wealthy entrepreneurs, having forged commercial links with fellow returnees in the ports of the Slave Coast.[62]

By the nineteenth century the quarters of Kinka, Nleshi, and—to a somewhat lesser extent—Osu had become complex territorial and political rather than purely kinship-based entities. This is reflected in the emergence of the *mantse* as the leading officeholder in each of the seven *akutsei* of Kinka and Nleshi. Retreating to their coastal settlements after 1677 as groups of harried refugees, the *Ga mashi* readily incorporated "strangers" (*gboi*, sing. *gbo*) into their shattered social and political order.[63] The subsequent growth of Accra can be seen as the demographic reconstruction of the Ga polity through the incorporation of free immigrants and slaves, a process fueled by the expansion and commercialization of the urban economy. Traders, artisans, canoemen, and refugees displaced by military conflict continued to circulate between the urban centers of the Gold and Slave Coasts. Fante settlers, widely credited with introducing sea fishing to the Ga, were over time perhaps the largest group of voluntary immigrants in Accra, where they came to form a significant component of the Abola *akutso*. Like other immigrants, such as the Alatas and later settlers from the Slave Coast, the Fante were largely assimilated into Accra society, adopting the Ga language and marrying into *Ga mashi* lineages.[64]

A vital step in the acquisition of Ga cultural identity for both free and unfree migrants was the adoption of male circumcision. In Ga minds, circumcision was the custom that more than any other distinguished them from their Akan neighbors.[65] Indeed, indigenous readings of the causes of the war of 1677 turn on Okaikoi's circumcision of an Akwamu prince residing with the Ga.[66] Three centuries later the lament could still be heard in Accra: *Nye ha foloi eha Nkranpon fee*—"You let uncircumcised people snatch Great Accra."[67] In the process of "becoming Ga," however, Akwamu, Fante, and other Twi-speaking settlers left a strong residue of Akan cultural traits that had a profound impact on the making of the town. The maxim *Ablekuma aba kuma wo*, "May strangers be added onto us," encapsulates the ideology of urban expansion that underpinned this historical process.

The census of 1891 recorded the population of Accra—the three towns of Kinka, Nleshi, and Osu together with the new colonial administrative district of Victoriaborg—as 19,999.[68] Despite an attempt at a scientific count, this figure should be treated with some caution, while earlier estimates were never more than impressionistic guesses. The population of Kinka, Nleshi, and Osu was thought in 1841 to total about 15,000, while Basel Mission sources from the early 1880s suggest a figure of 16,800 with perhaps another 17,000 inhabiting villages attached to the three *majii*.[69] There is every indication that Accra maintained a relatively high degree of demographic stability from at least the late eighteenth century, a time of trade expansion and growing prosperity in the town.[70] Population growth through natural increase and inward migration may have been checked by disease, especially smallpox. Despite Ga efforts at inoculation, smallpox epidemics appear to have periodically swept Accra, with large numbers of deaths being reported in the town at the beginning of our period in 1865.[71]

POWER AND BELIEF

As noted in the Introduction, historians of Ghana have long relied on M. J. Field's ethnographic studies for a view of Accra's past. Her account of Ga social organization, based largely on research conducted in the small fishing community of Tema and largely divested of any notion of political power, concluded that chiefly officeholders, *mantsemei*, had at no stage exercised any substantial secular authority. They were, she argued, merely minor priests who in wartime embodied certain supernatural attributes of their stools. Mistaken by Europeans for kings and chiefs, but always recognized as so-called "small boys" by their fellow Ga, the *mantsemei* would have atrophied with the ending of warfare had it not been for the patronage of the British colonial administration.[72]

Field's interpretation was, of course, a product of its age and disciplinary imperatives. Her often uncritical extrapolation of data from Tema to the complex urban arena of Accra, from the social structure to the political arena, and from the 1930s into the distant past, has been noted in passing by subsequent scholars.[73] If her portrayal of an organic community bound together by the ritual and moral authority of household heads and priests was misplaced, Field was quite correct in arguing that the Ga polity was not merely a replication of the Akan kingdoms that had for many centuries exerted a powerful influence over Accra. Indeed, references to the unusual "republican" nature of Accra's town government recur throughout eighteenth- and nineteenth-century sources.[74] The suzerainty of Akan overlords, the division of Accra into European zones of influence, and the ethnically diverse and autonomous nature of the *majii* and their constituent quarters combined to prevent the reemergence of a centralized Ga polity following the Akwamu conquest. As a subject people occupying a lucrative but politically hazardous middleman niche, the Ga developed an eclectic urban culture characterized by the borrowing of institutions and motifs from both Akan and European models. This renowned eclecticism continued to shape the historical trajectory of Accra throughout the early colonial period, fueling political action that often turned on the questions that so concerned Reindorf in the 1880s and Field in the 1930s: What constituted Ga authenticity? Who governed the precolonial town?

Hierarchies of Authority in Accra

At the heart of this problem lies the role of Accra's "chiefs." As has been noted, by the nineteenth century *mantsemei* had emerged as the leading officeholders in the seaside towns, as well as in each of the seven quarters of Kinka and Nleshi. The symbolic representation of the office of *mantse* was—and remains—a stool (*sei*), generally acknowledged by the Ga as the most prominent item in the range of politico-ritual regalia borrowed from the Akan. As in the Akan kingdoms, Ga *sei* are wooden stools belonging to the founder of a lineage or quarter that are retained after his death as sacred objects embodying the collective spirit of the institution. Thus, the Alata stool, or Gbese stool, refers to the office of *mantse* in the respective quarter. Although the *mantse* stool has functions relating to the entire quarter, it "belongs" to the patrilineage (*we*) established by its original owner.[75] Succession to a stool is hereditary and tends to be patrilineal, although there are numerous recorded examples of matrilineal succession. Ga succession to office rests on a combination of ascribed and acquired status, the successor being chosen from all genealogically eligible candidates by an electoral body of elders, subject to approval by the *manbii* of the town or quarter. By our period a number of Accra stools, including the "paramount" Okaikoi or *Ga* stool, succeeded by rotating succession, the stool typically circulating between two or three lineages. Lineages that provided *mantsemei* in rotation were either branches of the original *we* of the founder, or those established by an outsider appointed to office in extraordinary circumstances, and thereby securing the right of his descendants to the stool.

The holder of the Okaikoi stool of the Abola *akutso* of Kinka was recognized as the senior officeholder in the Ga polity and titled *Ga mantse*. How and why the stool of the relatively small quarter of Abola emerged as *primus inter pares* among the *akutsei* of Accra remains unclear. There is every indication, however, that the high status attached to Abola predates Field's somewhat casual suggestion of a genesis for the position of *Ga mantse* in "about 1840."[76] Until the late nineteenth century the Alata *akutso*, the community founded by the powerful Wetse Kojo, appears generally to have been accepted as the senior of the three quarters of James Town, although this became a bitterly contested issue in the early colonial period. The Alata *mantse* was often referred to—at least by his supporters—as James Town *mantse*, and his stool as *Nleshi sei*, implying the extension of authority over Sempe and Akanmaji. The hierarchy of office in Osu, where *mantsemei* did not emerge to head each of the four *akutsei*, is somewhat different. The Osu *mantse* is chosen from two lineages in Kinkawe, while the Asante Blohum *akutso* provides a *mankralo* ("town guardian") for all four quarters. La, Teshi, Nungwa, and Tema to the east all replicate the pattern in Osu, with one *mantse* and one *mankralo* apiece.

A second political hierarchy in Accra was that associated with the town's function as a center of military institutions. As part of *kromotsu*, the rite marking the passage from childhood to adulthood, every Ga male was initiated into an *asafo* company.[77] The Ga military companies (pl. *asafoi*) in many ways resembled those of the Akan coastal towns, and it has generally been assumed that they were derived from a Fante or Akwamu model.[78] However, the Accra *asafo* organization appears to have differed from its Akan counterparts in one fundamental respect. Whereas in towns such as Cape Coast and Elmina the companies were associated with particular quarters or wards, the Ga *asafoi* resembled broad age grades, each spanning a number of different *akutsei*. Sources from the early colonial period name a total of eight Ga companies, all bearing titles derived from the Twi language. The "age grades" were regularly mobilized for a variety of civic functions during peacetime, but appear to have divided when Accra went onto a war footing, their members joining the men of their own lineage and marching with the leaders of their respective *akutso*. Although the Ga rarely united as one army, the seven *akutsei* of Kinka and Nleshi together with the towns from Osu to Tema constituted, along Akan lines, a center, a left wing, and a right wing.[79] More importantly in terms of town politics, the *asafoi* were seen as the institutional expression of "commoner" interests, ready to defend the rights of the ordinary *manbii* and keep in check the prerogatives of chiefs. This balance of power in the body politic was commonly expressed by the *asafobii* as "the Chiefs are the head and we are the legs of the town."[80] The *asafoi* possessed an established hierarchy of hereditary offices. The sections of the companies in each *akutso* were headed by *asafoatsemei* ("fathers of the *asafo*"), or "captains," who were in turn answerable to one *shipi*. The military leader of each *akutso* was the *akwashon onukpa*. One powerful lineage, Kpakpatsewe of Asere, provided the *akwashontse*, or *akwashon mantse*, theoretically the senior military commander of all the Ga.

The *wulomei*, or "priests," formed a third formal structure of authority in the town. Like Ga culture generally, religion and belief in Accra was characterized by a high degree of eclecticism. Four main types of deities and respective modes of worship (called by Field "cults") may be identified, three of which are non-Ga in origin. *Me* was originally a Dangme, *otu* a Fante, and *akon* an Akuapem cult, while the fourth, *kple* or *kpele*, was associated with a mixture of migrant Ga and autochthonous deities. As early as 1760, Römer shrewdly warned of the dangers

Figure 1.3 Town leaders at Prampram, c. 1880. The Ligble *wulomo* (Dangme: *wono*), his wives, and the *mantse* and chiefs of Prampram (Gbugbla): a portrait of sacred and secular authority in Ga-Dangme society. (Courtesy of the Foreign and Commonwealth Office Library, London.)

of portraying Ga belief as an essentialized, systematic "religion": "For most . . . [Ga] never bother to think about such things, and the elderly among them who do, are, in most cases, of such varied opinions as East is from West."[81] In her study of the symbolism of the songs of the *kple* cult, Kilson criticizes Field's 1937 monograph as a "somewhat haphazard catalogue of deities and rites in different Ga towns" that misleadingly downplays the role of the supreme being, Nyonmo.[82] In line with her concern to reveal the authentic forms of Ga culture divested of corrupting outside influences, Field was certainly ready to dismiss any prominence given to Nyonmo as being due to the influence of Christianity. Yet her stubbornly localized account may in fact be a rather accurate reflection of the historical realities of Ga religion, in which discordant voices and the rise and fall of local cult complexes were of more importance than a systematic belief system focused on an unchanging pan-Ga pantheon. Field also draws out the crucial distinction between the great civic gods, revered to some extent by all Ga and around whose cults grew powerful public offices, and those deities worshipped in a more intimate and personalized manner by smaller groups of devotees, or *agbamei*.[83]

Ga cosmology was intertwined with the mental mapping of the physical world. The Ga identified a distant, "withdrawn" supreme being, Nyonmo, who was associated with the physical phenomenon of rain.[84] As in many African societies, everyday worship was directed toward more accessible "gods of the world" (*jemawojii*, sing. *jemawon*), the most powerful of an array of supernatural forces (*wojii*, sing. *won*) jostling for space with mankind's living, dead, and unborn. Just as the known world was bounded by the omnipresent sea and attendant rivers, so spiritual power was phrased by the fluidity, ambiguity, and coolness of water. An account by Barbot of a ceremony at the edge of Osu's Klote lagoon in 1679—at the very genesis of the seaside polity—provides the earliest commentary on the salience of water in Ga thought.[85] Subsequent sources are replete with references to water in all its physical and metaphorical forms. Paradigmatically, Accra's three great tutelary deities were all reified as bodies of water: Nai, the god of the sea, and the lagoon gods Sakumo and Koole (Korle). Water—and its highly potent variation, alcohol—served to mediate relations between man and the gods, between the living and the dead, between the known and unknown.[86] The afterworld, Zimmermann's informants in the 1850s supposed, lay "on the islands of and beyond the River Volta"—at the fluvial margins of the Ga-Dangme world.[87]

The authority of the *wulomei* was founded on esoteric knowledge of this ritual topography and its manipulation in the cause of ecological management. Like its secular counterpart, priestly office was hereditary and the preserve of particular lineages. Nai and Koole were historically associated with the Gbese and Sempe *akutsei*, respectively, acknowledged as the earliest Ga settlers at Accra who therefore established a privileged relationship with the local *jemawojii*. However, by the mid-eighteenth century the shrines of Nai, Sakumo, and Koole were all located in the Gbese *akutso*, the *wulomo* of each god provided by three Gbese lineages. The concentration of ritual authority in Gbese is an important element in the political evolution of Accra and seems to be associated with the rise of Okaija following his conflict with the Otublohums and Aseres in the late 1730s.[88] Tradition holds that the gods were "removed" from Asere to Gbese, although access to three other prominent deities, Dantu, the "time-keeping god," Naa Dede Oyeadu, the goddess of birth and death, and Gua, the blacksmith god, continued to be mediated by *wulomei* from Asere lineages. A final *jemawon* should be added to the list of great "national" gods: Lakpa, the tutelary deity of the town of La. Revered throughout the Ga country and beyond for its oracular powers, Lakpa competed with its fellow war god, Sakumo, as a source of ritual knowledge and power.[89]

Public Office and Private Power

In addition to these formal hierarchies of secular and sacred functionaries, authority in Accra was wielded by "big men" who held no established office. We have seen how the accumulation of wealth and power enabled entrepreneurial "strangers" like Wetse Kojo and Otu and his descendants to establish their own royal stools that became the focal point of new quarters. By about the mid-eighteenth century, for reasons that remain unclear, the rise of powerful accumulators no longer led to the foundation of new *akutsei*. These men, whose wealth was derived primarily from European maritime trade, instead founded private stools, known variously as "rich man's stools," "palanquin stools," or *oblempon* stools.[90] It appears that the right to "cut" a private stool and to display chiefly regalia was either purchased from or granted by the recognized officeholders. The right to be borne in an Akan-style palanquin (*akpakai*) visibly distinguished the mercantile prowess of the *oblempon* from the sacrally derived authority of public officeholders, for whom walking on the ground symbolized guardianship of the land.[91] The most salient characteristic of *oblempon* stool holders, however, was their control over large retinues of retainers or slaves. Many *mantsemei* are also remembered as wealthy traders and slave owners, but their office was based on a ritually sanctioned relationship with the freeborn members of their *akutso* rather than necessarily with accumulation and control over people. Arhin has identified a similar diffusion of authority among the Fante, arguing that relatively open access to wealth resulted in the dissolution of the established Akan rank system.[92] It is clear that compared to the more centralized forest kingdoms of the interior, the private accumulation of wealth and status was an integral feature of the entrepôt towns on the Gold Coast.

What, then, was the political position of office-holding chiefs in precolonial Accra? In what ways can their material and ideological resources be distinguished from those of "private" accumulators? The first point to consider is the exercise of judicial authority. The right to administer law and order in the town was historically contested between Akan suzerains, the European forts, and indigenous Ga leaders.[93] With the consolidation of the town quarters, cases involving civil dispute and criminal justice were heard by tribunals in each *akutso* presided over by the *mantse*.[94] The right to take part in public court proceedings was an important benchmark of civic status, and was limited to those members of the male community styled *anobulo* (pl. *anobua*), usually rendered as "councillors" or "grandees."[95] Various fees and fines levied by the court were retained by the *mantse* and his functionaries, representing an important component of stool revenue. Debt and adultery are cited as the most common causes of litigation, with penalties for the latter varying according to the rank of the wronged husband.[96] In line with his position as *primus inter pares* among the *mantsemei*, the *Ga mantse*'s court was regarded as senior, often resorted to by parties from neighboring Dangme and even Twi-speaking areas. In addition to the tribunals in each quarter, there also existed two bodies that acted as courts of appeal: *Mojawe* and the *akwashon. Mojawe* (lit. "house of blood," from the Twi *mmogya*, blood) was also presided over by the *Ga mantse* and appears to have been the only court with the right to impose capital punishment. Composed of the seven *akwashon onukpai* of Kinka and Nleshi, presided over by the *akwashontse*, and with certain rights regarding the conduct of the *Ga mantse*, the *akwashon* was an important element in the balance of judicial authority between *mantsemei* and military officials, and between the Abola and Asere quarters.

Officeholders also maintained their position through the exercise of warfare. Whereas in the commercial sphere they had little apparent advantage over private traders, the ascribed military role of *mantsemei* was based on the authority to mobilize the citizens of the *asafo* companies for war. The rewards of military success came in two forms: the attainment of status and virtue through feats of arms, and the accumulation of material wealth, usually in the form of captives. Although the coastal Ga polity was not particularly militaristic compared to some of its neighbors on the Gold and Slave Coasts, from the 1780s to the 1870s military expeditions were regularly mounted against neighboring states, a primary objective being the capture of booty and slaves. The ritual aspect of the military role of chiefs was stressed by Field, who argued that "as a human being a *mantse* had . . . no authority."[97] Office holding, ritual power, and warfare certainly were intimately connected in precolonial Accra. As we shall see in the next chapter, however, there is ample evidence that chiefs did act "as human beings," utilizing their office in the pursuit of status and wealth through war.

How did the authority of secular officeholders interact with that wielded by the *wulomei*? In theory, Field is again correct in insisting that the office of *wulomo* was superordinate to that of *mantse*. The differentiation between the two estates was conveyed by a range of cultural symbols implying the subordination of chiefs to priests. The most striking of these signifiers was the association of the color red (*tsuru*) with chieftaincy as opposed to the color white (*ye*) with sacral power.[98] Precolonial sources are replete with references to the peculiar religiosity of the Ga, and to the extensive influence of *wulomei* in Accra. On the one hand, this influence served to underpin the chiefly hierarchy. "The chiefs knew how difficult it was to make people observe a law made simply by them," a literate Ga observed in 1884 of the distant past, "and so called in the alliance of the fetish to enforce it, and this was the more easy as the chief then was often the fetishman."[99] On the other hand, the authority derived from access to esoteric ritual knowledge—dominated but far from monopolized by the *wulomei* of the great civic deities—could also be mobilized in opposition to that of the *mantsemei*.[100] Tensions between the sacred and secular estates periodically erupted over the accumulation of wealth in people, slaves being able to remove themselves from the control of an unjust master by fleeing to the sanctuary of a shrine (*gbatsu*) and attaching themselves to the household of the officiating *wulomo*.[101] The Ga called this transaction *no-he ke won*, "to dash (i.e., to give) one's self to the god."[102] *No-he ke won* was of particular benefit to the house of the war god Sakumo, recognized as a special guardian of slaves, and by 1834, the Sakumowe was said to control a retinue of 500 such *wonwebii*.[103] Its influence was dramatically demonstrated in the 1820s, when the oracle advanced one of its own "servants," the future *Ga mantse* Taki Kome, to lead the Ga armies against the Asante, an incident explored in more detail in Chapter 2.

The exercise of authority in precolonial Accra, both private and public, sacred and secular, was fundamentally shaped by gender relations. Although senior women possessed a high degree of autonomy and authority within the domestic arena, they were largely excluded from formal political discourse. Women were jural minors, whose subordination to men was expressed by a variety of symbols and social observances.[104] However, the very ways in which men regarded women as potentially threatening in itself suggests that the latter were willing and able to breach the barrier between the domestic and public realms. Women were viewed as inherently deceitful (*lakaloi*) and "left-handed" (*abekuloi*), and it is interesting to note that oral tradition portrays the only woman to rule over the Ga, Dode Akabi, as a ruthless tyrant. Not only did women in Accra have considerable economic clout, they also featured prominently in ritual networks as both *agbamei* and specialized religious functionaries. Most notable were the *woyei* (sing. *woyo*), "mediums" who provided direct mediation with the spiritual realm.[105] The public voice of the medium when possessed was, admittedly, that of the *jemawon* rather than her own, yet it was a role that was translated by many *woyei* into social status and material wealth. Precolonial sources are largely silent on these issues, but it is possible to speculate that the proximity of women to the divine and supernatural realms injected a certain tension— and, on the part of men, anxiety—into relations between the sexes.[106] In common with many societies, this anxiety emerges in the belief that women had a greater propensity to engage in witchcraft. In the political arena it emerges in the uninhibited and outspoken part that women often played in informal public discourse.

HOUSEHOLD AND LINEAGE

Field lays great emphasis on the agnatic patrilineage, the *we* or *weku*, as the major arena of Ga social activity. Her unequivocal characterization of Ga descent as patrilineal, however, has been qualified by later anthropologists. Kilson in particular argues that kinship is cognatic, with the emphasis only on patrilineal affiliation.[107] An individual, in other words, could "belong" to the lineage of either his or her parents or grandparents, affiliation depending on a range of social and political variables.[108] There is much historical evidence to suggest that succession and inheritance through the matrilineal line in Accra was far from uncommon. All things being equal, Ga children belonged to the *we* of their father. The *we*, however, was a nonresidential group dispersed in various households (*shiai*; sing. *shia*) in different quarters of Accra and in rural outposts. This residential pattern created a variety of bonds that crosscut the framework of patrilineages, serving to undermine the corporate nature of the normative agnatic *we*.

The "traditional" Ga household was characterized by the residential separation of male and female adults. The core of the male *shia* was typically a patrilineage of short span, say three generations, headed by the *shiatse* or *shia onukpa*, the "house elder." The female *shia* comprised matrilineally related women together with their young children of both sexes.[109] A third type of household occupied a single dwelling divided into two sections, one for men and the other for women who were either patrilineally affiliated to the *shia* or the wives of the adjacent men. The term *shia* also means the dwelling itself (*yeiashia*: women's house; *hiiashia*: men's house), or can refer to the lineage based in it, in both cases becoming broadly synonymous with the word *we*. It appears to have been quite common, however, for a man to reside with his mother's male relatives, and it was in this situation that matrilineal kinship ties would often come into play.[110] Both the male and female *shia* in Accra were typically augmented by domestic slaves of the same sex, who were to varying degrees incorporated into the social life of the household. No numerical data on the size of households exist before 1891, when the census recorded an average of just over twelve people in each of Accra's 1,663 dwellings.[111]

As a physical structure, the *shia* itself was resonant with cultural meaning. The original architectural norm in Accra was a round house made of swish and topped by a conical roof, a form preserved into the twentieth century in the shape of *gbatsui*, shrines.[112] Circular houses were still common in the early nineteenth century, but by the 1850s most dwellings in Accra

Figure 1.4 Women grinding corn in the courtyard of an Osu *agbonaa*, "compound house," 1870s. (Copyright Basel Mission Archive, Basel, Switzerland. Ref. No. D-30.01.047. Reproduced with permission.)

were of a rectangular design.[113] They comprised a series of rooms built around one or more courtyards, the former occupied by adult household members, and the latter by children, slaves, and other dependants. The courtyard of the *yeiashia* served as the kitchen, the women taking the cooked food to their husbands and sons in the *hiiashia*. The latter contained the shrines to the household gods, (male) indigenous readings invariably pointing to this division in ritual management as the origin of residential segregation. The gendered ordering of space in Accra lay at the heart of indigenous notions of domesticity, the set of ideas that associated women with the domestic realm and underpinned the hierarchical distribution of power in the favor of men.[114] At the same time, it reinforced women's social and economic autonomy, facilitating the creation of female community networks beyond the reach of husbands and kinsmen.

Nineteenth-century sources contain numerous descriptions of the imposing residences of wealthy traders and chiefs. Often built of stone hewn from local quarries, two to three storeys high, and brightly whitewashed, these so-called storey houses stood in dramatic contrast to the mass of single-storeyed swish "compound houses" (*agbonaa*) from which they rose. They continued to be built around multiple courtyards that housed retinues of slaves and followers, the ground floor serving as a warehouse and trading depot. Although members of the emerging Euro-African merchant elite were often coresident with their spouses, the storey houses built by Ga "big men" appear to have continued to be characterized by a separation of the sexes.[115] Commercial expansion in the nineteenth century meant that real property acquired quantifiable value in terms of rents, outright sale, and security for credit. Yet dwellings in Accra continued to have great cultural significance over and above their economic value. The building of a *shia* typically led to the establishment of a new lineage, both of which would eventually take the name of the founder and serve as a mnemonic for his success in furthering the expansion of the community. The house became the *adeboo shia*, the "ancestral house," the focal point in the social life of the *we* to which all members would return during the *Homowo* festival to honor the ancestors. Its social and ritual importance heightened by the Ga custom of intramural sepulture, the *shia*, as Kilson writes, was "a means of perpetuating one's identity within the otherwise highly fluid cognatic descent system."[116]

As in other established West African trading entrepôts, Accra's urban economy was marked by the active participation of women in the marketplace. Within each *we* the male hierarchy was ultimately superordinate to the female. Nevertheless, the ability of male lineage and household heads to call on the labor of women, and perhaps that of junior males who continued to reside with their mother or her family, appears to have been limited by the considerable autonomy of the *yeiashia*. By the mid-nineteenth century if not earlier Accra possessed a flourishing market, monetized by the use of cowries and dominated by women selling agricultural produce, fish, and a wide variety of cooked food. There is little evidence to show that senior men exercised control over this range of enterprises, managing the household as a single economic entity.[117] Field's observations of the domestic arena in the 1930s are instructive in this respect. She provides much evidence of distinct male and female economic networks, with seniors exercising control over cohabiting juniors and senior women retaining considerable control over their own wealth and labor.[118] A clear manifestation of this autonomy was the Ga custom of women inheriting property, including farms, houses, fishing canoes, and slaves from their mothers. Field's analysis of relative female economic autonomy has been further developed in Robertson's pioneering study of changing gender relations in twentieth-century Accra.[119] The prominent role of Ga women in the marketplace served to enhance their political clout, and nineteenth-century observers began to note the assertive—and often disruptive—influence of the ubiquitous "market women" in town affairs.

The considerable autonomy of female households and economic networks in Accra was closely related to the dynamics of the institution of marriage. Marriage was essentially a transaction between two families, conferring on a man exclusive rights over the sexuality and reproductive capacity of a woman. As the prominence of adultery cases in precolonial judicial action indicates, these rights were jealously guarded, and control over women was a key element in the accumulation of wealth and status. The word marriage, however, describes a wide range of contractual relations, ranging from the fully sanctified "six-cloth" marriage (*boi-ekpa*) to less formal arrangements that shade into the term "concubinage." Increasing social differentiation was probably reflected in the widening of this spectrum, poorer families often forgoing the considerable costs of *boi-ekpa*, with the result that "the woman is less amenable to the jurisdiction of her partner, less subject to restraint, and may at any moment leave him with her progeny."[120] "Seldom you meet with a Labadie or Teshi man living with a concubine," Reindorf reported in 1881, but "the Accras do the contrary."[121] The earliest records of the British courts reveal that by the 1850s many Ga women were both willing and able to shape gender relations by contesting male dominance of the institution of marriage. The number of cases involving divorce, the rights of concubines, and the control over children clearly suggest an established independence of action, which in the early colonial period would provoke expressions of patriarchal alarm.

PATTERNS OF HISTORICAL CHANGE

The chapter thus far has focused on the spatial and institutional forms of precolonial Accra, making only passing reference to actual historical events. The aim of this final section is to locate these structures in a broad pattern of historical change, briefly charting the development of Accra from the rupture of the 1670s to the eve of the colonial consolidation of the 1870s. Throughout this period two powerful external forces interacted with internal developments to fashion the making of the town: the shifting balance of power among the Akan forest kingdoms to the north, and the dynamics of the Atlantic economy.

Accra Under Akan Overrule

Despite the destruction and depopulation resulting from the expansion of the Akwamu kingdom to the coast, those remaining under Akwamu overrule in Accra between 1681 and 1730 retained a significant stake in the mercantile economy. Inexperienced on the coast and lacking the linguistic skills necessary to negotiate with the European forts, the Akwamu—the "coarse peasants" of Tilleman's account—left much of the profitable middleman activity to their Ga subjects.[122] By the 1740s, Römer's informants recalled the Akwamu years as a "glorious period" when, as slave brokers supplying the forts with "*sika din,*" "black gold," "we earned more in one day than we do now in a year."[123] Accra occupied an important position in the Akwamu imperial system, which at its height stretched for 250 miles from Agona in the west to Whydah in the east. The mercantilist empire was broken in 1729–1730 by a combination of internal revolt and the rising power of the Akyem kingdoms, which combined in 1730 to oust Akwamu from its coveted position between themselves and the coast. The Ga, who participated in the uprising under the leadership of Ayikuma Teikuba of the old ruling dynasty at Great Accra, regained some degree of political independence due to the inability of the Akyem to establish a firm presence on the coast.[124] The weakness of Akyem control seems to have created something of a power vacuum in Accra. Much of their twelve-year period of overrule was characterized by recurring conflict between various Ga factions, which, as we have seen, shaped the emerging configuration of Accra's town quarters. Political tensions may have been generated by the rising demand for slaves on the Gold Coast, as established ritual authorities, secular "big men," and the European forts jostled for advantage in the increasingly lucrative trade. The expansion of the slave trade also fueled the growing confrontation to the north between the Akyem and the expansionist Asante kingdom. Rising conflict culminated in the military defeat of Akyem in 1742 and the incorporation of Accra into the southern provinces of the Asante empire.

Accra and the Ga country remained under nominal Asante rule from 1742 until the mid-1820s.[125] Reindorf's detailed account of the period, emphasizing what he saw as the special relationship between the two peoples while at the same time pointing out the tyrannical aspects of Asante rule, reflects the deep ambivalence that many Ga must have felt toward their powerful overlords.[126] This ambivalence is succinctly captured in a Ga maxim recorded by Zimmermann in the 1850s: *Asantemei wonu no, si no fo mli tso*—"The soup of the Asante is tasteful, but there is too much salt in it."[127] As a result of ongoing hostilities between Asante and the Fante states that repeatedly blocked the trade routes from Kumase to Elmina and Cape Coast, the "great road" to Accra was from the 1740s to 1816 the Asante's principal route to the coast. For the period of peak slave exports from the Gold Coast, therefore, Accra was the only port with continuous access to the interior, becoming the main Asante entrepôt for guns, ammunition, salt, and other imports.[128] By the last quarter of the eighteenth century, traders from Asante and other inland and coastal states were flocking to Accra. There is no doubt that many Ga claimed a portion of the proverbial "Asante soup," profiting from this period of ris-

Figure 1.5 Wealthy Ga women wearing imported cloth and elaborate "rolled" hair styles. A studio portrait from the late nineteenth century. (Copyright Basel Mission Archive, Basel, Switzerland. Ref. No. QQ-30.101.0047. Reproduced with permission.)

ing commercial activity.[129] The consumption of imported goods rose, urban growth and the demand from slave-trading vessels stimulated agricultural production in the Accra hinterland, and the local economy became increasingly monetized with the importation of cowries.[130] One observer noted that Accra's flourishing free trade with Asante "diffuses money among every class."[131]

As in other West African middleman states, however, the impact of the Atlantic slave trade on Accra was complex and ambiguous.[132] Accra paid for its profitable relationship with Asante by incurring the periodic hostility of the neighboring Akyem, Akuapem, Krobo, Obutu, and Fante, all of whom staged military incursions at one time or another into Ga country.[133] These examples of organized violence were part of a more general insecurity throughout the eighteenth century, a time remembered by Reindorf's informants as one of endemic kidnapping by gangs of "siccadingers." Militias such as Odshofoi, the "iron-hearted company," were organized to protect the Accra plains, where farmers stood guard over villages called Ologobi, "to evade a pursuer," and Sowotuom, "hold your gun."[134] Whether levels of domestic slavery in Accra rose during the peak years of slave exports between 1730 and 1790 remains unclear, although this appears to have been the case in neighboring Cape Coast.[135] Evidence suggests that increasing commercialization took its toll on the weaker and more vulnerable members of society, Isert noting the close connection between debt, pawning, slavery, and violence in Accra in the 1780s.[136] Despite Meredith's impression of an air of general prosperity about town, new forms of wealth served to increase inequality. The range of clothing styles and bodily decoration in Accra is a reflection not only of the power of imported commodities and the rich culture of public display, but also the extent of socioeconomic differentiation.[137]

The decision by the Ga leaders to terminate eight decades of generally good relations with their suzerains in Kumase by joining the British-led alliance of coastal states against Asante in 1822–1826 represents a critical juncture in the history of Accra. Why by the 1820s had Asante rule finally become unpalatable? The Ga country had been spared the depredations wrought by a series of Asante military operations against the Fante beginning in 1806 and, indeed, Asante forces had protected Accra from incursions by the hostile Fante. Yet there are indications that Asante overrule in Accra—like that of Akwamu a century before—was becoming increasingly exacting by the early nineteenth century, perhaps fueled by the short-term disruption created by the British abolition of the Atlantic slave trade in 1807.[138] The dislocation of commerce at Accra and the diversion of much Asante trade to Elmina after 1816 meant that the benefits of the *pax Asante* had become less tangible.[139] The Ga switch of allegiance proved judicious. Hostilities culminated in a large set-piece battle on August 7, 1826 between an invading Asante army and an allied force on the open plains at Katamanso, some twenty miles northeast of Accra. The Asante were routed, effectively ending their overrule on the Gold Coast littoral and paving the way for the rise of Britain as an alternative regional power.

Nineteenth-Century Urban Transitions

The history of the trading towns of the Gold Coast during the first three quarters of the nineteenth century has generally been analyzed in the context of the transition to "legitimate" (i.e., nonslave) commerce, the rise of a new indigenous merchant elite, and the fitful extension of British influence.[140] The degree to which the decline of slave exports represented a "crisis of adaptation" for local states and the links between the commercial transition and the subsequent imposition of full-blown colonial rule has formed one of the central debates in the historiography of West Africa.[141] While most historians now agree that the coastal middleman states tended to weather the shift to legitimate commerce without experiencing significant disruption, the impact of the transition on Accra remains open to debate. Reynolds argues that in political terms 1807 marks the beginning of an inexorable decline in the power of the traditional rulers on the Gold Coast relative to the rising wealth and influence of a new merchant elite.[142] However, the fragmentation of economic and political power in eighteenth-century Accra suggests a greater degree of continuity between the era of the slave trade and that of legitimate commerce than this paradigm allows. As we will see in the next chapter, the rise of new legitimate entrepreneurs did not necessarily imply a concomitant loss of authority for established officeholders, both groups having also to contend with the shifting priorities of protocolonial European administrations.

The extent to which the institution of slavery in Accra was transformed as a result of the commercial transition also remains unclear. Historiographical perspectives on nineteenth-century slavery are considered in Chapter 3, but it can be noted here that slavery appears to have undergone a quantitative if not a qualitative change in the town and its farming hinterland. By the mid-nineteenth century servitude existed in a variety of different forms throughout all strata of Ga society, even small farmers, fishermen, and women petty traders often owning one or two slaves.[143] "[By] my own computation," Reindorf estimated in 1862 as part of a robust defense of the institution of domestic slavery, "I can say that among all Ga people one half are real natives," implying that the bulk of the other half were of unfree origin.[144] The sporadic export of slaves continued until the 1850s, probably as a means of exercising control over expanding internal labor forces.[145] Small groups of slaves were marched east to points on the Dangme coast, the Anlo coast, and sometimes as far as the Slave Coast port of Little Popo, Reindorf insisting that "all the influential chiefs had their hands in it."[146]

Nevertheless, by the 1820s the export of slaves from Accra was in sharp decline, and the first generation of independent, literate Euro-African merchants began to rise to prominence in town affairs. Key figures were James

Bannerman (1790–1858), John Hansen (d. 1840), and William "Nanka" Bruce (d. 1856) of James Town, and Henry Richter (d. 1849) of Osu, all of whom probably owned in excess of 300 slaves who were used to expand agricultural production for domestic and export markets.[147] English-language sources refer to those of mixed European and African parentage as mulattos, a word incorporated into Ga as *mulatofoi*. The Ga also conferred the honorific *owula* on both Europeans and influential Euro-Africans. Derived from the Twi *wura*, "master," but with connotations of gentlemanliness, learning, and urbanity, the term *owula* distinguished the wealthy, literate Euro-African from the established Ga "big man," or *oblempon*.[148]

The emergence of literate African and Euro-African elites has been a central concern of historians of the nineteenth-century Gold Coast. While some treatments have emphasized sociocultural links stretching to Europe and to the anglophone Creole (or Krio) communities of trading towns from Freetown to Fernando Po, others have stressed the importance of local African affiliations.[149] The absence of significant groups of Sierra Leonian Krios on the Gold Coast certainly points to the relative strength of ties between the emerging literate elites and the indigenous communities from which they emerged. Moreover, Euro-Africans had long been a feature of Ga and Fante coastal towns, with an established role as brokers between indigenous hierarchies and the European forts.[150] According to Reindorf—himself a descendant of an eighteenth-century Danish trader—the lack of educational facilities in Accra meant that "mulatto children were forced to adopt the ways and habits of the natives," some becoming powerful chiefs who distinguished themselves as warriors.[151] The exceptions, he notes, were the offspring of the Danes at Osu, where the boys attended a school opened in 1722 before being employed as soldiers. The Danish administration encouraged unions between its employees and Ga women, and herein lies the origin of the large, self-conscious Euro-African community of nineteenth-century Osu.[152] In Reverend Reindorf's reading, just as *mulatofoi* notables of the past had delivered their people from the Akwamu and Asante enemy, so too would the Euro-African modernizing elite of Victorian Accra lead the Ga into a new era of Christian enlightenment. For robustly secular figures like James Bannerman and his sons, however, it was education in Europe rather than Christian instruction that created new aspirations, life-styles, and identities, which, if not irreconcilable with those forged by participation in indigenous institutions, were quite distinct from them.

The rise of palm oil exports, the extension of credit to local traders by British consignment houses, and the transition from sail to steam in European maritime trade from the 1850s drew increasing numbers of Ga into the exchange economy. The chain of credit extended from the big commodity brokers down to a mass of petty traders, the majority of

Figure 1.6 The Osu cabinetmaker Bannerman and his workers, c. 1900. Bannerman poses in his workshop with the altar and pulpit for the new Basel Mission church. (Photograph by Max Schultz, Basel Mission. Copyright Basel Mission Archive, Basel, Switzerland. Ref. No. QQ-30.122.52. Reproduced with permission.)

whom were probably women.[153] New opportunities for accumulation were not limited to trade. Equally important in the social and economic history of Accra was the migration of skilled tradesmen to the trading towns of the Bights of Benin and Biafra, Fernando Po, and ultimately as far as the Congo Independent State.[154] The emergence of Ga artisans as the best and most abundant on the coast has been attributed to the establishment by the Basel Mission of a workshop at Osu in the late 1850s. Considerable numbers of coopers, carpenters, masons, and blacksmiths were trained at the mission workshop, although apprenticeship and guild-like craft organization soon became an indigenous Ga affair. Working at "the Bights" became an important source of wealth and status for large numbers of Ga tradesmen, resources utilized by many to attain public office on their return to a sedentary life in Accra. Their role as agents of new ideas and technologies is exemplified in the career of the most famous of all Ga tradesmen, Tete Quashie (c. 1842–1892), a Basel Mission–trained blacksmith who returned from Fernando Po in the late 1870s with the seeds with which he would establish the first successful cocoa farm on the Gold Coast.[155]

The incorporation of Accra into a framework of colonial rule was a drawn-out, negotiated affair, which ebbed and flowed throughout the nineteenth century. The British, Danish, and Dutch forts struggled to exercise a vague jurisdiction over their respective *majii* and ill-defined hinterlands, and the ability of officials to enforce their will in town affairs was prone to constant fluctuation. Until the British consolidation of the 1860s–1870s, the forts are best understood not as alien outposts of colonial rule but as integral components of Accra's fragmented political arena, sometimes cooperating and at other times competing with a variety of indigenous hierarchies to secure influence and revenue. Drawing on the Ga middleman tradition, literate Euro-Africans emerged as crucial brokers within this pattern of overlapping jurisdictions. Hansen and Bannerman both served as British magistrates and commandants of James Fort, the latter famously becoming Lieutenant-Governor of the Gold Coast in 1850–1851. By the 1840s, this equation included the slowly expanding influence of two missionary societies, the Basel Mission based at Osu and the Wesleyan Methodists at James Town. A combination of literacy, Christianity, and legitimate commerce was beginning to define the town's emergent merchant elite.

Despite a peace settlement with Asante in 1831 and the vigorous regime of Governor Maclean in the 1830s, British policy on the Gold Coast was constrained by fluctuating revenues, official parsimony, and indecisiveness.[156] In 1850, the British purchased the Danish settlements between Accra and the Volta, leaving Kinka as an isolated Dutch enclave in what became the Eastern Districts of the Gold Coast Protectorate. An attempt to secure a revenue base by the imposition of a poll tax, however, was fiercely resisted by the Ga of the leeward coast, hostilities culminating in a naval bombardment in September 1854 that destroyed the town of Osu with great loss of life.[157] The failure of the poll tax led to a short-lived experiment with municipal institutions. Governor Pine hoped to create a "strong native Government" that combined the authority of chiefs with the rising influence of the "large class of Native Merchants."[158] In May 1858 the *manbii* of James Town elected a seven-man Town Council headed by the younger James Bannerman, which, despite its collapse less than two years, later provided a model for the rising aspirations of the indigenous elite. For the British administration the 1860s was a time of renewed uncertainty. Faced with an anticolonial lobby at home that questioned the need to maintain a dilapidated string of coastal forts and a series of recurring military crises that tested the limits of its ill-defined jurisdiction, the inchoate colonial project appeared to be foundering. For the townspeople of Accra, changing conditions presented both threat and opportunity, a variety of interest groups seeking to defend the hard-won gains of the past in the face of new challenges.

CONCLUSION

Accra's urban identity was based on its function as a site of exchange, transaction, and power. Despite the fragmentation of Ga political authority following the rupture of 1677–1681, town notables in the three Accra *nshonamajii*, "seaside towns," fashioned a lucrative middleman role in the exchange networks of the Gold Coast and its forest hinterland. In the mid-1860s, Accra stood on the cusp of a new era in its long history. The consolidation of British rule would transform the nucleus of Ga state and society, as the three *majii* became the core of an expanding colonial port city. Despite this transformation, the chronology of urban change should neither obscure the continuity of precolonial forms, nor overemphasize the role of the metropole in the reconfiguration of social processes in the city. For two centuries or more, the Ga had drawn on a variety of endogenous and exogenous sources in the creative task of making the town. Danes, Dutch, English, Akan, Dangme, Ewe, "Alatas" from the Slave Coast, Sierra Leonian Krios, Muslim Brazilian returnees, German, Swiss, and West Indian missionaries: all had contributed to Accra's precolonial urban culture. The expansion of colonialism and capitalism did not mean that British rulers suddenly became the dominant force shaping Ga state and society. As we shall see in the following chapters, Accra's established role as a nexus of political, military, and sacral power would continue to fashion the social history of the early colonial town.

NOTES

1. A song from the *kple* religious cult, from Marion Kilson, *Kpele lala. Ga religious songs and symbols* (Cambridge, MA, 1971), 239. I have amended the orthography and translation of this song with the assistance of Mr. David Henderson-Quartey.

2. Ga proverb, from Zimmermann, *Grammatical sketch*, Vol. 1, 158.

3. For the political and cultural configuration of the coast at the start of our period, see Public Record Office, London [hereafter PRO] CO 96/41, Pine to Labouchere, No. 35, dd. James Fort, Accra, 30 Apr. 1857.

4. Reindorf, *History*, 11. Margaret Field's list of the seven coastal towns conflates Nleshi and Kinka as Accra and adds Kpon, or Kpone, situated to the east of Tema on the vague borderland between Ga and Dangme settlement, and which most sources identify with the latter: Field, *Religion and medicine*, 1. Whether or not Nleshi (or James Town) and Kinka (or Ussher Town) are to be considered separate entities historically has been a highly contested issue that was at the center of much political conflict in early colonial Accra.

5. C. Wise, "Climatic anomalies on the Accra plain," *Geography*, 29 (1944); H. P. White, "Environment and land use in the south eastern savannas of the Gold Coast," *West African Institute of Social and Economic Research: Annual Conference Proceedings, March 1956* (Ibadan, 1956).

6. On the prolonged dry period from 1816 to 1832 and the use of famine foods in Accra, see Reindorf, *History*, 274–277; on recurring drought in the 1860s resulting in food shortages and hunger, see *The African Times*, 23 Nov. 1863 and 23 Apr. 1866; Wesleyan Methodist Missionary Society Archives [hereafter WMMS] Gold Coast Correspondence [GCC], Box 263, File 1863-4, No. 86: John Plange to General Secretaries [GS], 12 Dec. 1864. On the Ga diet, see P. E. Isert, *Letters on West Africa and the slave trade: Paul Erdmann Isert's "Journey to Guinea and the Caribbean Islands in Columbia" (1788)*, trans. and ed. by Selena Axelrod Winsnes (Oxford, 1992), 125–127; M. J. Field, "Gold Coast food," *Petits Propos Culinaires*, 42 (1993 [1931]).

7. See Dakubu, *Korle meets the sea*; for the Slave Coast, and its links with Accra, cf. Robin Law, *The Slave Coast of West Africa 1550–1750: The impact of the Atlantic slave trade on an African society* (Oxford, 1991).

8. R. A. Kea, "Trade, state formation and warfare on the Gold Coast, 1600–1826," Ph.D. thesis, University of London, 1974, 196–197.

9. Reindorf, *History*, 269; Law, *Slave Coast*, 41–42.

10. PRO CO 96/729/31201/1, Hodson to Ormsby-Gore, No. 356, 24 June 1936, enclosed: "Report on a survey of the fishing industry at Labadi with some reference to Teshie and Accra," by A. P. Brown; F. R. Irvine, *The fishes and fisheries of the Gold Coast* (London, 1947), 23–24; Isert, *Letters on West Africa*, 126.

11. *Report on the Census of the Gold Coast Colony for the year 1891* [hereafter *1891 Census*], 134.

12. For detailed material on economic, social, and ritual aspects of fishing in Accra, see National Archives of Ghana, Accra [hereafter NAG] ADM 11/1/1474 Fishing Industry, 1900–1923.

13. For some discussion, see Robertson, *Sharing the same bowl*, 80–92.

14. Kwame Yeboa Daaku, *Trade and politics on the Gold Coast 1600-1720* (London, 1970), 25–26; I. B. Sutton, "The Volta River salt trade: The survival of an indigenous industry," *JAH*, 22 (1981).

15. Jean Barbot, *Barbot on Guinea: The writings of Jean Barbot on West Africa 1678-1712*, ed. by P.E.H. Hair, Adam Jones, and Robin Law (London, 1992), 579–586; Reindorf, *History*, 271.

16. Kilson, *Kpele lala*, 181–182.

17. See Basel Mission Archive [hereafter BMA] D-1, 60/76 "Slavery and pledge," by Peter Anteson, n.d. [1893].

18. M. E. Kropp Dakubu, *One voice: The linguistic culture of an Accra lineage* (Leiden, 1981), 14.

19. William F. Daniell, "On the ethnography of Akkrah and Adampé, Gold Coast, Western Africa," *Journal of the Ethnological Society*, 4 (1856), 2; Thomas J. Hutchinson, *Impressions of Western Africa* (London, 1858), 65; Rev. J. G. Christaller, Rev. Ch. W. Locher, and Rev. J. Zimmermann, *A dictionary, English, Tshi (Asante), Akra* (Basel, 1874), 16.

20. Reindorf, *History*, 11–12; see also *The Gold Coast Independent*, 24 Nov. 1928, "What is in a name? Notes on Accra." by C. Mills-Lamptey.

21. Zimmermann, *Grammatical sketch*, Vol. 2, 97–100.

22. Ibid., 190–193.

23. Kilson, *Kpele lala*, 238; idem, "The Ga naming rite," *Anthropos*, 63/64 (1968–1969).

24. Field, *Religion and medicine*, 1–2; for the alternative interpretation, cf. Marion Kilson, *African urban kinsmen: The Ga of central Accra* (London, 1974), 3.

25. *Manbii* is typically rendered as "citizens," although often more exclusively defined as males of military age or older.

26. Zimmermann, *Grammatical sketch*, Vol. 2, 159. Zimmermann worked in Accra from 1850 to 1876 and was the Mission's leading scholar of Ga language and culture. On this set of distinctions in Asante thought, cf. Kwame Arhin, "Peasants in 19th-century Asante," *Current Anthropology*, 24 (1983); McCaskie, *State and society*, 294–295. For an early reference to Ga coastal town dwellers regarding their Akwamu rulers as nothing but "coarse peasants," see Erick Tilleman, *En kort og enfoldig beretning om det landskab Guinea og dets beskaffenhed (1697): A short and simple account of the country Guinea and its nature*, trans. and ed. Selena Axelrod Winsnes (Madison, 1994), 28.

27. See Abrams, "Towns and economic growth;" Leeds, *Cities*, 51–69; Peel, "Urbanization and urban history."

28. Cf. David Parkin, *Sacred void: Spatial images of work and ritual among the Giriama of Kenya* (Cambridge, 1991).

29. NAG SCT 2/6/2 High Court Records, Accra, Judgement Book, Vol. 2, Part 1, *Labadi v. Christiansborg*, 1902, evidence of Carl Reindorf.

30. Rev. A. W. Hanson, "On the grammatical principles of the Ghā (Accra) language," *Journal of the Ethnological Society*, 4 (1856), 85; Reindorf, *History*, 4–11; A. B. Quartey-Papafio, "The native tribunals of the Akras of the Gold Coast," *Journal of the African Society* [hereafter *JAS*], 10 (Apr. 1911); Noa Akunor Aguae Azu, "Adangbe (Adangme) history," *Gold Coast Review*, 2 (1926); J. M. Bruce-Meyers, "The origin of the Gãs," *JAS*, 27 (Oct. 1927), and 28 (Jan. 1928); Field, *Social organization*. The earliest written account of Ga traditions is that of Römer, a Danish factor stationed at Christiansborg from 1739 to 1749: L. F. Römer, *Tilforladelig efterrenning om Kysten Guinea* (Copenhagen, 1760). I have used translations of Chapter 3 of Römer by Irene Odotei, "On the Negroes' religion in general," Institute of African Studies, University of Ghana, Legon [hereafter IAS] *Research Review*, New Series, 3 (1987), and Chapter 4 by Kirsten Bertelsen, *The coast of Guinea: Part IV. African history, customs and ways of life* (IAS, Legon, 1965); see too L. F. Römer, *Le Golfe de Guinée 1700–1750: Récit de L. F. Römer marchand d'esclaves sur la côte ouest-africaine*, trans. by Mette Dige-Hesse (Paris, 1989).

31. Paul Ozanne, "Notes on the early historic archaeology of Accra," *Transactions of the Historical Society of Ghana* [hereafter *THSG*], 6 (1962); idem, "Notes on the later prehistory of Accra," *Journal of the Historical Society of Nigeria*, 3 (1964); J. Anquandah, *Rediscovering Ghana's past* (London and Accra, 1982), 113–125; M. E. Kropp Dakubu, "Linguistic pre-history and historical reconstruction: The Ga-Adangme migrations," *THSG*, 13 (1972); idem, *Korle meets the sea*, 100–113; J. H. Kwabena Nketia, "Historical evidence in Ga religious music" in J. Vansina, R. Mauny, and L. V. Thomas (eds.), *The historian in tropical Africa* (London, 1964).

32. *Ga mashi* is evidently a contraction of *Ga manshishi* (lit. "under [i.e. sheltered by] the town of *Ga*"); for an alternative etymology, see Reindorf, *History*, 6–7; on *Ganyo kron*, see Kilson, *African urban kinsmen*, 6–7.

33. See Quaye, "The Ga," 12; Anquandah, *Rediscovering Ghana's past*, 113; and cf. Philip S. Zachernuk, "Of origins and colonial order: Southern Nigerian historians and the 'Hamitic hypothesis' c.1870–1970," *JAH*, 35 (1994).

34. Reindorf, *History*, 4–5; Field, *Social organization*, 143; Quaye, "The Ga," 29–31; Ozanne, "Early historic archaeology," 69; John Vogt, *Portuguese rule on the Gold Coast 1469–1682* (Athens, GA, 1979), 125–126.

35. For the material basis of the urban-centered polities on the Gold Coast in this period, see Kea, *Settlements*.

36. Reindorf, *History*, 111–128, esp. 113.

37. Ibid., 115–116; see too Quaye, "The Ga," 28–29.

38. Kea, *Settlements*, 24; see also Thierry Rivière, "Economie et politiques des peuples *ga* d'Accra (Ghana) au XVIIe siècle," Ph.D. thesis, University of Paris, 1994.

39. Kea, *Settlements*, 199, 216–223; Law, *Slave Coast*, 46–47.

40. Quaye, "The Ga," 42–70.

41. For a description of the forts in c. 1680, see Barbot, *Barbot on Guinea*, 430–453.

42. Ivor Wilks, "Akwamu 1650–1750: A study of the rise and fall of a West African empire," M.A. thesis, University of Wales, 1958; idem, "The rise of the Akwamu empire, 1650-1710," *THSG*, 3 (1957).

43. Römer, *Tilforladelig*, trans. Bertelsen, "African history," 5–6; Reindorf, *History*, 20–22; Wilks, "Akwamu 1650–1750," 1–39; Quaye, "The Ga," 95–119. Reindorf misdates the death of Okaikoi to 1660 (followed by Dakubu, *Korle meets the sea*, 103, 126), and maintains that he committed suicide on the battlefield—a highly noble act—rather than face defeat and capture.

44. For the Ofori dynasty at Little Popo, see Law, *Slave Coast*, 226–317.

45. Many songs of the *kple* religious cult thus represent meditations on the turmoil of the Akwamu wars: Kilson, *Kpele lala*, 100–101, 258–259.

46. See Reindorf, *History*, 28–29; NAG ADM 11/1/1673, Notes of evidence of the Commission of Enquiry into the Tribal Organization of the Gas, 1907 [hereafter 1907 Enquiry]; NAG ADM 11/1/1756, Report . . . into the Tribal Organization of the Gas, 1907 [hereafter 1907 Report]; Field, *Religion and medicine*, 85–91; idem, *Social organization*, 142–195; Quaye, "The Ga;" R.J.H. Pogucki, *Gold Coast land tenure. Vol. 3. Land tenure in Ga customary law* (Accra, 1955); A. A. Amartey, *Omanye Aba* (Accra, 1969); Irene Odotei, "External influences on Ga society and culture," IAS *Research Review*, New Series, 7 (1991).

47. The etymology of the terms Kinka and *Kanka* remains obscure. Zimmermann lists *kinka* as meaning a Dutch person; see too Furley Collection, Balme Library, University of Ghana, Legon, Dutch Diaries and Correspondence [hereafter FC] N82, Van Hein to Governor, dd. Accra, 27 Aug. 1858.

48. William Smith, *A new voyage to Guinea* (London, 1744), 135 (emphasis in original); see also Wilks, "Akwamu 1650–1750," 69–71.

49. Zimmermann, *Grammatical sketch*, Vol. 1, 165; Reindorf, *History*, 128.

50. Dakubu, *One voice*, 1–36.

51. On Okaija, see Reindorf, *History*, 103–111; Ivor Wilks, "Akwamu and Otublohum: an eighteenth-century Akan marriage arrangement," *Africa*, 29 (1959); Albert Van Dantzig (trans. and ed.), *The Dutch and the Guinea Coast 1674–1742: A collection of documents from the General State Archive at the Hague* (Accra, 1978), 320–326.

52. Reindorf, *History*, 27.

53. Law, *Slave Coast*, 24–25. By the nineteenth century the name Alata was often identified as a Twi-Fante word meaning someone from "down the coast," but had be-

come specifically associated with Lagos and with Yoruba people: Reindorf, *History*, 29; NAG ADM 11/1/1673, 1907 Enquiry, 19.

54. For Wetse Kojo, see Reindorf, *History*, 29; Field, *Social organization*, 149–150, 192–194; Quaye, "The Ga," 257.

55. Cf. Daaku, *Trade and politics*, 96–143, on the rise of "merchant princes" in the Fante towns to the west of Accra.

56. The adoption of the title *wetse*, lit. "father of the house," emphasizes Wetse Kojo's role as the progenitor of a new "royal" lineage.

57. The goddess Koole was associated with the lagoon to the immediate west of Nleshi, usually rendered in anglicized form as Korle. Throughout, I use Koole to refer to the deity and Korle to the lagoon.

58. A copy of a "Note" dated 1737 confirming the payment of ground rent for James Fort to the occupant of the Sempe stool is found in NAG ADM 11/1/823 Sempe Fetish "Oyeni"; Reindorf, *History*, 11.

59. See Wilks, "Akwamu and Otublohum".

60. See FC Dutch Diaries and Correspondence, N75, N76, and N77 passim.

61. FC N77, Journal, 13 Aug. 1836, and Lans to Ancra, dd. Elmina, 19 Aug. 1836; A. Addo-Aryee Brown, "Historical account of Mohammedanism in the Gold Coast," *Gold Coast Review*, 3 (1927); S Y. Boadi-Siaw, "Brazilian returnees of West Africa" in Joseph E. Harris (ed.), *Global dimensions of the African diaspora* (Washington, 1993); NAG SCT 2/4/59 Divisional Court Civil Record Book [hereafter Div. Court] Vol. 46, *Jemima Nassu v. Basel Mission Factory and Victoria Van Hein*, 1915.

62. *Governor Carstensen's diary* (IAS, Legon, 1965), entry dd. 13 May 1845. The name Tabon is said to derive from the Portuguese "*está bom?*" ("are you well?", or as '*tabom*: "all's well"), used by the newly arrived returnees to reply to any enquiry directed to them in Ga: Zimmermann, *Grammatical sketch*, Vol. 2, 283.

63. It is significant that *gbo*, the most commonly used Ga term for "stranger," is also the word for "guest": for some contextualization, see M. E. Kropp Dakubu, "Creating unity: The context of speaking prose and poetry in Ga," *Anthropos*, 82 (1987).

64. See Dakubu, *Korle meets the sea*, 113–114.

65. BMA D-1, 60/77 "Circumcision in our congregations," by Jeremias Engmann, dd. Christiansborg, 19 Nov. 1884; Reindorf, *History*, 24, who notes that slaves were circumcized between the ages of six and ten along with Ga boys; Zimmermann, *Grammatical sketch*, Vol. 2, 79, on the term *folo*, "an abusive name for men of surrounding tribes who have not the custom of circumcision."

66. Reindorf, *History*, 20–21; Römer, *Tilforladelig*, trans. Bertelsen, "African history," 5.

67. Kilson, *Kpele lala*, 259.

68. *1891 Census*, 42–43.

69. Marion Johnson, "Census, map and guesstimates: The past population of the Accra region," *African historical demography* (Edinburgh, 1977); Rev. J. G. Christaller, *A dictionary of the Asante and Fante language called Tshi (Chwee, Twi)* (Basel, 1881), 649; *Christian Messenger* [published in Ga as *Sika-nsona Kristofoia Sanegbalo*], Apr. 1887, 16; a useful guide is E.V.T. Engmann, *Population of Ghana 1850–1960* (Accra, 1986).

70. Kwamina B. Dickson, *A historical geography of Ghana* (Cambridge, 1969), 255.

71. Henry Meredith, *An account of the Gold Coast of Africa* (London, 1812, reprinted 1967), 194; *The African Times*, 23 Feb. 1865; see too PRO CO 96/45, Bird to Bulver

Lytton, No. 43, 11 July 1859, enclosed: "Medical Report for the year 1858," dd. 10 May 1859.

72. Field, *Social organization*, 71–81, 142–199.

73. Quaye, "The Ga," 261–262; Diana Gladys Azu, *The Ga family and social change* (Leiden, 1974), 1; Dakubu, *One voice*, 19. For a critical contemporary response to Field's work, see NAG SNA 306/38, Dr. J. B. Danquah to Dr. M. J. Field, 3 June 1941.

74. See Isert, *Letters on West Africa*, 133; Meredith, *An account of the Gold Coast*, 193–194; James Africanus B. Horton, *West African countries and people* (London, 1868), 136–151.

75. See Dakubu, *One voice*, 16–17.

76. Field, *Social organization*, 156–158.

77. Ibid., 186, 191–195.

78. Reindorf, *History*, 111–128; NAG ADM 11/1/1086, Report of the Commissioner of Police on the town companies of Accra, 20 May 1895; ADM 11/1/1673, 1907 Enquiry; Field, *Social organization*, 92–96, 168–173; Abraham Akrong, "Integration and adaptation: A case study of La and Osu asafo religious culture," *THSG*, New Series, 2 (1998); for the debate on the origins of the Akan *asafo*, see Ansu K. Datta and R. Porter, "The *asafo* system in historical perspective," *JAH*, 12 (1971).

79. There were no words in Ga for these formations, which retained their Twi terminology: NAG ADM 11/1/1673, 1907 Enquiry, esp. 4, evidence of Tete Kwaku.

80. See esp. PRO CO 96/41, Pine to Labouchere, No. 40, dd. James Fort, 14 May 1857.

81. Römer, *Tilforladelig*, trans. Odotei, "On the Negroes' religion," 115.

82. Kilson, *Kpele lala*, 7–8; and see Field, *Religion and medicine*, esp. 61–63.

83. Richly suggestive material is also located in BMA D-10, 4, Miscellaneous Ghana Manuscripts, a series of essays written by pupils of the Basel Mission school in Osu in the early 1870s under the heading "Name and describe the Gods and Fetishes of the Accra natives."

84. In addition to ethnographic sources already cited, see Ako Adjei, "Mortuary usages of the Ga people of the Gold Coast," *American Anthropologist*, 45 (1943); E.T.A. Abbey, *Kedzi afo Yordan* (Accra, 1967), trans. M. E. Kropp Dakubu, "When the Jordan is crossed: Ga death and funeral celebrations," MS, 1971; Joshua N. Kudadjie, "Aspects of religion and morality in Ghanaian traditional society with particular reference to the Ga-Adangme" in J. M. Assimeng (ed.), *Traditional life, culture and literature in Ghana* (New York, 1976); Joyce Engmann, "Immortality and the nature of man in Ga thought" in Kwasi Wiredu and Kwame Gyeke (eds.), *Person and community: Ghanaian philosophical studies, I* (Washington, 1992).

85. Barbot, *Barbot on Guinea*, Vol. 2, 576.

86. See Marion Kilson, "Libation in Ga ritual," *Journal of Religion in Africa*, 2 (1969); Dakubu, "Creating unity"; and on the spiritual power of alcohol, Emmanuel Kwaku Akyeampong, *Drink, power and cultural change: A social history of alcohol in Ghana, c. 1800 to recent times* (Portsmouth, NH, 1996), 21–46.

87. Zimmermann, *Grammatical sketch*, Vol. 2, 97–100; suggestive material is found in files NAG ADM 11/1/1474 Fishing Industry, 1900–1923, ADM 11/1/823 Sempe Fetish "Oyeni," NAG ADM 11/1/1054 Lagoons.

88. Reindorf, *History*, 110–111; A. B. Quartey-Papafio, "The Gā Homowo festival," *JAS*, 19 (Jan. 1920).

89. A valuable precolonial source for Lakpa is Römer, *Tilforladelig*, trans. Odotei, "On the Negroes' religion;" one of the Dane's closest Ga associates and informants was the powerful Lakpa *wulomo* Wetse Odoi Kpoti (d. 1757). See too NAG ADM 11/1/1118 Labadi Native Affairs Vol. 1; A. K. Quarcoo, "The Lakpa—principal deity of Labadi," IAS *Research Review*, 3 (1967).

90. *Oblempon* is the Ga form of the Twi *obirempon*, "rich man," "notable," or "man of distinction," and is broadly synonymous with the Ga *niiatse*, or *sikatse* (lit. "father of money").

91. The historical meanings of palanquins became highly contested in the early colonial era, and much relevant material is found in the Supreme Court Civil Record Books: see esp. NAG SCT 2/4/41 Div. Court Vol. 30, *Land at Accra re Public Lands Ordinance 1876*, 1907, and Chapter 5.

92. Kwame Arhin, "Diffuse authority among the coastal Fanti," *Ghana Notes and Queries*, 9 (Nov. 1966); idem, "Rank and class among the Asante and Fante in the nineteenth century," *Africa*, 53 (1983); cf. T. C. McCaskie, "Accumulation, wealth and belief in Asante history. I. To the close of the nineteenth century," *Africa*, 53 (1983).

93. Quaye, "The Ga," 124–145.

94. Quartey-Papafio, "Native tribunals," 323.

95. Ibid., 328; Reindorf, *History*, 326; Field, *Social organization*, 166.

96. Isert, *Letters on West Africa*, 133–135; Daniell, "Ethnography of Akkrah," 13–14; PRO CO 96/41, Pine to Labouchere, Conf., 1 Oct. 1857.

97. Field, *Social organization*, 73.

98. Kilson, *Kpele lala*, 91–92.

99. *The Gold Coast Times*, 9 Sept. 1884.

100. For one dramatic eighteenth-century manifestation of this tension, the suicide of a powerful chief when accused of incest by the Lakpa oracle, see Römer, *Tilforladelig*, trans. Odotei, "On the Negroes' religion," 124; and for general insights, J.D.Y. Peel, "History, culture and the comparative method: A West African puzzle" in L. Holy (ed.), *Comparative anthropology* (Oxford, 1987).

101. Reindorf, *History*, 115; A. B. Quartey-Papafio, "The use of names among the Gäs or Accra people of the Gold Coast," *JAS*, 13 (Jan. 1914).

102. Zimmermann, *Grammatical sketch*, Vol. 2, 338.

103. FC N76, Maclean to Lans, 25 July 1834; N78, Van der Eb to Pel, 13 Feb. 1844. *Wonwebii*, lit. "children of the god's house," rendered by Zimmermann as "fetish domestics."

104. See Kilson, *African urban kinsmen*, esp. 19.

105. Field, *Religion and medicine*, 100–109.

106. See Römer, *Tilforladelig*, trans. Odotei, "On the Negroes' religion," 132; this theme is further developed in Chapter 5.

107. Kilson, *African urban kinsmen*, 16–36.

108. On the ramifications of cognatic kinship, see Meyer Fortes, *Kinship and the social order: The legacy of Lewis Henry Morgan* (London, 1969), 122–137.

109. A report by the Town Planning Department in 1953 found that unisexual households still predominated in the old quarters of Ussher Town, although Kilson noted that ten years later they occurred fairly infrequently: Acquah, *Accra survey*, 47; Kilson, *Kpele lala*, 12.

110. Field, *Social organization*, 6–12; Azu, *The Ga family*, 19.

111. *1891 Census*, 135.

112. Reindorf, *History*, 272.

113. For a description of Accra architecture in c. 1850, see Daniell, "Ethnography of Akkrah," 27–28.

114. See Hansen, "Domesticity in Africa."

115. See Paul Jenkins's Abstracts from the Gold Coast Correspondence of the Basel Mission [hereafter Jenkins's Abstracts], typescript, 3: "Plan and description of house of Teshie merchant, Atufu, 1851."

116. Kilson, *African urban kinsmen*, 30–31.

117. See Isert, *Letters on West Africa*, 136; Daniell, "Ethnography of Akkrah," 29; and compare the absence of an active market in precolonial Kumase, where the Asante urban elite was provisioned largely by lineage and slave production: McCaskie, *State and society*, 31–37.

118. Field, *Social organization*, 7, 54–64.

119. Robertson, *Sharing the same bowl*.

120. Daniell, "Ethnography of Akkrah," 13.

121. BMA D-1, 33/119A, Reindorf to Committee, dd. Mayera, 28 Dec. 1881; detailed material on Ga marriage compiled in 1905 is located in NAG ADM 11/1/1457 Marriage.

122. Quaye, "The Ga," 120; Kea, "Trade, state formation and warfare," 196–199.

123. Römer, *Tilforladelig*, trans. Bertelsen, "African history," 8, on the supply of captives to the Ga by gangs of kidnappers dubbed "siccadingers."

124. Reindorf, *History*, 84; Wilks, "The rise of the Akwamu empire," 111–112; Quaye, "The Ga," 216–217.

125. On Asante and its southern provinces, see J. K. Fynn, *Asante and its neighbours 1700–1807* (London, 1971).

126. Reindorf, *History*, 160–219, esp. 176–178; see too T. C. McCaskie, "Asante and Ga: The history of a relationship" in Jenkins, *The recovery of the West African past*.

127. Zimmermann, *Grammatical sketch*, Vol. 1, 172.

128. Yarak, *Asante and the Dutch*, 122–123; S. Tenkorang, "The importance of firearms in the struggle between Ashanti and the coastal states, 1708-1807," *THSG*, 9 (1968), 6.

129. Yarak, *Asante and the Dutch*, 143; J. T. Lever, "Mulatto influence on the Gold Coast in the early nineteenth century: Jan Nieser of Elmina," *African Historical Studies*, 3 (1970).

130. The cowrie zone of the Slave Coast and the gold zone of the Gold Coast met at Accra, the only point on the West African littoral where both currencies were regularly used: see Jan Hogendorn and Marion Johnson, *The shell money of the slave trade* (Cambridge, 1986), 106, 133.

131. Meredith, *An account of the Gold Coast*, 190.

132. For a useful summary, see Marion Johnson, "The Atlantic slave trade and the economy of West Africa" in Roger Anstey and P.E.H. Hair (eds.), *Liverpool, the African slave trade, and abolition* (Liverpool, 1976); and more generally, Paul E. Lovejoy, "The impact of the Atlantic slave trade on Africa: A review of the literature," *JAH*, 30 (1989).

133. Tenkorang, "The importance of firearms," 6.

134. Reindorf, *History*, 100, 149–150, 276; see also Ray A. Kea, "'I am here to plunder on the general road': Bandits and banditry in the pre-nineteenth-century Gold Coast" in Donald Crummey (ed.), *Banditry, rebellion and social protest in Africa* (London, 1986).

135. George Metcalf, "A microcosm of why Africans sold slaves: Akan consumption patterns in the 1770s," *JAH*, 28 (1987), 392.

136. Isert, *Letters on West Africa*, 133–134.

137. See ibid., 112–118, for vivid descriptions of clothing, jewelry, and elaborate coiffures in Accra.

138. Reindorf, *History*, 170.

139. Meredith, *An account of the Gold Coast*, 216; Yarak, *Asante and the Dutch*, 143; Ivor Wilks, *Asante in the nineteenth century: The structure and evolution of a political order* (Cambridge, 1975), 171–173.

140. The literature includes Edward Reynolds, *Trade and economic change on the Gold Coast, 1807–1874* (London, 1974); Susan Kaplow, "African merchants of the nineteenth century Gold Coast," Ph.D. thesis, University of Columbia, 1971, idem, "The mudfish and the crocodile: Underdevelopment of a West African bourgeoisie," *Science and Society*, 41 (1977); idem, "Primitive accumulation and traditional social relations on the nineteenth century Gold Coast," *Canadian Journal of African Studies*, 12 (1978); Raymond E. Dumett, "John Sarbah, the elder, and African mercantile entrepreneurship in the Gold Coast in the late nineteenth century," *JAH*, 13 (1973); idem, "African merchants of the Gold Coast, 1860–1905: Dynamics of indigenous entrepreneurship," *Comparative Studies in Society and History*, 25 (1983); McCarthy, *Social change*; Martin Lynn, *Commerce and economic change in West Africa: The palm oil trade in the nineteenth century* (Cambridge, 1997).

141. For an overview, see Robin Law, "The historiography of the commercial transition in nineteenth-century West Africa" in Toyin Falola (ed.), *African historiography: Essays in honour of Jacob Ade Ajayi* (London, 1993); and for recent contributions, Robin Law (ed.), *From slave trade to "legitimate" commerce: The commercial transition in nineteenth-century West Africa* (Cambridge, 1995).

142. Reynolds, *Trade and economic change*, 114–118.

143. Daniell, "Ethnography of Akkrah," 14.

144. BMA D-1,13B, Akropong 1862, No. 6A, Reindorf to Josenhans, 5 Mar. 1862.

145. PRO CO 96/23, Hill to Grey, No. 87, 24 Nov. 1851.

146. Reindorf, *History*, 152.

147. Great Britain Parliamentary Papers [hereafter PP] 1842 XII [551-II] *Report from the Select Committee on the West Coast of Africa [1842 Report]*, Appendix 3, 32; Kaplow, "African merchants," 25–54; Reynolds, *Trade and economic change*, 31–71.

148. For the term *owula*, see *The Gold Coast Times*, 13 Aug. 1881; Christaller et al., *A dictionary*, 156; Field, *Social organization*, 143; for further discussion, John Parker, "*Mankraloi*, merchants and mulattos: Carl Reindorf and the politics of 'race' in early colonial Accra" in Jenkins, *The recovery of the West African past*.

149. For the former emphasis, see Margaret Priestly, *West African trade and coast society: A family study* (London, 1969); Gocking, "The historic Akoto;" and for the latter, Arhin, "Rank and class"; Dumett, "African merchants"; Kimble, *Political history*. For a useful overview of the literature, see Jenkins, "Gold Coast historians," 43–90; on Lagos, cf. Mann, *Marrying well*, 3–32.

150. Quaye, "The Ga," 251–252.

151. Reindorf, *History*, 97.

152. Isert, *Letters on West Africa*, 156–157.

153. See G. A. Henty, *The march to Coomassie* (London, 1874), 258–260, for a description of women traders and the importance of cowries in facilitating small-scale commercial transactions in Accra's bustling marketplace in 1873.

154. *The African Times*, 23 Sept. 1868; *The West African Herald*, 22 Aug. 1871; John Hartford, "A voyage to the Oil Rivers twenty-five years ago," appendix in Mary Kingsley, *West African studies* (London, 1899), 571–572; NAG SCT 2/4/17 Div. Court 1889–1891 Part 2, *Jacob Ankrah v. Aryee Kumah*, 1891; on the large numbers of Ga goldsmiths—reputedly the most prestigious trade in Accra—see Hutchinson, *Impressions*, 69.

155. On the contested introduction of cocoa into the Gold Coast, see Polly Hill, *The migrant cocoa-farmers of southern Ghana* (Cambridge, 1963), 170–176.

156. The best source for the vicissitudes of British policy remains G. E. Metcalfe, *Great Britain and Ghana: Documents of Ghana history 1807–1957* (Accra, 1964).

157. Events chronicled in Reindorf, *History*, 329–341; Zimmermann, *Grammatical sketch*, Vol. 1, 187–193; BMA D-1, 6, "The bombardment of Christiansborg, Western Africa" by Rev. J. Stanger, n.d. [1855].

158. PRO CO 96/43, Pine to Labouchere, No. 44, dd. James Fort, 7 May 1858.

2

DEFENDING THE TOWN: WARFARE, WEALTH, AND CIVIC VIRTUE, 1866–1874

Bu-aso, bu-aso ne yen; kurotwiamansa ba, mmu no abofra!
(We are axe-breakers; a leopard cub should not be deemed a boy!)[1]

Asiedu Ketekre, Kotoko wokoro ko, Wokoro obata?
(Great Accra, are you going to battle, or are you going to trade?)[2]

In October 1907, the British administration held a Commission of Enquiry to investigate the "tribal organization" of the Ga people. In the course of preparing a new Native Jurisdiction Bill that would for the first time be applied to Accra, it became apparent to officials that, although the town had been the headquarters of the Gold Coast Colony for thirty years, very little was known about the political institutions of its indigenous people. For five days, a group of fifty or so Ga notables gathered each morning in the district courthouse in James Town, where the two British commissioners, allowing vigorous cross-examination from those in attendance, gathered evidence from a succession of witnesses.[3] All were men, mostly elderly, nonliterate traders, farmers, or artisans; *anobua*, "men of influence." Many were respected war veterans, who as young men had fought in the series of military campaigns that had dominated the transition to full-blown colonial rule in Accra and the southeast Gold Coast in the late 1860s and early 1870s.

The picture these men drew of state and society in Accra is a striking one. Time and time again, their testimony returns to the importance of military organization and of warfare in determining the form of Ga institutions and the dynamics of political competition. Indeed, their reliability as witnesses—as repositories of knowledge regarding town affairs—was often established by inquiring of their first-hand experience of war.[4] It would be all too easy to dismiss the resulting image of Ga history as based on the vainglorious reminiscences of a group of old warriors. Women would certainly have provided a different perspective, as would have members of Accra's literate elite, few of whom took part in the proceedings. Despite its lacunae, the Enquiry indicates the extent to which Ga political authority in the nineteenth century had been linked to the social status derived from feats of arms. It had been over three decades since the *manbii*, the townspeople or "citizens," had been mobilized for war. Yet the period of heightened military conflict on the Gold Coast, which precipitated the formalization of British rule in the 1870s, continued to shape the contested political terrain of early colonial Accra.

This chapter examines war, trade, and politics in Accra in the period of transition between the era of informal imperialism and formal colonial rule. To understand why a warrior ethos remained so important in Accra long after the imposition of colonial peace, we look first at the historical connections between war and civic virtue in Ga thought, and how these ideas were central to the making of Accra as a moral community. Ga concepts of morality and political authority are further explored in an analysis of the office of *Ga mantse* in the mid-nineteenth century. This also serves to introduce the figure of *Ga mantse* Taki Tawia, who, from his enstoolment in 1862 until his death in 1902, played a key role in the history of early colonial Accra. The following account of the three wars fought by the Ga and their allies between 1866 and 1874 aims to locate the town firmly in its wider regional context. Accra emerges as a fulcrum around which turned a variety of economic and political transactions between the polities of the southeastern Gold Coast: Ga, Dangme, Akyem, Akuapem, Ewe, and the inchoate British colonial regime. Changes in these wider networks in turn shaped the evolution of the town, the established Ga middleman role coming under threat from the gradual expansion of colonial control.

WARFARE AND CIVIC VIRTUE IN GA THOUGHT

The role of warfare as an agent of political and economic change, and in particular the links between firearms, state formation, and the transatlantic slave trade, has long been a concern of historians of precolonial West Africa.[5] It is generally accepted that the exigencies of military organization played a central role in the emergence and subsequent development of states on the Gold Coast and in its forest hinterland. Less attention has been paid to the various indigenous meanings of warfare, and to the social implications of the ending of organized violence with the imposition of colonial rule. Precolonial Accra did not exhibit a particularly high degree of militarism. Indeed, the historical record tends to suggest the opposite: that the Ga

sought to alleviate political and military domination by their Akan neighbors to the north by exploiting their position as coastal middlemen, engag-
ing in a largely peaceful commerce with the interior. Arhin has explored this
issue within Akan culture, drawing a sharp contrast between the militarism
of Asante and the commercialism of the Fante.[6] Nevertheless, in common
with other precolonial middleman states of the Gold and Slave Coast, an
elaborate ideology of warfare played a central role in the dynamics of Ga
political power and social change. There is much evidence to suggest that
commercial wealth and a military ethos, intimately connected since the seventeenth-century expansion of the slave trade, continued to coexist in Accra
in the era of legitimate commerce. This mercantilist tradition was observed
in the 1850s to be explicitly reflected by the device worn by Ga men on
their marriage, a girdle of miniature elephant tusks, war equipment, and
cowries, all finely worked in metal.[7] Warfare was more than simply a method
of material accumulation. It was also an important determinant of collective
identity, social status, political authority, and the gendered construction of
ideas of masculinity.

Military service was historically one of the principal vectors for the incorporation of "strangers," *gboi*, into Accra. It should be repeated that those
Ga who survived the destruction of the centralized state at Ayawaso by the
Akwamu in 1677 fled as refugees to the forts of their European trading partners at Nleshi, Kinka, and Osu. As a defeated people concerned above all
with institutional and demographic reconstruction, the Ga were particularly
receptive to the incorporation of both free and unfree migrants. Yet they have
also been acutely conscious of their distinctive identity, particularly with
regard to their Twi-speaking Akan neighbors to the north and west. Joining
Accra's military units, the *asafo* companies, Reindorf argues, was an essential first stage in the acquisition of citizenship for settlers: "Alatas in each
town formed their own quarter . . . and were acknowledged as citizens of
the place by joining the established band [i.e. *asafo*] in the towns."[8] The role
of warfare in the conferring of fundamental civic rights on strangers is repeatedly confirmed by testimony given in court cases in the early twentieth
century, when who was and who was not a "true Ga" (*ganyo kron*) began to
be contested in the colonial courts.[9] To fight in defense of the town was a
vital element in the process of becoming Ga. "The Otooblohums were
Akwamus," one elder succinctly argued in 1918, "[but] they became Gas as
they fought with the Gas."[10]

At the center of this complex of ideas are Ga notions of civic virtue and
of the town as a moral community.[11] To have fought as a warrior (*tabilo*)
was an essential component in the social identity—the reputation—of the
"virtuous" or "brave" man, *mokpakpa*.[12] Writing in the early eighteenth century, the Danish pastor Rask noted that "in the olden days" a Ga man could

not become a "caboceer" without first having been to war or killing a selection of wild animals, but observed that this rule was no longer strictly adhered to.[13] While never rigorously applied, this tradition of candidates succeeding to public office after proving themselves in war continued to recur in times of military conflict into the mid-nineteenth century. It is unclear how far the acquisition of moral authority (*jenba*) through having been to war was due to the accumulation and redistribution of plundered wealth, or to a more nonmaterial notion of civic virtue. Wealth and virtue were so intimately bound together that the two cannot easily be separated.[14] Wealth, primarily in the form of slaves who bolstered the population and military capability of Accra, enabled ambitious outsiders such as the progenitor of the Alata *akutso*, Wetse Kojo, to enter the Ga ruling hierarchy. Wetse Kojo's rise to power was vividly described in these terms by his descendant, Alata *mantse* Kojo Ababio IV: "When the Aquamoo [Akwamu] war broke out and Wetse Kojo . . . fought very hard, and the Aquamoo were driven away, they said 'Oh we have got a man,' and they all made him their manche [*mantse*] . . . and Wetse Kojo was called the King of James Town."[15]

The idea of the virtuous man as successful warrior was not entirely subsumed into an ideology of material accumulation. It was also fashioned by the tension between individual morality on the one hand and the influence of divine and supernatural forces on the other. Field addresses this tension in her discussion of the Ga *asafo* companies.[16] If supernatural guidance was regularly sought in order to chart a successful path through quotidian affairs, its importance was heightened by the hazardous occupation of war. The efficacy of ritual preparation and the protective charms worn into battle was ultimately dependent on the personal morality of the warrior. "If the owner of a medicine deceives or lies," Field argues, "his medicine 'spoils' and will fail him in time of need." She goes on: "Tribal wrongdoing brought wholesale death, individual wrongdoing brought family death. When the orientation was towards war ideas swung on exactly the same pivot—life was to him who was good and upright, death to the wrongdoer."[17] To return triumphant from the dangers of war was more than just proof of a man's bravery and civic-mindedness; it also suggested a divinely blessed morality or "goodness." Conversely, to return home in shame and defeat bordered on the unthinkable. Like their Akan neighbors, the Ga regarded suicide as the only virtuous alternative. This code of honor was enshrined in the traditional recension of the death of King Okaikoi in 1677 and it extended beyond the battlefield to shape everyday notions of male honor.[18]

It was office-holding *mantsemei* and their war captains who were responsible for the defense of their quarters (*akutsei*) and, collectively, for the territorial integrity of Accra and its hinterland. The holders of *oblempon* stools, often successful middlemen in the slave trade, were also well equipped to utilize retinues of slaves as armed militias to defend and enhance their position in the community as independent entrepreneurs. In 1829, for example, *makelaar* Ankra of Otublohum was appointed by *Ga mantse* Taki Kome to lead an army to Krepi, the Ewe-speaking region east of the River Volta. Despite having stated diplomatic objectives, the campaign functioned as a large slave-raiding exercise. "A Portuguese slaver being in the roads at that time," Reindorf explains, "chief Ankra . . . obtained a large amount of goods, arms and ammunition, on credit, payable . . . in prisoners after the expedition."[19] Ankra returned to Accra in April 1830 with "an immense number of prisoners; several of them were presented . . . to all the chiefs and elders...that had sent a contingent."[20] Those captives not sold to slavers were settled in a farming village that became known as Awudome (or Adidome), the name of the Volta town at the center of the campaign. Yet large retinues of slaves could be difficult to manage, and those who had secured a degree of citizenship through "fighting for the town" were likely to defend those hard-won rights with vigor. Ankra died in 1840 and was succeeded as both Dutch *makelaar* and head of the Dadebanwe by his younger brother Okanta. Two years later, Okanta was in open conflict with his own slaves. For reasons that remain obscure, but that we can surmise arose from the new *wetse*'s attempt to restructure rights and obligations within the Dadebanwe, 300 heavily armed slaves rose against Okanta in December 1842.[21] Fleeing to the safety of Fort Crèvecoeur, he was able to emerge only after two weeks of stiff negotiations.

By the second quarter of the nineteenth century, the economic dominance of slave brokers like Ankra and Okanta in Accra was beginning to be superseded by the "legitimate" commercial activities of merchants such as James Bannerman, John Hansen, Henry Richter, and William "Nanka" Bruce. Like the occupants of *oblempon* stools, these Western-educated Euro-Africans were large slave owners, also willing to mobilize armed retainers in pursuit of political goals.[22] Although the Euro-African notables ("*owulai*") appear to have retained control of their own warriors outside the established *asafo* structure, the distribution of arms and ammunition was crucial in retaining their influence as "influential natives"—in the words of Reindorf.[23] A petition from *Ga mantse* Taki Tawia to the British administration in 1873 stresses the political importance of such largesse in order for "Kings . . . , Chiefs and our principal native gentlemen . . . to command the services of the masses."[24] Testimony given in the 1907 Enquiry further underlines the importance of the distribution of munitions in determining the social status of individuals and the political seniority of stools.[25]

The possession of a gun was, with the exception of circumcision, the most fundamental indicator of male adulthood in Ga society.[26] Famously unreliable, the long-barreled muskets, commonly known as "Dane guns," were usually fired at arm's length with the face averted as a precaution against injury from exploding barrels. The utility of the Dane gun on the battlefield was ultimately less important than the social status gained from its owner-ship. Reindorf's comments on codes of masculinity are suggestive: "Every youth of the age of sixteen is bound to buy a gun or gets one from his fa-ther, otherwise he is never esteemed a man worthy of his country, and the company . . . look down upon him."[27] The testing cross-examination during a court case in 1918 of Abossey Okai of the Akanmaji *akutso*, on the subject of the Anglo-Ga expedition against the Krobo in 1858, vividly demonstrates the connection between firearms, masculinity, and adulthood:

Q: You were a boy then?

A: I was grown up, I carried a gun, I also carried my father's load.

Q: Did you go as a warrior or a carrier?

A: I went with my father to the war.

Q: Did you hold your father's gun?

A: My father had his gun and I carried mine . . .

Q: At the time of the Marko case [1880] you were a boy?

A: I had gone to the Bights more than ten times.[28]

Abossey Okai's shift from defending his manhood in terms of having borne arms to war to having traveled repeatedly to the Bights is revealing. The upsurge and then final termination of organized violence between 1866 and 1874 coincided with the growth of skilled-labor migration from Accra, and a high proportion of elders and officeholders in the early colonial pe-riod had both served as warriors and worked at the Bights. What emerges from the testimonies of men of this generation is a striking similarity be-tween the ways in which the two experiences are described. A certain heroic quality emerges from accounts of hazardous journeys down the coast in search of work. This quality is captured in the language used to describe the peripatetic movement of workers: *ete nshon* ("he is gone to the sea") and *edshe nshon* ("he comes from the sea"), phrases that evoke both the original Ga migrations and the spiritual hazards of the ocean.[29] It is in this context that the link between status and wealth can be broadened to include the ac-cumulation of less easily identifiable social assets such as prestige and civic virtue. Neighboring coastal societies in the mid-nineteenth century displayed similar traits. King Aggrey of Cape Coast and King Ghartey IV of Winneba, for example, were both adventurers who as young men had gone to sea be-fore succeeding to office.[30] Field also noted the connection between politi-cal authority and migrant work with regard to the "big men" of Tema in the

1930s, most of whom "in their youth left the town and travelled, many of them doing surf-boat work at various ports all around West Africa."[31] The accumulation of social prestige through labor migration appears to have replaced to some extent that hitherto gained by the test of warfare.

Women played a central role in shaping this discourse of masculinity and male civic virtue. Although Ga women are largely absent from accounts of precolonial military conflict, the vigor with which they participated in informal political action in colonial Accra provides a clear indication of their ability to mold the public reputations of men. The outspoken manner in which women urged their kinsmen on to feats of arms was matched in its fluency only by the public ridicule reserved for those identified as less than courageous. Women's exhortations took formal shape in ritual war dances called *asayere*, in which they took on the persona of their warrior kinsmen.[32] Isert witnessed these exuberant displays in 1783, noting how the women "acted out the battle by fencing with wooden swords [and] by sitting in the canoes . . . on the beach and pretending to paddle."[33] Reindorf's description of *asayere* before the battle of Katamanso in 1826 was likely based on his own observations of the campaigns in the 1860s and 1870s: "The women in camp and those at home had since the marching out of the warriors each assumed the dress and tools of her husband and imitated his work, dancing in company, and singing to keep the spirits of their husbands lively. . . . One of their war songs is . . . 'Sons of heroes, get hold of your guns!'"[34]

As these accounts indicate, *asayere* was performed both in camp and at home. Women played a crucial role in military campaigns as carriers and supporters, sometimes going into the firing line to reload muskets and even picking up the gun of fallen kinsmen.[35] Field attended several funerals in the 1930s of women accorded full military honors due to famous feats in the wars of the 1860s–1870s. Such women had charged into the enemy lines, "terrifying the warriors not only by the horrible ferocity and strength of her onslaught, but by the conviction that supernatural powers were driving her."[36] What these extraordinary actions had in common with the ritual exhortations of *asayere* was the startling inversion of gender roles. Women were also capable of turning the power of their sexuality onto their own kinsmen. An extreme form of ridicule was for women to publicly remove their clothes before those they wished to shame, the implication being that the latter were not men.[37] Nudity and cross-dressing were also employed by the young men of the *asafo* companies during the *Homowo* festival, suggestively mirroring the ritualized sexual ambiguity of the female *asayere*.

As rising tensions in the trading economy of the eastern Gold Coast escalated into military conflict in the mid-1860s, debates over this complex of ideas linking war, identity, gender, social status, morality, and political power rose to the fore in Accra. The termination of organized violence with the extension of British rule in 1874 did not mean that these debates ended. Indeed, the imposition of colonial peace appears to have made them even more important, the contested meanings of war remaining at the center of Ga politics in the colonial town.

MORAL AND RITUAL PROPERTY:
TAKI KOME AND TAKI TAWIA

Ga mantse Taki Tawia, recognized by the British as the "King of the Accras," died on July 14, 1902. Aged 68 at his death, Taki had occupied the Ga (or Okaikoi) stool for forty turbulent years. His funeral two days later was attended by an estimated 10,000 mourners, including large numbers of "bush people," *kosebii*, who had come into town from the villages of the Accra plains. "All over the town . . . there was incessant firing of guns, women even holding muskets; and all who could . . . manage to do so wore the colour of blood."[38] The government having proscribed intramural sepulture in 1888, Taki was the first *Ga mantse* not to be buried under the floor of his *abedoo shia* and was instead interred in a mausoleum on the outskirts of Accra to the north of the Korle lagoon. The ritual firing of sixty-two kegs of gunpowder continued for two weeks, officials being somewhat irked that the chiefs had requested only twenty kegs with which to mark the coronation of Edward VII.[39] The high esteem in which the departed *mantse* was held, the astute Governor Nathan reported, "was due in part to the name he made for personal bravery in his early wars, in part to his reputation as a fetish priest, being credited with supernatural powers, and in part to a kindly disposition."[40] Always the pragmatist, it was said that on his deathbed Taki had sent for Wesleyan pastors and had died a Christian.[41] Obituary notices in the Gold Coast press emphasized not only Taki's struggles with outside enemies and with the colonial regime, but also his often troubled relationship with the *manbii* of Accra. "The late King suffered a great deal at the hands of his own people," reported the *Leader*, "for often in endeavouring to please them he excited the hostility of the Government," while the *Chronicle* concluded that "although he might have had troubles with the Accras . . . he invariably succeeded in adjusting every difficulty by his patience and sagacity."[42]

Taki Tawia was born about 1834 in the Abola *akutso* of Kinka, or Dutch Accra. His genealogy is both complex and contested, yet provides crucial insights into the working of the office of *Ga mantse* in the nineteenth century. He was enstooled on September 12, 1862 as successor to Yaote of Amugiwe (1859–1862), who had succeeded Ofori Kakpo of Teiko Tsuruwe (1856–1858). By midcentury succession to the Ga stool

Figure 2.1 *Ga mantse* Taki Tawia and his household in 1891. Photograph by R.R.C. Lutterodt. Probably Accra's first professional photographer, Lutterodt began business in 1889, later working in Cameroon, Gabon, Fernando Po, and São Tomé before returning to Accra in 1900. (Copyright Basel Mission Archive, Basel, Switzerland. Ref. No. QD-30.030.0058. Reproduced with permission.)

rotated between three Abola patrilineages: Teiko Tsuruwe, Amugiwe, and Taki Komewe.[43] In a genealogical table based on oral evidence collected in the 1930s, Field places Taki Tawia and his father Teiko in Teiko Tsuruwe.[44] However, in 1902, Ga notables stated clearly that he was a grandson of *Ga mantse* Taki Kome (c. 1826–1856) and a member of the *we* he founded and that bore his name.[45] It seems likely that Taki was eligible for the Ga stool through more than one line of descent and was linked to both Teiko Tsuruwe and Taki Komewe.[46] The relevance of Taki Tawia's descent is not limited to the mechanics of cognatic kinship. By succeeding to the office of *Ga mantse* through his descent from Taki Kome, he also inherited the "moral and ritual property" of his revered grandfather.[47] "Because you have the same *kla* as your grandfather," Field was informed, "when your grandfather dies all his bravery comes into you."[48] That Taki's contemporaries chose to emphasize his descent from Taki Kome indicates a certain status derived from the latter's role as the founder—under extraordinary circumstances—of a third "stool house" in the Abola *akutso*.

The emergence of Taki Kome as *Ga mantse* and the creation of a third line of succession to the Okaikoi stool was a key event in the political evolution of nineteenth-century Accra that continued to have ramifications throughout the early colonial period. It provides a graphic example of the connections between military, ritual, and political authority in Ga thought, and underlines the function of urban Accra as a site where these structures of power were located. The rise of Taki Kome occurred at a critical point in Accra's history: the decision by the Ga leaders to join the British-led alliance against their Asante suzerains in the early 1820s. Although this period of conflict culminating in the Asante defeat at Katamanso is well documented, only one source, an oral tradition recorded by Field in the 1930s, details the process by which Taki Kome became *Ga mantse*.[49] According to Field's informant(s), the leaders of the seven quarters of Kinka and Nleshi gathered before the shrine of the oracular war god Sakumo in order to determine who should lead the Ga forces to war. Sakumo advanced one Taki Kome, who would march with the Abola *akutso* and would succeed to the Ga stool of that quarter. The leaders of the powerful Asere quarter were dismayed. Taki Kome, the account insists, was a lowly "servant" of the Sakumowe, one of the many escaped slaves and other fugitives who sought refuge at the *gbatsu* of Sakumo through the exercise of *no-he ke won*, "giving oneself to the god."[50] "But you, *Asere*, every year must give the *hewale* (strength, power, authority) of the *mantse* to *Taki Komi* [sic]," the Sakumo oracle continued. "You shall be the father of the Gã *mantse*."[51]

Field deploys this narrative to illustrate her contention that *mantse* stools had no authority other than as "war fetishes" and that the position of *Ga mantse* was merely a temporary wartime expediency.[52] As already argued, the view that precolonial *mantsemei* were merely minor priests cannot be sustained. Field presents her oral evidence uncritically, seemingly unaware that the tradition—clearly emanating from Asere informants—was shaped by contemporary political conflict between that quarter and the Ga stool.[53] Taki Kome may well have been a *wonwebi* attached to the Sakumo shrine—indeed, the connection between the authority of the Ga stool and that of the Sakumo cult in the nineteenth century is well documented.[54] Yet, despite Asere opposition, Taki's success in war enabled him to accumulate real political authority. The combination of ritual authority and military prestige was confirmed by the Ga lawyer A. B. Quartey-Papafio to be central to the ability of what he calls the "Takyi dynasty" of Abola to consolidate their hold on the Ga stool and preside over a period of demographic advance in Accra: "They have had their wars, but in all, excepting the first Awuna war, they have been successful. It is most likely that their connection with the old priesthood and that of the new Fetish Sakumo gave the Takyis such a strong and lasting hold on the people."[55]

By the mid-nineteenth century, the *Ga mantse*—"the King of Dutch Accra"—was widely recognized as the senior military leader among all the states, Ga, Dangme, and Akan, of the southeast Gold Coast.[56] This status rested in part on Accra's position as a conduit of armaments to the interior and on the role of its chiefs as regional brokers with the European forts. The Ga struggled to contain the erosion of this middleman role, arresting and fining *Okuapehene* Kwao Dade of Akuapem in 1857 for accepting munitions directly from the British.[57] Moreover, if within Accra Taki Kome's success at Katamanso consolidated the right of the Abola *akutso* and the Taki Komewe to the Ga stool, then the role played by the combined Ga forces greatly enhanced their reputation as a military force to be reckoned with. As Africanus Horton pointed out in 1868, since Katamanso the Asante had "regarded the Gas with a certain degree of fear."[58] This was confirmed by the well-informed Basel missionary Elias Schrenk, who believed that bitter experience had taught the Asante never again to tackle the Ga and their allies on the Accra plains.[59]

A close reading of Reindorf's narrative of the military conflicts of the 1820s allows a more textured interpretation of this aspect of the Asante-Ga relationship. The standard explanation for the wariness with which the Asante regarded the Ga has stressed the former's unfamiliarity with combat on the open coastal plain. Yet this widely reported attitude may have had less to do with military strategy than with the realms of cognition and belief. In short, the Asante perceived the Ga to possess exclusive access to a potent array of supernatural forces: "Before the battle of Katamanso, several of the Asante monarchs used to apprize the kings of Akra and their fetishes of any projected expedition, and receive in return fetish leaves and war-medicines. On the return from such expeditions large presents of prisoners and spoils were sent to the Akras."[60] Reindorf goes on to recount how in preparation for the campaign against Accra and the eastern Gold Coast, *Asantehene* Osei Yaw Akoto consulted, in turn, Asante oracles associated with the river Tano, Muslim diviners, and finally the renowned Dente shrine at Krache. Tano, the most powerful of all Asante *abosom*, warned that "he had been defeated on the coast by Akra fetishes," while the Muslim diviner Kramo Koko also failed to "catch" any of the elusive Ga *jemawojii*.[61] British accounts of the Asante defeat of August 7, 1826 emphasize the decisive role of European-led regulars and the firepower of their military hardware. But for the Asante, and for the Ga under the command of the divinely ordained Taki Kome, the outcome confirmed the power of the Ga *jemawojii* and their watery supernatural allies.[62] Reverend Reindorf again: "It was God in heaven who mercifully defended our country. But our deluded people attributed the victory not only to their fetishes, but also to every cartilaginous, spinous, and testaceous creature in the sea, which they consider, to the present day, as warriors of their fetish Nai (the sea) and suppose to have taken part in the engagement and even, in some instances, to have got wounded."[63] The superior culture of the Ga south—backed by the ritual power of the sea itself—had finally triumphed over that of the rustic, terrestrial, Akan north. It was a key moment in the remaking of Accra's identity after the defeats of the past.

WAR AND TRADE ON THE VOLTA

In the decades following the watershed of the 1820s, the middleman role of the Ga evolved from that of brokers in the slave trade to that of brokers in the new legitimate commerce. Although intermittent slave exports from the leeward coast lingered on to midcentury, by the 1850s Accra's external commerce was dominated by palm oil. The main regional producers were the Akuapem, a predominantly Akan-speaking people occupying the forested hills to the north of Accra, and the Krobo, a Dangme-speaking people inhabiting rich farming country further to the northeast. Expanding trade enabled Accra to enhance its position as an entrepôt for imported goods, and by midcentury leading Ga and Euro-African merchants were extending their business operations east to the Dangme ports of Prampram (known to the Ga as Gbugbla) and Ada. The political configuration of this trading region shifted in 1850 when Britain purchased the Danish forts between Osu and the Volta, inheriting a vague jurisdiction over the oil-producing states of the hinterland. The British attempt to pay for expanding colonial commitments by the imposition of direct taxation backfired in 1854 when the Ga of Osu, La, and Teshi rose in a short-lived but violent rebellion. Krobo resistance to British taxation erupted four years later, resulting in an Anglo-Ga military expedition against the rebels and the imposition of a fine of over £8,000, payable in palm oil. Efforts by the Krobo to circumvent the collection of the fine resulted in the diversion of oil away from Accra and Prampram to the Volta route, where, by the early 1860s, fierce competition ensued over access to supplies at a time of falling prices.[64] As the region's main port town, Accra was at the center of these economic and political tensions, which in 1866 drew the Ga into large-scale military intervention on the lower Volta.

The 1866 Awuna Campaign

Remembered by the Ga as the Awuna (Anlo) War and by their Anlo Ewe adversaries as the Datsutagba War, the 1866 conflict opened a succession of confrontations focused on the Volta River that continued until 1874.[65] This period of war and insecurity on the eastern Gold Coast and western Slave Coast can be analyzed in a number of contexts. Part of a long tradition of rivalry between the middleman states on either side of the Volta dating back to the mid-eighteenth century, it must be located in the changing economic and political conditions wrought by the rise of legitimate commerce.[66] To some extent, the wars also represent a "crisis on the periphery" of informal empire. As rising competition over the control of legitimate commerce placed trading relations on the coast under increasing strain, the British were drawn into a cycle of conflict that ended only with the consolidation of colonial rule in 1874. Within this broad historiographical paradigm, the focus here is on the changing political terrain of urban Accra and the connections between the town and its trading hinterland. Particular attention is paid to the shifting relationship between established Ga officeholders, the rising entrepreneurs of Accra's merchant community, and the British administration. What resources, ideological, moral, and material, were these groups able to draw on to meet their political and economic objectives? What was the role of warfare in reshaping the contours of authority and influence in Accra?

The proximate cause of the first Awuna war was a dispute in April 1865 between the Ewe entrepreneur Atitsogbi, better known as Geraldo de Lima, and an Ada debtor. Already established as a leading slave trader on the lower Volta, Geraldo was well positioned to take advantage of the expanding palm oil trade following the Krobo boycott. In a situation of competition for palm oil between Geraldo and the Anlo on the one hand and merchants based at Ada, Prampram, and Accra on the other, the dispute escalated into open hostilities between the Anlo and Ada states. According to the combined African and European merchant community at Accra, the result was the complete collapse of trade throughout the Eastern Districts of the Protectorate.[67]

The complex and well-documented negotiations leading to the 1866 campaign provide an entry into Accra's fragmented political arena in the transition to full-blown colonial rule. By September 1865, the commandant of Fort Crèvecoeur, the influential Euro-African merchant William A. Lutterodt, was urging the Dutch governor to resolve an ongoing dispute with the chiefs of Kinka in order that the Ga might take the field in support of their Dangme allies at Ada. This request fell on deaf ears at Elmina, despite Lutterodt's warning that if not able to fight "the Dutch Town Accra will lose their name as the head of the whole country."[68] Throughout 1865, the *mantsemei* of Kinka had been locked in dispute with the Dutch over the issue of legal jurisdiction in the town. To avoid arrest, Taki Tawia was forced to retreat to "the bush," the refusal of the chiefs to surrender the fugitive *Ga mantse* resulting in a Dutch bombardment of Kinka in December.[69] Accra's beleaguered merchants, already urging the *mantsemei* to mobilize the town for war, found the rival British administration more receptive to their pleas for assistance.[70]

The first half of the 1860s had been a time of uncertainty and retreat for the British administration on the Gold Coast. A shambolic attempt to defend the Fante country from an Asante incursion in 1862–1863 exacerbated metropolitan hostility toward the ramshackle Protectorate, leading the Colonial Office to reiterate the old policy of nonintervention in African military disputes. This proved insufficient to disarm parliamentary critics, and although the anticolonial lobby failed in their attempt to secure complete withdrawal from the Gold Coast through the 1865 Select Committee, the emphasis of the resulting report was on a gradual reduction of commitments.[71] The fragility of the British presence at Accra in the mid-1860s reflected this general malaise. Despite criticizing the Dutch for their lack of control over the unruly enclave of Kinka, British authority in James Town, Osu, and the surrounding hinterland was maintained by a solitary Civil Commandant presiding over a handful of locally recruited functionaries and a garrison of ill-disciplined troops.[72] The problems faced by the British in maintaining order in the coastal towns began within the ranks of their own coercive apparatus. When, in 1862, the ex-slaves of the Gold Coast Corps mutinied at Cape Coast and were reported to be marching on Accra, the Commandant was forced to appeal for help from Ga chiefs and merchants to protect the town from the threat of a rampaging colonial soldiery.[73] As a result of the mutiny the Gold Coast Corps was disbanded, its garrison duties taken over by detachments of the West India Regiment. In 1865 a new police force, the so-called "Fanti Police," was created and eleven constables were for the first time stationed permanently at Accra.[74] Both European powers struggled to maintain a degree of law and order within their respective towns by negotiation and compromise, punctuated by the resort to crude coercion as in the bombardments of Osu in 1854 and Kinka in 1865.

Turning a blind eye to recent pronouncements from London in the aftermath of the 1865 Report, Administrator Conran sailed from Cape Coast to Accra with a detachment of the Third West India Regiment in February 1866. There, he encouraged the Ga to defend the Protectorate and its trade by distributing 1,200 muskets to Kojo Ababio, Alata *mantse*, or King of James Town (1844-1871), and Frederick Noi Dowuona, Osu *mantse*, or King of Christiansborg (1854–1866).[75] However, problems arose when Conran threatened to withdraw the firearms unless the Ga forces departed for Ada immediately.[76] This meant foregoing full ritual preparation for war, in particular the gathering of the warriors before the Sakumo shrine where the *wulomo* would "boil the battle" (*ta hoo mo*) to ensure a favourable outcome.[77] Torn between the material and supernatural requisites for combat it appears that many Ga townsmen were forced to curtail the latter, and on February 18 the warriors of Nleshi began to depart for the Volta.

In an attempt to keep British participation in the 1866 conflict to a minimum, Conran insisted that the leading merchants of James Town and Christiansborg supply their own contingents of fighting men. There is every indication that these private militia were composed largely of slaves. In a letter to Africanus Horton, James Bannerman advocated a greater role in local government for the literate, Western-educated elite on the basis of their recent war effort: "The Kings of Accra, unlike the Fantees, have very few, if any, personal followers, and next to nothing of—what is equal to any amount of slaves—the sinews of war. The educated natives alone can aid the kings with followers in times of war, the men or slaves whom they possess having descended to them from their fathers."[78] Bannerman is correct in stating that compared to the big merchants, Ga officeholders did not necessarily own large retinues of slaves. That they possessed a mandate to mobilize the free-born *manbii*, however, is apparent from the events of 1866. Kojo of Nleshi and Dowuona of Osu had each assembled some 3,000 men on the Volta when on March 20 Taki Tawia, having circumvented Dutch and British efforts to prevent his participation, arrived with a force of 4,000 fighting men of Kinka.[79] Accra, denuded of its male population, had temporarily become a female domain. As the warriors departed, *asayere* companies took control of the streets, the women "marching uninterruptedly the whole day under a deafening shouting."[80]

The *Ga mantse*'s entry into the campaign subverted the attempt by Conran to retain control over his African allies. An initial inconclusive engagement on the Volta was followed by heated disagreements over tactics, resulting in the withdrawal of the colonial regulars to Ada. The force eventually crossed the river to Adidome, from there setting off in pursuit of Geraldo and the Anlo. On April 12, the Ga and their allies were drawn into a well-laid ambush. "Here we were, 15,000 men, who boasted of having conquered the Ashantees, well armed and no doubt brave, flying before at most 8,000 Awoonlahs [Anlos]."[81] The fleeing Ga rallied only when the Akuapem, who had been marching separately, fell upon the Anlo at the rear. Although by the end of the day some 1,500 Anlo men had been killed and decapitated, the initial rout seriously damaged the self-confidence of the Ga.[82] A reversal of such magnitude could mean only one thing: inadequate divine and supernatural support. The reported evaporation of morale can be understood only in these terms, and there are hints that the hasty, ritually ill-prepared departure from Accra was identified by many as the cause of the fiasco.[83] The three *mantsemei* of Kinka, Nleshi, and Osu subsequently fell back on Ada, while the bulk of their forces disbanded and returned shamefaced to Accra. The ambush of April 12, 1866 would be enshrined as *Awuna So*, "Awuna Thursday," one of the most potent Ga oaths uttered to enforce judicial obedience by evoking the specter of military disaster.[84]

To what extent was Accra's established chiefly hierarchy attempting to bolster its wealth and authority in the era of legitimate commerce by reverting to accumulation through warfare? Evidence on this point is contradictory. Taki Tawia and Kojo Ababio remained at Ada with their immediate households for almost three years, not returning to Accra until January 1869.[85] British officials suspected that personal enrichment was the primary motive for this prolonged residence at the mouth of the Volta. Herbert Ussher, who replaced Conran as Administrator in 1867 and displayed an immediate hostility toward African authorities, ordered the *mantsemei* to return to Accra, convinced that they remained at Ada "solely for plunder."[86] The attraction of the town for the Ga war leaders was also noted in 1874, when it was reported that Taki and his fellow *mantsemei* were again "levying imposts on produce passing down the river."[87] Despite the British role, moreover, the taking of war captives remained an important part of the Awuna campaigns. Captured enemy warriors tended to be decapitated, but many women and children were either enslaved or held for ransom.[88]

Neither the war nor the stubborn refusal of the *mantsemei* to quit Ada can be explained simply by the logic of material accumulation. Kojo Ababio himself suggests more complex motives in a letter from Ada arguing against peace with the Anlo. Its jagged syntax should not obscure a revealing insight into the fine line between rights and obligations negotiated by Ga officeholders:

> Government brought me to this war . . . [but] you have return[ed] . . . . I have [to] fight with the Awhoonahs and my business must be done. If I . . . [do not] catch Geraldo I can't go to Accra. It looks rather too shame for us if we return to Accra and not to fight with Awhoonahs and by doing [that] I am nobody and I can't command no more nation and then I am not on the Throne and half breaking the law [of] our Country.[89]

If warfare presented an opportunity for the accumulation of material wealth and moral authority—for plunder and prestige—it also carried the danger of failure and of shame. All forms of high status in Accra were precarious at the best of times, and even more so during the hazardous occupation of war. Kojo's fear was that if he returned to Accra following the retreat of *Awuna So* and with Geraldo still at large, he would be treated at best as a "nobody." The women of Accra, who had tirelessly performed *asayere* in ritual support of the campaign, were now reported to be waiting angrily to hold the *mantsemei* to account for their lost kinsmen.[90]

War, Slavery, and Civic Rights

At the opposite end of Accra's social spectrum, slaves had much to gain from their role in defending the town. The role of warfare as a mechanism that could accelerate the incorporation of slaves into Ga society was demonstrated by a series of cases in the Supreme Court in 1872. At issue were the rights of a group of slaves who had fought in the Awuna Wars. An Osu woman, Anna Lutterodt, brought charges against members of the Akomfode *asafo* to the effect that they had "beaten gong-gong" in the streets of the town, unilaterally announcing the manumission of all her domestic and plantation slaves.[91] After inheriting the slaves from her late husband, Danish merchant George Lutterodt, she had begun to dispose of them, selling thirty-three people before the intervention of the *asafo*. According to Badu Asonko, the *otsiami* of the Osu stool: "the slaves and Companies combined amongst themselves and made a law that they (the slaves) would no longer serve Mrs. Lutterodt. . . . We the chiefs gave leave to beat the gong-gong . . . for the purpose of telling the people that good ladies [i.e, *owulai*] in Christiansborg [should] . . . not sell slaves in lot, if they did so the Town would be broken."[92] Losing the first action, Anna then charged five Osu chiefs with responsibility for the manumission. "If [Anna Lutterodt] owe any money no one is to touch any of her slaves on account of the debt," she testified the chiefs decreed. "If [she] sell any more of those slaves the party who will buy them will be considered to be touching Christiansborg people."[93]

The ethnicity of the slaves is an important consideration here, and, as in most court cases involving slavery, remains obscure. The above statement, however, suggests that these slaves had not hitherto been considered as "Christiansborg people." If this was the case, and a group numbering at least thirty-three must have been one of diverse origin, what forged this solidarity between free-born Osu notables and the slaves? One of the defendants, Aiku, the *otsiami* of the Osu *mantse*'s tribunal, explained the manumission as follows: "When [the Chiefs] were going to war some years ago all these people helped the war. They were at the war twice. And that is the reason for our beating the Gong Gong."[94] By participating in the fighting, Anna Lutterodt's slaves had earned the right to be considered "Christiansborg people," on whose behalf leading Osu officeholders were prepared to intercede during a dispute with their Ga owner. Two years later we find Anna offering to hand all her people over to the Basel Mission in return for monetary compensation, which would "allow me . . . to hire [other] peoples to . . . work for me."[95] The slaves had not only successfully resisted sale and dispersal, but appear to have removed themselves from the effective control of their mistress.

The Departure of the Dutch from Kinka

The expansion of British rule in Accra from 1868 brought these issues of slavery, law, and civic identity to the forefront of town affairs. The exchange of territory on the Gold Coast between the British and the

Dutch came into effect on January 1, 1868. First suggested in 1857, the agreement replaced the mosaic of interdispersed forts and jurisdictions with two contiguous administrative units divided at the Sweet River between Elmina and Cape Coast.[96] Four days later, Governor Blackall arrived in Accra to preside over the transfer of Kinka to the British. Fort Crèvecoeur was renamed Ussher Fort and the surrounding town officially became Ussher Town. In an address to the people of Accra Blackall reaffirmed the "outlaw" status imposed by Ussher on the absent Kojo Ababio and imposed the same on Taki, now effectively a British subject. Blackall warned his audience that support for the two kings would result in "severe punishment under English law."[97]

The immediate threat of the punitive application of English law reflects the beginning of a more effective colonial presence in Kinka following the many years of minimal Dutch control over their solitary outpost on the eastern Gold Coast.[98] Import duties were increased and for the first time imposed on traders operating from Kinka.[99] Reflecting on the exchange some two decades later, Taki suggests that the Ga of Kinka viewed 1868 as the effective beginning of colonial rule: "At that time the land belonged to my grandfathers and I didn't see any white man here . . . and my own uncle was the Commandant of the Fort. . . . When this country was taken by the White man I was absent from town and I heard that their flag was up. I was then at Awoonah."[100] Unable to enforce its writ as far east as Ada, the British government was again forced to change its policy of coercion toward the two outlawed chiefs to one of co-option. In November 1868, Taki and Kojo, under pressure from Accra's merchants, reluctantly signed a British-sponsored peace treaty with the Anlo, paving the way for their return.[101] The two *mantsemei* finally reentered Accra on January 2, 1869, Taki declaring that only William Addo's influence persuaded him to return before he "had finished the war."[102]

THE DUFFO WAR AND THE "ACCRA CONFEDERACY"

The second Awuna War, or Duffo War, occurred against the background of the Asante invasion of the Ewe country between 1869 and 1872. The immediate aim of the Asante army was to suppress an attempt by the Ewe-speaking peoples of the Krepi region to throw off the last vestiges of Akwamu overrule. The goal of *Asantehene* Kofi Kakari and the "war party" in Kumase appears to have been to shore up their Akwamu and Anlo allies in order to secure continued access to the Volta trade route, and in particular the flow of firearms controlled by these two states.[103] Ga military involvement in this destructive conflict was minimal, limited to a successful assault against an Asante and Akwamu garrison on Duffo island in the Volta, a victory that for the Ga gave the war its name. The continuing insecurity in the southeast Gold Coast, however, had a great impact on politics in Accra.

The most notable development during this period was the creation of the ephemeral "Accra Confederacy," an attempt by the indigenous merchant elite to assert their influence over the established *mantsemei*. In a brief treatment, Kimble views the Accra Confederacy essentially as a short-lived by-product of the Fante Confederation, locating both movements under the rubric of an emergent African nationalism.[104] The changing idiom of elite political aspirations is indeed important, but this analysis remains overly weighted toward the impact of political developments among the Fante to the west at the expense of economic factors on the Volta to the east. It tells us very little, moreover, about the reformulation of authority and status within Accra's volatile political arena.

The opening of the Asante assault in Krepi early in 1869 confirmed the fears of Accra's chiefs and merchants that diplomatic efforts on the part of the British administration had done little to reopen the Volta or overland trade routes. The conclusion of a treaty with the Akwamu in March by Administrator Simpson was reported to be greeted with derision in Accra by everyone "from King Tackee to his pipe-bearer."[105] The Akwamu and Anlo, town leaders complained, continued to prevent Krobo palm oil and Krepi cotton from reaching Accra. A number of Ga merchants had invested in the cotton trade from Krepi in response to rising world market prices in the early 1860s. The most notable was Julius C. Briandt of Osu, whose factories containing gins and presses at Anum, Peki, and Adidome were lost during the Asante invasion.[106] The disruption to trade was exacerbated in the minds of the African merchants by competition from the Basel Mission Trading Company, founded in 1859 as the commercial arm of the missionary enterprise. The Mission's policy of opposing armed intervention was widely suspected to be on account of its own commercial interests in the region, in particular the continued ability of its agents to receive cotton and oil deliveries at the Anlo ports of Keta and Dzelukofe.[107] A letter from an Osu trader to the *African Times*, published under the title "The injurious trading operations of the Basle Mission," conveys the intensity of commercial competition: "There is now not one educated native buying palm oil in this place. With their large means they undersell everyone here, and . . . have wrested the trade from our hands. Even the latest (palm-oil kernel) trade they have taken from our hands. . . . They maintain this false peace in order to have the interior for themselves."[108] Hostility toward the Basel Mission was shared by the *mantsemei*, who must have been particularly antagonized by the ongoing attempt to prohibit church members from taking disputes to African tribunals.[109] Taki Tawia warned the British that he did not want the Mission involved in the negotiations with Akwamu because "their palaver was not good."[110]

Figure 2.2 Counting cowrie shells for the Basel Mission Trading Company at Osu, 1860s. (Copyright Basel Mission Archive, Basel, Switzerland. Ref. No. QD-30.011.0068. Reproduced with permission.)

The mutual antagonism between sections of the Accra trading community and the Basel Mission in this period is striking, qualifying the implicit connection between legitimate commercial elites and Christianity found in much of the literature. Much of this tension was no doubt due to the Mission's aggressively competitive commercial operations. A deeper and more complex antipathy, phrased by the missionaries' suspicion of Accra's urban milieu and by changing European attitudes regarding race, is revealed in a letter by Rev. Elias Schrenk: "We have a number of half-bankrupt . . . native merchants, mulattoes. These people are crying for war to have an excuse for not paying [their debts]. . . . If you read their articles you might really think to listen to reformers; but . . . many of them [are] lazy and lustful men, whose morality is often lower than a simple negro."[111] The lack of Christian morality displayed by many of the merchants clearly caused consternation among the strictly pietistic Swiss and German missionaries. Although a number had been highly educated in Britain or Sierra Leone, most Euro-African men were little more than nominal Christians. Many were prone, like the tiny group of resident Europeans with whom they often socialized, to hard drinking, gambling, and occasional outbursts of violent behavior.[112] Many practiced polygamy, and most were considerable slaveowners. *"Rationalism* and *licentiousness,"* the West Indian Methodist missionary Henry Wharton thundered from James Town in 1869, "are the governing principles of the more intelligent classes!"[113]

Continuing regional conflict and disruption to trade provided the impetus for these "more intelligent classes" to attempt to formalize their political influence in Accra. On his return from Akwamu in March 1869, Simpson extracted an agreement from Taki, Kojo Ababio, and the new Osu *mantse* Naku (c. 1868–c. 1883) to provide contingents of warriors to aid the beleaguered Krepi. However, the authority of the *mantsemei* to call the quarters to war had been sorely undermined by the debacle of *Awuna So.*[114] When, by August, it was reported that Akwamu forces had crossed the Volta into the British Protectorate and no Ga army had yet been mobilized, the merchant community—said by James Bannerman to number "about sixty respectable persons"—decided to act. A six-man "Managing Committee" was established to advise the chiefs on the organization of the war effort under the leadership of William A. Lutterodt, "the acknowledged head of the educated natives of Accra."[115] The other members were Lebrecht Hesse and J. E. Richter of Osu and George Cleland, William Addo, and James Bannerman of James Town, with Edmund Bannerman, James's younger brother, serving as secretary.

What motives lay behind the formation of the Managing Committee of a putative Accra Confederacy? As with the better-known Fante Confederation, a crucial ideological impetus was the charter for a modernizing, independent African statehood advanced by the Sierra Leonian army surgeon James Africanus Horton. In response to the 1865 Select Committee's recommendation for ultimate British withdrawal from West Africa, Horton (1835–1883) advocated self-government for the political communities of the coastal enclaves in *West African Countries and Peoples* in 1868.[116] Proposing that the Gold Coast be divided into two nation-states, a Kingdom of Fante and a Republic of Accra, Horton argued that the latter should encompass all of the southeastern Gold Coast and be ruled by a president chosen from the educated elite of Accra—he suggested Lebrecht Hesse.[117] Kimble argues that the goal of the Accra merchants was "to supersede the traditional rulers" by the creation of "an alliance which they hoped might be the germ of the republican form of government advocated by Horton."[118]

The influence of the Fante Confederation is certainly apparent from the surviving letters that passed between the Accra committee and the Fante leaders at Mankessim.[119] However, there is little evidence to indicate the existence of any widespread "republican" sentiment among the African merchant community of Accra. The reformist rhetoric of the committee's existing correspondence suggests the influence of two very atypical individuals, James and Edmund Bannerman. James (c. 1830–c. 1875) and Edmund (1832–1903) were two of the ten children of the late James Bannerman and *oheneba* Yaa Hom, the daughter of *Asantehene* Osei Yaw famously captured on the battle-field of Katamanso in 1826. Highly educated and articulate, they and their elder brother Charles (1828–1872) were the first members of Accra's Euro-African elite to establish themselves in fields other than trade, all three work-ing as colonial civil servants and attorneys before falling out with the Brit-ish authorities in the 1860s and being branded as meddlesome "mulattos."[120] Among Accra's elite leadership only the two Bannermans had strong links with the Cape Coast milieu that spawned the Fante Confederation. Charles had long resided at Cape Coast and played a key role in local politics, airing his grievances against the petty injustices of British and chiefly rule alike in the *West African Herald*, the Gold Coast's first newspaper, which he founded in 1857.[121]

Despite the influence in town affairs of these scions of Accra's most prominent Euro-African lineage, economic interests appear to have out-weighed overtly political motives in the formation of the Accra Confederacy. The careers of the other members were based largely on the export of palm oil, while Cleland and Addo were intimately connected with the established political order of Nleshi. It is significant that only when reports reached Accra that the Akwamu and Asante threatened the Krobo palm oil region was action finally taken.[122] The fact that the Ga and Euro-African merchants formed the committee to the exclusion of their European counterparts does provide some indication of a new type of elite African political identity. Nevertheless, their basic demand remained the same as that of expatriate merchants: not the withdrawal, but the extension of British authority in or-der to protect trade.[123]

What the merchants did attempt to do was to attach new conditions to the established obligation of "big men" to supply the town quarters with arma-ments in wartime. Yet events suggest real limits to their ability to usurp the functions of the Ga officeholders. Informing the British of the formation of the committee, Lutterodt explained that the educated community planned to raise a force to defend Krobo themselves, as the chiefs clearly had no power to do so.[124] One month later, however, their plans were revised significantly: they were now simply supplying the chiefs with funds to rearm the *asafo* companies.[125] The educated merchant elite had clearly failed in its attempt to circumvent the established authority of the "traditional rulers," and by the end of 1869 the Managing Committee along with the envisaged Accra Con-federacy had faded from view. The failure of the experiment may have been due to the fact that the limited economic objectives of the merchants were secured following the success of the second Awuna campaign. Nevertheless, the short-lived Accra Confederacy represents an early struggle between the acquired wealth and status of the emergent literate elite on the one hand and the ascribed status of the *mantsemei* on the other. It is a struggle that would continue to influence town politics throughout the early colonial period.

The successful outcome of the second Awuna War served to alleviate the lingering sense of shame in Accra and to bolster the bruised authority of the *mantsemei* after the disaster of *Awuna So*. By October 1869, the Ga *asafo* companies had again marched for the Volta, the long campaign culminating in an assault on an Asante and Akwamu garrison on Duffo Island on June 19, 1870. The Ga reportedly killed 400 of the enemy and took 650 prisoners of war, while *Ga mantse* Taki gained control by rights of conquest over the Volta ferry crossing at Bator.[126] The prestige of military success was translated into further material gain on Taki's arrival back in Accra, when he unilaterally raised the charges for oaths uttered before his tribunal from the traditional 32 shillings to a hefty 110 shillings.[127] By early 1871 the Krobo, who had secreted several seasons worth of palm oil in underground pots, were again head-loading large amounts of oil to Accra. "It is . . . astonishing to see the . . . articles which the bushmen now take in exchange," reported the *Herald*: "expensive straw hats, beaver hats, silk handkerchiefs, Crimean shirts, flanel vests, walking sticks and whips, looking glasses and pictures and even . . . 'Moselle.'"[128] The campaign had succeeded in reopening the interior trade routes so vital to Accra's middleman economy.

THE "GLOVER WAR" AND
THE END OF ORGANIZED VIOLENCE

The Anglo-Asante war of 1873–1874 accelerated the process of British consolidation on the Gold Coast, which began with the 1868 exchange of territory and continued with the takeover of the remaining Dutch possessions in 1872. The large-scale military intervention, with its resulting loss of European life and cost to the metropolitan taxpayer, led directly to the creation of a formal Crown Colony, the abolition of slavery, and, in 1877, the transfer of the seat of government from Cape Coast to Accra.[129] The events of 1873–1874 are well known and will not be repeated here.[130] It should be stressed, however, that the Ga took part in a very different war to that involving the Asante and Fante. For the Fante, the conflict became known as the *Sagrenti* War, after the commander of the British expeditionary force, Sir Garnet ("*Sagrenti*") Wolseley. It was remembered in Accra as the *Glover ta*, the Glover War. This distinction reflects more than the fact that the African forces in the Eastern Districts were commanded by Captain John Glover, the Administrator of Lagos. While European accounts portray the expedition to the Volta as a minor sideshow to the real action, Wolseley's advance on Kumase, for the Ga and their Dangme allies the Volta region continued to be the locus of conflict in what was regarded as a third Awuna War.[131]

On arriving at Accra in September 1873, Glover found no enthusiasm for a confrontation with Asante.[132] Throughout 1873, the main concern in the town had not been the threatened Asante advance southward at all, but rather the British move to pay for the defense of the Protectorate by raising import duties on spirits at the beginning of the year.[133] The importance of the alcohol trade to the local economy was reflected in the vigor with which the townspeople mobilized against the new tariff, a petition warning of the threat posed to the livelihood of the "vast numbers" of women "who manage to eke out an existence solely by retailing spirits."[134] In such circumstances, the *Ga mantse* warned, the British should not expect any great war effort from Accra. Antipathy toward war with Asante was exacerbated by Glover's clumsy attempts to subvert the established role of the Accra chiefs as middlemen in the distribution and sale of munitions to the states of the interior. Determined to bypass Taki Tawia and the new Alata *mantse* Kofi Oku (1871–1885), he traveled inland to Akuropon in order to deal directly with the Akuapem and Akyem leaders. This strategy was undermined by *Okyenhene* Amoako Atta of Akyem Abuakwa, who insisted that Accra was the customary location for a war council with Europeans.[135]

Glover's recruiting strategy caused chaos in Accra. Wishing to be independent of the Ga military hierarchy, he decided to recruit local volunteers for his so-called Hausa Police Force from Lagos.[136] The arrival of a detachment of 200 "Hausa" regulars caused considerable agitation among the large *odonko* slave population in Accra and its agricultural hinterland.[137] Slaves began to flock to the forts to enlist, resulting in a confrontation between Glover's troops and the slave-owning citizenry of Accra. Opposition on the part of the Ga to the recruiting campaign mounted daily, culminating in a violent clash on October 1 between the Hausa soldiers and armed townsmen. Many *odonkofo* were physically constrained from enlisting, "every man of local consequence," Glover observing, "having a domestic lockup for his slaves."[138] Taki Tawia's own prison was broken down by Hausa troops, who released slaves wishing to enlist. Fearing the collapse of his entire campaign, Glover authorized that owners be paid five pounds for each slave who volunteered for the force.[139] This measure, he admitted, was only partially successful in restoring harmony: "Houssa [i.e., *odonko* slave] women wished to accompany the men, and at every embarkation of a detachment for the camp at Addah, the whole town came down to the beach to resist the departure of the women."[140]

These dramatic events indicate the magnitude of slavery in Accra. The eagerness with which so many *odonkofo* attempted to join the colonial troops, moreover, shows that many actively sought to resist the conditions of their servitude. Glover was shocked by the legal recognition of slavery in the British courts, and by the way in which government employees "shamelessly came forward to be paid for the slaves of their wives and sisters."[141] On learning of this arrangement, the Colonial Office ordered the termination of such payments, fearing that they would be construed as the buying of slaves.[142]

Although the compensation agreement together with the distribution of munitions finally succeeded in placating the slave-owning *manbii*, Glover's difficulties in generating a martial fervor continued. When, in early October, news reached Accra that the Anlo had plundered and burnt some Ga trading stores at Keta, the town leaders, together with their Ada and Krepi allies, saw the opportunity of replacing a march on Kumase with a campaign against their old enemies on the Volta.[143] The analysis of the Ga and Dangme attitude by the early historian and ethnographer of the Gold Coast, A. B. Ellis, is well observed: "they cared very little about making war on Ashanti— which had not troubled them during the late invasion—and a great deal about making war upon the Awunas, . . . and they simply made use of Captain Glover."[144]

The negotiating position of the Ga *mantsemei* was undermined by the *konor* of Manya Krobo, Sakite, who to their fury had unilaterally agreed to follow Glover to Kumase. On October 12, 1873, the chiefs of the southeastern Gold Coast met Glover at a ceremonious public gathering in James Town. Azu's firsthand account confirms the analysis offered by Ellis:

> All the chiefs with the exception of King Sakitey consulted together and said: ". . . we are bound to follow his example or we shall lose the favour of the whiteman, yet the rub is that even during the time of our forefathers, nobody has dared to attack the Ashantees on their soil." "I am going to tell the governor", said Ga Manche Taki, "that the Ashantees and the Awunas are allied and the latter would certainly attack us during our absence . . . so we would fight the Awunas first and then proceed on to Ashantee; but . . . we can clear ourselves when the Awuna war is over by saying that we are tired of warfare."[145]

That, indeed, was how the Ga proceeded to conduct their final military campaign. The leading Accra merchants again mustered and led their private armed militias.[146] Their wives, meanwhile, supplied their female domestics as carriers for the head-loading of supplies, mainly cases of gin, between Accra and Akyem, receiving twenty shillings for each slave provided.[147]

As in the earlier campaigns, once the decision-making process had resulted in a collective understanding that Accra was at war, it was socially imperative that every able-bodied man take part. On arriving at Accra, G. A. Henty, correspondent for the *London Standard*, found the town "denuded of its male population, almost all the men who could carry arms having left to join Glover."[148] Reindorf reported a similar situation in the hinterland, adding that once the women "commence to dance and sing war songs, [not] much could be done during the whole time this war may last."[149] The status associated with the bearing of arms was such that the issue erupted into open conflict within the ranks of the Ga *tabiloi,* warriors. On November 4, Glover authorized that fighting men would receive three pence a day for subsistence, compared to the lucrative sum of one shilling a day for carriers.[150] Even this proved insufficient to induce any *tabilo* to give up the chance of carrying a gun. "It is the opinion of the women that . . . influences the men," Henty perceptively reported.[151] The men knew that howls of female derision awaited them if they returned to Accra having done the work normally assigned to slaves, women, or children. It is in this context that the questioning of Abossey Okai in 1918 in order to establish his role as warrior or carrier—as "man or boy"—can best be understood.

CONCLUSION

The late 1860s and early 1870s was a period of transition in the history of Accra. The town's historical role as a conduit of firearms and other goods from the Atlantic economy had been a vital factor in enabling Ga office-holders to establish themselves as political brokers between the European forts and the African states of the interior. Their recognized status as regional war leaders was further enhanced by the accumulation of ritual power and by the Asante defeat of 1826. The restructuring of Accra's middleman role with the transition from the slave trade to legitimate commerce created new opportunities for the accumulation of wealth and status in the town. By the late 1860s, established authority began to be contested by an emerging literate, predominantly Euro-African, merchant elite. The outcome of this contest was inconclusive, as it was subsumed by the rise of a third, increasingly autonomous, political actor: British imperial power. These contests within Accra were shaped by a series of military conflicts on the lower Volta River generated by rising tensions within the regional trading economy. The events of the three Awuna Wars provide graphic evidence of the intimate connection between warfare, wealth, and civic virtue in Ga thought and action. Even as British power moved toward a consolidation of colonial rule, warfare was continuing to shape indigenous notions of Accra as a moral community. As the termination of organized violence after 1874 began gradually to refashion male civic virtue, defending that moral community became a more complex affair. No longer could the Ga raise a returning warrior such as the eighteenth-century hero Wetse Kojo to high office with the cry of "Oh, we have got a man!" The realities of the new imperial age for the *mantsemei* of Accra must have appeared closer to the situation feared by Wetse Kojo's successor

Kojo Ababio, who wrote in 1866 that defeat would mean "I am nobody and I can't command no more nation."

NOTES

1. Drum motif and battlefield motto (in the Twi language) of the Asonko *asafo* company of Accra, which conveys the link between warfare and male adulthood: Reindorf, *History*, 120–121.

2. *Obonu* (talking drum) motif in the Twi language, said to have been drummed by opposing warriors in order to mock the Ga: Dakubu, *One voice*, 375.

3. NAG ADM 11/1/1087, "List of Chiefs and others present at the Maxwell-Crowther Commission," n.d. [1907]; ADM 11/1/1673, 1907 Enquiry; ADM 11/1/1756, 1907 Report; for the background to the enquiry, see ADM 11/1/9 Accra Native Affairs, 1907, and Chapter 5.

4. See esp. NAG ADM 11/1/1673, 1907 Enquiry, evidence of Ato Kwai Fio, cross-examined by Alata *mantse* Kojo Ababio, 3.

5. For the Gold Coast, see R. A. Kea, "Firearms and warfare on the Gold and Slave Coasts from the sixteenth to the nineteenth centuries," *JAH*, 12 (1971); idem, "Trade, state formation and warfare"; idem, *Settlements*; Robert S. Smith, *Warfare and diplomacy in pre-colonial West Africa* (London, 1976); Tenkorang, "The importance of firearms"; Metcalf, "Microcosm of why Africans sold slaves"; for regional comparisons, see Law, *Slave Coast*; Boubacar Barry, *Senegambia and the Atlantic slave trade* (Cambridge, 1998).

6. Kwame Arhin, "Rank and class"; on the ideology of warfare in Asante culture, see idem, "The Asante praise poems: The ideology of patrimonialism," *Paideuma*, 32 (1986).

7. Daniell, "Ethnography of Akkrah," 7.

8. Reindorf, *History*, 29.

9. See, for example, NAG SCT 2/4/50 Div. Court Vol. 39, *Mantse D. P. Hammond v. Mantse Ababio*, 1912.

10. NAG SCT 2/4/66 Div. Court Vol. 50, *Land for Accra Water Works*, 1918, evidence of James Allotey Wayo.

11. For comparative insights, see John Lonsdale, "The moral economy of Mau Mau: Wealth, poverty and civic virtue in Kikuyu political thought" in Bruce Berman & John Lonsdale, *Unhappy valley: Conflict in Kenya and Africa* (London, 1992); Ali A. Mazrui, "The warrior tradition and the masculinity of war" in A. Mazrui (ed.), *The warrior tradition in modern Africa* (Leiden, 1977); Fortes, *Kinship and the social order*, 87–153.

12. The term *kpakpa* or *kpakpo* (good, brave, or virtuous) was occasionally awarded to individuals for outstanding feats; notable examples from early colonial Accra include Pedro Kpakpo Ankra (d. 1888), William Kpakpo Brown (1846–1922), and William Quartey-Papafio [Kwatei Kpakpa-fio] (d. 1889).

13. Quaye, "The Ga," 256–257; caboceer, from the Portuguese *cabeceiro*, "headman." Cf. McCaskie, *State and society*, 43–44, on the possible link between the early Asante *abirempon* and the killing of an elephant.

14. On eighteenth-century Accra, see Quaye, "The Ga," 256.

15. NAG SCT 2/4/68 Div. Court Vol. 52, *Land for Accra Water Works*, 1918.

16. Field, *Social organization*, 170–171.

17. Ibid.; see also Kudadjie, "Aspects of religion."

18. For an eighteenth-century commentary on the code of martial honor and the intense shame borne by those men whose "ancestors' heads are in the hands of the enemy," a condition often resulting in depression and heavy alcohol use, see Römer, *Tilforladelig*, trans. Bertelson, "African history," 11.

19. Reindorf, *History*, 254.

20. Ibid., 257; see too FC N75, Last to Minister, 3 Jan. 1830.

21. FC N78, Outforts 1842–1845, Accra 1842; detailed oral material on the history of the Dadebanwe is located in NAG SCT 2/4/17 Div. Court 1889–1891 Part 2, *John Vanderpuye v. Dadaye, W. A. Solomon, Ankra Fio, Pappoe*, 1890.

22. Reindorf, *History*, 206, 261–263.

23. Ibid., 203–204.

24. PP Mar. 1874 XLVI [C.891], No. 126: Harley to Kimberley, 13 Aug. 1873, enclosed: King Tackee and others to Administrator, 20 Feb. 1873.

25. NAG ADM 11/1/1673, 1907 Enquiry, 4, 33.

26. Kilson, *African urban kinsmen*, 22; Field, *Social organization*, 130.

27. Reindorf, *History*, 118.

28. NAG SCT 2/4/67 Div. Court Vol. 51, *Land for Accra Water Works*, 1918, evidence of Abossey Okai; cf. Fortes, *Kinship and the social order*, 149–150.

29. Reindorf, *History*, 5–6; and see esp. NAG ADM 11/1/1673, 1907 Enquiry; NAG SCT 2/4/68, *Land for Accra Water Works*, 1918.

30. McCarthy, *Social change*, 50.

31. Field, *Social organization*, 105–106.

32. On *asayere* and its Akan version, *mmobomme*, see Adam Jones, "'My arse for Akou': A wartime ritual of women on the nineteenth-century Gold Coast," *Cahiers d'Etudes Africaines*, 132, 33 (1993).

33. Isert, *Letters on West Africa*, 136.

34. Reindorf, *History*, 211; cf. BMA D-1, 25, Abokobi 1873, No.17, Reindorf to Committee, dd. Mayera, 17 Nov. 1873; FC N84, De Jeune to Governor, 22 Mar. and 29 Mar. 1866. On the vestiges of *asayere* dance groups, described to Field in the 1930s as "the women's *asafo*," see Field, *Social organization*, 103.

35. See *African Times*, 22 Sept. 1866; cf. Kwame Arhin, "The political and military role of Akan women" in Christine Oppong (ed.), *Female and male in West Africa* (London, 1983).

36. M. J. Field, "Spirit possession in Ghana" in John Beattie and John Middleton (eds.), *Spirit mediumship and society in Africa* (London, 1969), 12.

37. See esp. Winwood Reade, *The African sketch-book* (London, 1873), Vol. 2, 174.

38. *Gold Coast Leader*, 26 July 1902.

39. NAG ADM 11/1/1086, "Amount of gunpowder distributed by Captain Codjoe during the funeral of King Tackie," n.d. [Aug. 1902].

40. PRO CO 96/397, Nathan to Chamberlain, Despatch No. 313, 22 July 1902.

41. Ibid.; NAG ADM 11/1/1775, interview between Nathan and P. C. Randolf, n.d. [May 1903].

42. *Gold Coast Leader*, 26 July 1902; *Gold Coast Chronicle*, 18 July 1902.

43. NAG ADM 11/1/1086, P. C. Randolf and others to Secretary for Native Affairs [hereafter SNA], 28 Jan. 1903; ADM 11/1/1086, *Gold Coast Chronicle*, 1 Aug. 1902, "Mode of electing to the Accra stool;" Field, *Social organization*, 180–185. The three "stool houses" were also known as Kpatashi, Ajamankese, and Akropong, respectively,

while a fourth subdivision of Abola, Wemprakwa, provided the quarter's military officeholders, the *shipi* and *asafoatsemei*.

44. Field, *Social organization*, 181; see also Kilson, *African urban kinsmen*, 23, citing evidence from an inquiry into the Ga stool in 1932 that states that Taki was descended from Teiko Tsuru through his father's mother.

45. NAG ADM 11/1/1772, interview between Governor Nathan and Noi Ababio and others, 12 Jan. 1903; ADM 11/1/1086, P. C. Randolf and others to SNA, 28 Jan. 1903; see also ADM 11/1/1086, *Gold Coast Chronicle*, 1 Aug. 1902; ADM 11/1/1088, Report on Enquiry into Destoolment of Tackie Obile, Ga mantse, by J. T. Furley, 21 Oct. 1918.

46. This was suggested by Osu *mantse* Noi Ababio: NAG ADM 11/1/1772, interview dd. 12 Jan. 1903.

47. The phrase is borrowed from Meyer Fortes, *Oedipus and Job in West African religion* (Cambridge, 1983), 5; the closest Ga concept would be *jenba*, "morality" or "moral authority."

48. Field, *Social organization*, 129–130. *Kla* (Twi: *kra*) can be translated in the broadest terms as "spirit" or "soul."

49. Ibid., 154–157.

50. See Chapter 1.

51. Field, *Social organization*, 157. The "*hewale*" was symbolically renewed each year at *Homowo* by the presentation of a *yo* hat, made from the skin of a duiker antelope, by the Asere *mantse*.

52. Field, *Social organization*, esp. 73–75.

53. See Chapter 6.

54. Kilson, *Kpele lala*, 162; FC 81, Journal of Governor Shonerus, 18 Mar. 1856; PRO CO 96/38, Connor to Labouchere, No. 23, dd. James Fort, 22 Mar. 1856.

55. Quartey-Papafio, "Native tribunals," 324.

56. Daniell, "Ethnography of Akkrah," 2; PRO CO 96/41, Pine to Labouchere, No. 35, 30 Apr. 1857; Zimmermann, *Grammatical sketch*, Vol. 1, ix; PP 1865 V [C.412] *Report from the Select Committee on Africa (Western Coast)* [hereafter *1865 Report*], 137; FC N84, W. A. Lutterodt to Governor, 25 Aug. 1865; Reindorf, *History*, 118.

57. FC N81, Coulon to Governor, 30 May 1857; PRO CO 96/41, Pine to Labouchere, Conf., 31 Aug. 1857; see too the commentary by *Ga mantse* Taki Tawia on Accra's middleman function reported in the *West African Herald*, 20 May 1871.

58. Horton, *West African countries*, 136.

59. PP 1865 V [C.412] *1865 Report*, 137.

60. Reindorf, *History*, 177. For further insights, see Field, *Religion and medicine*, 124–125, who observes that the Ga in turn regarded ritual medicines from Dahomey, Krobo, and the northern savannas as particularly potent.

61. Reindorf, *History*, 200–201; on Tano see McCaskie, *State and society*, 117; on the Dente oracle, D.J.E. Maier, *Priests and power. The case of the Dente shrine in nineteenth-century Ghana* (Bloomington, 1983).

62. Compare the Asante explanation for the loss of the 1873–1874 conflict as being due to the loss of a potent war charm: McCaskie, *State and society*, 17, 344–345.

63. Reindorf, *History*, 217; see also WMMS Box 260, File 1846, No. 20, Edward Addison to GS, dd. British Accra, 11 June 1846.

64. D.E.K. Amenumey, "Geraldo de Lima: A reappraisal," *THSG*, 9 (1968); Reynolds, *Trade and economic change*, 139–142; Louis E. Wilson, *The Krobo people of Ghana to 1892: A political and social history* (Athens, OH, 1991), 100–114; Greene, *Gender, ethnicity, and social change*, 127–134; Lynn, *Commerce and economic change*, 112.

65. See the firsthand accounts of warriors of both sides in NAG ADM 11/1/1673, 1907 Enquiry; ADM 11/1/1661, Notes of Evidence. Commission of Enquiry. Awuna, Addah, and Akwamu, 1912.

66. Economic competition on the lower Volta resulted in a similar conflict in 1784, the Sagbadre War: see Isert, *Letters on West Africa*, 31–77; and Reindorf, *History*, 130–137, who draws an interesting parallel between the causes of the two conflicts.

67. PRO CO 96/70, Conran to Cardwell, No. 39, 10 Mar. 1866; see too NAG SCT 5/1/46 Letter Book (William Addo) 8 Mar. 1866–15 June 1867. William Addo—trader, farmer, cattle merchant, surfboat contractor, proprietor of Accra's first hotel, labor recruiter, and "Government Interpreter"—was a key figure in Accra until his death in 1876. This one extant volume of Addo's correspondence provides an intimate glimpse into his commercial and social life. One of the private merchants to whom the British farmed out the collection of the Krobo fine in 1859, Addo was still owed 1,330 gallons of oil (value £1,919) in 1866.

68. FC N84, Lutterodt to Governor, 25 Sept. 1865. William Augustus Lutterodt (d. 1880), popularly known as "Owula Vielhelm," was a wealthy trader-farmer of Ga and Danish parentage residing at Kinka. An independent trader since 1830, he emerged as a political broker between the Ga and the Dutch fort, acting as commandant from June to November 1865.

69. See FC N84 passim, esp. Coulon to Governor, 7 Dec. 1865.

70. The Ga merchants at the forefront of the campaign for armed intervention on the Volta were Lutterodt, Addo, James and Edmund Bannerman, Lebrecht Hesse, George Cleland, J. C. Briandt, C. VanLare, J. E. Richter, W. G. Bruce, and J. H. Badu. All were Euro-Africans except Badu and Addo, who appear to have had no European ancestry, and all were literate except Addo.

71. PP 1865 V [C.412] *1865 Report*; Metcalfe, *Great Britain and Ghana*, 291–331.

72. The civil establishment of British Accra in 1871 consisted of three officials, the Civil Commandant, a Colonial Surgeon, and a Clerk of Customs: PRO CO 38/8 Colonial Office List, 1871. For the militia and police presence, see W. H. Gillespie, *The Gold Coast police 1844–1938* (Accra, 1955); David Killingray, "Guarding the extending frontier: Policing the Gold Coast, 1865–1913" in David M. Anderson and D. Killingray (eds.), *Policing the empire: Government, authority and control, 1830–1940* (Manchester, 1991).

73. *African Times*, 22 Nov. 1862.

74. Gillespie, *Gold Coast police*, 7.

75. NAG ADM 11/1/1769, meetings of 8, 12, and 13 Feb. 1866. Educated and baptized in Denmark, Dowuona had returned to Accra with the first Basel Missionaries in 1828, accepting the position of *mantse* in 1853 only after prolonged negotiations with Osu elders had enabled him to retain some elements of his Christian faith: see Jenkins's Abstracts, 17–18, Zimmermann's Quartel Bericht, 7 Oct. 1853; Hans W. Debrunner, *Presence and prestige: Africans in Europe* (Basel, 1979), 181–182.

76. *African Times*, 22 Sept. 1866, letter dd. Christiansborg, 10 June 1866. This letter to the London monthly, a graphic account of the war written by an anonymous participant—possibly Edmund Bannerman—is reprinted in abbreviated form in Africanus B. Horton, *Letters on the political condition of the Gold Coast* (London, 1870, reprinted 1970), 78–89.

77. On "boiling" or "cooking" the battle and other ritual preparation for war, see Reindorf, *History*, 122–123; Field, *Social organization*, 153; idem, "The *otutu* and the *hionte* of West Africa," *Man*, 43 (1943); NAG ADM 11/1/832 Sempe Fetish "Oyeni," Sempe *mantse* Anege Akwei to SNA, 17 Sept. 1923.

78. Horton, *Letters*, 34–36, James Bannerman to Horton, dd. Cape Coast, 21 Sept. 1869.

79. The total force, including 4,000 Akuapem led by *Okuapehene* Kwao Dade, numbered some 16,000 men: *African Times*, 22 Sept. 1866.

80. FC N84, Le Jeune to Governor, 22 Mar. 1866.

81. *African Times*, 22 Sept. 1866.

82. The *African Times* correspondent puts casualties among the allied force at 65 killed and 320 wounded, of whom 150 subsequently died.

83. NAG ADM 11/1/1673, 1907 Enquiry, 5; NAG SCT 5/1/46 Letter Book, Addo to Taki, Codgoe, and Dorwoonah, 25 May 1866, on arrangements for the sacrifice of bullocks by the Ga *wulomei* in order to begin ritual reconstruction after the defeat; FC N84, Weytingh to Governor, 24 Mar. 1867, on the hiring of a renowned "foretelling priest" from the Fante town of Mumford to consider the merits of further military action.

84. NAG ADM 11/1/1756, 1907 Report, appendix B.

85. *African Times*, 23 Feb. 1869. Frederick Noi Dowuona disappears from the historical record in late 1866; by mid-1867 *otsiami* Aiku was acting Osu *mantse* at Ada, and by June 1868 Naku had succeeded to the Osu stool. The complete documentary silence regarding the fate of such a prominent figure is unusual and mysterious.

86. PRO CO 96/74, Blackall to Buckingham, No. 36, 13 June 1867.

87. PP Feb. 1875 LII [C.1140], No. 65: Hewett to Secretary to the Admiralty, 19 June 1874; see too *African Times*, 30 July 1974.

88. PRO CO 96/71, Blackall to Secretary of State, No. 7, 20 June 1866, enclosed: Herbert to Donelan, 28 May 1866; *African Times*. 22 Sept. 1866.

89. PRO CO 96/72, Blackall to Carnarvon, No. 67, 26 Dec. 1866, enclosed: King Cudgoe to Conran, 1 Nov. 1866; see also CO 96/71, Blackall to Secretary of State, No. 7, 20 June 1866, enclosed: Hesse to Colonial Secretary, 2 May 1866.

90. See FC N84, Accra Journal, 25 April 1866; NAG SCT 5/1/46 Letter Book (William Addo), Addo to King Tackee, 13 July 1866.

91. NAG SCT 2/4/10 Div. Court Vol. 3C, *Anna M. Lutterodt v. Adjaye Codgoe and Lartaye*, 29 Oct. 1872.

92. Ibid. *Otsiami* (from Twi *okyeame*): spokesperson or "linguist" for a chief; "to beat gong-gong": to beat an iron bell in order to draw the public's attention to an important announcement.

93. Ibid., *Anna Maria Lutterodt v. Baddo Assonkor*, 1872.

94. Ibid.

95. BMA D-1, 26/81, Anna Lutterodt to Josenhans, 7 Aug. 1874.

96. See Kimble, *Political history*, 223–224.

97. *African Times*, 23 Apr. 1868.

98. See ibid., 22 July 1865. The Dutch ceded their remaining territory on the western Gold Coast to Britain in April 1872.

99. PP Mar. 1873 XLVI [C.890], No. 85: Harley to Kimberley, 31 May 1873.

100. NAG ADM 11/1/1086, interview between Col. White and King Tackie, 12 Oct. 1887. Taki's "uncle" is a reference to his kinsman William A. Lutterodt.

101. PRO CO 96/79, Kennedy to Granville, No. 29, 9 Feb. 1869; *African Times*, 23 Apr. 1869.

102. *African Times*, 23 Feb. 1869.

103. Donna J. E. Maier, "Asante war aims in the 1869 invasion of Ewe" in Enid Schildkrout (ed.), *The Golden Stool: Studies of the Asante centre and periphery* (New York, 1987).

104. Kimble, *Political history*, 239–240; see too, from a strong protonationalist perspective, Francis Agbodeka, "The Fanti Confederacy 1865–69: An enquiry into the origins, nature and extent of an early West African protest movement," *THSG*, 7 (1964).

105. *African Times*, 23 Apr. 1869. On Ga participation in the Volta trade, see Marion Johnson, "Ashanti east of the Volta," *THSG*, 8 (1965).

106. *African Times*, 30 Dec. 1872.

107. Ibid., 23 July 1868; Reynolds, *Trade and economic change*, 148–150.

108. *African Times*, 22 Aug. 1868. One response to the problems in the palm oil trade was the development of palm kernel oil as a supplementary commodity; 1868 saw the first substantial exports from the Gold Coast: Lynn, *Commerce and economic change*, 120.

109. *African Times*, 23 Nov. 1864, C. L. [Locher] to editor, dd. Abokobi, 10 Oct. 1864.

110. Ibid., 23 Jan. 1869.

111. Schrenk's letter, written to the *Anti-slavery Reporter*, was reported in the *African Times*, 23 May 1868; see further Chapter 5.

112. For commentaries on the propensity for gambling in Accra, see John Duncan, *Travels in Western Africa in 1845 and 1846* (London, 1847), Vol. 1, 89; PRO CO 96/43, Pine to Labouchere, No. 1, 1 Jan. 1858; WMMS, Synod Minutes, Box 267, No. 68, Report of the religious state of the . . . Akrah Circuit for . . . 1872.

113. WMMS GCC, Box 264, File 1869, No. 34: Wharton to GS, 21 Apr. 1869 [emphasis in original]; for an indigenous Ga commentary on the educated elite's "natural antipathy to religion," see *African Times*, 28 Feb. 1873.

114. PP Mar. 1874 XLVI [C.892], Berkeley to Kimberley, 12 Sept. 1873.

115. Horton, *Letters*, James Bannerman to Horton, dd. Cape Coast, 21 Sept. 1869, 38; see too PRO CO 96/81, Kennedy to Granville, No. 93, enclosed: Lutterodt and others to Russell, 14 Aug. 1869.

116. See Christopher Fyfe, "Africanus Horton as a constitution-maker," *Journal of Commonwealth and Comparative Politics*, 26 (1988); Lonsdale, "European scramble and conquest," 700; Basil Davidson, *The black man's burden. Africa and the curse of the nation-state* (London, 1992), 21–51.

117. Horton, *West African countries*, 124–137.

118. Kimble, *Political history*, 239–240.

119. WMMS GCC, Box 264, File 1868-9, No. 56, Rev. J. A. Solomon to Rev. W. B. Boyce, 22 Nov. 1869, enclosed: Tackee Tawiah and others to the President, Kings, and Chiefs of the Fantee Confederacy, 21 Sept. 1869, and W. A. Lutterodt to the President and Kings of the Fantee Confederacy, 14 Oct. 1869.

120. For some discussion, see Kimble, *Political history*, 68–70.

121. See *West African Herald*, 13 July 1859, "The recollections of an old sinner," an autobiographical account of Charles's early career; on the *Herald*, see K.A.B. Jones-Quartey, *History, politics and early press in Ghana* (Accra, 1975). A fourth brother, Robert, was a large merchant based at Ada, while the five Bannerman girls, Helen Hansen, Emma Mills, Sarah Smith, Anna Sackey, and Elizabeth Bruce, all married into notable Accra families.

122. PRO CO 96/81, Kennedy to Granville, No. 93, 17 Sept. 1869, enclosed: W. A. Lutterodt and others to Russell, 18 Aug. 1869, and Julius Ungar and others to Simpson, 31 Oct. 1869.

123. See ibid., Kennedy to Granville, No. 98, 9 Oct. 1869, enclosed: Ungar to Simpson, 31 Aug. 1869.

124. Ibid., Kennedy to Granville, No. 93, 17 Sept. 1869, enclosed: W. A. Lutterodt and others to Russell, 14 Aug. 1869.

125. Ibid., Kennedy to Granville, No. 98, 9 Oct. 1869, enclosed: W. A. Lutterodt and others to Simpson, 13 Sept. 1869.

126. *African Times*, 23 Aug. 1870, E. B. [Edmund Bannerman] to editor, dd. Doffor, River Volta, 1 July 1870. Taki was continuing to extract revenue from the ferry in 1886: see the *Western Echo*, 11 Sept. 1886, E. Bannerman to editor.

127. NAG ADM 11/1/1673, 1907 Enquiry, 12, evidence of Kojo Ababio; ADM 11/1/1756, 1907 Report, appendix B.

128. *West African Herald*, 20 May 1871.

129. See Raymond E. Dumett, "Pressure groups, bureaucracy, and the decision-making process: The case of slavery abolition and colonial expansion in the Gold Coast, 1874," *Journal of Imperial and Commonwealth History*, 9 (1981).

130. From a large selection of contemporary accounts, see for example the "official" history by Henry Brackenbury, *The Ashanti war: A narrative* (London, 1874, reprinted 1968).

131. See BMA D-1, 25/17, Reindorf to Committee, dd. Mayera, 17 Nov. 1873; NAG ADM 11/1/1089, statement by Joseph Quartey-Papafio, 6 Dec. 1929.

132. Royal Commonwealth Society Collection [hereafter RCS], Glover Papers, File 6, 3, MS by Glover, n.d. An important indigenous source for this period is Noa Akuonor Aguae Azu, "Adangbe (Adangme) history" [part 3], *Gold Coast Review*, 4 (1928).

133. Ordinance No. 1 of 1873 raised duties on spirits from 1 shilling to 2 shillings 6d. per gallon, up from the 6d. per gallon in force from 1868 to April 1872.

134. PP Mar. 1874 XLVI [C.890], No. 85: Harley to Kimberley, 31 May 1873, enclosed: Petition from King Tackee Tawiah and others, 8 May 1873; for the organization of the liquor trade, see the detailed findings of the commission appointed to look into the grievances: PP March 1874 XLVI [C.892], No. 21, Berkeley to Kimberley, 12 Sept. 1873.

135. RCS Glover Papers, Files 15–16, MS by Deputy Commissioner Goldsworthy, n.d.

136. RCS Glover Papers, File 6, 3, MS by Glover; PP Mar. 1874 XLVI [C.893], No. 20: Wolseley to Kimberley, 13 Nov. 1873, enclosed: Glover to Wolseley, 6 Nov. 1873; A. B. Ellis, *A history of the Gold Coast of West Africa* (London, 1893), 315.

137. RCS Glover Papers, File 6, 3, MS by Glover. *Odonko* (Ga pl. *odonkofo*) was the Twi word also used by the Ga for a non-Akan person from the savanna north of Asante and specifically for a slave from that region (see Chapter 3 for a full lexicon of Ga terms for slaves and slavery). Hausa was also a generic term, used by both the British and coastal Africans to describe Muslims of the central Sudan, specifically those recruited as colonial soldiers due to supposed martial qualities.

138. Ibid.

139. PP Mar. 1873 XLVI [C.893], No. 20. The average value of a slave at Accra at this time was reported as $40, between £8 and £9: NAG ADM 1/12/3, Lees to Colonial Secretary [CS],22 June 1872.

140. RCS Glover Papers, File 6, 3, MS by Glover.

141. PP Mar. 1874 XLVI [C.893], No. 20.

142. Ibid., No. 25: Kimberley to Wolseley, 17 Dec. 1873.

143. Ellis, *History of the Gold Coast*, 315–316. Christian Rottmann, the Basel Mission agent at Keta, insisted that the act was committed not by Anlos but by Ga *agents provocateurs*: RCS Glover Papers, File 12, Rottmann to Glover, dd. Keta, 16 Oct. 1873.

144. Ellis, *History*, 316–317.

145. Azu, "Adangbe history" [part 3], 5. Sakite's younger brother and literate advisor, N.A.A. Azu (1832–1917) was—like his fellow amateur historian Carl Reindorf—a protégé of the Basel Mission.

146. RCS Glover Papers, Files 15–16.

147. Ibid., File 7, J. Bannerman to Glover, 6 Jan. 1874.

148. Henty, *The march to Coomassie*, 261.

149. BMA D-1, 25/17, Reindorf to Committee, dd. Mayera, 17 Nov. 1873.

150. RCS Glover Papers, File 6, 3.

151. Henty, *The march to Coomassie*, 270–271.

3

LAW, SLAVERY, AND COLONIAL RULE, 1874–1880

Alomte ke "mlikpano no," hewo ni ehee nyon.
(The cat says "stretching is sweet,"
so it does not buy a slave.)[1]

Moni tsuo nii hao le, eyan ke emusu flo.
(He who works for you does not go with an empty belly.)[2]

The period from 1874 to 1880 saw the beginning of the transformation of Accra from three largely autonomous Ga towns to a colonial city. For the people of Kinka the colonial presence had become more focused when the British supplanted the Dutch in 1868, remembered by *Ga mantse* Taki Tawia as the year "when this country was taken by the White man."[3] Six years later, the Asante War of 1873–1874 acted as the catalyst for the consolidation of British sovereignty throughout the Gold Coast, transforming a fluctuating, ill-defined jurisdiction into a steadily expanding colonial project. This chapter explores law and slavery as they reflect the struggle for control over Accra between colonial administrators and local leaders, and within the Ga community itself. If the imperial decree that created the Crown Colony of the Gold Coast and Lagos on July 24, 1874 meant little to the average townsman and woman, then the British decision to abolish the legal status of slavery at the end of that year and to relocate the colonial headquarters to Accra in 1877 were actions that had a significant impact on the fabric of urban life.

In the last chapter we located Accra at the center of a network of political, economic, and military exchanges in the southeast Gold Coast during the opening phases of the transition to colonial rule. In this chapter, the focus narrows to the town itself, and to the restructuring of the relationship between the urban center and its immediate hinterland. We begin by considering urban Accra as a site of legal jurisdiction, and look at how conflicting concepts of law shaped the reformulation of political authority in the town with the expansion of colonial rule. In the second half of the 1870s, the institution of slavery became the principal focus of British legal intervention into Ga society. We first consider transformations in slavery in the era of legitimate commerce, and go on to examine the impact of abolition on Accra and its hinterland. A fundamental turning point in the trajectory of Ga history came with the elevation of Accra to colonial capital in 1877, a status that served to intensify struggles for control of the town and its cultural space. The willingness of the British to intervene in Ga state and society was dramatically demonstrated in 1880, when *Ga mantse* Taki Tawia was summarily arrested and imprisoned without trial at Elmina.

LAW, ORDER, AND POLITICS IN ACCRA IN THE 1860s–1870s

By the mid-nineteenth century, European concepts of law had begun to make themselves felt in Accra. Throughout the era of the Atlantic slave trade, European, African, and Euro-African brokers in the entrepôt ports of West Africa had formulated sets of ad hoc legal codes in order to manage commercial transactions. The opening of the campaign against the slave trade in the 1810s–1820s signaled a shift to a more interventionist approach to questions of law and legality on the part of the British, Danes, and Dutch on the Gold Coast. Using a mixture of persuasion and the threat of force, European officials gradually stepped up efforts to expropriate from the indigenous authorities of the coastal towns the right to try serious criminal offences committed within their respective spheres of influence. It is likely that the Accra forts, especially the more assertive British presence at James Town, had some impact on limiting "morally objectionable" customs such as human sacrifice even before the so-called Bond of 1844 clarified the legal jurisdiction of the British Crown on the Gold Coast.[4] By signing the Bond, the chiefs of the British enclaves consented to the trial of serious crimes such as murder by the Queen's judicial officers.[5] The British further created a Supreme Court in 1853, from which date the Judicial Assessor, whose role was to advise the chiefs on the "just application" of indigenous law, simultaneously presided over the exercise of English law as Chief Justice.[6]

The creation of British and Dutch courts was prompted not only by a desire to impose a degree of law and order in the coastal towns, but by the need to regulate property relations, debt, and credit in the increasingly competitive world of legitimate commerce. In the 1860s, the Chief Justice/Judicial Assessor traveled from Cape Coast to hold court in James Town as infrequently as once or twice a year. In between times, British justice continued to be administered in a makeshift fashion by the Commandant or a local Euro-African resident commissioned as a Justice of the Peace. For the British administration at least, there is evidence that the generation of scarce revenue was as important as the dispensing of justice. When asked in 1862 to account for a fall in judicial receipts, Commandant de Ruvignes complained that he was losing valuable business to the tribunal of the James Town merchant George F. Cleland, to whom Alata *mantse* Kojo Ababio had recently deputed authority to settle cases.[7] A further obstacle to attracting litigants to the British court was the judicial clout of both Ga tribunals and the Dutch court in Kinka, where, according to de Ruvignes, "an immense number of cases are settled."[8]

British officials had long been concerned about what they considered to be the disruptive influence exercised by the *mantsemei* and *wulomei* of Dutch Accra over the inhabitants of James Town and, after 1850, Osu.[9] Despite their own tenuous presence, the British regarded the Dutch outpost as an ill-governed enclave of lawlessness where the writ of African chiefs and "fetish priests" ran large, a haven where both European and African merchants evaded British import duties and criminals and slave dealers sought refuge from British law. The rhetoric of colonial rivalry aside, the identification of Kinka as a stronghold of tradition was shared to a large extent by the Ga themselves. Rooted in the identity of the *Kinkabii* as *Gamei kron*, or "true" Ga, this perception was reinforced by the status of the Ga stool of the Abola quarter. It was further influenced by the ritual topography of Kinka, its heavy concentration of sacred sites serving to enhance the authority and visibility of the *wulomei* of the great civic cult systems.

Kinka was indeed less subject than Nleshi and Osu to the forces of social change resulting from the presence of European merchants, officials, and missionaries. Few members of Accra's literate Euro-African elite had roots in Kinka, whose leading entrepreneurs tended to be either Ga with closer links to the established sociopolitical structure or members of the Brazilian "Tabon" community of Otublohum.[10] The uneven emergence of literate elites was further shaped by the absence of missionary endeavor, and therefore European educational facilities, in Kinka. By the 1840s, the Wesleyan Methodists and the Basel Mission were operating primary schools in James Town and Osu, respectively, yet throughout the period of Dutch rule Kinka remained without a school.[11] This became a major issue in Accra in the years following the departure of the Dutch, when notables of all three towns, led by the Wesleyan-educated Brazilian returnee Francisco Ribeiro, repeatedly demanded improved access to English-language education for their children.[12] With fewer established intermediaries able to broker transactions,

British efforts to assert control over Kinka after 1868 were often characterized by misunderstanding and mutual hostility.

Law and Slavery

No one issue captures the contradictions of Accra's complex judicial arena
in the mid-nineteenth century better than that of slavery. As wealth in people
constituted one of the major forms of property, British officials found themselves adjudicating a variety of disputes involving the rights and obligations
of slaves and slave owners.[13] During his visit to the Gold Coast in 1842,
Commissioner Madden had proclaimed that the holding of slaves by British
subjects within the vaguely defined limits of the Forts and Settlements was
illegal. Except in cases of extreme cruelty, however, official policy continued to be one of noninterference in the institution of slavery. The British
and Dutch cooperated in the return of runaways to masters, and efforts to
extract slaves who had attached themselves to shrines as *wonwebii* was a
major source of friction between the three towns. Slaves and pawns occasionally used the British courts to challenge the conditions of their bondage,
but failure to prove ill treatment invariably resulted in litigants being handed
back to their owners.[14] If released on the order of a court, slaves and pawns
were required either to redeem themselves by paying their debt, purchase
price, or value, or to find another master who would do so. British courts
were also resorted to by slave owners, who sometimes chose to counter resistance to their authority by laying charges against recalcitrant slaves.[15]

By the mid-1860s, the legal status of slavery in Accra was becoming increasingly contentious. This was in part due to the decision in 1861 by the
Basel Mission to break with the laissez-faire tradition among Europeans on
the coast and abolish slave holding among its Christian converts.[16] The Mission established a Slave Emancipation Commission to oversee the transformation of slaves into bonded laborers, who were to work for their erstwhile
owners until they had paid off their purchase price or agreed value.[17] The
missionaries met with some resistance from Christian slave owners, including Carl Reindorf, who wrote a lengthy apology for domestic slavery before
resigning as a catechist over the issue.[18] None of the larger slave owners in
Accra were members of the Basel church, and the number of people directly
affected, both free and unfree, remained small. Yet there are indications that
both the ideology and mechanics of slavery started to become a conscious
issue in the minds of some free-born people in Accra. This only served to
highlight the contradictions of the British position, with exposés of the way
in which English law upheld the rights of slave owners beginning to appear
in the columns of the London-based *African Times*.[19] These prompted the
occasional rejoinder from Accra, such as the 1867 letter from wealthy Osu

cotton exporter Julius C. Briandt, who, like Reindorf, contrasted the benevolent treatment of the "so-called slaves" with the cruel fate of sacrificial victims at the hands of heathen masters in Asante. "The question of slavery," Briandt wrote, "is the current topic among the educated community of this place."[20]

The question of slavery became even more pronounced with the arrival in Accra in 1868 of a new Chief Justice, W. A. Parker. Parker, for motives that seem to have included animosity toward people of mixed race, resurrected the moribund proclamation outlawing slave holding by British subjects and launched an aggressive judicial assault upon the Euro-African elite in Accra.[21] A total of fifty-six people, notably Sarah Smith and her siblings Emma Mills and James, Edmund, and Robert Bannerman, were shipped to Cape Coast to stand trial on charges of slave dealing and ownership.[22] Replying to protests from Osu *mantse* Naku, Parker tried to reassure Ga officeholders that he had "no intention to interfere with the family and domestic institutions of the chiefs and people," the proclamation only applying to British subjects "who are not under any native chief."[23] But it was far from clear exactly who was and who was not a British subject in Accra. "If you will allow us to rectify that point," replied *mantse* Naku and *mankralo* Tete Wuruku, "we consider that the educated and uneducated natives here are, as one body, subject to their representative Chiefs."[24]

Despite succeeding in briefly imprisoning the Bannerman brothers, Parker's efforts foundered on the confusion as to the legal status of those accused of slave dealing. The impunity with which the aggressive jurist ordered the detention of leading Accra residents alarmed the Governor at Freetown, who in early 1869 hastily arranged his transfer to an even more remote outpost of empire, St. Helena. Although regarded as extreme, Parker's behavior betrays the beginnings of the late Victorian shift in attitudes toward race so intimately connected with the New Imperialism of the 1880s and 1890s. The systematic exclusion of Africans from the upper echelons of the colonial bureaucracy was still some decades away, but the petty racialism that characterized the ongoing tribulations of the Bannerman brothers in the 1860s would have been unknown in the time of their late father.[25]

Tribunals, Prisons, and Colonial Rule

Rising conflict over the role of the *Ga mantse*'s tribunal in the early 1870s is an indication of the importance of judicial authority in the transition to colonial rule in Accra. As we have seen, Taki Tawia sharply increased the fees for uttering oaths before his tribunal in the aftermath of his success in the Duffo War.[26] Payment for legal services took a variety of forms: cash in the form of currency, gold, or cowries, livestock, cloth, utensils, and occasionally slaves or labor services. Shortly after his return to Accra in 1870, Taki heard an appeal from one Aba Ashong after she had been found guilty of theft in a case initially adjudicated by Asere *mantse* Akrama (c. 1869–1896).[27] Taki, according to Aba, had demanded that she hand over a female domestic slave as security for any expenditure incurred in the case. Two years later, with the "palaver" not yet settled and the slave still working in the *Ga mantse*'s household, Aba lodged another appeal, this time to the British Judicial Assessor, to secure the return of her property. The process of appeal also moved in the other direction, from British to Ga tribunals, causing the Civil Commandant to complain in 1873 that Taki was "constantly interfering in matters connected with the Court."[28] In one case from that year, Philip Randolf, a literate Euro-African from the Gbese quarter, sued a debtor named George in the British Magistrate's Court. Unhappy with the terms of repayment ordered by the court, Randolf appealed to Taki Tawia to imprison George in order to extract the outstanding debt. The Commandant intervened and secured the release of George, who in turn successfully sued Randolf for damages. Randolf's response was to appeal yet again to the *Ga mantse*, who advised him not to comply with the British court and not to pay the damages.

The picture that emerges in the 1870s is of a highly competitive free market in judicial services, with litigants moving freely between different African and European courts in order to secure a successful outcome to a particular dispute. The distinction between these legal sites, moreover, was far from clear-cut. As Ga litigants began to use the Supreme Court as an alternative to indigenous tribunals, *mantsemei* and other notables were invited to act as advisers in cases that turned on details of local custom.[29] The legal strategies of Aba Ashong, Philip Randolf, and many others show that the British court was emerging as a viable alternative for Ga litigants unsuccessful in the tribunals of the *mantsemei* and, increasingly, as a court of first instance. They also indicate the potential for conflict between colonial and Ga authorities. Accra's commercialized trading economy based on complex chains of credit meant that a large proportion of civil cases heard by the British court were concerned with debt. The Civil Record Books indicate that cases involving issues such as marriage, adultery, control over slaves and pawns, and a variety of conflicts concerning the religious and supernatural realms tended to arrive at the British court following initial attempts at adjudication by various Ga tribunals. Aside from the *mantse*'s tribunal in each quarter, moreover, *wulomei* also commanded considerable judicial clout, utilizing their religious expertise both independently of and in conjunction with the secular chiefs. Just as by uttering a military oath (such as "*Awuna So*") associated with a particular stool a litigant was effectively consigning the dispute to that *mantse*, the public evocation of a certain *jemawon*—often referred to as "putting someone in fetish"—meant that the case would be heard by that deity's *wulomo*.[30] *Wulomei* and other religious specialists were also responsible for administering a variety of trials by ordeal, an integral part of the legal process often resorted to when other channels of adjudication had proven fruitless.[31]

Questioned in 1886 about Accra's judicial arena, George Cleland confirmed that he had established his private tribunal—"I first began to exercise my power"—in the year 1862.[32] A member of the Nii Atowe of the Alata *akutso* and a descendant of Kofi Akrashi, Wetse Kojo's successor as *mantse* of Alata or James Town, Cleland (1830–1887) was a wealthy Euro-African businessman who moved with ease between the Ga political structure of Nleshi and the social milieu of the literate merchant elite. The expansion of his business activities into law and order met with considerable success, and to enforce his rulings he operated his own prison.[33] Whether Cleland's extensive judicial authority was derived primarily from his close association with the Alata stool or from his status as a successful merchant with a considerable entourage of retainers is difficult to tell. *Mantsemei* used imprisonment in cells, called *kpabui* (sing. *kpabu*), to extract fines set by their tribunals. Glover's observations from 1873 suggest that private merchants also possessed *kpabui*, using them to enforce obedience among their slaves.[34] What is clear is that as well as dispensing Ga law in his own tribunal, Cleland also played a prominent role as juror, litigant, and magistrate in the fledgling British legal system.

British moves to clarify and extend colonial jurisdiction following the Asante War served to increase tensions within this fragmented legal arena. In a move that reflected the altered political climate of 1874, officials sought to place limits on the power of imprisonment of the *Ga mantse* and questioned the propriety of George Cleland's role in both colonial and Ga courts. When, in April 1874, a debtor who had been detained by Taki Tawia brought charges of assault, robbery, and false imprisonment against his accuser and jailor in the colonial court, Chief Justice Marshall launched an inquiry into the operation of the *Ga mantse*'s *kpabu*.[35] Testimony from local attorneys James and Edmund Bannerman established that most imprisonments began as cases of petty debt, which then accumulated with the swearing of oaths until the accused owed as much as 500 heads of cowries and his or her family became liable for detention.[36] Allegations of inhuman conditions in Taki's lockup carried an air of hypocrisy given the deplorable state of the jail in James Fort, condemned by an inquest jury—which included George Cleland—following the death of a European prisoner in 1868.[37] Nevertheless, Marshall urged that the *Ga mantse*'s powers of detention be curtailed.

Cleland had emerged as a key intermediary between the Ga and British during the Awuna Wars. In late 1873 he had been appointed as a magistrate, an office which gave him jurisdiction over British subjects and that it was believed made Cleland himself a British subject.[38] The difficulty, in the words of the Chief Justice, was that "Mr. Cleland as a native Chief, holds a Court . . . in Accra which . . . is more resorted to than any other of the native Courts."[39] This position, Marshall believed, was incompatible with that of a magistrate of the British court, overlooking the fact that as Chief Justice and Judicial Assessor, he too was charged with the execution of both English and African law. The Colonial Office ruled that Cleland was in fact not a British subject, but as a Justice of the Peace was free to adjudicate "strictly native cases" within the Forts and Settlements. Direct intervention against *Ga mantse* Taki was also frustrated by the Secretary of State, who was "not disposed to consider . . . the exercise of civil jurisdiction by him . . . as an usurpation."[40] Taki was merely warned from London to exercise justice "with some regard to equity and humanity," and his tribunal and prison continued to function without overt interference from the British until 1880.[41]

The creation of a formal colony on July 24, 1874 was an attempt by the government in London to tackle these long-standing contradictions. On that date the old Forts and Settlements were separated from Sierra Leone to form the Crown Colony of the Gold Coast and Lagos, while a proclamation the following month empowered the local government to enact laws for the adjacent Protectorate.[42] Pressure from metropolitan business interests for colonial expansion, as Dumett has shown, was negligible.[43] Far more strident were members of the Euro-African mercantile communities of the main coastal towns, who throughout the 1860s had filled the letter columns of the *African Times* with calls for a formalization of British responsibilities in order to protect the Gold Coast's urban trading network from the perceived Asante menace. This desire for more rather than less European government is also apparent in local petitions from the *mantsemei* of Accra, who argued in the early 1870s that if the townspeople were required to pay increased customs duties they expected a concomitant expansion of British power in order to further protect trade.[44] The chiefs and merchants had little warning that the expansion of colonial power would be manifested in a direct attack on their property rights as slave holders, when in 1875 the Gold Coast became the first British colony in tropical Africa to abolish the legal status of slavery.

SLAVERY AND EMANCIPATION IN ACCRA

On November 5, 1874, Governor Strahan announced to a gathering of the "kings and chiefs" of the Eastern Districts at Ussher Fort that he intended to outlaw slave dealing and to emancipate slaves and pawns throughout the Colony and Protectorate. Ordinances 1 and 2 of 1874, "To provide for the abolition of slave dealing" and "To provide for the emancipation of persons holden in slavery," signaled a new willingness on the part of the British to intervene in the social structure of the African states of the Gold Coast.[45] Accounts of the meeting, coming two days after a similar pronouncement at Cape Coast, differ considerably. After brief consideration, the Governor reported, *Ga mantse* Taki Tawia, speaking on behalf of the assembled chiefs, "came forward and expressed . . . their readiness to do as the Queen told them."[46] According to the newly established Cape Coast newspaper, the *Gold Coast Times*, the alarmed chiefs requested three days to deliberate the matter. Strahan, the *Times* reported, "would not allow them to leave the Fort till they had given their consent, which the poor fellows . . . gave."[47] Despite the acquiescence of the chiefs, the correspondent continued, "I am afraid not much regard will be had to His Excellency's speech. I know that people here will continue to buy and sell slaves and take pawns. . . . I have slaves and I do not yet see what is to prevent me from selling any of them. Let the Government pay us for our slaves, and let employment be found for them, and . . . few of us will grumble."[48] How accurate was the prediction of this anonymous Accra slave owner that the British would be unable to enforce the new laws? What was the impact of the ordinances on Ga society in early colonial Accra? Before these questions can begin to be answered, it is necessary to consider the nature of slavery in the town and its immediate hinterland on the eve of abolition.

Slavery in Accra: Historiographical Perspectives

There are two broad schools of thought on the character of nineteenth-century slavery and its demise on the Gold Coast. Both have contributed to and drawn from the wider debate on slavery in Africa.[49] The first was informed by the contemporary reports of European officials and merchants, which, as Dumett notes, "concluded, by almost any comparative historical standard, 'slavery' . . . in a majority of the Akan coastal states appeared more like . . . patron-client relationships."[50] The anthropologist R. S. Rattray came to a similar conclusion regarding the forest kingdom of Asante, laying the foundations for the "functionalist" or "assimilationist" view of African slavery, which emphasized the sociopolitical imperatives and the reciprocal nature of the relationship between free and unfree. The fusion of functionalist anthropology and historical methodology reached its apotheosis in the influential thesis by Miers and Kopytoff, who viewed African slavery above all as an "institution of marginality."[51] Social institutions, they argued, functioned to maintain the marginal status of the slave, as he or she gradually traversed a continuum from servile outsider to partial or in some cases full membership of local kinship groups. The paternalistic domestic slavery described by most nineteenth-century observers suggested that the ideology of absorption described by Miers and Kopytoff characterized the societies of the Gold Coast littoral. The abolition of slavery by the British, the argument runs, therefore caused little socioeconomic or political dislocation, many slaves, clients, or dependents choosing to remain as part of the household of their erstwhile masters.

This view of Gold Coast slavery as a relatively benign and essentially domestic institution was subsequently challenged by scholars who argued that the nature and extent of slavery on the West African littoral underwent considerable change following the ending of the Atlantic slave trade in the first decades of the nineteenth century.[52] The loss of the overseas market resulted in a sharp fall in the price of slaves, leading, the revisionist argument contends, to a wider and more rational exploitation of servile labor in the domestic economy and an implied deterioration in the conditions of slave life. Manning argues in a recent survey that the rapid termination of export demand on the Gold Coast resulted in a transition to something resembling a "slave mode of production," as slave labor was reorientated toward agricultural production on coastal plantations.[53] Rejecting the implication of the functionalist-assimilationist thesis that slave-owning societies were defined by a coherent ideology based on the "reduction of marginality," the second wave of scholarship stressed instead the resistance of slaves to their bondage and to the extraction of their labor. According to McSheffrey, the slaves' "increasingly oppressive lot in society" resulted in widespread social and economic disruption following abolition in 1874.[54] McSheffrey's reassessment of the impact of abolition has in turn been subjected to a persuasive critique by Dumett and Johnson, who demonstrate its empirical weaknesses and misreading of key Basel Mission sources.[55] Contrary to McSheffrey's portrayal of a widespread and spontaneous reaction on the part of the slave and pawn population to the abolition ordinances, Dumett and Johnson conclude that there is little evidence to suggest any significant socioeconomic or political dislocation in the Akan, Ga, or Dangme coastal states.

Two fundamental problems face any attempt to locate slavery and abolition in Accra within this debate. First, there is a problem of historiographical bias toward the Akan. As Dumett points out, practically nothing has been written on either internal slavery or participation in the Atlantic slave trade by the Ga, Dangme, and Ewe peoples.[56] Second, there is the difficulty in differentiating between the nature of servitude within "traditional" Ga lineage groups on the one hand and the large retinues of Accra's merchant elite on the other. Despite flimsy and often contradictory evidence, there is a tendency throughout the literature to suggest that slavery was more oppressive in the coastal towns and their immediate hinterlands, where the drive for accumulation on the part of the big merchants resulted in a more rational exploitation of slave labor by the mid-nineteenth century.[57] The distinctive social structure and complex urban economy of Accra means that the extrapolation of evidence on the nature of slavery from neighboring Akan areas may be highly misleading. Yet it is equally misleading to think in terms of an ethnically defined "Ga slavery," any notion of which must be carefully differentiated in terms of the occupation, residential location, gender, and sociopolitical role of both the slave and slave owner. "Domestic slavery," Africanus Horton observed of Accra in 1868, "exists in all its forms."[58]

The Language of Servitude

The Ga language provides the first clues to the nuanced perceptions of servitude in mid-nineteenth-century Accra. The general Ga term for slave was *nyon* (pl. *nyojii*), derived from the verb *nyo*, meaning "to fall," "to sink," or "to go down."[59] *Nyo* also provides the root for *nyomo*, "debt," and the verb *nyomoje*, "to take a pledge or pawn." This etymology is highly suggestive of a close link between debt, pawning, and slavery, in terms of both socioeconomic process and Ga concepts of servitude. Although it is difficult to establish a firm causal link between one and the other, an increase in indebtedness and pawning in Accra may have coincided with the period of high slave exports and increasing commercialization during the second half of the eighteenth century. Zimmermann points out that by the 1850s the word *nyon* was seldom openly used, and "a more common and less offensive expression" for slaves was *tsujii* (more correctly *tsuloi*; sing. *tsulo*), "servants," or *webii*, literally "children of the house."[60] Whereas the Twi word commonly translated as "slave," *akoa*, implied subordination rather than servitude and is perhaps better defined as "subject," *nyon* suggests a more narrowly defined economic relationship rather than one based on rank or status.[61] This may reflect the highly commercialized and less hierarchical nature of nineteenth-century Accra relative to the Akan forest states, a distinction only partially disguised by the euphemistic use of the language of kinship common to many African societies.

Other categories of Ga servitude appear to have relied on loan words from Twi. The most prominant was *odonko* (Ga pl. *odonkofo*, Twi pl. *nnonkofoo*), which, as noted in Chapter 2, refers to a non-Akan person from the savannas to the north of Asante and more specifically to a slave from that region. Other terms that appear are *awoba* (or *ahoba*), from the Twi *awowa*, "pawn," and *okrawa*.[62] *Okrawa*, according to Wilks, was used in Asante to describe "a class of female servants of the Asantehene having to do with his spiritual well-being."[63] No such class of women existed in Accra, although the word *okrawa* is used in one courtroom discussion from 1915 to describe female slaves purchased specially as concubines for the sons of a family.[64] A further, important distinction was made between slaves who were acquired through purchase or other economic transaction and those who were captured during warfare. Called *agbanbii* or *ojotjaloi*, captives or "plundered slaves" appear to have had certain rights of refuge denied to other *nyojii*, and under Ga law could attach themselves to any new master without fear of return.

Transformations in Slavery

How does slavery in Accra and its hinterland fit into the analytical framework outlined above? There is certainly some evidence to suggest that the extraction of labor for production increased as a result of the transition to legitimate commerce. The fall in slave prices after 1807 appeared to be followed by the reorientation of unfree labor to larger-scale agricultural production for both overseas markets and consumption within Accra by Danish merchants and Euro-Africans such as James Bannerman and John Hansen.[65] By the 1860s, a number of Ga and Euro-African merchants of the next generation owned sizable farms on the more fertile northwestern reaches of the Accra plains, Horton mentioning the coffee plantations of W. A. Lutterodt, Lebrecht Hesse, J. C. Briandt, John Dodu, Rev. T. B. Freeman, and one of the prominent Bruce family—probably William G. Bruce—of James Town.[66] There is little information on how labor was organized on these plantations. However, given their size—between 10,000 and 30,000 coffee trees—and the fact that all these figures with the exception of Freeman owned considerable numbers of slaves, it must be assumed that these farms were at least partly worked by unfree labor.[67] It was reported in 1864 that members of the Brazilian Tabon community controlled a flourishing trade in slaves from Krepi, who were "readily bought" as farm workers.[68]

Transportation is a second sector of the economy within which unfree labor has been identified as playing a more regimented role by the mid-nineteenth century. Head-loading trade goods and rolling casks of palm oil to and from the interior was an arduous task that often fell to the slaves of the Accra merchants. It was also common practice for slave owners—both large and small—to hire out their "people" as farm laborers, artisans, canoemen, or carriers. The European forts, the two missions, and expatriate merchants were often dependent on these workers.[69] The distinction between the British administration and the merchant elite in midcentury was often hazy, Euro-African slave owners such as the elder James Bannerman and his sons serving as Civil Commandants at the forts of the Eastern Districts at various times throughout the 1850s and 1860s. Zimmermann records the word for wage laborer in the 1850s as *niitsulo* (lit. "wage slave"), clearly suggesting continuity with the concept of slavery. His fellow Basel missionary Schrenk reported in 1865 that while some masters allowed their slaves to retain a portion of their earnings, others took all of the pay.[70]

Zimmermann's observations on slavery and abolition in the Accra area, which contrast the treatment of domestic slaves incorporated into family groups with that of those owned by the big farmer-merchants, provide perhaps the strongest evidence for the revisionist thesis. "The situation of the slave is different with educated slave-owners, the merchants of the coast, mulattos and the great princes among the Twis," he noted. "Such people do not work and eat with their slaves, and in general stand further away from them. Among such people slavery has more or less lost the character of a mild house-slavery, and often seems similar to American slavery."[71] The official British view of a benign, paternalistic slavery, moreover, was far from monolithic. In 1857, the energetic Governor Pine mounted a vigorous attack on the prevailing laissez-faire attitude, critiquing the "apologist" argument of Cruickshank's *Eighteen Years on the Gold Coast*. While implicitly conceding that the institution of slavery remained overwhelmingly domestic, Pine argued that domestic slaves—especially recently purchased *odonkofo*—were often worked hard and treated brutally.[72] This is an important distinction. Slaves born in Accra probably spoke Ga, were circumcized (if male), and had acquired a certain degree of civic rights, possibly by participation in the town's military organization. Newly purchased *odonkofo* were more open to abuse as alien "outsiders," and were likely to have been acquired by the rising merchant class as farm workers. It was *odonkofo*, it will be remembered, who rose in rebellion with the arrival of Glover's "Hausas" in 1873.

Some of the harsher aspects of slave life in Accra can be glimpsed in British court records. Although relatively few cases of resistance on the part of slaves reached the Supreme Court, a considerable proportion of those that did involved complaints against brutal or unjust treatment by Euro-African merchants or their wives.[73] The resistance by Anna Lutterodt's slaves in 1872 discussed in Chapter 2 reveals considerable antipathy on the part of Ga office holders toward the wealthy slave-owning Euro-African community, the so-called "good ladies" of Osu. "The educated and the wealthy classes," a petition from a group of Ga women reminded the Secretary of State in 1897, "were the great upholders in the past of domestic slavery in our midst."[74] Indigenous defenders of domestic slavery, moreover, had some trouble in avoiding the fundamental subordination that underlay the institution. "So-called slaves . . . stand in the same . . . position as true children in almost all families," protested Reindorf, *"provided they are faithful."*[75]

Evidence from a variety of sources therefore confirms Zimmermann's contention that conditions of servitude in Ga society did not always conform to the stereotype of "a mild house-slavery." However, it is not sufficient to sustain McSheffrey's unequivocal claim that "a new form of slavery and a new class of slaves [clearly] did emerge in the nineteenth-century Gold Coast out of the traditional mould in response to economic change."[76] It is far from clear that the expansion of slave holding led to increasing levels of regimentation or "oppression." Nineteenth-century sources tend to use the term "plantation" to describe all Ga farms, *nmojii* (sing. *nmo*), on the Accra plains. Although the scale of some of these *nmojii* certainly increased, there is no firm evidence to suggest a concomitant change in relations of production resulting in slaves working in gangs under supervision. With the possible exception of the half dozen or so large coffee plantations mentioned above, there is every indication that the majority of slaves and pawns on the Accra plains in the 1860s resided in semiautonomous villages from which a surplus of food crops, rather than labor, was extracted.[77] Zimmermann's evidence is itself contradictory: elsewhere he refers to a work regime on the landholdings of the "mulatto" merchants involving slaves working three days of the week for their master, as well as paying him part of their produce in return for the right to farm the land for their own subsistence.[78]

McSheffrey's contention that the "assimilation of slaves was unprofitable and . . . impractical" seems misplaced in its dual assumption that the rational extraction of labor was the only concern of Accra's slave owners and that assimilation was a process that they could regulate at will.[79] Slaves could be reduced to economic chattels, he argues, because by the nineteenth century "the bulk, if not all, of the slave population in the Colony . . . was composed of *nnonkofoo* or alien slaves imported from the northern regions in recent times."[80] In the case of Accra and its hinterland this appears to be incorrect. Many slaves in Accra were *odonkofo*, but others were of Akan, Ga, Dangme, or, especially, Ewe origin.[81] Many of the latter were *ojotjaloi*, war captives, such as the large number settled by Ankra in "Ahodome" village in 1830. The numerous references to Krepis made by Basel Mission agents stationed on the Accra plains in the early 1870s indicate that the number of Ewe-speaking slaves was further increased by the Asante campaign across the Volta between 1869 and 1872.[82] Over time, *odonkofo* too could acquire a degree of assimilation in Ga society. It was not uncommon for Ga men from all levels of society to take female *odonko* slaves as wives or concubines, one well-documented example being William Lutterodt, who had a number of children with his domestic slaves including the Grushi woman Ajadom.[83]

The Unraveling of Slavery in Accra

What was the impact of the Governor's declaration of November 5, 1874? Evidence points neither to the historiographical polarities of continuity or rupture, but rather to a whole range of responses often involving ongoing negotiation between master and slave, patron and client, household head and dependent. Although Ordinance No. 2 provided for the "emancipation of persons holden in slavery," the law was actually framed to end only the "legal status" of slavery. Under this system—first used by the British in India in 1843—the courts simply no longer recognized the existence of slavery as an institution. The onus of emancipation was placed on the individual slave or pawn, who was required to approach a magistrate or District Commissioner and request his or her freedom. Response was therefore fashioned to a large extent by specific domestic relationships and by the range of options available to those in servitude, rather than by the overt intervention of the colonial apparatus.

Of those slaves who chose to liberate themselves through official channels in the first months after abolition, the vast majority were reported to be recent war captives who retained links with their area of origin.[84] By August 1875, Reindorf began to lose Ewe-speaking slaves from his pastoral flock at Mayera on the Accra plains, many of whom chose to "go back to their country."[85] Chief Magistrate Chalmers noted in contrast that "the much less numerous class of imported slaves . . . have scarcely . . . appeared before the Courts," although he believed that many *odonkofo* had left their masters to form independent farming communities.[86] This was apparent on the Accra plains, where by mid-1875 *odonko* and Krepi villages were appearing in an area that had for many years contained scattered settlements of runaway slaves and other fugitives.[87] By the 1890s, a dozen villages inhabited by a variety of northern ethnic groups, most prominently "Grushi," were reported in the neighborhood of Abokobi, although many of the inhabitants had fled from servitude not in Accra but in Asante.[88] Many appear to have been recently arrived captives who in subsequent decades would maintain a distinctive Grushi identity, while at the same time forging a variety of patron-client ties with urban notables in Accra.[89]

Zimmermann's observations on the large farms he likened to American plantations indicate that, far from widespread desertion, masters and slaves arrived at a variety of new—and clearly negotiable—social and economic relationships. Some slaves ran away, and these had the option of returning home, establishing their own farms, or finding wage employment, especially as soldiers or policemen, in Accra. Others continued to work for themselves on the same land, no longer giving the owner part of their produce or their labor for three days a week as before.[90] Some slave owners began to pay their men and women wages: six to nine pence for an eight-hour farming day, one to two shillings a day as carriers and canoe crews, and a higher but unspecified figure as hammock carriers.[91] This appears to have been the regularization of an existing system of wage earning by slaves, many of whom had utilized "free" days to hire themselves out or had retained a portion of their wages when hired out directly by their masters.[92] Chalmers's measured report of 1878 captures something of the ongoing restructuring of socioeconomic relationships, a process that in many cases did not involve a clear transition from unfree to free:

> It is said to be more difficult to obtain hired labour in the towns on the coast. . . . Formerly the householder, possessed of a large retinue of retainers for whose maintenance he was considered responsible, was always ready to hire out the services of his people . . . and he had means of enforcing on them a certain degree of attention to the work. . . . Many of these retainers have emancipated themselves, or, at least, are so much out of any real control by their head, that [he] cannot induce them to work except on their own terms.[93]

The absence of major social and economic dislocation in Accra did not therefore mean that abolition had little impact, or that, as some historians have posited, it "failed."[94] Insofar as the aim of the legislation was limited to emancipating those slaves and pawns who actively wished to leave their masters, without disrupting either mutually acceptable patron-client relationships or the running of the domestic economy, then abolition—from the British point of view—was relatively successful. Initial opposition from Accra's slave owners, as the *Gold Coast Times* correspondent predicted, was focused on the issue of compensation.[95] However, opposition was muted, an angry petition from Fante chiefs demanding compensation having no equivalent in Accra. Resistance on the part of the slave-owning Euro-African merchants was constrained by an often strident espousal of Victorian ideas of civilization and progress. Attempts to defend in writing the institution of slavery in Accra, typically comparing its benevolence with the harsh treatment of slaves in Asante, only betray the difficulty that the literate elite faced in rationalizing their role as the "great upholders of slavery."[96] The feared disruption of the local economy, moreover, failed to materialize, and palm oil, the mainstay of many of the big Accra merchants, continued to move to the coast.[97]

There is little evidence to suggest that the majority of domestic slaves residing within Accra and belonging to Ga families or lineages did not remain as part of the *shia* or *we* into which they were brought or born. Just as deviations from recognized norms of behavior on the part of masters had triggered resistance by slaves in the period before 1875, so the dynamics of individual domestic relationships fashioned the reactions to the abolition ordinance. Some slaves subjected to what they considered unjust treatment approached the District Commissioner to demand manumission, an action that was occasionally resisted by their owners. In one court case, a woman named Abiuah successfully charged her ex-mistress, Botchey, with attempting to retain her as a slave by taking her before *Ga mantse* Taki to "drink fetish," thereby preventing her from approaching government officials on pain of death.[98] Accra court records contain few manumission cases, Robertson locating only nineteen instances of slaves or their relatives actively applying for emancipation between 1874 and 1880.[99] Some slaves in Accra applied for manumission, but, finding it difficult to carve out an independent niche in the competitive urban economy, decided to return to their masters.[100] Despite this retreat from "freedom," ongoing restrictions in the labor market enabled many slaves in Accra—as on outlying farms—to renegotiate new terms of service.

Court records do indicate that the buying and selling of slaves, mainly female children, continued discreetly into the first decades of the twentieth century.[101] Despite these prosecutions, the long governorship of Sir William Brandford Griffith (1885–1895) was characterized by a reluctance on the part of British officials to interfere in African domestic relations, marking a virtual return to the old laissez-faire tradition with regard to slave holding.[102] Pawning, which Dumett and Johnson argue acted as a buffer enabling chiefs and "big men" throughout the Gold Coast to weather the transition from slave to free labor without great loss of prestige or income, also continued in Accra.[103] "We are afraid of buying slaves," wrote Basel Mission catechist Peter Anteson when asked in 1893 if Christians continued to take pawns, "but not . . . of this," while the *Gold Coast Independent* reported toward the end of the decade that "notwithstanding the utmost vigilance and the most stringent enforcement of the laws against domestic slavery, that branch of the institution known as pawns continues . . . in full swing . . . in Accra."[104] Whether pawning actually increased in magnitude after 1875, as Dumett and Johnson suggest, or merely began to appear more often in the historical record, remains inconclusive. Evidence suggests that the dynamics if not the scale of pawnship in Accra changed as a result of the loss of control over slave labor, the value of pawns rising at a time when the emergence of wage labor was advancing only fitfully.[105]

What implications did the abolition of slavery have for the making of early colonial Accra? Just as the slave trade and the incorporation of unfree settlers had been central to the reconstruction of the precolonial *majii*, so the gradual unraveling of the institution of slavery was central to social and economic change in the late nineteenth- and early twentieth-century town. While much evidence points to continuity rather than rupture, this does not mean that servile members of Ga *wei* simply continued to acquiesce to a benign assimilationist ideology of family and lineage heads. The many court cases throughout the early colonial era in which subordinate family members of slave origin contested Ga laws of succession and inheritance provide ample evidence that the ongoing absorption of servile outsiders was a process shaped by both conflict and accommodation. The changing meanings of servitude and status continued to be debated, family heads often seeking—to use the terminology of Miers and Kopytoff—to maintain the marginality of those descended from slaves. In 1914, Alata *mantse* Kojo Ababio was questioned on the impact of the abolition ordinance. "There are many sons and grandchildren of slaves living in Accra," he answered. "Since the emancipation those who chose to go away have gone. Those who remained are still in the houses and are not treated as slaves, but they are subject to the Accra custom because they have married and have had children and grandchildren. . . . Here when you die a slave is entitled to your property."[106] But Kojo Ababio added an important qualification: "If he sleeps with me, he is still my slave."

THE TRANSFER OF THE COLONIAL CAPITAL TO ACCRA, 1877

In the months following the announcement of the abolition of slavery, the British began to consider the possible relocation of the headquarters of the new Gold Coast Colony. Both Accra and Elmina were advanced as alternatives to Cape Coast, which had long been considered by European officials to be a particularly unhealthy town. The open grassland behind Accra, together with the proximity of the Akuapem hills, was thought to constitute an environment more suitable for European residence, permitting exercise and sport in the form of horse riding and shooting.[107] Accra's commercial prospects were promising, particularly with regard to the reinvigorated palm oil export trade. By 1875, with a total population of approximately 20,000, the three Accra towns formed the largest trading center on the Gold Coast, contributing in customs receipts nearly one-third of the colony's revenue.[108] Its main drawback, besides the lack of an adequate prison, courthouse, or hospital, was its rocky shorefront, which made the landing of goods and people through the surf a hazardous exercise. The health factor ultimately outweighed these problems and in mid-1875 the decision was made in favor of Accra.[109] Work began on the renovation of the dilapidated Christiansborg Castle, which was to be the seat of the Governor. Meanwhile, the open land between Osu and Kinka, dubbed by the British "New Site" and later Victoriaborg, was earmarked as a suitable location for the offices of the enlarged colonial bureaucracy.[110] A large block of land was transferred by the *Ga mantse* and the chiefs to the Crown, and by the end of the year government buildings—most emblematically a new courthouse—began to rise along the sides of the old road between the two *majii*.[111] On March 19, 1877,

Figure 3.1 James Town (Nleshi), c. 1880. Urban landmarks penciled in include from left to right: James Fort, the Police Court, Addo's hotel, the Colonial School, G. F. Cleland's house, the customs office, Hansen's Hall, F. & A. Swanzy's factory, and the Wesleyan Chapel, which marked the boundary between Nleshi and Kinka. (Courtesy of the Foreign and Commonwealth Office Library, London.)

Accra officially became the headquarters of the Gold Coast Colony, thereby ending a two-hundred-year period during which Cape Coast had been the seat of British power.

The relocation of the colonial capital interacted with the decline of slavery to accelerate an existing process whereby land in and around Accra was emerging as an economic commodity and a political resource. Historically, the relationship between Ga town and country had been phrased by the institution of slavery, "ownership" of farming land on the outskirts of Accra and beyond having been largely determined by the settlement of slaves in *aklowai*. As control over slaves declined, the concept of property gradually shifted from wealth in people to wealth in land.[112] "Vacant" land was customarily managed by town quarters, although as demand rose the question of whether ultimate guardianship lay with the *mantsemei* or with the sacrally derived rights of the *wulomei* emerged as a key area of contention. Writing in the 1880s, Reindorf noted that the "power of the priest over lands and revenues is gradually falling into the hands of the kings."[113] Nevertheless, the collective granting of "town" or "stool" land to a family or an individual

Figure 3.2 Ussher Town (Kinka), c. 1880. In front of Ussher Fort the large stone houses of the Brazil quarter rise from the thatched roofs of compound houses. (Courtesy of the Foreign and Commonwealth Office Library, London.)

tended to initiate a process whereby such land became recognized as the property of the latter to be henceforth disposed of as they wished.[114] Written transactions detailing the transfer of land by Osu officeholders to the Basel Mission date to the 1830s, while the outright sale of privately owned urban real estate was under way by at least the 1850s.[115] The commoditization process, coupled with the recognized rights of officeholders as real estate brokers, meant that the issue of control over urban land emerged in this period at the very center of Ga politics. The mechanism through which the colonial regime entered this equation was the Public Lands Ordinance of 1876, promulgated to facilitate the spatial reordering of the new headquarters by providing for the compulsory purchase of land required by the government.

The Reordering of Urban Space

By the late 1870s, issues of disease and medicine began to join those of law and order in official efforts to reshape the cultural space of Accra. Indeed, "sanitation" and "order" became linked by an emerging imperial ideology in which the new concern with tropical medicine contained a variety of encoded messages about wider social control.[116] At the center of the debate over the transfer of the colonial capital was the belief that the sanitary condition of Accra's "native town" could be improved.[117] Lacking the resources to clean, let alone effectively control, the old town quarters, the administration foisted the task onto the chiefs in general and the unfortunate *Ga mantse* in particular. Failure to maintain the degree of cleanliness in the streets required by colonial officials now resulted in arbitrary fines, Taki Tawia suffering the indignity of being fined ten pounds in November 1877.[118]

The drive to clean up Accra soon extended beyond mere street sweeping to a desire to rid the town of activities deemed unsuitable for the seat of imperial power. Herein lay a tension that would shape the making of colonial Accra: the town was both the British capital and the sacral epicenter of an African state. Much of the effort on the part of the colonial state to impose order on its new headquarters was directed toward the elimination of so-called "fetish practices" or "customs." Officials were particularly alarmed by the annual *Homowo* festival, which they referred to as "Black Christmas" or—misleadingly—the "Yam Custom."[119] Such African rituals, it was repeatedly opined, were best conducted in the "bush," not in the envisaged urban showcase of expatriate enterprise and ordered modernity. On the eve of the first *Homowo* season since the transfer, Freeling summed up the prevailing British attitude in an exchange with Alata *mantse* Kofi Oku: "I cannot allow these indecent customs in the towns. People get drunk and riotous. Go into the country if you want them."[120] Accra, in other words, was no place for the display of African custom, effectively reversing Ga notions of urban civilization. After some negotiation Kofi Oku persuaded the Governor to sanction the festival, on the condition that dancing be restricted to the interior of people's courtyards. "If there is drunkenness in the streets," Freeling warned, "I will hold the Kings and Chiefs responsible." Colonial rule was also beginning to impose new notions of public and private space.

The equation linking urban sanitation with urban order emerged in legislative form the following year in the Towns, Police, and Public Health Ordinance. A diverse set of regulations designed to control the use of space in towns, the ordinance included clauses requiring permits to be obtained for such important ritual—and recreational—activities as the discharging of firearms and the beating of drums.[121] One of the most important sanitary provisions of the ordinance in the eyes of officials was to rid Accra of roaming pigs, which, after a number of failed attempts, were finally banned from the town centers in 1884. Pig rearing was an almost exclusively female occupation, and—like later attempts to end fish smoking within the town—this measure represented a direct attack on the livelihood of many Ga women. The result was two large female deputations to Christiansborg Castle, pro-

Figure 3.3 An (unnamed) Accra *mantse* with his musicians, late nineteenth century. The tall drums are *obonu*; the man at the back beats an iron "gong-gong." (Copyright Basel Mission Archive, Basel Switzerland. Ref. No. D-30.01.042. Reproduced with permission.)

tests that succeeded in extracting concessions from the British regarding the application of the anti-pig legislation.[122]

The reformulation of cultural space in Accra was not simply contested between the colonial state and the collective upholders of Ga tradition. An increasingly diverse range of social groups, Ga townsmen and women, ex-slaves, newly arrived migrants, Christian converts, Muslim traders, British officials, all possessed contrasting visions of the colonial city. The columns of the Gold Coast press and the *African Times*, as we have seen with regard to the issue of slavery, reveal the deep ambivalence with which members of the literate African elite regarded the expansion of colonial control. Although cultural affiliations and attitudes toward British rule began to shift in response to the racism of the New Imperialism, many continued to be ardent proponents of a robust Victorian civilizing mission, as opposed to the activities of so-called "fetish priests" as any expatriate official.

One early example may be cited to illustrate this point. Only months after the transfer of 1877, the *African Times* published a series of letters from Accra demanding stern action against the functionaries of the Naa Dede Oyeadu *gbatsu* in Asere.[123] Just as death during *Homowo* was seen to sow grave spiritual confusion at a time when the gods were "in the town," so the

death of a woman in childbirth represented a horrific conflation of the carefully mediated passage between biological and otherworldly existence.[124]
Such an occurrence occasioned a general trauma throughout Accra. The
corpse was cast unburied into the bush, the dead woman's family forced to
bear the heavy cost of the purification rites conducted by the *wulomo* and
woyo of Naa Dede Oyeadu. A complex of potent ideas linking water, fluidity, sexuality, and liminality was apparent in the power of the goddess, who
was physically manifested within the *gbatsu* as a pot of water containing a
live black river fish, *ajen*.[125] To the *African Times* correspondents, all of this
was nothing but "abominable fetish custom." "Now that Accra has become
the . . . seat of British government," the newspaper editorialized, "this, and
kindred fetish abominations . . . can no longer be overlooked and winked
at."[126] As in subsequent incidents, the reforming modernity of the indigenous—and increasingly Christian—elite outpaced that of the colonial administration, and it would not be until 1905 that the latter moved to suppress the Naa Dede Oyeadu cult.[127]

MO DIN SANE: "AFRICAN AFFAIRS" AND COLONIAL POWER

The transfer of the seat of government to Accra also occurred against a
background of British efforts to redefine the judicial powers of the colonial
state and its African subjects. The 1876 Supreme Court Ordinance abolished
the office of Judicial Assessor and provided for the application of English
Common Law in a new Supreme Court, while the old magistrate's courts
were replaced by courts presided over by District Commissioners. The Native Jurisdiction Ordinance of 1878 represented the first effort to formally
set out the powers of the colonial government vis-à-vis African rulers, by
defining the role of indigenous tribunals.[128] That the implementation of the
ordinance was delayed for five years was due in large part to rising political
tension within the new colonial capital.[129]

One cause of this tension was the erosion of the Ga chiefs' established
role as political brokers between Europeans and the states of the interior. In
June 1877, a letter from Taki Tawia on the subject of the turbulent state of
affairs in Asante in the aftermath of the recent war appeared in the *African
Times*.[130] The *Ga mantse* was particularly concerned about the fate of
Dwabenhene Asafo Agyei, whose attempt to secede from Asante overrule
ended in military defeat in late 1875. Asafo Agyei and his followers fled
south to Akyem Abuakwa in the Gold Coast Protectorate, and by 1877 large
numbers of Dwaben refugees were encamped in the vicinity of the modern
town of Koforidua, some forty miles north of Accra.[131] The Ga were determined, Taki wrote, to assist their ally Asafo Agyei in returning to Dwaben
to continue the struggle against the Asante enemy.

This goal brought the *Ga mantse* into conflict with the British administration, which had resumed its policy of nonintervention in Asante following the 1873–1874 war.[132] On discovering—although only with the arrival of the *African Times* on the mail boat from London—that hostility toward Asante continued to exist in Accra, Governor Freeling (1876–1879) summoned Taki Tawia, *Okyenhene* Amoako Atta of Akyem Abuakwa, and *Dwabenhene* Asafo Agyei to a palaver at Christiansborg Castle on July 16, 1877.[133] Freeling lambasted Taki for sending a belligerent message to *Asantehene* Mensa Bonsu and "mixing himself up in affairs outside the Protectorate," alleging that William Quartey-Papafio, an influential member of the Kpakpatsewe of the Asere *akutso*, had advanced Asafo Agyei £350 for the war effort. This sum had in turn been passed to Taki to organize the purchase of ammunition at the old Ga colony of Little Popo on the Slave Coast.[134] The arms-trading efforts of the *Ga mantse* and William Quartey-Papafio were part of the historical Ga middleman identity. However, the Governor ordered Taki to return the money, fined him twenty ounces of gold (£72), and threatened to remove him from the stool unless he stopped conspiring against Asante. Freeling subsequently ordered the arrest of Asafo Agyei, who was deported to Lagos at the end of 1877.

In 1880, the colonial regime, once again under the robust leadership of Herbert Ussher, launched a renewed assault on the authority of officeholders in Accra. The implementation of the Native Jurisdiction Ordinance had been referred to Ussher on his return to office in 1879, yet the hostility toward indigenous rulers that he had demonstrated during his first stint as governor from 1867 to 1872 remained undiminished.[135] Early in 1880, Ussher forwarded a dossier of documents to London concerning the "habitual proceedings of King Taki," which he believed called into question the suitability of African rulers throughout the Gold Coast to be "entrusted with the working" of the ordinance.[136] The *Ga mantse* had recommitted two grave offenses. First, he and Osu *mantse* Naku had sent messengers out of the Protectorate to the chiefs of Kwawu, voicing support of the latter's attempts to resist the reimposition of Asante overrule. Second, it became apparent that Taki continued to preside over a tribunal and to enforce his judgments through the use of his prison. The tension between Accra's identity as colonial capital and as African city-state is clear, the Governor informing the *Ga mantse* of his doubts as to whether "a chief of your character is the proper person to represent the natives of the Headquarters of the Gold Coast."[137]

Ussher remained uncertain whether under the 1876 Supreme Court Ordinance African tribunals could legally operate in a town equipped with a District Commissioner's court. His hostility towards Ga law was somewhat tempered by Chief Justice Marshall, who believed that there was "much in the native laws and customs . . . which is good and suitable to the people . . . and so long as fetishism and polygamy exist . . . there are many matters which . . . could not well be taken into our courts."[138] Yet "native laws and customs" had begun to change in response to the expansion of colonial rule and its alternative legal system. Those fined in Taki's court were being forced to sign a written document binding them to payment. Many cases, moreover, were now heard in the privacy of the chiefs' houses rather than outdoors before the public as had hitherto been the tradition.[139] British officials considered a number of regulations designed to keep African jurisdiction "out in the open," including a rule that each town should possess only one native court. To this end Ussher suspended the *Ga mantse*'s court, temporarily allowing "a committee of Chiefs" to dispense justice under the supervision of George Cleland. Four months later the *mantsemei* received confirmation of the "abrogation of all native courts in Accra."[140]

Ussher's stated aim was to depose and deport Taki, but he was worried about the impact this would have in Accra and the surrounding Eastern Districts. He was further constrained by the Colonial Office, which, sensing added responsibilities and expenditure, urged extreme caution in dealing with courts in Accra.[141] Yet George Cleland would later remember the Governor's intervention as decisive: "Governor Ussher . . . told me that I must only arbitrate cases and not hold Court as before and finding that I could not enforce my judgement I discontinued holding a Court."[142] By September 1880, the *Ga mantse* was petitioning the administration for compensation for the damaging loss of revenue derived from legal fees and fines.[143] Ussher recommended that this request be acceded to, suggesting a stipend of £75 per annum and acknowledging grudgingly that Taki's widespread influence could be useful to the government.

The Deportation of Taki Tawia

Despite this compromise, a dramatic sequence of events in the closing months of 1880 culminated in the arrest and deportation of the *Ga mantse* by the colonial regime. The proximate cause of the conflict was the repatriation of Asafo Agyei from Lagos in October 1879, Ussher allowing the deposed chief to rejoin his people in their refuge of "New Dwaben."[144] By early 1880, the British began to suspect that the *Dwabenhene* had again joined forces with his Ga allies in order to reopen hostilities against Kumase. In September, a bitter conflict over the possession of the ritually blackened stools of Dwaben—and the future direction of Dwaben policy with regard to Asante—erupted in Accra between Asafo Agyei and his daughter Akosua Afrakuma.[145] Underlying the so-called "Asafo Agyei affair" was Accra's dual urban identity as the locus of both indigenous and colonial political power.

While the Ga hierarchy supported Asafo Agyei, Ussher backed the claims of Afrakuma, who the British hoped would make peace with Kumase.[146]

It was at this juncture that the rising contest between African and European power in Accra became the central issue. While Afrakuma appealed to the Governor for assistance against her father, Asafo Agyei turned to his ally the *Ga mantse* for adjudication. Despite the fact that Taki, in the words of Ussher, had been "deprived of all power and . . . expressly forbidden to exercise any authority whatsoever," he agreed to settle the case.[147] Afrakuma refused to submit to the *Ga mantse*'s tribunal, reporting to Ussher that Taki Tawia and her father were conspiring to kill her. Ussher later wrote that he had received intelligence from the town that Taki had come to an understanding with Asafo Agyei to settle the case in the latter's favor. When the *Ga mantse* attempted to coerce Afrakuma to attend a hearing, the British intervened. The Governor had Taki Tawia arrested and detained in the old Dutch castle in Kinka that since 1868 had borne his name, Ussher Fort.

Events took an ominous turn when, following the detention of the *Ga mantse*, Afrakuma fell seriously ill. In spite of the efforts of the British Medical Officer, her condition steadily deteriorated and she died on October 26. In the atmosphere of political intrigue and rising tension in Accra, her death was widely considered to have been the result of ritually induced "poisoning." "The general impression in Accra," Ussher wrote, "was that there was foul play."[148] A postmortem—the findings of which were announced to the Ga townspeople—found that death was due to natural causes. However, the concept of natural causes carried little or no weight in a belief system where sudden death was invariably the result of divine or supernatural intervention. Even the Governor felt sure that Afrakuma's demise was "hastened by fear."[149] Later that day he detained her father, on a charge, according to "G. A. Maashie," "of having caused the death . . . by fetish charms."[150]

On November 9, in disputed circumstances and with dubious legality, the *Ga mantse* and the *Dwabenhene* were deported to Elmina and Lagos, respectively. Amid rumours that the *asafo* companies of Accra were about to mount an attempt to release the *Ga mantse*, the Hausa Constabulary surrounded Ussher Fort.[151] Taki, without trial and hastily designated a "State Prisoner," was transported by gunboat to Elmina Castle, where he was locked in the turret that sixteen years later would be occupied by the deposed *Asantehene* Agyeman Prempe. "As he is to a certain extent a British subject," a Colonial Office official noted, "he ought to be tried in a proper form. . . . At the same time I doubt if any jury could be got to convict him . . . and it might be well . . . to dispense with the ordinary forms of law and deal with him out of hand."[152] The day after Taki's removal from Accra, Ussher sat down in Christiansborg Castle to justify his actions to the Colonial Office. In an uncanny coincidence, he too took sick, never completing his dispatch. He died three weeks later, on December 1, 1880. On the demise of Ussher our sources are silent. Nevertheless, in the light of the foregoing events and Taki's acknowledged intimacy with the supernatural realm, the popular perception in Accra must have been that the governor, like Afrakuma, was the victim of a ritual poison.[153]

The deportation of Taki Tawia can be analyzed in a variety of contexts. On one level, it is part of the shifting relationship between the colonial regime, the African states under British rule, and the independent Asante kingdom to the north. Ussher was convinced that Ga leaders were encouraging the Dwaben to attack Asante, a view that was shared in Kumase and that contributed to the "war scare" of early 1881.[154] The correspondents to the *African Times* dismiss as ludicrous the charge that Taki was conspiring against Asante, ridiculing the need for him to be spirited away without trial. It would have been impossible, they argue, for Taki or any other Ga chief to even contemplate such a course without the knowledge of the *manbii*.[155] "G. A. Maashie" further details how the Asante-Dwaben conflict was linked to politics within Accra. He writes that the information against Taki Tawia and Asafo Agyei was supplied to the British in 1877 and again in 1880 by a resident of Accra, a paid agent of the *Asantehene* striving to "create an incident whereby the Government should . . . cast off the protection of the Djuabins."[156] This version of events was confirmed six years later by George Cleland. It was common knowledge in Accra, Cleland informed Governor Griffith, that the evidence that led to the deportation of Taki was furnished by Edmund Bannerman.[157] This is quite feasible. Bannerman, as we will see in the next chapter, was a consummate politician and arch intriguer who maintained links with the court in Kumase through his mother, the Asante princess *oheneba* Yaa Hom.[158]

The episode also points to the way that political action within Accra had begun to be fashioned by the town's ambiguous identity as colonial capital and African state. The British saw the removal of Taki Tawia as a vital step in the imposition of political control over their new headquarters. For the Ga, however, the Dwaben dispute at the heart of the conflict was seen to lie outside the remit of the colonial authorities. It was regarded, to use a vernacular construction, as "*mo din sane*," an "African affair" (lit. "black man's palaver"). The concept of *mo din sane*—social action beyond the realm or comprehension of European overlords—is crucial to the social and political history of early colonial Accra. What the events of 1880 demonstrate is that what the Ga saw as a "black man's palaver" the colonial state also regarded as its legitimate concern. Backed by the coercive arm of the colonial state in the form of the Hausa Constabulary, British rulers were increasingly able to impose their will within Accra.

CONCLUSION

The deportation of the *Ga mantse* in 1880 was a clear indication of the consolidation of colonial rule in Accra. This is not to argue that in the space of a few years the British presence suddenly became the dominant force molding Ga state and society. Far from being abruptly terminated, the compromises, evasions, and negotiations of the past continued to characterize Accra's political arena into the new imperial age. An expanding and increasingly assertive colonial regime was certainly more willing to intervene in local society, most clearly with the abolition of slavery, the attempts to curb the judicial powers of chiefs, and the efforts to impose control over urban space. Yet the negotiations that resulted from British legislative intervention proceeded largely between Africans themselves, outside the reach of colonial rulers and based on political idioms long established in Ga culture. Moreover, the truncation of Ga chieftaincy was temporary, Taki Tawia being returned to Accra and "reinstated" as *Ga mantse* in 1883. It was the transfer of the colonial capital to Accra in 1877 that proved to be the key moment in the historical trajectory of the city. Like the gradual and contested unraveling of slavery, the full meaning of the relocation was not immediately apparent. In time, however, the evolution of the colonial capital would have a profound impact on Ga state and society. Ga state and society would also shape the nature of the colonial city, as well as that of the wider colonial project. As the events of the late 1870s demonstrate, Accra's turbulent political arena often had a disproportionate influence on the evolution of the official mind on the Gold Coast. Imperial conceptions of town and country closely informed the emerging ideology of indirect rule, a policy that never fully came to terms with the existence of an African state in the very heart of the colonial capital.

NOTES

1. Ga proverb, from Zimmermann, *Grammatical sketch*, Vol. 1, 162, commenting on the troubles that slave owning can entail.

2. Ibid., 171.

3. See Chapter 2.

4. For a review of the evidence, see John Parker, "The cultural politics of death and burial in early colonial Accra" in David M. Anderson and Richard Rathbone (eds.), *Africa's urban past* (Oxford, 2000); for an introduction to the interaction of European and African concepts of law, see Kristin Mann and Richard Roberts (eds.), *Law in colonial Africa* (Portsmouth, NH, 1991).

5. Kimble, *Political history*, 193–195; for the Dutch, see R. Baesjou, "Dutch 'irregular' jurisdiction on the nineteenth-century Gold Coast," *African Perspectives*, 2 (1979).

6. PRO CO 879/6 Gold Coast No. 47, *Domestic slavery: The jurisdiction of the Judicial Assessor, and the legal character and limitations of British power upon the Gold*

Coast, memorandum by E. Fairfield, 24 Mar. 1874 [hereafter *Fairfield Memorandum*]; A. N. Allott, "Native tribunals in the Gold Coast 1844–1927," *Journal of African Law*, 1 (1957).

7. NAG ADM 11/1/1088, Magistrate and Civil Commandant, James Fort, to CS, 3 Mar. 1862.

8. Ibid.; for competition between Dutch and African courts within Kinka, see FC N81, Governor to Nagtglas, 15 July 1854.

9. See PRO CO 96/41, Pine to Labouchere, No. 35, 30 Apr. 1857; CO 96/84, Kennedy to Granville, No. 41, 16 Apr. 1870, enclosed: Ussher to Kennedy, 11 Feb. 1870; Baesjou, "Dutch 'irregular' jurisdiction," 55.

10. See Chapter 4.

11. See WMMS GCC, Box 264, File 5, Penrose to Committee, 26 Apr. 1875.

12. NAG ADM 1/12/3, Commandant to CS, 28 Oct. 1872; PP Mar. 1874 XLVI [C.892], No. 21, Berkeley to Kimberley, 12 Sept. 1873, enclosures 9 and 10; on the emergence of the English language in Accra, see Dakubu, *Korle meets the sea*, 149–161.

13. PRO CO 879/6, *Fairfield Memorandum*, 10–12.

14. See, for example, NAG SCT 2/4/1 Div. Court Vol. 1, 12 May 1859, and *J. E. Richter v. Assahinahueato*, 27 May 1859.

15. See ibid., *Case of Mrs. George Lutterodt*, 21 July 1859; SCT 2/4/9 Div. Court Vol. 3B, *Ashearkoo Macarthy v. Maylay*, 2 July 1872.

16. See Hans W. Debrunner, *A history of Christianity in Ghana* (Accra, 1967), 172–173.

17. PP 1865 V [412] *1865 Report*, evidence of Elias Schrenk, 142.

18. BMA D-1, 13B/6A, Reindorf to Josenhans, 5 Mar. 1862; Peter Haenger, "Reindorf and the Basel Mission in the 1860s" in Jenkins, *Recovery of the West African past*.

19. *African Times*, 23 Nov. 1863 and 23 Nov. 1864.

20. Ibid., 23 Apr. 1867.

21. Ibid., 23 July 1868.

22. Ibid., 22 Aug. and 23 Sept. 1868; NAG SCT 2/4/4 Div. Court Vol. 2A, *Queen v. Mrs. Sarah Smith*, 20 May 1868.

23. *African Times*, 23 July 1868, Parker to King and Chiefs of Christiansborg, dd. 16 June 1868.

24. Ibid., Naku to Parker, dd. 20 June 1868.

25. For some discussion, see Kimble, *Political history*, 65–70.

26. See Chapter 2.

27. NAG ADM 1/12/3, Lees to Administrator, 8 Oct. 1872, enclosed: Abbah Ashong to Administrator, 18 Sept. 1872.

28. Ibid., Paul to CS, 25 Aug. 1873.

29. On 26 May 1869, for example, five months after the Dutch departure from Kinka, Chief Justice and Judicial Assessor W. A. Parker assembled twenty-four chiefs representing all three Accra *majii* to advise on the Ga law of succession in the case *Akosua v. Orbadie*: see NAG SCT 2/4/6 Div. Court 1868–1871. For commentary, see J. M. Sarbah, "Maclean and Gold Coast Judicial Assessors," *JAS*, 9 (Apr. 1910); A.B. Quartey-Papafio, "Law of succession among the Akras or the Gã tribes proper of the Gold Coast," *JAS*, 10 (Oct. 1910).

30. Field, *Social organization*, 16–17. As early as 1858 the British—with the support of some chiefs—issued a proclamation banning "putting into fetish," but the practice continued throughout our period: PRO CO 96/43, Bird to Stanley, No. 56, 10 June 1858.

31. For descriptions of the *odom* trial, involving the swallowing of an extract of the bark of the *odom* tree mixed with copious amounts of water, see WMMS GCC, Box 263, File 1862, No. 58, J. A. Solomon to GS, dd. James Town, 12 Nov. 1862, and Box 262, File 1857, No. 34, H. Wharton to GS, dd. James Town, 30 Dec. 1857; PRO CO 96/41, Pine to Labouchere, No. 75, 2 Nov. 1857; NAG ADM 11/1/1673, 1907 Enquiry, evidence of Tete Kwaku, 14–15; NAG ADM 11/1/1437, "Suppression of objectionable Customs," by S. D. Codjoe, n.d. [c.1930].

32. PRO CO 96/191, Griffith to Knutsford, No. 116, 10 April 1888, enclosed: Memorandum on Native Prisons, 3 Dec. 1887, "Questions put to Mr. Cleland Chief of James Town," 30 Apr. 1886.

33. NAG SCT 2/4/10 Div. Court Vol. 3C, *Nimpah Bayadan v. Tettay Arkoe*, 1872, and *Francis Addy v. Oyakey*, 1872; PP Feb. 1875 LII [C.1140], No.6: Johnston to Carnarvon, 18 Apr. 1874.

34. Quartey-Papafio, "Native tribunals," 80; RCS Glover Papers, File 6, 3.

35. PP Feb. 1875 LII [C.1140], No. 6: Johnston to Carnarvon, 18 Apr. 1874, enclosed: Marshall to Johnston, 9 Apr. 1874, and "Joe Mason's case," by James Bannerman.

36. Ibid., *Quow Ouchin v. Tawiah and Quaye*, 13 Apr. 1874. By the 1870s, 500 heads of cowries was equivalent to about £25: Marion Johnson, "The cowrie currencies of West Africa: Part II," *JAH*, 11 (1970).

37. *African Times*, 23 Sept. 1868.

38. PP Feb. 1875 LII [C.1140], No. 6, enclosed: Goldsworthy to CS, 16 Oct. 1873.

39. Ibid., enclosure 6.

40. Ibid., No. 24, Carnarvon to Officer Administrating the Government, 5 June 1874.

41. PRO CO 96/130, Ussher to Hicks-Beach, No. 24, 26 Jan. 1880.

42. Kimble, *Political history*, 302–306.

43. Dumett, "Pressure groups," 202, points out that by the 1870s only two European firms of any significance, Alexander Miller Brothers and F.& A. Swanzy, were involved in direct trade with the Gold Coast.

44. PP Mar. 1874 XLVI [C.892], No. 21: Berkeley to Kimberley, 12 Sept. 1873, enclosed: "Grievances of the Kings, Chiefs, merchants and people of Accra," 13 Aug. 1873; *African Times*, 1 Dec. 1875.

45. For transcripts of the Governor's address and the ordinances, see PP 1875 LII [C.1139] *Correspondence relating to the Queen's jurisdiction on the Gold Coast, and the abolition of slavery within the Protectorate.*

46. Ibid., No.13: Strahan to Carnarvon, 7 Nov. 1874; see also PRO PRO 30/6/24 Carnarvon Papers, Strahan to Carnarvon, 6 Nov. 1874.

47. *Gold Coast Times*, 30 Nov. 1874.

48. Ibid.

49. For discussion, see Raymond Dumett and Marion Johnson, "Britain and the suppression of slavery in the Gold Coast Colony, Ashanti and the Northern Territories" in Suzanne Miers and Richard Roberts (eds.), *The end of slavery in Africa* (Madison, 1988); Raymond E. Dumett, "Traditional slavery in the Akan region in the nineteenth century:

Sources, issues and interpretations" in David Henige and T. C. McCaskie (eds.), *West African economic and social history* (Madison, 1990); Larry W. Yarak, "West African coastal slavery in the nineteenth century: The case of the Afro-European slaveowners of Elmina," *Ethnohistory*, 36 (1989).

50. Dumett, "Traditional slavery," 9. This "official" view of servitude on the Gold Coast was stated definitively in the Fairfield Memorandum written in early 1874 and which drew heavily on Brodie Cruikshank's *Eighteen years on the Gold Coast of Africa* (London, 1853). For an indigenous Ga version of the same argument, see BMA D-1, 13B/6A, Reindorf to Josenhans, 5 Mar. 1862.

51. Igor Kopytoff and Suzanne Miers, "African 'slavery' as an institution of marginality" in S. Miers and I. Kopytoff (eds.), *Slavery in Africa: Historical and anthropological perspectives* (Madison, 1977).

52. Martin A. Klein and Paul E. Lovejoy, "Slavery in West Africa" in Henry A. Gemery and Jan S. Hogendorn (eds.), *The uncommon market: Essays in the economic history of the Atlantic slave trade* (New York, 1979); Paul E. Lovejoy, *Transformations in slavery: A history of slavery in Africa* (Cambridge, 1983), 159–160; Gerald M. McSheffrey, "Slavery, indentured servitude, legitimate trade and the impact of abolition in the Gold Coast, 1874–1901: a reappraisal," *JAH*, 24 (1983); Patrick Manning, *Slavery and African life: Occidental, oriental, and African slave trades* (Cambridge, 1990), 144.

53. Manning, *Slavery*, 144.

54. McSheffrey, "Slavery," 351.

55. Dumett and Johnson, "Britain and the suppression of slavery"; see also Yarak, "West African coastal slavery," 45–46.

56. Dumett, "Traditional slavery," 8.

57. For this tendency on both sides of the historiographical divide, see McSheffrey, "Slavery," 354; Dumett and Johnson, "Britain and the suppression of slavery," 90.

58. Horton, *West African countries*, 125.

59. Zimmermann, *Grammatical sketch*, Vol. 1, 242; Christaller et al., *A dictionary*, 221.

60. Zimmermann, *Grammatical sketch*, Vol. 2, 318.

61. See NAG ADM 11/1/975, Memorandum on the vestiges of slavery in the Gold Coast, by J.C. deGraft Johnson, 17 Oct. 1927; Dumett and Johnson, "Britain and the suppression of slavery," 75.

62. Christaller et al, *A dictionary*, 186, 221.

63. Ivor Wilks, *Forests of gold: Essays on the Akan and the kingdom of Asante* (Athens, OH, 1993), 341.

64. NAG SCT 2/6/5 Judgement Record Book Vol. 3 Part 1, *G. A. G. Lutterodt v. A. G. Lutterodt*, 31 July 1915.

65. On the collapse of slave prices on the Gold Coast after 1807 and the internally driven recovery by about 1820, see Paul E. Lovejoy and David Richardson, "The initial 'crisis of adaptation': The impact of British abolition on the Atlantic slave trade in West Africa" in Law, *From slave trade to "legitimate" commerce*, 36–37; Ray A. Kea, "Plantations and labour in the south-east Gold Coast from the late eighteenth to the mid nineteenth century" in ibid.; PP 1842 XII [551-II] *1842 Report*, which notes that the 400 to 500 slaves owned by the late John Hansen had been "severely worked"; cf. Yarak, "West African coastal slavery."

66. Horton, *West African countries*, 133; on Dodu's farm, see *African Times*, 23 July 1866. A number of these leading trader-farmers came together with other members of the literate elite under the chairmanship of T. B. Freemen to found the "Eastern District Agricultural Association" in 1871: *West African Herald*, 13 June 1871.

67. Jenkins's Abstracts, 1, Extracts from Stanger's diary, 1848, and 586–587, Report by Zimmermann, dd. Abokobi, 26 July 1875; Kea, "Plantations and labour."

68. *African Times*, 23 Nov. 1864.

69. PRO CO 96/6, Hill to Stanley, No. 23, 7 Mar. 1845; PP 1865 V [412] *1865 Report*, 144; PP 1878 LV [C.2148] *Report by Sir David Chalmers on . . . the abolition of slavery within the Protectorate*; NAG SCT 2/4/9 Div. Court Vol. 3B, *William Addo v. Mayee*, 22 May 1871; NAG SC 2/45, Lees to Bannerman, 2 Feb. 1871.

70. PP 1865 V [412] *1865 Report*, 144.

71. Jenkins's Abstracts, 586–587, Report by Zimmermann, 26 July 1875.

72. PRO CO 96/41, Pine to Labouchere, Conf., 1 Oct. 1957. Pine drew on oral information from the experienced Wesleyan missionary T. B. Freeman, who was convinced that slave holding had expanded in recent decades.

73. See, for example, NAG SCT 2/4/1 Div. Court Vol. 1, *Kotey v. Svannikier*, 25 June 1858, and *J. E. Richter v. Assahinahueaho*, 27 May 1859; SCT 2/4/4 Vol. 2A, *Queen on prosecution of Amanfill v. Mrs. Robert Bannerman*, 18 June 1867; SCT 2/4/10 Vol. 3C, *Queen v. Mrs. Thomas Cheetham*, 7 Feb. 1873.

74. PRO CO 96/298, Maxwell to Chamberlain, No. 386, 4 Sept. 1897, enclosed: Akole Ankrah and others to Chamberlain, 31 May 1897.

75. BMA D-1, 13B/6A, Reindorf to Josenhans, 5 Mar. 1862 [emphasis added].

76. McSheffrey, "Slavery," 364.

77. On this distinction, see Frederick Cooper, "The problem of slavery in African studies," *JAH*, 20 (1979), 115.

78. Jenkins's Abstracts, 586–587, Report by Zimmermann, dd. Abokobi, 26 July 1875.

79. McSheffrey, "Slavery," 364.

80. Ibid., 363.

81. See Claire C. Robertson, "Post-proclamation slavery in Accra: A female affair?" in Claire C. Robertson and Martin Klein (eds.), *Women and slavery in Africa* (Madison, 1983), 22; Dakubu, *Korle meets the sea*, 114–115.

82. BMA D-1, 25/17, Reindorf to Committee, dd. Mayera, 17 Nov. 1873; D-1, 26/ 126B, Reindorf to Committee, dd. Mayera, 25 Nov. 1874; *African Times*, 30 Dec. 1872. Although Ga forces entered the fray in support of Krepi allies, slaves continued to be traded down the Volta via Ada to Accra.

83. NAG SCT 2/4/57 Div. Court Vol. 45, *Georgina Lutterodt v. Annanfio*, 1914; Robertson, "Post-proclamation slavery," 225.

84. PRO PRO 30/6/24, Strahan to Carnarvon, 7 Dec. 1874; PP 1875 LII [C.1343], No. 42: Strahan to Carnarvon, 6 Mar. 1875, enclosed: Chalmers to Strahan, 6 Mar. 1975.

85. BMA D-1, 27/125, Reindorf to Committee, dd. Mayera, 17 Nov. 1875; see too D-1, 27/135, Reindorf to Committee, dd. Mayera, 10 Feb. 1876.

86. PP 1875 LII [C.1343], No. 42, Chalmers to Strahan, 6 Mar. 1875.

87. Jenkins's Abstracts, 586–587, Report by Zimmermann, dd. Abokobi, 26 July 1875.

88. Ibid., 306, Report by Schopf, 23 May 1893; J. G. Christaller, "Sprachproben vom Sudan Zwischen Asante und Mittel-Niger (Specimens of some Sudan languages),"

Zeitschrift für Afrikanische Sprachen, 3 (1889), 107-111; BMA D-1, 60/76 "Slavery and pledge" by P. Anteson, n.d. [1893]. Grushi (or Gurunsi) is an ethnic label collectively applied by outsiders to a group of small stateless societies that straddle the present-day border of Ghana and Burkina Faso.

89. Jean Rouch, *Migrations au Ghana* (Paris, 1956), 23–24; NAG SCT 2/4/57 Div. Court Vol. 45, *Georgina Lutterodt v. Annanfio*, 1914; and see file NAG ADM 11/1/1185 Grunshi Community.

90. Jenkins's Abstracts, 586–587, Report by Zimmermann, 26 July 1875, and 585B–585C, Hermann Rottman to Basel, dd. Accra, 30 June 1875.

91. Ibid., 586–587, Report by Zimmermann, 26 July 1875; cf. ibid., 585B–585C, Rottmann to Basel, 30 June 1875; 583–585, Dieterle to Basel, dd. Aburi, 22 June 1875; 585–585A, Eisenschmid to Basel, 26 June 1875.

92. Ibid., 585C–586, Binder to Mader, dd. Ada, 3 July 1875; and see above.

93. PP 1878 LV [C.2148] *Chalmers Report*.

94. Robertson, "Post-proclamation slavery;" McSheffrey, "Slavery," 357.

95. PRO PRO 30/6/24, Strahan to Carnarvon, 22 Jan. 1875.

96. *The African Times*, 23 Apr. 1867; *Gold Coast Chronicle*, 22 Dec. 1894, "The so-called slaves."

97. PP 1875 LII [C.1159], No. 2: Strahan to Carnarvon, 8 Jan. 1875; PP 1875 LII [C.1343], No. 42: Strahan to Carnarvon, 6 Mar. 1875; PP 1878 LV [C.2148], No. 2: Lees to Hicks-Beach, 5 July 1878; *Gold Coast Times*, 17 Nov. 1877, Cudgoe Mensah to editor, dd. Anomabo, 3 Nov. 1877.

98. NAG SCT 17/4/2 District Court Civil Record Book [hereafter Dist.Court], *Abiuah v. Botchey*, 3 Nov. 1875.

99. Robertson, "Post-proclamation slavery," 222.

100. Jenkins's Abstracts, 587–588, Fritz to Basel, dd. Christiansborg, 28 July 1875.

101. Robertson located seventy-nine court cases from Accra involving slavery charges between 1881 and 1918, most of which were for slave dealing: Robertson, "Post-proc-lamation slavery," 222–224.

102. See PP May 1891 LVII [C.6354] *Correspondence respecting the adminis-tration of the laws against slavery in the Gold Coast Colony*; and for some discus-sion, Kwabena Opare-Akurang, "The administration of the abolition laws, African responses, and post-proclamation slavery in the Gold Coast, 1874–1940," *Slavery and Abolition*, special issue on "Slavery and colonial rule in Africa," 19 (1998), an analysis that identifies the weakness of the colonial state as a reason for the limited impact of the abolition laws.

103. Dumett and Johnson, "Britain and the suppression of slavery," 106; Jenkins's Abstracts, 129–130, Mohr's report for the first quarter of 1880; for an overview, see Toyin Falola and Paul Lovejoy (eds.), *Pawnship in Africa: Debt bondage in historical perspective* (Boulder, 1994).

104. BMA D-1, 60/76 "Slavery and Pledge" by P. Anteson, n.d. [1893]; *Gold Coast Independent*, 30 Sept. 1898.

105. See the detailed treatments in BMA D-1, 60/76 "Slavery and pledge," by P. Anteson [1893], and D-1, 60/85 "Interest of money," by William Buckmann, 19 Nov. 1894.

106. NAG SCT 2/4/57 Div. Court Vol. 45, *Georgina Lutterodt v. Annanfio*, 1914.

107. PP Feb. 1875 LII [C.1140], No. 50: Rowe to Carnarvon, 1 July 1874, No. 54: Lees to Carnarvon, 9 June 1874 and No. 81: Glover to Carnarvon, 3 Aug. 1874.

108. PRO CO 96/115, Strahan to Carnarvon, Conf. Despatch, 5 Mar. 1875.

109. *African Times*, 1 June 1875.

110. Ibid., 1 Oct. 1875.

111. On the land acquisition, see PRO CO 96/181, White to Holland, Conf., 18 June 1887, enclosed: interview with King Tackie, Chief Akramah, and W. Quartey-Papafio, 11 May 1887.

112. See Parker, "Ga state and society," 194–199.

113. Reindorf, *History*, 117.

114. For an example of this process, see NAG SCT 3/4/12 Div. Court Vol. 4B, *Edmund Bannerman v. Christian F. Swannikier*, 20 Jan. 1878. For a detailed and histori-cally sensitive overview of Ga land tenure, see Pogucki, *Gold Coast land tenure*; some discussion is also found in S. S. Quarcoopome, "Urbanisation, land alienation and poli-tics in Accra," IAS *Research Review*, New Series, 8 (1992); Firmin-Sellars, *The trans-formation of property rights*, 36–58.

115. BMA D-31, 3/1 Indentures Book, and 3/2A Indentures 1845–1885.

116. Philip D. Curtin, "Medical knowledge and urban planning in tropical Africa," *American Historical Review*, 90 (1985); David Arnold (ed.), *Imperial medicine and in-digenous societies* (Manchester, 1988); K. David Patterson, "Health in urban Ghana: The case of Accra 1900–1940," *Social Science and Medicine*, 13B (1979); idem, *Health in colonial Ghana: Disease, medicine, and socio-economic change 1900–1955* (Waltham, MA, 1981).

117. PRO CO 96/115, Strahan to Carnarvon, Conf., 5 Mar. 1875.

118. NAG ADM 1/9/2, Freeling to King Tackie, 22 Nov. 1877; PRO CO 96/122, Freeling to Carnarvon, No. 259, 26 Nov. 1877.

119. Corn, not yam, was the main Ga staple and symbolic focus of that part of Homowo celebrating the new crop. Gods purchased or incorporated from the Akan, however, continued to be ritually "fed" yam, in contrast to the corn- or millet-eating autochthonous deities.

120. NAG ADM 11/1/1770, interview dd. 15 Aug. 1877.

121. PRO CO 97/2, Towns, Police, and Public Health Ordinance, No. 10 of 1878, 5 July 1878. For the implementation of the ordinance, see the account by A.B. Ellis, then DC at Accra, in *The land of fetish* (London, 1883), 254–255; for similar legislation against ritual and recreational drumming in early colonial Brazzaville, cf. Phyllis M. Martin, *Leisure and society in colonial Brazzaville* (Cambridge, 1995), 37.

122. PRO CO 96/155, Rowe to Derby, Despatch No. 86, 2 Feb.1884.

123. *African Times*, 1 Aug. 1877, "Heathenism at Accra," and letter to editor, dd. Accra, 30 May 1877, "Abominable fetish custom at Accra"; and 1 Nov. 1877, "A na-tive" to editor, dd. Accra, 17 Sept. 1877.

124. See Parker, "The cultural politics of death and burial."

125. NAG ADM 11/1/1437, "Suppression of objectionable customs," by S.D. Codjoe, n.d. [c.1930]; *Gold Coast Chronicle*, 4 Nov. 1899.

126. *African Times*, 1 Aug. 1877.

127. See Chapter 5.

128. Kimble, *Political history*, 304–306, 460–461. The title District Commissioner had replaced that of Civil Commandant in 1875.

129. Cf. Firmin-Sellars, *Transformation of property rights*, 37–38: "The passage of the Native Jurisdiction Ordinance in 1878 transformed the loose federation of Ga republics into a rigid hierarchy." This recent analysis of the emergence of conflict over land rights in Accra in the context of the creation of indirect rule is flawed by a rigidly instrumentalist reading of Ga politics and a simple misreading of the evidence: the passage of the first NJO was delayed until 1883, and was not actually applied to Accra until its amendment in 1910.

130. *African Times*, 1 June 1877.

131. R. Addo-Fening, "The background to the deportation of King Asafo Agyei and the foundation of New Dwaben," *THSG*, 14 (1973); Wilks, *Asante*, 509–516; on the links between the Dwaben exiles and Accra, see McCaskie, "Asante and Ga," 142.

132. Metcalfe, *Great Britain and Ghana*, 404.

133. PRO CO 96/121, Freeling to Carnarvon, No. 181, 18 July 1877.

134. The Kpakpatsewe was linked to Asafo Agyei through the marriage of Kwale, the sister of William Quartey-Papafio, to the *Dwabenhene*: NAG ADM 11/1/1089, statement by R. W. Quartey, 6 Dec. 1929; BMA D-1, 46/97, Reindorf to Committee, dd. Christiansborg, 12 Apr. 1888.

135. Kimble, *Political history*, 460–461.

136. PRO CO 96/130, Ussher to Hicks-Beach, No. 24, 26 Jan. 1880.

137. Ibid., enclosed: Ussher to King Taki, 23 Jan. 1880.

138. Ibid., enclosed: "Taki's prison and the Jurisdiction of Chiefs," memorandum by J. Marshall, 24 Jan. 1880.

139. The distinction between *kweshi* ("under the eaves") and *blohum* ("in the street") tribunals was firmly established in the Ga towns by the 1930s: Field, *Social organization*, 93.

140. PRO CO 96/131, Ussher to Secretary of State, No. 149, 10 May 1880.

141. PRO CO 96/130, Ussher to Hicks-Beach, No. 24, 26 Jan. 1880; CO 96/131, Secretary of State to Ussher, 23 June 1880.

142. PRO CO 96/191, Griffith to Knutsford, No. 116, 10 Apr. 1888, enclosed: "Questions put to Mr. Cleland Chief of James Town," 30 Apr. 1886.

143. PRO CO 96/131, Ussher to Kimberley, No. 244, 25 Sept. 1880.

144. See Addo-Fening, "The background to the deportation."

145. *African Times*, 1 Apr. 1881, "G. A. Maashie" to editor, dd. Accra, 14 Feb. 1881. The pseudonym of the writer is a play on words of *Ga mashi*, the term for the Ga of Kinka and Nleshi. See also PRO CO 96/397, Nathan to Chamberlain, No. 313, 22 July 1902; and for the background to the conflict between Afrakuma and her father, R. S. Rattray, *Ashanti law and constitution* (Oxford, 1929), 174.

146. PRO CO 96/132, Griffith to Secretary of State, No. 312, 14 Dec. 1880, enclosed: Ussher to Secretary of State, 10 Nov. 1880.

147. Ibid.

148. Ibid.

149. Ibid.

150. *African Times*, 1 Apr. 1881; see also ibid., 2 May 1881, John Cup to editor, dd. Accra, 28 Feb. 1881.

151. Ibid., 1 Jan. 1881.

152. PRO CO 96/132, Griffith to Secretary of State, No. 312, 14 Dec. 1880, minute by A. Herbert, 21 Jan. 1881; see too NAG ADM 11/1/1086, Inspector General, Gold Coast Constabulary to CS, 9 Nov. 1880.

153. On Taki's supernatural powers and unrivaled knowledge of medicines and charms, see PRO CO 96/397, Nathan to Chamberlain, No. 313, 22 July 1902; *Gold Coast Leader*, 26 July 1902.

154. Wilks, *Asante*, 523–527.

155. See esp. *African Times*, 2 May 1881, Tom Gray to editor.

156. Ibid., 1 Apr. 1881, "G. A. Maashie" to editor.

157. PRO CO 96/179, Griffith to Stanhope, Conf., 20 Jan. 1887.

158. On this crucial link between Kumase and Accra via the Bannermans, see McCaskie, "Asante and Ga;" idem, "*Konnurokusem*: Kinship and family in the history of the *Oyoko Kokoo* dynasty of Kumase," *JAH*, 36 (1995), 383–384.

4

BETWEEN TWO FIRES: ECONOMIC CHANGE AND POLITICAL POWER, 1880s–1890s

"To be a king or a chief in Accra is no enviable position, as you will very frequently find yourself between two fires—the Government on one side, and the people on the other."[1]

Ohiafo ebuu man.
(A poor man does not watch over the town.)[2]

In March 1901, the new Governor of the Gold Coast, Sir Matthew Nathan, traveled from the colonial headquarters at Accra to Kumase, his first visit to Asante since the Yaa Asantewa uprising of the previous year. Nathan's journey was designed to aid the formulation of British jurisdiction in Asante and in the recently acquired Northern Territories. Six months later, in September 1901, a series of Imperial Orders in Council linked the two regions with the established Colony, creating the foundation of twentieth-century Gold Coast/Ghana. Contemplating the role of African chiefs in the new colonial framework as he journeyed north across the coastal plain, Nathan considered the political situation among the Ga of Accra after many decades of British rule:

The first twenty miles of my march was through the Accra country under King Tackie whose power for any useful purpose has practically disappeared. He no longer has a court in which to sell justice at Accra and so has no revenue. He also has no powers of punishment and so no means of making his nominal subjects obey him. He is an old man with the recollection of great former importance and of an influence extending over all the Ga-talking people and he naturally resents the new order of things and is not inclined to assist the government that has brought it about. He declined to help with carriers for the Kumasi relief expedition; he has sent me very few men for the railway while . . . Chief Kwadjo Ababio of James Town—an educated chief of a later type—has collected nearly 300. When I asked Tackie for carriers for this journey he gave me four. . . . I believe however it was want of ability and not of will that produced so poor a result.[3]

This chapter examines the evolution of Accra in the 1880s and 1890s, focusing on the connections between the changing urban economy and town politics. Following the concerted expansion of British rule between 1874 and 1880, the last two decades of the century represent something of a lull in the development of the colonial city. As imperial energies became directed toward the scramble for interior hinterlands, Nathan's "new order of things" emerged only gradually in Accra. Judging by the Governor's appraisal of the waning authority of Taki Tawia, the established Ga political order was the clear loser in this process. Their judicial powers and ability to wage war expropriated by the British, their control over people eroded by the abolition of slavery, and their roles as political and economic brokers undermined by the growing literate elite, the *mantsemei* struggled to defend their position in the changing colonial order. That they were to some degree successful in this struggle is an indication of the continuing resilience of Ga state and society in the colonial capital. Despite Nathan's dismal prognosis, indigenous urban institutions proved remarkably adaptable in the changing conditions of the new imperial age.

We begin by outlining the main shifts in the urban economy in the 1880s and 1890s, a time of downturn in trade and the erosion of the Ga's middleman role by the expansion of expatriate commerce. The focus is then narrowed to the careers of two of Accra's most powerful merchant "Chiefs," Ajaben Ankra and John Quartey. Both skillfully negotiated the shifting economic waters of the late nineteenth century, although their success in the wider community created new tensions within their respective domestic domains. We then turn to a series of political conflicts in which a variety of interest groups advanced conflicting claims to be part of the remaking of the colonial town. The *Agbuntsota*, the "smoked herring war," of 1884 was a factional conflict fought out in the established idioms of Ga political action. Subsequent struggles witnessed the emergence of new political idioms, as rising elite aspirations intersected with popular protest against the demands of the colonial state. Underlying the political narrative is a concern to stress the importance of interlinking patterns of economy and culture in Accra's urban history.[4]

THE CHANGING URBAN ECONOMY

Early colonial Accra was shaped by a complex variety of economic forces, from changes in the global capitalist economy at one extreme to the restructuring of social relationships within individual Ga households on the other. The first half of our period, roughly the last quarter of the nineteenth century, was a time of depression in international trade on the West African coast. This period has been identified by historians as one that witnessed the eclipse of the indigenous merchant elite on the Gold Coast by expatriate enterprise.[5] A pattern of rise and decline in the fortunes of African traders in Accra is certainly discernible, although the dynamics and periodization of this process remain far from clear. The midcentury widening of the "entrepreneurial niche" was closely linked to the trade in palm oil and, from the late 1860s, palm kernels. The concerted efforts on the part of Accra's merchants in the 1860s and 1870s to maintain access to supplies of oil and kernels from the interior reflects the importance of these commodities, which in the period 1881–1885 continued to account for 73 percent of total Gold Coast exports.[6] Although supply-side problems were alleviated by the termination of military conflict after 1874, coastal middlemen remained at the mercy of the fluctuating world market price for vegetable oils. In 1885, prices fell sharply and thereafter remained low, causing a deterioration in terms of trade and mounting debts for many merchants.[7]

The problems facing Accra middlemen were exacerbated by changes in the "trust" system, the great network of credit on which international trade was based. As cutthroat competition and narrowing profit margins resulted in rising levels of bad debt, commission houses became reluctant to extend credit to independent African traders. British and German firms began instead to appoint salaried agents, and, from the 1890s, to open their own branches in Accra and other towns. The 1890s, the apex of the New Imperialism, appears to have been the key decade in the relative decline of the African mercantile enterprises that had risen to prominence in midcentury. The cartelization of European shipping to West Africa in 1895 was a major development in the trend toward price fixing that worked to the benefit of better capitalized expatriate firms to the exclusion of their smaller, often family-based, African rivals. The impact of these changes on urban society was described by the European president of the newly created Accra Town Council in 1900:

The condition of Accra has altered very greatly of late. Ten years ago there were at least half a dozen wealthy families in Accra trading some on their own account but chiefly as Agents for Big Firms at home doing a very large business and as in the case of the late Chief John Quartey maintaining a retinue of some three or four hundred people. Bad times came, value of produce decreased . . . but competition increased on the Coast; less and less moneys worth was sent home until the profits became so small that the Firms took . . . the Coast business into their own hands through European agents and the rich middlemen . . . found their occupation gone. [T]he destruction of the credit system threw hundreds of poor people for want of a patron on their own resources and the rich Merchants became poor and in many cases hardly able to live. The poor people then eked out a precarious livelihood by farming, fishing and petty trading.[8]

This report paints a graphic picture of downturn in Accra's middleman economy. However, it seems mistaken in suggesting that the dislocation and in some cases dissolution of patron-client networks was caused solely by the onslaught of European mercantile competition. Many of the "people" of powerful merchants such as John Quartey—both before and after 1875— were slaves and pawns. Abolition triggered an unraveling of rights and obligations that enabled many slaves and pawns to move out of the orbit of their master, toward independent farming, petty trading, or urban employment. Such retinues typically comprised also wives and concubines, other junior family members, and independent small traders. The distinction between these groups was often blurred, with many petty traders becoming tied to a *sikatse*, "rich man," by the extension of credit or other debt. Commercial transactions involving the extension of credit also intersected with the institution of marriage. Wives were often sought specifically by Ga merchants to act as storekeepers or market traders, and spouses running separate business enterprises entered into a variety of contractual arrangements, loaning each other money secured by pawns and mortgages. By the late 1880s, growing numbers of commercial/marital disputes were appearing before the colonial courts.[9] A wide variety of social relations, therefore, underpinned commerce in Accra.[10] These relations were also undergoing change and renegotiation in the late nineteenth century, change that both coincided and interacted with the increasingly competitive commercial climate.[11]

The credit system underpinning Accra's economy was evolving, but it was far from destroyed. By the 1870s, urban real estate had joined human pawns as collateral and a mechanism to extract interest on loans.[12] Interest rates varied, with European firms charging between 5 and 10 percent on cash advances, but anything from zero up to 100 percent being charged by African creditors. The often-quoted norm of 50 percent does suggest some de-

Figure 4.1 Building Accra's new Salaga Market, early 1880s. (Courtesy of the Foreign and Commonwealth Office Library, London.)

gree of integration in the local credit market.[13] Elite voices occasionally inveighed against the socially corrosive impact of high interest rates, focusing their ire on the indebtedness and pawning resulting from expenditure on funerals and other "customs."[14]

The Town Council's impression of an absolute contraction in economic activity in Accra may also be misleading, as a number of countervailing factors served to offset the generally depressed decades of the 1880s and 1890s. First, the Asante defeat and the consolidation of colonial rule in 1874 accelerated the realignment of interior trade away from the northern savannas and toward the coast.[15] In the aftermath of the war the British were keen to attract the trade of the northern entrepôt of Salaga away from Kumase and directly toward Accra. Despite some Asante success in enforcing an embargo on the movement of kola, by 1882 a sizable traffic was passing between the two towns.[16] The importance of the northern trade is reflected in the emergence of a new name for Accra's expanding marketplace: Salaga Market. Growing numbers of Muslim merchants settled in Accra, building their own quarter, or "*zongo*," just beyond the northern boundary of Kinka. By the late 1880s, Hausa settlers controlled a thriving kola trade based on seaborne exports to Lagos.[17] Urban population growth created a buoyant market for foodstuffs from the agricultural hinterland, where not all farmers by any means "eked out a precarious livelihood." It was noted in 1889 that "all the land around . . . Accra is being fast put under cultivation to meet the demands of the growing community."[18]

Second, a new export commodity emerged in the form of wild rubber, which served as a crucial bridge between the declining palm produce trade and the rise of the twentieth-century cocoa economy. The rubber trade was pioneered by Cape Coast merchants, but its focus moved gradually to Accra, which in the 1890s became the principal port of export for supplies from Krepi, Kwawu, and as far away as the Brong states.[19] The brief but spectacular rubber boom offered new opportunities for a younger generation of Ga entrepreneurs, notably George Owoo and William A. Q. Solomon. Two of the most successful businessmen in early twentieth-century Accra, both made their fortunes as middlemen in the rubber trade of the 1890s. Owoo (1861–1934) built up a large trade by mortgaging family property in Kinka to secure advances of up to £2,000 from the Basel Mission Trading Company, investing profits in urban real estate.[20] Solomon (1868–1936), whose maternal family milieu is examined in greater detail below, entered the rubber trade with his sister in 1883 at the age of 15.[21] Rubber also generated income for numerous small-scale Ga middlemen and women, and for wage laborers. It was reported in 1890 that a German firm at Accra, probably a reference to J. J. Fischer, was purchasing £400 worth of rubber daily and employing 120 women in its preparation for export.[22]

A third factor was the expansion of the infrastructure of colonial rule, which generated a rising demand for literate clerks and other local auxiliaries. Following the burst of activity of the mid-1870s, the colonial state grew slowly in the 1880s. The downturn in trade coupled with an unwillingness to again risk direct taxation resulted in declining government revenues throughout the decade, slowing the construction of a colonial bureaucracy.[23] A growing deficit was tackled in 1890 by the imposition of a 10 percent *ad valorem* duty on most imports. This funded the creation of new branches of government to add to the Medical and Sanitary Departments created in 1885 and 1888, respectively: Roads (1890), Education (1890), Telegraph (1891), and Prisons (1891). The new duty was greeted with hostility in the coastal towns, Africans and Europeans combining to protest to London that the administration continued to spend little or nothing on public works in Accra or elsewhere. Governor Griffith refuted the allegations, identifying many of the signatories of the petition as nothing but "clerks, petty native traders, mostly hucksters, . . . auctioneers, carpenters, drunkards, labourers, schoolmasters, bankrupts, convicts, goldsmiths, photographers, servants, shoemakers, tailors"—an interesting snapshot of Accra's diverse urban crowd.[24] By 1891, the colonial bureaucracy at Accra totalled 826, already half the number of the 1,615 men recorded by the census as being fishermen.[25] Although not all

African civil servants were local Ga, the widening of salaried employment and its linkages to other sectors of the urban economy contrasted sharply with the old headquarters of Cape Coast, where government employees numbered a mere 68.

Fourth, the West African coastal trading diaspora continued to offer lucrative employment opportunities for many Ga tradesmen, as well as growing numbers of literate clerks. Artisanal wages were rising, prompting the cooper's guild in 1889 to increase the severance fee paid to masters by trained apprentices from 32 dollars to 32 pounds. The "freeing" of an apprentice was the occasion for a solemn ceremony, the master craftsman parading through the streets of Accra sporting the silk cloth, felt hat, and umbrella presented by his acolyte.[26] It was access to unskilled rather than artisanal labor, however, that became a contentious issue in the colonial capital in this period. The commoditization of labor in the decades following the abolition of slavery was a slow and uneven process. As ties between master and slave unraveled, it became more difficult to obtain wage labor, particularly for the low-status and arduous task of head-loading goods. The unwillingness of Ga men to enter the local labor market became a standard complaint on the part of mercantile firms, many of which instead recruited Kru migrants from Liberia. Firms were forced to pay local canoemen in advance, yet continued to face difficulties in securing regular labor for this vital task in the import/export economy. In 1888, the German firm J. J. Fischer sued a crew of canoemen who had failed to report for work after being paid up front to load ten tons of rubber. "The last time a steamer came in," the headman of the crew explained, "all the youngsters had gone fishing."[27] Six years later, the Wesleyan missionary Dennis Kemp was forced to send to the Kru coast to obtain a mere twelve carriers. "The native labourers are too proud," he railed. "A mighty famine might perhaps make them work—but nothing else."[28]

It took less than a famine to induce the Ga to work for wages. Laborers began to join their skilled kinsmen in traveling to the Bights in the aftermath of the abolition of slavery, a movement that accelerated with the carving out of colonial empires in Equatorial Africa in the 1890s.[29] "The Congo and French settlements . . . possess an extraordinary . . . fascination . . . these days for native labourers," reported the *Chronicle* in 1894. "Every steamer . . . has on board . . . scores of men who have resolved to better their 'lot' by going abroad."[30] Fierce competition arose between local recruiting agents such as cocoa pioneer Tete Quashie, who in 1892 was involved in a dispute over the supply of men to Matadi.[31] Local labor shortages resulted less from excessive pride on the part of Ga men than from their decision to opt for the higher wages, advances, and long-term contracts offered by firms such as the Congo Railway

Company, the largest recruiter of migrant workers in Accra in the 1890s.[32] When reports of atrocities led the British to ban recruitment by the government of the Congo Independent State in 1896, a group of Ga women protested that migrants' wages had "done much to counteract the . . . depression which has gone on for years."[33] In Accra, as elsewhere in West Africa, the limitations of the local labor market would force the British to resort to direct compulsion and to the authority of chiefs to mobilize manpower.[34]

THE GA MERCHANT AS TOWN "CHIEF"

The nature of Ga state and society in early colonial Accra can begin to be located in the changing economic context outlined above by looking in more detail at the lives of individual "big men." Who were the half dozen powerful Accra families referred to in the Town Council report that in the 1880s stood at the center of extensive but fragile networks of clients and dependents? Periodization of the rise and decline of individual mercantile fortunes is important, particularly in the light of Dumett's observation that family-based enterprises on the nineteenth-century Gold Coast often did not survive the death of a dynamic founder.[35] Leading members of the generation of merchants that emerged in the middle decades of the century and played such a prominent role in the conflicts of the period were passing away by the 1870s: Lebrecht Hesse in 1874, William Addo in 1876, and W. A. Lutterodt in 1880. George Cleland continued to exert a powerful influence in Ga affairs until his death in 1887.[36] So too did Thomas F. Bruce (d. 1897), who emerged as the most prominent member of the extensive Bruce family of the Sempe *akutso* when he inherited Addo's diverse business operations. Yet the indigenous hierarchy of trade in Accra in the 1880s and 1890s was dominated less by members of the literate Euro-African elite than by more "traditionalist" Ga merchants, men such as Ajaben Ankra, John Quartey, and Daniel Annan. Members of influential lineages at the center of Ga political power, these men, while not succeeding to the public office of *mantse*, became known popularly as "Chiefs." The English word Chief appears to be a late-nineteenth-century version of *niiatse*, *sikatse*, or *oblempon*.[37] Like these Ga terms for "rich man," the honorific "Chief" was part of a highly nuanced vocabulary of civic virtue. It was bestowed by the community on members whose outstanding success at material accumulation lent them considerable moral authority, authority that could readily be converted into political power. We will here consider the careers of Ajaben Ankra and John Quartey, widely regarded in 1890s Accra as two of the outstanding figures of their generation.[38]

Chief John Quartey

Chief John Quartey (d. 1896) was a member of Kpakpatsewe, the Asere lineage that controlled the office of *akwashontse*. His father was Kwatei Kojo, a commander of the Ga warriors at Katamanso and a notable slave owner who had strengthened the position of Kpakpatsewe at the center of political power in Kinka. By the late nineteenth century, Kwatei Kojo was regarded as the greatest of all *akwashontsemei*.[39] He had married three wives, whose descendents formed distinct branches of the *we* between which the office of *akwashontse* circulated after his death in about 1833. John Quartey's mother was Naa Amponsa, a daughter of Otublohum *mantse* Amponsa. His half-brother was Kpakpafio, or William Quartey-Papafio, who succeeded to the office of *akwashontse* in the early 1880s after the death of the eldest son and John Quartey's full brother, Kpakpa Kakadan.[40] William Quartey, the son of Naa Odarkor of Lamte Janwe, was a third paternal half-brother, also a successful trader who succeeded William Quartey-Papafio to office on the latter's death in 1889. Unlike his brothers, William Quartey (d. 1895) received a mission education, and became known as Owula Kpakpa Brofonyo, a name rendered by his son in 1929 as "the educated, good master."[41]

Although Chief John Quartey belonged to one of the oldest and most influential *wei* in Kinka, according to his obituary in 1896 he was "purely a self made man."[42] As one of the younger sons of Kwatei Kojo he neither succeeded to public office, nor, apparently, inherited family wealth in the form of slaves or other property. Quartey's matrilineal connection to the Otublohum *akutso* often appeared more salient than his patrilineal membership of Kpakpatsewe of Asere. Many considered him to be an Otublohum man, and even by the 1880s to have jurisdiction over that *akutso*. This identity was reinforced by the location of his residence and trading store on Otu Street, then the heart of Kinka's retail trade.[43] His mother Naa Amponsa was a strong early influence, actively preventing him from continuing a youthful career as a fisherman by placing him as a junior trading agent with a Spanish merchant resident in Kinka.[44] In a career path common to many Ga merchants, the business acumen he developed working as an agent was subsequently applied to independent enterprise.

Both William Quartey and William Quartey-Papafio enter the historical record rather earlier than their younger brother. By the late 1850s the former was a prominent palm oil exporter based at Prampram, while the latter's reputation was firmly established by his role as a military leader during the Glover War.[45] The three half-brothers ran quite separate trading enterprises, their interests occasionally coming into conflict. In 1869, for example, John sought recourse to the British court to recover a debt of 205 heads of cowries from William Quartey.[46] In a more acrimonious dispute two years later, William Quartey-Papafio, a close ally and advisor of Taki Tawia, had his brother William incarcerated in the *Ga mantse's kpabu* for debt, the latter bringing countercharges in the colonial court.[47] That the mechanisms for dispute settlement within the Kpakpatsewe proved insufficient to deal with the conflicts of its most powerful members is as much a reflection of the loosely articulated nature of the Ga lineage as of the fiercely competitive commercial climate. Austin's claim that in much of West Africa it was "not considered possible for a debt to exist between members of the same lineage" is clearly not applicable to Accra, and may indeed require qualification with regard to other coastal societies.[48]

The documentary record yields little information on the business activities of John Quartey until the last decade of his life, by which time he was perhaps the leading moneylender in Accra. Land title registers from the 1890s record loans of between £100 and £1,500, most of which were for four years, at 10 percent interest per annum and secured by mortgages of houses and land.[49] Through foreclosures and purchases he came to acquire some of the best-known properties in Accra, including Addo's old hotel in James Town and W. A. Lutterodt's residence in Osu. No records exist of the transactions shaped by established idioms of patron-clientage by which Quartey's nexus of followers must have been further enlarged. In light of the well-documented continuation of the institution of pawnship, however, it is likely that large numbers of petty traders would have secured credit from powerful patrons by using pawns as collateral. Quartey's economic and social clout in Accra appears to contradict the Town Council's suggestion that his credit-based personal entourage collapsed in the 1890s due to expatriate competition. It is more likely to have fragmented after his death in 1896, when his estate was inherited by his sister Oyo and his nephew Frederick A. Ankra, son of Antonio Ankra of the Dadebanwe of Otublohum.

Chief Ajaben Ankra

Ajaben Ankra (d. 1887) was a scion of the powerful Dadebanwe, one branch of the descendants of the eighteenth-century Akwamu governor Otu. Like John Quartey, he was a nonliterate merchant who despite his family connections enjoyed the reputation of being a self-made man. The clout of Dadebanwe had been firmly established by his uncle, Kwaku Ankra (d. 1840), the Dutch *makelaar* and Accra's leading slave broker in the final years of the overseas slave trade.[50] Ajaben's father was Ankra's elder brother Ayi, and his cousin Antonio Ankra (d. 1897)—also a successful merchant and prominent "Chief"—was the son of Ankra. His mother was Aku, a woman from Sempe *akutso* and one of Ayi's five or more wives.[51] Ajaben's marginal position in the family as a young man may be connected to the fact that Aku "was born in Old Ankra's home," an indication that she was of servile status.[52] Both "Old Ankra" and his brother Ayi founded *oblempon* stools, paying for the right to be borne through the streets of Accra in a palanquin by their retainers during *Homowo* and to display umbrellas and other chiefly regalia.[53] This right of public display was the most visible signifier of *oblempon* status. It set "rich men" apart from *mantsemei*, whose strictly pedestrian movement about Accra signified their sacred role as custodians of Ga land.[54] Antonio Ankra was in no doubt about Ajaben's status as a self-made *sikatse*: "Ajaben was carried about . . . not because he had the right but because he had the power—he did not take the old stools but his own. . . . The gold he wore was his own."[55]

The importance attached to the notion of the self-made man in this period reflected more than a vague cultural approval of entrepreneurial skill. As opportunities for accumulation through independent trade and skilled labor migration grew from the 1850s onward, the distinction between "family-owned" and "self-acquired" property became increasingly contentious. Following the abolition of slavery, much of this property took the form of houses. As few people in this period left wills, inheritance became a highly contested issue, confused by the cognatic strain in Ga kinship. Intrafamily conflict over inheritance also evolved in the context of the ongoing reformulation of social relations, as junior men, women, ex-slaves, and other subordinates used the colonial courts to challenge patriarchal authority. One such dispute within the Dadebanwe resulted in the suit *Vanderpuye v. Dadaye* in 1890, which provides a glimpse into the architecture of domestic power that lay behind the public displays of authority by wealthy "Chiefs."

Like many family disputes that entered the public arena in early colonial Accra, the material focus of *Vanderpuye v. Dadaye* was a house, the *adeboo shia* ("ancestor house") built by Ayi opposite the western end of the Dutch fort. The contest turned on who in the Dadebanwe had the authority to dispose of family-owned property. What emerges from the testimony is that Ajaben, as one of the younger sons of Ayi, struck out on his own in business, building a small swish-and-thatch dwelling as a residence and trading store. Ajaben returned to live in the *adeboo shia* after the death of first his father and then Old Ankra, whose joint property, including the village of Ahodome and its slave inhabitants, passed to the third brother, Okanta. The young Ajaben was not close to his uncle Okanta, whom he approached cautiously through cousin Antonio for permission to move into the house. This was granted, although, significantly, Ajaben lived in the more rudimentary ground floor quarters of the storey house cheek by jowl with his slaves. It was only after Okanta's death shortly before the Awuna War of 1866, Antonio recalled, that Ajaben "moved upstairs and gave the downstairs rooms to his people."[56] Yet they remained very much "his" people. Pedro, Ayi's eldest son and the new *wetse*, led the Dadebanwe slaves and retainers to the Awuna campaign, but Ajaben, in true *oblempon* fashion, commanded a separate militia of his own followers.

Despite the insecurity of the 1860s, Ajaben's business was flourishing. His almost complete absence from land and legal records indicates that his methods were largely "traditional," underpinned by established sociopolitical rights and obligations. "Being an illiterate man," he told a British commission in 1873, "I keep no books."[57] By that time he was one of the few traders to secure quarterly credit facilities with H.M. Customs at Accra, a reflection of his huge turnover in spirits as much as his credit-worthiness.[58] Ajaben's growing stature was further enhanced by the Glover War, when the size of his personal militia earned him recognition as one of Accra's leading warriors. This status facilitated his acquisition of urban and periurban properties in the late 1870s, when records show that *Ga mantse* Taki Tawia began to convey land outright to influential allies and to followers.[59] Ajaben's reputation with the British was secured by advancing Glover the sum of £1,500, "without security," an act of generosity repeated in 1881 when he supplied Captain Lonsdale with fifty ounces of gold dust for his journey to Salaga and Kumase.[60] In 1883, having requested "not a present of money but some personal ornament . . . he can wear on state occasions," Ajaben was presented with a silver collar from Queen Victoria in recognition of his services to the colonial administration.[61] In Accra's eclectic culture of public display with its uninhibited use of exotic motifs, there can have been few more potent symbols of *oblempon* status.

Personal accumulation not only reshaped the position of successful merchants in the community, but also altered social relations within the domestic realm. On the death of Pedro, the senior member of Dadebanwe was Ammanua, a daughter of Ayi. According to Antonio, Ammanua "had no power, being a woman, so I acted for her with her consent."[62] Ammanua herself viewed the situation somewhat differently: "I have never given up my right or appointed anyone to act for me. . . . Having no means I have not exercised my right as head of the family. Ajaben being a man of substance acted as head."[63] As in the case of John Quartey and his brothers, a degree of tension emerged between Ajaben, the marginal family member made good, and Antonio, his senior but distinctly less wealthy cousin. At some stage, perhaps in the late 1860s, Ajaben built his own storey house adjacent to the *adeboo shia*, his personal entourage growing to such an extent that he later "connected the two houses and his people lived partly in one . . . and partly in the other."[64] This is a striking image: the slaves of the self-made man gradually taking over the domestic space of the ancestral house. Other slaves were settled in a farming village on land acquired from Taki Tawia to the north of Accra and which he named "Philadelphia."[65]

Ajaben Ankra died in 1887, leaving his property to W.A.Q. Solomon, the dynamic nineteen-year-old rubber-trading son of his sister Dede. The contested balance of domestic authority within Dadebanwe reemerged a few years later, when a demand for 400 carriers passed from the colonial regime via Taki Tawia to the *mantsemei* and "Chiefs" of Accra, including Antonio Ankra. When Antonio summoned family retainers residing in the Otublohum house and in various farming *aklowai*, "they simply refused," arguing that they had "belonged" not to him but to Ajaben.[66] Antonio's difficulty in establishing his position as head of the Dadebanwe contains a striking echo of the slave revolt faced by his uncle Okanta in 1842.[67] Clearly, domestic power structures had long been fashioned by a fine line between rights and obligations. As the institution of slavery evolved into new forms of patron-clientage in the late nineteenth century, established rights and obligations were undergoing extensive renegotiation. The death of a "big man" like John Quartey or Ajaben Ankra, who had built up retinues of hundreds of followers and whose careers straddled the consolidation of colonial power, appears to have been a key moment in this process.

The case studies of John Quartey and Ajaben Ankra demonstrate the ways in which the accumulation of power and influence in the town by individual entrepreneurs could reshape relations within families. They also suggest that change within households was a key part of the reshaping of the colonial city. Ga *wei* were complex organisms, and the view from inside was often very different from that from outside. Although members of prominent slave-owning lineages, both Quartey and Ankra were self-made men who in their younger years had occupied relatively low positions in their respective domestic hierarchies. In the wider urban community, however, they were able to trade on the "social assets" derived in part from their kin connections.[68] "A Ga *we* is like the fat of a crocodile," an old maxim warned; "rub it on, and your skin will crack."[69] But as Asere *mantse* Akrama put it in 1890 when questioned about the inner workings of the Dadebanwe, "Nobody . . . knows what goes on in another family."[70]

AGBUNTSOTA: THE SMOKED HERRING WAR

In 1880, a dispute between the Alata quarter of James Town and the Asere quarter of Kinka over the control of land and people on the western fringe of the Accra plains came before the Supreme Court. The decision went to Alata *mantse* Kofi Oku (a.k.a. Edward Solomon), who succeeded in demon-

strating that the villages in question had been established some decades before by slaves attached to his *akutso*.[71] The case *Solomon v. Noy* is important in the history of early colonial Accra. It was the first in a long sequence
of Supreme Court confrontations between the Ga leaders of James Town
(Nleshi) and Ussher Town (Kinka), endlessly cited as a benchmark decision
in legal debates over the balance of power between—and within—the two
adjoining *majii*. The ongoing dispute was the most salient feature of politics
in Accra from the 1880s to the 1920s, involving a shifting kaleidoscope of
alliances between individuals, families, lineages, and town quarters. Although the dispute was shaped by the political economy of British rule and
often intersected with Ga struggles with the colonial state, it was essentially
mo din sane, an "African palaver." What was seen to be at stake was control
over the remaking of the Ga state in Accra.

The tensions between Kinka and Nleshi that emerged in the colonial
courtroom in 1880 resurfaced four years later in the form of a violent
confrontation known as the *Agbuntsota*. A clash between the *asafo* companies of Abola on the one hand and those of the three quarters of James
Town on the other, the *Agbuntsota* was comparable to the conflagrations
that periodically engulfed the coastal towns to the west of Accra in the
early colonial period. Whereas the Fante *asafo* organization was characterized by endemic conflict, however, the 1884 incident is notable as
being the only major battle between the Ga military companies.[72] This
may explain why the *Agbuntsota* was remembered in Accra as a full-scale
"war," cited with Katamanso, the bombardment of Osu, and the Awuna
campaigns as a key reference point in the calculation of time. It became
a defining moment in popular perceptions of the ongoing *manso* ("town
strife," "civil war") between Kinka and Nleshi, which came to define Ga
politics in the early colonial period.

What is immediately striking about the *Agbuntsota* is its name: the "the
smoked herring war."[73] Its etymological genesis lies in a cardinal event
in Accra politics: the return of *Ga mantse* Taki Tawia from imprisonment
in Elmina in 1883. Throughout his exile, Taki Tawia and Ga leaders in
Accra continued to protest the extrajudicial nature of his detention.[74]
However, Gbese *mantse* Ama (c. 1880–c. 1891), who, in line with established practice, headed the chiefly establishment in the absence of the
Ga mantse, appears to have tried to take advantage of Taki's removal by
the British. A letter to the *Gold Coast Times* reported that serious charges
had been brought against two chiefs who had usurped the *Ga mantse*'s
prerogatives by acting as intermediaries in the sale of Accra land.[75] This
incident was recalled in 1925 by the Gbese *akwashon onukpa* as an historical example of the rights of the *asafo* as the mouthpiece of "commoner" interests:

About forty years ago . . . we learnt . . . the *mantse* had sold a certain
land. The Gbese *Asafoiatsemei* [sic] and *Asafoi* met . . . dressed only in
loin-cloth with cutlasses and called upon the *mantse* to explain why he
sold the land and did not give them the money. They sent messengers . . .
and he refused to come. So the people said they would destool him. Not
long after they saw the *mantse* in front of two messengers carrying two
demi-johns of rum. [The people] drank the rum and were satisfied because
the *mantse* had . . . come to them.[76]

Contrasting these Ga legal proceedings with those of the British, the *Times*
correspondent emphasized that "these charges are made openly *before the
public*, and not in any underhand manner." "If we are thus to be imprisoned," he demanded, "for what are we paying Judges, Queen's Advocates,
District Commissioners, and the whole staff of the judicial machinery?"[77]
Such reminders of Taki's summary exile made the subject one of particular
sensitivity with the British. Moreover, unlike Ussher, Governor Rowe
(1881–1884) favoured drawing African chiefs into the framework of colonial rule, and during a visit to Elmina on March 9, 1883 he ordered Taki's
release.[78] The next day Taki was "reinstated" as *Ga mantse* at a huge assembly outside James Fort. "At night there were great rejoicings among the
people," reported the *Times*, "and singing and dancing kept up until a late
hour."[79]

Despite the rejoicing throughout Accra on Taki's return, the
Agbuntsota was sparked by an open display of hostility toward the *Ga
mantse* from the fighting men of James Town. We are fortunate to have a
record of the conflict in the form of a diary kept by Kwaku Niri, a trader
resident in Abola.[80] Although hardly an impartial account—the writer was
charged with the death of the one person to be killed in the bloody street
fighting—the diary provides a unique perspective on the early colonial
courtroom and a glimpse of how Ga family affiliations functioned during a time of town conflict. The riot occurred toward the end of the 1884
Homowo festival on Monday, September 8, during what was probably
the annual homage of the Accra *asafo* companies to the *gbatsu* of the
war deity Sakumo in Gbese. The men of James Town marched into Kinka
beating an iron "gong-gong" of a type hitherto exclusive to the Kinka
asafo and waving long poles used to carry fish, a mocking allusion to
malicious rumors that the *Ga mantse* had been forced to support himself
during his exile in Elmina by hawking smoked herrings.[81] None of our
sources indicate why the Nleshi *asafobii* chose to ridicule Taki Tawia,
beyond the fact that provocative inversions of the social order were an
integral part of the carnivalesque interludes of *Homowo*. A pitched battle
erupted when their way into Kinka was blocked by the Abola *asafo*.

Figure 4.2 The *Homowo* festival, c. 1883. A swirling procession enters the court-yard of Christiansborg Castle during the annual *Homowo* celebrations. (Photograph by J. W. Rowland. Copyright Royal Geographical Society, London. Neg. No. T1363. Reproduced with permission.)

Despite attempts by Taki Tawia and George Cleland to placate the two sides, the fighting left 1 man dead, 30 wounded, and 47 arrested. As in the wars of the 1860s–1870s, women played an uninhibited role in inflaming the martial qualities of their kinsmen. Cleland, acting as Alata *mantse* due to the declining health of Kofi Oku, informed the government that "nothing would have happened had not the women brought stones and egged on the men." The Colonial Secretary agreed that this was "always the case."[82]

Kwaku Niri records how conflicting family interests prevented him from taking active sides in the battle. His father was a member of Nii Atowe of Alata and his mother a daughter of the late *Ga mantse* Taki Kome, and therefore a member of the Taki Komewe of Abola. Although in terms of patrilineal descent Kwaku was a member of his father's *we*, he associated himself with the Abola *akutso*, residing at the time in his

mother's *adeboo shia* on King Street. He claims that he refrained from
venturing outdoors for the duration of the fighting as he "belonged" to
both quarters. A revealing aspect of Kwaku Niri's account is his need to
justify his caution to various callers that day, his conversation with Mrs.
Adoley Vanderpuye providing an intimate glimpse of how Ga women
monitored and judged the actions of men. Adoley enquired why Kwaku
was lurking in an upstairs room while the *asafobii* bravely confronted
each other in the streets outside. "We cannot mingle ourselves into such
matter," he explained. "The Co. of Jamestown they are my Father's relatives as well as Abolar Co. So I have no right to join any of them. . . .
'All right . . . good' she said to me."[83]

The following morning, however, patrilineal kinsmen from Kwaku
Niri's father's house came to the Taki Komewe to inform him that he
was being accused in James Town of striking down the Nleshi man killed
in the fighting. The accusation reached the British authorities, and later
that day Kwaku Niri was arrested. On September 12 an inquest jury found
that there was evidence that he had indeed struck the fatal blow, and he
was committed for trial, seemingly on a charge of manslaughter.[84] The
sole surviving source for the legal aftermath of the riot is the diary of
the accused, who relates how a series of false witnesses testified against
him. Although the veracity of this account must remain open to question, there is little doubt that it was George Cleland who orchestrated the
campaign against Kwaku Niri. Given Cleland's political influence in
James Town this is hardly surprising. What is striking is that as a leading member of the Nii Atowe, he was a patrilineal kinsman of Kwaku
Niri. Kwaku Niri recorded that Cleland was quite aware that he had nothing to do with the riot, but was motivated by his—Kwaku's—affiliation
with Taki Komewe and the rival Abola *akutso*.[85] On September 24 the
jury returned a verdict of not guilty, and as Cleland drove home in his
carriage from the Supreme Court in New Site he was loudly "hooted" as
he passed through the streets of Kinka.[86]

What were the causes and meanings of the *Agbuntsota*? The solitary
outbreak of urban rioting in late nineteenth-century Accra stands in sharp
contrast to the recurring *asafo* violence in many of the Fante coastal
towns to the west. Although the dynamics of the internecine conflict in
the Fante towns remain far from clear, this contrast further suggests the
differences rather than the similarities between the Ga and Fante *asafo*
organization.[87] Although during wartime the Ga appear to have fought
not in their "age grades" but in kinship or residential groups, the regular
mobilization of the *asafoi* for a variety of social functions created affiliations that to some extent cut across those of *shia*, *we*, and *akutso*.[88]

While these structural factors may to some extent account for the relative harmony of the Ga *asafo*, they fail to explain why the *Agbuntsota* did occur. It is significant that the two famous "wars" between Kinka and Nleshi, on September 6, 1846 and September 8, 1884, both occurred at key points in the yearly cycle of *Homowo* rites, a time when the *asafobii* paraded in their kinship and *akutso*-based fighting groups. Aside from a succession of highly formalized religious observances, *Homowo* was also a time of controlled chaos, when normal codes of conduct were suspended and outrageous behavior was sanctioned. Most prominent was the sexually exuberant *oshi* dance, which brought nudity, cross-dressing, and displays of giant phalli to the streets of Accra.[89] There was a close link between the *asafo* and the *oshi* dance groups, which in the anarchic, alcohol-fueled atmosphere of *Homowo* openly ridiculed rivals in a way that would normally have been deemed unacceptable.[90] The wearing of women's clothes, jewelry, and cosmetics by the young men was considered to be among the most outrageous methods of lampooning rivals, and may be seen as a mirror image of female cross-dressing in the wartime *asayere* dances. But chaos could be difficult to control. In the confines of a densely populated, face-to-face urban environment where honor and reputation were all-important, such public ridicule and insult could provoke a violent reaction.

Why did the companies of Nleshi choose to display such open hostility toward Taki Tawia in September 1884? Far from representing an atavistic residue from the era of precolonial warfare, the *asafo* conflict was fueled by the strains of urban development in the colonial capital. Underlying the rising tension between Nleshi and Kinka was the need to establish control over the physical space of the town as urban land underwent rapid commoditization. Control over urban land and rural villages, an issue that emerged in the case *Solomon v. Noy* four years earlier, was becoming increasingly contested by a variety of Ga officeholders. Land lay at the heart of the 1882 challenge to Gbese *mantse* Ama, whose prudent act of pacification succeeded in defusing the angry *asafoi*. In the highly charged atmosphere of *Homowo*, Accra's "youngmen" could mount a further challenge on what was seen as the arbitrary land dealing of their leading officeholders. Despite these manifestations of distinct "commoner" interests, it was the cleavage between Kinka and Nleshi rather than that between "youngman" and "chief" that emerged as the more salient political fault line in early colonial Accra. Social and economic change certainly created new tensions between generations and the sexes, yet these intersected with political factionalism shaped by the structure of town quarters.

"CARING FOR THE TOWN": NATIVE POLICY, ELITE ASPIRATIONS, AND POPULAR PROTEST

Native Jurisdiction in the Colonial Capital

The arrest and exile of Taki Tawia in 1880 sent a clear signal to the people of Accra that a new political dispensation was firmly in place in the town. At a meeting of "Accra natives" at T. F. Bruce's Anglo-American Hotel in James Town in March 1886, the *Ga mantse* reflected on this shift in the balance of power that had taken place since the 1860s. Speaking from bitter personal experience, he observed that: "Twenty years ago meetings of this kind were convened regularly . . . at the house of the late Mr. Lutterodt, at which Europeans . . . and natives . . . used to pull together; . . . now it was not so. Some people hate each other and will go and tell the whiteman that this man is bad, or that man is bad, merely to get the whiteman to hurt an innocent man."[91]

Despite Taki's anxieties, it would be misleading to draw too firm a contrast between a Ga polity racked by uncertainties and divisions on the one hand, and a coherent colonial project able to exert an increasing level of control over Accra on the other. "Native policy" on the Gold Coast took legislative form for the first time with the Native Jurisdiction Ordinance (NJO) of 1883. The Ordinance sought to define the nature and limits of African jurisdiction in the regions where it was applied, making judgements in indigenous tribunals subject to appeal to the British courts.[92] Yet the administration remained uncertain over how to approach the question of governing Accra. As colonial officials stumbled toward an early form of indirect rule, their thinking was influenced by a perceived distinction between the "traditional" forest kingdoms of the interior and the hybrid urban milieux of the coastal towns. Ready access to colonial law in the latter was considered to render legally sanctioned African tribunals unnecessary, and it was twenty-seven years before the NJO was finally applied to Accra, in modified form, in 1910.

If the *Ga mantse*'s removal was a graphic demonstration of colonial power, then his return to Accra two and a half years later suggested very real limits to that power. Indeed, British indecision over the role of chiefs in Accra helped create a space for Taki to reestablish his judicial prerogatives soon after his return in 1883. When in August 1885 it was reported that he and other *mantsemei* continued to preside over tribunals, officials were unsure how to proceed. "The question of what if any jurisdiction native chiefs have is in a very undecided state," the Queen's Advocate wrote.[93] That decision came the following year, when the Full Court ruled that "native Kings" to whom the NJO was not applied continued to have the legal right to hold court and to imprison their subjects.[94] The whole question was one on which the colonial regime was deeply divided. While some officials subscribed to the maxim of "rule through the chiefs," others, most prominently the governor's son William Brandford Griffith Jr., hoped that African jurisdiction in Accra and the other coastal towns would simply wither away. In November 1887, as the government was formulating a response to the court ruling, two debtors escaped from Taki's *kpabu*, lodging complaints about their treatment with the DC. One man was from Krepi and the other Asante, alerting the British to the fact that Taki's coercive powers extended to those who were not even his own "subjects."[95] Griffith Jr., the Queen's Advocate, eagerly grasped the opportunity for restrictive legislation. The Native Prisons Ordinance of 1888 empowered the government to regulate and if need be to suppress prisons, and in September 1890, on the advice of the Chief Medical Officer, the *Ga mantse*'s *kpabu* was finally closed.[96]

British officials entertained a vague hope that African courts in Accra would continue to function as arenas of informal arbitration. With the loss of coercive powers, however, the chiefs found it difficult to enforce their judgments. The dire consequences of the resulting loss of income were explained in an unsuccessful appeal for financial aid by Gottfried Alema Dowuona, a Basel Mission catechist who in 1887 was enstooled as Osu *mantse*: "It is very hard for me, because I do no work and I sit at one place, and my business is to care for the town, and I get nothing at all to maintain myself, and . . . if you are a Chief or King and you have *nothing* the people . . . under your control do *not regard you*."[97] The loss of court revenues was such a heavy blow because the business of "caring for the town" was regarded as a full-time job, incompatible with commercial or artisanal activities. Material wealth was a key consideration in the selection of a *mantse*, yet once enstooled he was expected to desist from the occupation by which that wealth had often been generated.[98] Yet events in 1886 indicate that the British fully expected the *mantsemei* to continue to command the regard of the townspeople. At a time of economic downturn and rising popular discontent, this was an increasingly tall order to fill.

Elite Political Aspirations and Popular Protest

If the 1880s–1890s saw a shift in the Gold Coast trading economy in favor of expatriate commerce, it also marked a more general restructuring of relations between African and European. Only sixty-eight Europeans resided in the colonial capital in 1891, with officials outnumbered by merchants and missionaries, many of whom were German. Advances in tropical medicine together with a more assertive, racist imperial ideology resulted in the growth of the official European population during the following decade and a more systematic exclusion of Africans from senior administrative posts.[99] As Taki Tawia hinted in 1886, social interaction between black and white—first and foremost interracial marriage—declined dramatically. Rising racial discrimination interacted with a set of indigenous intellectual developments to dilute the unashamedly anglophile worldview of the coastal elites, the decline and then final removal of the Asante menace playing an important role in a new willingness to embrace rather than reject "traditional" Africa.

In strictly economic terms, the impact of these changes remains ambiguous. Those members of the established elite who were excluded on racial grounds from official posts began to move into new and more lucrative professions, most notably law. At the same time, the growing overall demand for literate auxiliaries in the public and private sectors offered employment and status opportunities for a new generation of young men—and some women. The result was a growing and increasingly differentiated, Western-educated, urban elite. The most visible signifier of social change was clothing, the wearing of imported or locally tailored European-style garments setting the so-called "frock" or "frock coat" class apart from the traditionalist "cloth portion" of town. Although all literates were popularly referred to as "scholars," the social identity of the younger generation began to diverge from that of the old merchant elite. New identities and aspirations emerged most clearly in "youngmen" organizations, beginning with the Accra Young Men's Free and Mutual Improvement Society in 1873 and the Accra Social Union founded in the late 1880s.[100]

Some of the political implications of Accra's shifting socioeconomic landscape began to emerge in 1886, when conflict over a plan to send a deputation to London to protest the lack of African representation in the colony's Legislative Council escalated into a major town crisis. The so-called "deputation scheme" has been treated by Kimble as a manifestation of early Gold Coast nationalism.[101] There is no doubt that for the main proponents of the plan, notably the hard-hitting Cape Coast journalist J. H. Brew and his one-time brother-in-law Edmund Bannerman, African representation was a vital issue. Five Euro-Africans, beginning with Edmund Bannerman's father James, had served as members of the Legislative Council between 1850 and 1873, after which date none had been appointed. Yet protonationalism was not the sole motor of the turbulent events of 1886. Elite aspirations interacted with those of the common townspeople, producing political action that was neither unambiguously "modern" nor "traditional."

The idea of a deputation to the Colonial Office was first raised by Brew in the *Gold Coast Times* in 1882 and resuscitated in his new newspaper, the *Western Echo*, in 1885. The cause was championed in Accra by Edmund Bannerman, who at the age of fifty-four reemerges at the center stage of town politics. Popularly styled the "Boss of Tarkwa" (or "B of T") after his imposing James Town residence Tarkwa House, Bannerman had lost none of the aptitude for political intrigue that had defined his earlier years.[102] Despite the rumors regarding his shadowy role in the arrest of the *Ga mantse*, he was keen to secure Taki's support for the deputation, organizing a series of public meetings in 1886 designed to drum up popular support.[103] Bannerman himself spoke Ga poorly and relied on his brother Robert to translate his speeches, later admitting that "when I am speaking what I believe to be the best Accra I am nearly talking Greek to the people."[104] He and other scholars appear to have had little to say on the issue of representation on the Legislative Council, appealing instead to a range of economic grievances of more immediate concern to the townspeople: the abolition of slavery, new import duties on spirits, and customs controls on migrants returning from the Bights.[105] The women of Accra, robustly led by Bannerman's octogenarian mother, Yaa Hom, "announced their resolve to deal after their own fashion with any Chief or other individual, even if that individual was a husband, who might prove himself . . . false to 'the cause.'"[106]

That slavery suddenly resurfaced as a political issue a decade after abolition may have been related to the economic downturn following the collapse in the price of palm produce in 1885. Whether it was in fact a widespread popular grievance in Accra is unclear, although the proponents of the deputation certainly considered it worth publicizing. Other leading scholars, notably George Cleland, were hostile to the idea of a deputation and considered slavery to be a nonissue. Regarded by Griffith as "an upright and honourable man," Cleland—confirmed as acting Alata *mantse* following the death of Kofi Oku in 1885—clearly possessed the ear of the administration.[107] The Governor acted to head off the protest by recommending to the Colonial Office that Cleland and C. W. Burnett, a European agent for F. & A. Swanzy, be appointed as unofficial members of the Legislative Council. Cleland, the Governor claimed, "possesses the confidence of the native population of Accra, and is thoroughly acquainted with the wishes of the people."[108] In the wake of the *Agbuntsota*, however, tension between Kinka and Nleshi continued to run high, many *Kinkabii* regarding Cleland with the greatest suspicion. There was also a deep mutual antipathy between the Alata stool and sections of the Sempe *akutso*, in particular the prominent Bruce family. A number of Bruces were at the forefront of the deputation scheme and were vying for influence in James Town with Cleland, who advised the *manbii* to ignore the agitation.[109]

In September 1886, the simmering tension erupted into open conflict. The catalyst was the detention by colonial police on the night of September 9 of deputation scheme leader Alexander Bruce.[110] The following morning he appeared in the packed DC's courthouse charged with resisting arrest. Also in court that day was the *Ga mantse*, appearing as a witness in the case before that of Bruce. As Taki Tawia took the stand, the inexperienced young DC, C. K. Freeman, demanded that he remove his cloth from his shoulder and give evidence bare-chested.[111] When Taki refused to acquiesce to what would have been a deeply humiliating mark of deference, Freeman threatened to send him to prison for contempt of court, at which the enraged *mantse* threw his entire cloth to the floor.[112] When news of the altercation reached those outside, the courthouse was attacked by an angry crowd, which was kept at bay by Hausa soldiers with fixed bayonets. The *Ga mantse*, Edmund Bannerman, Alex Bruce, and a large crowd of townspeople proceeded directly to Christiansborg Castle to demand the DC's removal. On returning from Osu, the entourage was waylaid near the Muslim *zongo* on the outskirts of Kinka by Freeman and his soldiery. An ugly confrontation developed between Ga and "Hausa" women, the situation escalating with the arrival of the Nleshi *asafobii*, girded for action and accompanied by "at least 2,000" more angry women.[113] After sending telegrams to Taki and Cleland appealing for calm, Griffith drove in his carriage to Kinka, where he relieved Freeman of his duties and confined the Hausas to barracks. For days afterward "policemen on their beats . . . were pelted with stones thrown from houses and the . . . labyrinths of alleys in Accra," to which the British responded by mounting armed patrols of the town.[114] Thirteen years after the first violent encounter between the Ga and Hausa Constabulary, the steadily expanding coercive apparatus was one of the most visible indications of Accra's transition to colonial rule.

To the frustration of the Governor, the violence won support in Kinka for Bannerman's argument for a deputation, which became linked to efforts to seek redress for the events of September 9–10.[115] The latter, at least, met with some success. An enquiry condemned the actions of Freeman, recommending that Alex Bruce receive an official apology for his illegal arrest.[116] It was George Cleland, though, who decisively shaped the Governor's view of town affairs, reporting to the Castle details of what he portrayed as an unholy alliance between Taki and Bannerman. The latter were clearly rattled by Cleland's influence, declaring their loyalty in a letter of December 1886.[117] When a final ploy, a telegram sent directly to Buckingham Palace, failed to elicit any positive response, the protest began to falter. In April 1887 *Ga mantse* Taki, Bannerman, and their allies were summoned to the Castle to receive the Secretary of State's final word on the matter: that he would neither sanction a deputation nor entertain their grievances. Notices were posted around the town declaring that the abolition of slavery without compensation was absolute, the Hausa force would not be disbanded, and spirit duties were a matter for local legislation.[118] Although the leaders of the protest can hardly have been happy with the appointment of George Cleland to the Legislative Council, the *raison d'être* of the deputation evaporated with the restoration of unofficial representation.[119] On November 26, 1887, however, Cleland died after a short illness at the age of fifty-seven. His influence in Accra since the early 1860s had been extensive, and his death represented a serious blow for the interests of the Alata *akutso*.[120] Yet Cleland's demise opened the way for the emergence of an equally skillful political leader who would in turn dominate affairs in James Town for many decades, Alata *mantse* Kojo Ababio IV.

Alata *Mantse* Kojo Ababio IV (1892–1938)

On September 12, 1892, the Colonial Secretary was surprised to see a large crowd of people gathered about their chiefs and elders on the outskirts of Accra. Inquiring into the reason for the assembly, he was told by a bystander that the Ga people had gathered to witness King Taki receive the oath of allegiance from the newly enstooled King of James Town, Kwamin Amoako-Atta, who had taken the name Kojo Ababio IV.[121] What the British official had chanced upon was the final ceremony of an installation process that had begun nine months before on the night of November 29, 1891, when the 18-year-old schoolboy Kwamin was pulled from his bed and placed on the Alata stool.[122]

The ceremony at the ancient meeting place of Amugina was not merely a ritualistic "customary" procedure, but a product of current political circumstance. Ongoing tension between Nleshi and Kinka was exacerbated in 1891 by the murder of a son of the late Kofi Oku, a crime considered by many in Alata to be politically motivated.[123] In July 1892 a series of meetings was convened by representatives of the two towns, an initiative attributed by the *Gold Coast Chronicle* to "a few sensible and educated natives." A bullock was slaughtered and the meat shared between the *mantsemei*. The *Chronicle* editorialized that "the people of the two . . . quarters [sic] now look upon each other as proceeding from the same stock. . . . We do not believe in calling some natives 'Accras' and others 'Fantees' and some 'James Town people' and others again 'Ussher Town natives,' but we wish every native . . . to be looked upon as a Gold Coast native."[124] Kojo Ababio's oath was intended as a final normalization of relations by Kinka leaders, who informed the British that "the people of James Town and Ussher Town had mutually agreed that James Town should no longer be a separate town but that its chief should be . . . under King Tackie."[125]

On October 18, Taki took Kojo Ababio together with two other newly enstooled *mantsemei*, Okaija of Gbese and Allotei of Sempe, to Christiansborg Castle to be introduced to the Governor. There occurred in the "Palaver Hall" an exchange that would enter the corpus of Ga oral history, repeatedly reconstructed as a defining act in the troubled relationship between Kinka and Nleshi. An account from British records captures something of the moment:

> The Governor having . . . expressed his pleasure at the announcement that James Town and Ussher Town agreed to amalgamate and to become one town under King Tackie, congratulated Amoako Atta [Kojo Ababio] upon being elected chief of one of the quarters of James Town. Thereupon Amoako Atta, drawing himself up, said "I am not one of King Tackie's chiefs, I am King of James Town. James Town is an English Town and Ussher Town is a Dutch Town, and English people can't serve Dutch people."[126]

The government, which equated "tribal unity" with law and order, was not pleased by this startling rejection of the authority of Taki Tawia. It recognised Kojo Ababio not as a "King" but merely as a "Chief." This inferior status in the evolving colonial hierarchy was confirmed two months later, when Griffith, recognizing the continuing influence of Taki and Osu *mantse* Dowuona throughout the southeastern Gold Coast, decided to grant the two kings annual stipends of £180 and £72, respectively.[127]

Kojo Ababio's calculated appeal to the English antecedents of Nleshi and its historic autonomy from its Dutch neighbor would over time strike a chord with British officials who continued to view Kinka as a stubbornly tradition-bound and often hostile community. Kojo's personal qualities and upbringing in the more "modern" milieu of James Town enabled him to refine this discourse, and he was soon regarded as a progressive figure. His father, James Kwamin, an influential *asafoatse* and associate of Cleland and other Euro-African merchants, had sent him to the Government School in James Town. Unlike the majority of officeholders, he was fully literate and spoke English well. Kojo was also a professed Anglican, which as the "official" Church of the colonial state was emerging as the denomination of choice among the elite of James Town by the 1890s.[128] Despite his Anglicanism, in 1899 Kojo took the unusual step of allowing the Basel Mission to open a vernacular Sunday School in the courtroom of the *mantse we*, attending classes himself in order to improve his literacy in Ga.[129] As indicated by Governor Nathan's reflections on chieftaincy in Accra that began this chapter, Kojo Ababio's reputation as a modernizer also rested on his ability to mobilize scarce manpower. A new round of colonial state building in the late 1890s pushed the question of access to labor to the center of town affairs, the young Alata *mantse* emerging as a skillful leader and political thinker.

LABOR, TAXATION, AND MUNICIPAL GOVERNMENT

The development of Accra in the second half of the 1890s was dominated by two issues that exemplified the new imperial age in Africa: taxation and labor. Both emerged and became intertwined at the center of Ga politics as a result of two pieces of British legislation, the Town Councils Ordinance of 1894 (TCO) and the Compulsory Labour Ordinance of 1895 (CLO). The TCO was motivated less by a desire to build representative institutions than to relieve the colonial exchequer of some of the expense of governing Accra. It envisaged a municipal council consisting of half official and half elected members plus the DC as *ex-officio* president, empowered to raise revenue through a range of licenses and by a rate on property.[130] The two African members of the Legislative Council, the Ga businessmen Chief John Vanderpuye and J. H. Cheetham, raised objections to the imposition of rates during the passage of the bill, and it was this aspect of the ordinance that provoked popular opposition.[131] Protest meetings resulted in the formation of a committee headed by Edmund Bannerman but also featuring a younger generation of professionally qualified barristers: his son, C. J. Bannerman, his nephew, Thomas Hutton Mills, and William Addo, son of the late merchant. According to C. J. Bannerman, the common townspeople were simply "not sufficiently civilized" for a council.[132] For the *manbii* themselves, the issue was the repugnance of any form of direct taxation and they looked to their *mantsemei* to resist what were seen as unjust British demands at a time of economic difficulties. The chiefs found themselves in a tricky situation. "We are always ready to do everything in our power to assist the Government," Kojo Ababio explained, "but . . . any disposition on our part to help in the introduction of the Ordinance . . . would be greatly misconstrued by the people in our neighbourhood, who would . . . regard us as enemies."[133] The cautious Griffith had some sympathy with these arguments and was reluctant to implement the scheme, but in April 1895 his long governorship came to an end. He was replaced by Sir William Maxwell, a more aggressive imperialist of the 1890s mold with little patience for dissenting African opinion.

Maxwell's energies were soon directed toward the 1896 subjugation of the Asante kingdom, delaying the enactment of the TCO and leading to yet another set of demands on the Ga community. In order to secure carriers for the expedition to Kumase that resulted in the arrest of *Asantehene* Prempeh and the termination of Asante sovereignty, the British passed the CLO in December 1895. Based on the premise that "by native custom it is obligatory on persons of the labouring class to give their labour for public purposes on being called out by their Chiefs," the ordinance caused some turmoil in Accra, where the *mantsemei* had never exercized such authority.[134] "Recruiting of carriers in Accra," it was noted, "goes on very slowly."

> Kings Tackie and Dawuna are seriously handicapped by having their seats of administration in the Capital . . . where . . . legal requirements are amply filled by the Courts. The loss of Executive power with a Native King or Chief is almost synonymous with the loss of moral control, and it is not to be wondered at that these two Kings find themselves in a serious dilemma in the present crisis. They still retain their influence among their people in interior villages of their respective spheres of jurisdiction and it is in this direction that . . . their power must be directed.[135]

References to the divergence in the degree of control the chiefs exercised over the townspeople, *manbii*, and rural dwellers, *kosebii*, recur throughout the labor crisis of the 1890s. "We have no authority to force the people in town," Taki Tawia admitted.[136] "The men in the town are either carpenters, coopers, blacksmiths, fishermen, bricklayers or cooks," he later tried to explain. "Men who engage themselves as carriers are all from the bush."[137]

Yet just a week later, amid scenes reminiscent of the Awuna Wars, a martial spirit suddenly gripped Accra. "Even clerks have been called upon to give their services, and . . . the excitement has . . . taken a decided hold upon the women and the fetish priests."[138] As the town emptied of its young men, the *Independent* voiced concern that commerce would grind to a complete halt. "No sooner had it become known that special powers had been vested in the Chiefs by the Government," the newspaper reported, "the Accras almost *en masse* rushed to their Captains and with them to their Chiefs and with the latter to the King who suddenly found himself in a position of moral authority over his people."[139] In the light of the subsequent failure of the ordinance, the efficacy of government-vested powers proved somewhat less than that suggested here. Nonetheless, this analysis, neatly capturing the ebb and flow of moral authority, represents a perceptive contemporary interpretation of Ga politics. "The general impression has been," the *Independent* added with further insight, "that the men are going to fight, not to act as carriers." This may come closest to explaining the social forces propelling the mobilization, given the location of warrior and carrier at opposite ends of the spectrum of male status.

However, times had changed in the two decades since the Glover War. The Ga marched to Kumase not as warriors but as carriers, ignominiously lugging the ammunition of the colonial Hausa soldiery. When in February 1897 the *Ga mantse* was instructed to provide carriers for another detachment to Asante, the response could not have been more different. At a mass meeting called to discuss the TCO and CLO, Edmund Bannerman and other leading scholars urged compliance, Hutton Mills advising Taki that anyone "who was called 'Chief' or who called himself 'Chief' was liable under the Ordinance . . . to furnish his contingent."[140] This represented something of a switch in political strategy on the part of the aging Bannerman. Following the failure of the deputation scheme and the death of his rival Cleland he had adopted a less confrontational attitude toward the colonial regime, choosing instead to play the role of an elder statesman in town affairs.[141] The Ga women, he wrote disapprovingly, "displayed their [usual] pugnaciousness," driving on popular protest by loudly demanding resistance to government demands.[142] Taki chose to take the advice of the scholars, accompanying Bannerman back to Tarkwa House where the names of twelve Ga leaders liable to furnish carriers were added to the requisition forms provided by the government. These included three *oblempon* stool holders of the Otublohum quarter: Chiefs Antonio Ankra and John Vanderpuye of the Dadebanwe, and John A. Nelson, the leader of the Tabon community. In a striking display of the fragmentation of old patron-client networks, neither they nor the nine *mantsemei* listed were able to provide a single carrier. All were hauled off to court, and with the exception of Nungwa *mantse* Odai, who later came up with fourteen men, each fined £25.[143] As Chief Nelson bemoaned: "More troublesome people than those under me it would be difficult to find."[144]

Widespread hostility toward the CLO throughout the Gold Coast forced the government to discontinue its use in 1898. To secure labor for the construction of the Sekondi-Kumase railway that began that year a new approach was tried, the Accra chiefs being offered £20 for every hundred men supplied. Although even *kosebii* were now reluctant to act as carriers, large numbers of men from villages attached to the Alata *akutso* were recruited for the railway by Kojo Ababio.[145] The reasons for the success of the young *mantse* in mobilizing scarce manpower remain unclear. He certainly applied himself to the task with vigor, sending agents around the villages and keeping watch on the roads.[146] Kojo's clout was also a reflection of the pattern of authority on the Accra plains, evidence from court cases like *Solomon v. Noy* and from official surveys indicating the historic success of the Alata *akutso* in the planting of outlying villages. As one official observed in 1907, "While 33 towns, many of considerable size, owe allegiance to . . . James Town, the . . . five [sic] quarters of Kinka have only 25 towns under them."[147] As in the era of slavery, the relationship between Accra and its agricultural hinterland was crucial in shaping the dynamics of political power in the urban center.

The Accra Town Council

Maxwell returned to the implementation of the Town Council Ordinance in the second half of 1896, the limits of the municipality being defined to encompass Nleshi, Kinka, and Osu. As in 1886, women were at the fore-front of popular resistance to what was seen as an unjust imposition. An angry demonstration outside the Castle by the women of all three *majii* on December 1 was followed by an extraordinary printed petition to Secretary of State Joseph Chamberlain demanding that the ordinance be withdrawn. Municipal taxation would "only aggravate the already hard lot of women" and the "poorer classes" in general, the twenty-six female signatories argued, adding that the council would inevitably "fall into the hands of the so-called educated classes." The female community had decided to act, they wrote, because "our chiefs and headmen and the general male population have become enervated and demoralized. . . . They are afraid to speak their minds."[148]

We have seen the extent to which such gendered discourse historically shaped Ga politics. What the petition represented, however, was a quite unprecedented eruption of female action from the streets of Accra into the formal political arena. Not all the signatories can be identified, but the protest leaders appear to be women from prominent families who were traders in their own right. Notable figures include Kale Ankra, daughter of Ayi and mother of Chief John Vanderpuye, and Kai Ankra (1845–1947), wife of the late Ajaben.[149] Their efforts clearly had an impact. When in March 1897 Taki Tawia prevaricated on being requested to assist in the valuation of town properties, Maxwell withdrew his stipend until such time as he cooperated fully with the levying of the rate.[150] In the face of mounting popular hostility it would have been almost impossible for the *mantsemei* to be seen to support the TCO. By the end of the year an electoral register of 225 male property owners had been compiled, but no one on the list was willing to stand as a candidate. It was only with the greatest difficulty that Governor Hodgson, who inherited the scheme after the death of Maxwell, managed to persuade C. J.

Bannerman, E. W. Quartey-Papafio, and Alata *mantse* Kojo Ababio to accept nomination as councillors.[151]

The attempt by the newly inaugurated Town Council to collect the house rate, set at 2.5 percent of annual rentable value, met with the anticipated resistance. Taki responded to British demands that he be the first to pay by "beating gong-gong" through the streets of Kinka to the effect that he had no intention of doing so. Messages were sent to the bush instructing the *kosebii*—with only limited success—to come into Accra to aid their urban kinsmen and women. Meanwhile, Accra's fishermen stopped putting to sea in protest. On April 25, 1898, a meeting at the *Ga mantsewe* was dispersed by baton-wielding police, after which the government proscribed the sale of gunpowder. The situation came close to igniting on May 4, when a mass meeting was confronted by the Hausa soldiery. As in 1886, the civilian Muslim community again entered the fray, appearing "on the scene on the sound of the 'fall-in' bugle . . . ready to assist in the maintenance of order."[152] The prospect of violence began to alarm the town's property-owning elite, who attempted to defuse the situation by paying the rates owed by Taki and the new Osu *mantse* Noi Ababio. "The object of the mob," Edmund Bannerman warned the government, "is now merely to create disorder . . . so as to enable them to plunder the respectable houses and shops."[153] The arrest on May 6 of Gbese *asafoatse* Charles Kwamena for sedition caused the opposition to falter. Five days later, rate payers began to flock to the Municipal Office to forestall the British threat to double unpaid rates bills, clearly after a collective decision that further resistance would be futile.

Forty years after the first ephemeral experiment in new civic institutions Accra had its Town Council, but it was to be singularly unsuccessful in encouraging the municipal spirit so desired by Joseph Chamberlain. Few townspeople were happy paying rates, further protests succeeding in winning an exemption for individuals on the grounds of poverty.[154] The *manbii*, Taki insisted, had "got on very well without the municipality."[155] The Council failed, Governor Clifford argued in 1915, because Maxwell had thrust at bayonet point "upon a fiercely unwilling population a form of local government which they recognised as a mockery of self-government," imposing a direct tax "which could only produce an utterly insignificant revenue."[156] Nonetheless, it marked the beginning of a new phase in the history of Accra, which in the new century began to expand beyond the three old Ga *majii* into an increasingly complex colonial city. Taki Tawia's long tenure as "father of the town" was drawing to a close. Despite repeated requests, the British refused to restore the old chief's stipend, and his final years were blighted by a deepening yet dignified poverty. His death in July 1902 was followed nine months later by that of Edmund Bannerman. The relationship of these two dominant figures over the decades in many ways personified the complexities of town politics. Their deaths cleared the stage for a new generation of Ga leaders to confront the challenges of the twentieth-century colonial encounter.

CONCLUSION

The 1880s and 1890s witnessed the beginning of a decisive shift in the Gold Coast's urban network in favor of the new colonial capital. As Accra consolidated its position as the administrative and commercial headquarters of the expanding British colony, rival entrepôts experienced wildly fluctuating economic fortunes, port towns such as Ada, Prampram, Winneba, Anomabo, and Cape Coast entering a long period of relative decline.[157] Within Accra, the situation was more complex, and urban development brought both new opportunities and new threats. The expatriate commercial advance of the 1890s resulted in a restructuring of the established middleman role of Ga notables. Facing a serious erosion of their moral authority through the loss of judicial powers and revenues, officeholders began to forge a new role as brokers in the distribution of urban and rural land. In this shift to a more informal exercise of authority the *mantsemei* met with some success, although the commoditization of land threw up a new set of conflicts that would characterize the growth of the colonial city. The literate urban elite, meanwhile, confronted the economic competition and political closure of the late nineteenth century by employing a widening range of "modern" skills and techniques to maintain a key brokering role within the new colonial dispensation.

NOTES

1. *Gold Coast Leader*, 15 July 1902.

2. Ga proverb, from Zimmermann, *Grammatical sketch*, Vol. 1, 161.

3. NAG ADM 11/1/1086, Extract from the Governor's Conf. Despatch, 10 Mar. 1901.

4. Cf. Liss and Knight, *Atlantic port cities*, 2.

5. Kaplow, "African merchants," 85–126; Reynolds, "The rise and fall of an African merchant class"; Dumett, "John Sarbah, the elder"; idem, "African merchants"; Lynn, *Commerce and economic change*, 151–170.

6. H. J. Bevin, "The Gold Coast economy about 1880," *Transactions of the Gold Coast and Togoland Historical Society*, 2 (1956).

7. For prices and export figures, see Dumett, "John Sarbah, the elder," 663.

8. PRO CO 96/362, Hodgson to Chamberlain, No. 332, 28 July 1900, enclosed: Adams to CS, 30 July 1900.

9. See NAG SCT 17/4/12 Dist. Court, *Mattier v. Aryichoe*, 22 Aug. 1888, *Antonio Ankrah v. Mansah Affiaye*, 9 Mar. 1889, *John A. Nelson v. Amisah*, 1 Nov. 1889,

and *John A. Nelson v. Nah Din, Nah Churu, Kai*, 2 Nov. 1889; *Western Echo*, 22 Sept. 1886.

10. Cf. Kristin Mann, "The rise of Taiwo Olowo: Law, accumulation, and mobility in early colonial Lagos" in Mann and Roberts, *Law in colonial Africa*.

11. See Parker, "Ga state and society," 174–179.

12. Land Title Registry, Accra [hereafter LTR], Documents 1845–1866 Vol. 2, and Documents Registered 1877–1883; NAG ADM 5/3/9, Report upon the customs relating to the tenure of land on the Gold Coast, 1895, 18.

13. BMA D-1, 60/85, "Interest of money" by William Buckmann, 19 Nov, 1894; *Gold Coast Leader*, 13 Feb. 1904; for an overview, see Gareth Austen, "Indigenous credit institutions in West Africa, c. 1750-c. 1960" in G. Austen and K. Sugihara (eds.), *Local suppliers of credit in the Third World, 1750–1960* (London, 1993).

14. *African Times*, 18 Feb. 1873; PP 1890 XLVIII [C.5897-40] *Economic agriculture on the Gold Coast, 1889*, 10–11; on the link between "customs" and pawning in the 1920s, see *Gold Coast Independent*, 13 Sept. 1922.

15. R. Szereszewski, *Structural changes in the economy of Ghana 1891–1911* (London, 1965), 7.

16. PP 1882 XLVI [C.3386], No. 18: Rowe to Kimberley, 16 Jan. 1882; Wilks, *Asante*, 281–284.

17. *African Times*, 1 June 1880; *1891 Census*, 16; NAG ADM 11/1/1772, interview between Nathan and Native Officer Ali and Brimah, 27 Jan. 1903; Paul Lovejoy, *Caravans of kola: The Hausa kola trade, 1700–1900* (Zaria, 1980), 116. The total Muslim population in Accra in 1891, including police and soldiers, was recorded as 1,617.

18. PP 1889 LXXVI [C.5897], Sanitary report on the Accra station for the quarter and year ended 31 December 1888, by J. F. Easmon.

19. Raymond Dumett, "The rubber trade of the Gold Coast and Asante in the nineteenth century: African innovation and market responsiveness," *JAH*, 12 (1971).

20. LTR Register of Mortgages, Accra 1896–1898, esp. indenture of 28 Feb. 1896, 16–19; C. F. Hutchison, *The pen pictures of modern Africans and African celebrities* (London, n.d. [c.1930]), 144–145.

21. NAG SCT 17/4/19 Dist. Court, *James Kotey v. Jacob Vanderpuye*, 10 Dec. 1897.

22. PP 1890-91 LV [C.6270] *Further reports relative to economic agriculture on the Gold Coast*, 10.

23. Kimble, *Political history*, 306–315.

24. PRO CO 96/234, Griffith to Ripon, No. 171, 12 June 1893.

25. *1891 Census*, 134. This figure includes, however, soldiers and police; in 1901 civil servants were numbered at 258.

26. NAG SCT 2/4/17 Div. Court 1889–1891 Part 2, *Jacob Ankrah v. Aryee Kumah*, 1891; see also NAG ADM 5/2/3 1911 Census Report, 35–36: a generation later the once-powerful guild was reported to be "practically defunct" due to the decline in demand for coopers.

27. NAG SCT 17/4/12 Dist. Court, *J. J. Fischer and Co. v. Herman Wood*, 23 July 1888.

28. WMMS GCC 1893-4, Box 766, File 1, Kemp to Hartley, 6 May 1894.

29. NAG SCT 17/4/3 DC's Court Book No. 6, *J. A. Ribeiro v. Francisco Ribeiro*, 8 May 1876.

30. *Gold Coast Chronicle*, 11 Aug. 1894.

31. NAG SCT 2/4/18 Div. Court Vol. 7, *Wm. Tetteh Kwasshi v. Akrong*, 1892.

32. *Gold Coast Chronicle*, 5 Mar. 1897.

33. PRO CO 96/298, Maxwell to Chamberlain, No. 386, 4 Sept. 1897, enclosed: Akole Ankrah and others to Chamberlain, 31 May 1897; see also S.J.S. Cookey, "West African immigrants in the Congo 1885-1896," *Journal of the Historical Society of Nigeria*, 3 (1965).

34. See Anne Phillips, *The enigma of colonialism: British policy in West Africa* (London, 1989), 28–58.

35. Dumett, "African merchants," 691.

36. The remaining members of the Managing Committee of the 1869 Accra Confederacy, J. E. Richter and James Bannerman, disappear from the historical record in 1871 and 1874, respectively.

37. See NAG ADM 11/1/1086, Chief John Vanderpuye to CS, 2 Mar. 1897; and *Akwashontse* T. R. Quartey's reflections on the meanings of Chief John Quartey's title in NAG SCT 2/4/61 Div. Court Vol. 47, *R. S. Sackey v. H. B. Okantah*, 1916.

38. Ibid.; *Western Echo*, 29 July 1886; and see John Quartey's obituary in *West African Gazette*, 22 Feb. 1896.

39. Reindorf, *History*, 152, 305–314; Quartey-Papafio, "Law of succession," 67–68; PRO CO 96/507, Bryan to Harcourt, No. 233, 11 May 1911, enclosed: Quartey to Secretary of State, 27 Apr. 1911; interview with Nii Akwashon Mantse, R.K.M. Quartey, Accra, 12 Aug. 1992.

40. As the name Kwatei was rendered as Quartey, so Kpakpa Fio ("Kpakpa junior") became Papafio. Both forms, however, continued to coexist, sometimes within the same name.

41. NAG ADM 11/1/1089, statement by R. W. Quartey, 6 Dec. 1929; *brofonyo*, or *blofonyo*, is the Ga word for European.

42. *West African Gazette*, 22 Feb. 1896.

43. NAG SCT 17/4/17 Dist. Court, *Regina per Antonio Ankrah v. Daku*, 13 Jan. 1891, evidence of Antonio Ankrah.

44. Interview with Nii Akwashon Mantse, R.K.M. Quartey, Accra, 12 August 1992.

45. *West African Herald*, 18 Apr. 1859; NAG SCT 2/4/1, *William Quartaye v. Ashong*, 3 Feb. 1857; *Gold Coast Independent*, 19 Sept. 1896.

46. NAG SCT 2/4/5 Div. Court Vol. 2B, *John Quartey v. William Quartey*, 17 Apr. 1869.

47. NAG SCT 2/4/7 Div. Court Vol. 3, *William Quartey v. William Papa Feo*, 25 Apr. 1871.

48. Austin, "Indigenous credit institutions," 111.

49. LTR, Conveyances and Leases 1890–1993 Vol. 3, and Register of Mortgages, Accra 1892–1899 Vol. 2; and see *Gold Coast Independent*, 23 Sept. 1922, on Quartey's bank-rolling of the expatriate concern of Messrs Gallie, Flamang and Co.

50. See Chapter 1.

51. Interview with Sydney E. Heward-Mills, Accra, 14 Jan. 1993.

52. NAG SCT 2/4/17 Div. Court 1889–1891 Part 2, *John Vanderpuye v. Dadaye, W. A. Solomon, Ankra Fio, Pappoe*, 1890, evidence of Ofosua. To be "house born" (*webii* or *shiabii*) was a common euphemism for someone of slave descent.

53. Ibid., evidence of Antonio Ankra and James Henry Badu.

54. NAG SCT 2/4/41 Div. Court Vol. 30, *Land at Accra re Public Lands Ordinance 1876*, 1907, statement by A. B. Quartey-Papafio.

55. NAG SCT 2/4/17, *Vanderpuye v. Dadaye*, 1890.

56. Ibid.

57. PP 1874 XLVI [C.892], No. 21: Berkeley to Kimberley, 12 Sept. 1873, enclosure 2.

58. Ibid., enclosure 1.

59. LTR Documents Registered 1877–1883, 19 Jan. 1877; NAG SCT 2/4/19 Div. Court Vol. 8, *King Tackie v. R. Nelson*, 30 Sept. 1892.

60. NAG ADM 11/1/1770, 18 Oct. 1881.

61. PRO CO 96/139, Rowe to Kimberley, No. 122, 8 Apr. 1882; see too *Gold Coast Times*, 24 Mar. 1883.

62. NAG SCT 2/4/17, *Vanderpuye v. Dadaye*, 1890.

63. Ibid.

64. Ibid., evidence of Ofosua. The house, later leased to the firm of Pickering and Berthould and popularly known as "P & B," served as the Ussher Town police station until its collapse in the mid-1990s.

65. LTR Conveyances and Leases Vol. 2 1889–1891, 63–65.

66. NAG SCT 17/4/17 Dist. Court, *Regina per Antonio Ankrah v. Daku*, 13 Jan. 1891.

67. See Chapter 2.

68. On the concept of "social assets," cf. Peel, *Ijeshas and Nigerians*, 136–145.

69. Zimmermann, *Grammatical sketch*, Vol. 1, 172. "Used to warn people not to try to derive too much advantage of a Gā-family," Zimmermann noted.

70. *Vanderpuye v. Dadaye*, 1890.

71. NAG SCT 2/4/13 Div. Court Vol. 4C, *Solomom, King of James Town v. Noy*, 1880; for a full analysis of the case, see Parker, "Ga state and society," 194–199.

72. NAG ADM 11/1/1086, Report of the Commissioner of Police on the town companies of Accra, 20 May 1895; T. J. Johnson, "Protest: Tradition and change: An analysis of southern Gold Coast riots 1890–1920," *Economy and Society*, 1 (1972). The last outbreak of violence between Kinka and Nleshi had occurred in 1846: Reindorf, *History*, 324–326.

73. *Agbuntso*, smoked herring, is a contraction of *a gbu mli tso*, lit. "a skewer was put through it," the incident being rendered in some sources as the "war of the skewer": M. E. Kropp Dakubu, *Ga-English dictionary* (IAS, Legon, 1973), 30.

74. NAG ADM 11/1/1086, Ammah to CS, 22 July 1881, and King Tackie to Inspector General, Gold Coast Constabulary, 15 Apr. 1882.

75. *Gold Coast Times*, 10 June 1882.

76. NAG ADM 11/1/1756, Notes of evidence taken in connection with the enquiry into . . . whether Tackie Yaoboi, Ga mantse, has been destooled in accordance with native law and custom, 1925; for further suggestive evidence of land alienation by Gbese elders headed by the Nai and Koole *wulomei*, see LTR Documents 1877–1883, 24 June 1881, 254, and 21 Dec. 1882, 292–293.

77. *Gold Coast Times*, 10 June 1882 [emphasis in original].

78. PRO CO 96/149, Rowe to Derby, No. 97, 9 Mar. 1883; Kimble, *Political history*, 462.

79. *Gold Coast Times*, 24 Mar. 1883.

80. Marion Kilson (ed.), *Excerpts from the diary of Kwaku Niri (alias J. Q. Hammond) 1884–1918* (IAS, Legon, 1967), 1–15; see too Field, *Social organization*, 170–172; NAG ADM 11/1/1086, Griffith, DC, to CS, 11 Sept. 1884.

81. Kilson, *The diary of Kwaku Niri*, 3, 41; NAG SCT 2/4/50 Div. Court Vol. 39, *Mantse D. P. Hammond v. Mantse Ababio*, 1912, evidence of Taki Obili.

82. NAG ADM 11/1/1086, Griffith to CS, 11 Sept. 1884.

83. Kilson, *The diary of Kwaku Niri*, 3–4.

84. Ibid., 13; NAG ADM 11/1/1086, minute by Griffith, 16 Sept. 1884.

85. Kilson, *The diary of Kwaku Niri*, 15.

86. "Hooting" (the public howling down and shaming of an individual) was a prominent part of informal political action in the streets of Accra, and was a particularly important weapon in women's political armory: see NAG ADM 11/1/795 Alleged "Hooting" Campaign [1920].

87. See Chapter 1; on the Fante, see Arthur Ffoulkes, "The company system in Cape Coast Castle," *JAS*, 7 (1907–1908); J. C. de Graft Johnson, "The Fanti asafu" [sic], *Africa*, 5 (1932); Ansu Datta, "The Fante *asafo*: A re-examination," *Africa*, 42 (1972).

88. See Field, *Religion and medicine*, 186.

89. *Western Echo*, 11 Sept. 1886, "The great Accra custom"; Field, *Religion and medicine*, 48, 89–90; NAG ADM 11/1/1087, minute by SNA, 18 Aug. 1904; ADM 11/1/1437, "Suppression of objectionable customs" by S. D. Codjoe, n.d. [c.1930]; Victor Mensah Clottey, "Music and dance of Oshie ceremony in the Homowo festival among the Gas," thesis for Diploma in Dance, University of Ghana, Legon, 1968.

90. On the role of alcohol and dancing groups in the 1846 conflict, see Reindorf, *History*, 325; cf. Dakubu, *Ga-English dictionary*, 185: *oshieku*: "backbiting," "slander."

91. *Western Echo*, 10 Apr. 1886.

92. Kimble, *Political history*, 462–464.

93. NAG ADM 11/1/1086, minute by Simonds, 8 Aug. 1885.

94. PRO CO 96/191, Griffith to Knutsford, No. 116, 10 Apr. 1888, enclosed: Memorandum on Native Prisons, by W. B. Griffith, Jr., QA, 3 Dec. 1887.

95. Ibid.

96. NAG ADM 11/1/1086, minute by H. M. Hull, 6 Feb. 1890; Quartey-Papafio, "Native tribunals," 83; cf. Roger Gocking, "British justice and the native tribunals of the southern Gold Coast," *JAH*, 34 (1993), 98, which mistakenly states that it was not until 1910 that legislation regulated native prisons.

97. NAG ADM 11/1/1139, King G. A. Dawuonah to Griffith, 10 Dec. 1888 [emphasis in original].

98. See NAG ADM 11/1/1773, interview between Gov. Rodger and Taki Obili, Kojo Ababio, Okaija, and other chiefs, 10 Mar. 1904.

99. For some discussion, see Adell Patton, Jr., "Dr. John Farrell Easmon: Medical professionalism and colonial racism in the Gold Coast, 1856–1900," *International Journal of African Historical Studies*, 24 (1989).

100. *Gold Coast Chronicle*, 9 July 1896.

101. Kimble, *Political history*, 410–418.

102. The term "Boss," by which big men of the literate elite began to be known by this period, appears to be an English version of the Ga *owula*. See *Gold Coast Chronicle*,

9 Apr. 1897, for an evocative description of a "graphaphone" concert at Lutterodt Hall, Accra's principal elite social venue, where 118 guests were "provided with refreshment by the 'Bosses'"; and NAG ADM 11/1/1429, Salutations and greetings of various Gold Coast tribes, by J. C. de Graft Johnson, Asst. SNA, n.d. [1921].

103. *Western Echo*, 10 Apr. 1886; PRO CO 96/175, Griffith to Granville. Conf., 27 July 1886.

104. NAG ADM 11/1/1086, letter dd. 15 Feb. 1897.

105. PRO CO 96/179, Griffith to Stanhope, No. 24, 20 Jan. 1887.

106. *Western Echo*, 7 Aug. 1886.

107. PRO CO 96/179, Griffith to Stanhope, Conf., 20 Jan. 1887.

108. PRO CO 96/175, Griffith to Granville, No. 292, 27 July 1886.

109. PRO CO 96/179, Griffith to Stanhope, Conf., 20 Jan. 1887, esp. enclosure: Cleland to Griffith, 18 Jan. 1887.

110. PRO CO 96/175, Griffith to Stanhope, No. 357, 16 Sept. 1886; *Western Echo*, 22 Sept. 1886.

111. PRO CO 96/179, Griffith to Stanhope, No. 28, 21 Jan. 1887, enclosed: Notes of Evidence taken by Commission of Enquiry into Accra Disturbances.

112. Kimble, *Political history*, 415, is wrong in dismissing this as a "trivial incident." For a *mantse* or other dignitary to be publicly derobed was a potent symbol of the loss of authority, as recognized at the time by W. B. Griffith, Jr.: see Sir William Brandford Griffith, *The far horizon: Portrait of a colonial judge* (Ilfracombe, 1951). For the social distinctions implied by cloth being worn over the shoulder as opposed to merely around the waist, see PRO CO 879/20, No. 253, Young to Derby, 17 May 1884; and for discussion of this infamous incident some three decades later, see *Gold Coast Nation*, 12 Feb. 1914.

113. *Western Echo*, 22 Sept. 1886.

114. PRO CO 96/179, Griffith to Stanhope, No. 26, 20 Jan. 1887.

115. NAG ADM 11/1/1498, Taki Tawia to Governor, 25 Sept. 1896.

116. PRO CO 96/179, Griffith to Stanhope, No. 28, 21 Jan. 1887, enclosed: Report of Enquiry into Accra Disturbances, 1886.

117. NAG ADM 11/1/1086, King Tackie to CS, 29 Dec. 1886.

118. PRO CO 96/180, Griffith to Holland, No. 121, 7 Apr. 1887.

119. Kimble, *Political history*, 417.

120. On the impact on his family and followers of Cleland's death, see A. Addo-Aryee Brown, "Signs and omens," *Gold Coast Review*, 2 (1926). Cleland was replaced on the Leg. Co. by the Anomabo merchant John Sarbah.

121. NAG ADM 11/1/1086, CS to Governor, 19 Sept. 1892; *Gold Coast Chronicle*, 19 Sept. 1892.

122. Ibid., DC to CS, 30 Nov. 1891. Kojo Ababio vividly describes the intricate ritual process of his enstoolment in NAG SCT 2/4/68 Div. Court Vol. 52, *Land for Accra Water Works*, 1918.

123. NAG ADM 11/1/1086, CS to DC, 19 June 1891.

124. *Gold Coast Chronicle*, 18 July 1892. Accra's first weekly newspaper, the *Chronicle* was founded in 1890 by the Cape Coast journalist Timothy Laing. In 1894 it was bought by a group of Ga businessmen headed by brothers Chief John, Isaac, and Emmannuel Vanderpuye, and continued to appear until 1902.

125. NAG ADM 11/1/1086, minute by CS, 11 Oct. 1892.

126. Ibid., minute by CS, 21 Oct. 1892. Amoako Atta received his distinctively Akyem name on account of being born on October 12, 1873, the day that *okyenhene* Amoako Atta entered Accra for the war council with Glover. This is important, as his Ga ethnic credentials would later emerge at the center of much debate.

127. PRO CO 96/227, Griffith to Ripon, Secret, 26 Dec. 1992.

128. On the belated rise of Anglicanism in Accra, see Reindorf, *History*, 249–250.

129. NAG EC 6/7, "Report of missionary work at Accra, 1899," by Isaac Odoi, 31 Dec. 1899.

130. PRO CO 96/254, Griffith to Ripon, No. 35, 26 Jan. 1895; for legislative antecedents, see Kimble, *Political history*, 418–426.

131. Son of Jacobus Vanderpuye of Kinka and Elmina and Kale Ankra of Dadebanwe, Chief John Vanderpuye (1848–1925) made his fortune trading at Ada in the 1880s. He returned to Accra to succeed to his uncle Pedro Ankra's *oblempon* stool in 1888, serving on the Leg. Co. 1894–1904. J. H. Cheetham (1834–1902) of James Town was the labor agent for the Congo Independent State in Accra, and a Leg. Co. member 1893–1898.

132. PRO CO 96/268, Griffith to Maude, 3 July 1895.

133. PRO CO 96/254, Griffith to Ripon, No. 39, 30 Jan. 1895, enclosed: King, Chiefs, and Headmen of James Town to Governor, 22 Jan. 1895.

134. From the preamble to the Ordinance, reprinted in *Gold Coast Independent*, 21 Dec. 1895.

135. Ibid., 14 Dec. 1895. The *Independent*, edited by J. Bright Davies, was founded as a rival to the *Chronicle* early in 1895 by leading members of Accra's Sierra Leonian community after attacks in the latter on one of their number, Dr. J. F. Easmon: see Kimble, *Political history*, 97.

136. NAG ADM 11/1/1086, interview dd. 26 Apr. 1897.

137. NAG ADM 11/1/1772, meeting dd. 17 Apr. 1902.

138. *Gold Coast Independent*, 21 Dec. 1895; see also Kilson, *The diary of Kwaku Niri*, 16–22.

139. *Gold Coast Independent*, 21 Dec. 1895.

140. NAG ADM 11/1/1086, Bannerman to Hodgson, CS, 14 Feb. 1897.

141. Ibid., Bannerman to Hodgson, 24 Feb. 1897 and 4 Mar. 1897.

142. Ibid., Bannerman to Hodgson, 14 Feb. 1897.

143. Ibid., Hall to CS, 23 Feb. 1897.

144. Ibid., Nelson to CS, 24 Feb. 1897.

145. NAG ADM 11/1/1772, meeting dd. 3 Apr. 1902.

146. NAG ADM 11/1/1086, interview between Nathan and King Tackie, Noi Ababio, and others, 27 May 1901.

147. NAG ADM 11/1/9, Curling to SNA, 24 Oct. 1907. Only two years later the political geography of the Accra plains looked very different. The numbers of *aklowai* attached to each stool—no doubt inflated for political purposes—now read: Abola 14; Gbese 20; Asere 25; Otublohum 9; Alata 41; Sempe 13; Akanmaji 5: NAG ADM 8/1/13 The Gold Coast Civil Service List, 1909.

148. PRO CO 96/298, Maxwell to Chamberlain, No. 386, 4 Sept. 1897, enclosed: Akole Ankrah and others to Chamberlain, 31 May 1897. The petition was drafted for the mostly nonliterate women by the radical journalist J. Bright Davies, and—in an apparent attempt to retain a modicum of patriarchal authority—endorsed by Taki Tawia and some 2,000 other male signatories.

149. Interview with Sidney Heward-Mills (great-grandson of Kai Ankra), dd. Accra, 14 Jan. 1993.

150. PRO CO 96/294, Maxwell to Chamberlain, Secret, 9 June 1897. When Osu *mantse* G. A. Dowuona died on June 6, 1897, Maxwell also refused to extend the stipend to his successor.

151. PRO CO 96/318, Hodgson to Chamberlain, No. 282, 4 July 1898.

152. Ibid.

153. Ibid., enclosed: Bannerman to CS, 5 May 1898.

154. PRO CO 96/337, Low to Chamberlain, Conf., 4 Jan. 1899.

155. NAG ADM 11/1/1772, meeting dd. 26 Dec. 1900.

156. PRO CO 96/557, Clifford to Harcourt, Conf., 15 Apr. 1915.

157. Dickson, *Historical geography*, 254–259.

5

GOD'S PALAVER:
RELIGION AND POLITICS,
1860s–1920s

Nyonmo sane hi, si wonyen wofo nii ni
wotsemei le fe siwo le femo.
(God's palaver is good, but we cannot give up
doing what our fathers had done and left for us.)[1]

"Our fathers worshipped the fetish and were well practised with
charm-affairs and there came no riches nor peace into their lives,
therefore if we the children will continue on the same way, we shall
also share the same troubles and dangers in life as our fathers."[2]

The death of *Ga mantse* Taki Tawia in July 1902 was followed by an eigh-
teen-month interregnum during which Ga officeholders, sacred, secular, and
military, jostled for influence in town affairs. In life Taki's moral authority
may have been subject to sharp fluctuations as he negotiated a path between
the conflicting demands of the colonial regime and the Ga townspeople, but
in death he was sorely missed. After forty years on the stool, his demise
triggered a period of political uncertainty and dissonance in Accra. The process of succession to the Okaikoi stool demanded a careful engagement with
ritual custom, but custom was far from timeless and much had changed in
Accra since the 1860s. While established chiefs and priests renegotiated the
balance of sacred and secular authority, new interest groups—Christian converts, Muslim migrants, educated "scholars"—pressed their own claims to
be part of the ongoing making of the town. The ensuing political struggles
reveal that religion and belief remained at the center of Ga ideas of civic
virtue and urban identity.

This chapter deals with Accra as a sacral center, focusing on the connections between town politics and religious change. By the beginning of our period, Christianity was emerging as the principal form of religious innovation in the trading towns of the Gold Coast. However, the impact of Christianity on Accra's urban culture should not obscure the fact that indigenous structures of belief continued to evolve throughout the early colonial period and beyond. Religious change in Accra was more than simply a matter of conversion. As a recent essay points out, the analytical dominance of the rubric "African conversion" has encouraged the construction of traditional belief and world religion—whether Christianity or Islam—as if they were independent, opposed systems, to the neglect of the encounter and interaction between the two.[3] Indeed, far from being the site of a spectacular evangelical breakthrough, early colonial Accra was characterized by an ongoing, uneasy dialogue between Christianity and indigenous belief. The town was notable for being neither particularly receptive to Christianity, nor implacably hostile toward the new religion.

The chapter first turns back to the opening phase of the Christian encounter in the second half of the nineteenth century. The connections between religious change and town politics are then examined in an account of a dispute that gripped Accra in 1903 following the death of *Ga mantse* Taki Tawia. At issue was the political role of Accra's Muslim community, whose rapid expansion provides a graphic illustration of the growing ethnic and confessional diversity of the urban arena. We then look at the ways in which Accra's historical role as a sacral center shaped conflicting visions of the colonial city in the first decade of the twentieth century. Finally, the resilience of indigenous Ga belief is examined in the context of the resurgence of female possession cults in the town. The activities of Ga spirit mediums not only reinforced the established social and ritual power of women in Accra, but directly challenged notions of the colonial capital as a symbol of ordered modernity.

THE NINETEENTH-CENTURY CHRISTIAN ENCOUNTER

The Wesleyan Methodist and Basel Missions at Accra

European pastors had been dispatched intermittently to the Gold Coast forts from the mid-seventeenth century onward to cater to the religious and educational needs of expatriate traders and their Euro-African progeny, attracting a handful of African converts. Systematic evangelistic projects did not get under way at Accra until the 1840s, following the establishment of the Wesleyan Methodist Missionary Society at James

Town in 1838 and the consolidation of the tenuous Basel Mission Society presence at Osu in 1847. Both missions had an existing base of adherents on which to build. The Basel Mission had the "Christiansborg mulatto" community, many of whom were at least nominal Christians, while the Methodists had a group of young Ga men who had organized meetings for Bible study and worship after hearing the gospel preached in Fante towns in the 1830s. The leaders of the latter group were John Ahuma Solomon, John Plange, and Frederick France, all of whom were subsequently ordained. Together with Edward Fynn and Timothy Laing of Cape Coast they formed the first generation of indigenous Methodist pastors on the Gold Coast. Like Frederick Noi Dowuona, the Christian convert who in 1854 became Osu *mantse*, both Plange and Solomon came from families at the heart of political power in their respective *majii*. Plange (1820–1899) was a member of Teiko Tsuruwe of the Abola *akutso* whose father was remembered as a powerful slave trader, while Solomon (1818–1898) was the son of the Nleshi *mantse* Ahuma.[4]

Despite the prominence of these early Ga evangelists, throughout the nineteenth century the Accra circuit of the Methodist Society remained very much an outpost of its more fruitful field in the Fante country.[5] The missionaries found indigenous Ga belief an especially tough nut to crack, Henry Wharton despairing in 1849 that "the difference, in a moral point of view, betwixt Cape Coast and British Akrah, is as great as that betwixt the latter place and Kumasi."[6] In the early 1870s, after nearly four decades of labor, the James Town congregation still numbered less than 100 souls. Despite a rise to about 300 by the middle of the decade following the colonial consolidation and the construction of a school and chapel in Kinka, reports remained pessimistic. In 1875 the Ga were still reckoned to be "at least twenty years behind the other peoples of the Gold Coast; day after day the streets are disturbed by one or another of their many superstitious practices."[7]

Despite a superior organizational structure backed by the financial resources of its trading company, the Basel Mission at Osu experienced difficulties similar to those of the Wesleyans in attracting committed Ga converts outside its core congregation of Euro-Africans. Its goals were shaped by the doctrines of Württemburg pietism, which stressed the ideal of self-contained rural communities of "scholar-farmers," and the Mission distrusted what it considered to be the morally corrupting urban milieu of Accra. Instead it concentrated its efforts on the construction of a network of interior stations throughout the southeast Gold Coast, looking always—like the Methodists—to Asante as its ultimate goal.[8] For decades the Basel Mission avoided preaching in heavily populated Dutch Accra, only beginning to build a small, mostly non-Ga, congregation in the town following the removal of its Trading Company from Osu to new premises on Kinka's High Street in

1872.[9] Evangelistic efforts in Accra remained focused on the creation of a segregated Christian community, or Salem, to the north of Osu, morally and spatially removed from the seething "Babel" that was the old town quarters.

In common with British officialdom, the European evangelists of the Basel Mission betrayed a distinct rural bias in their view of African culture on the Gold Coast. Yet the Basel project, like its Methodist counterpart among the Fante of Cape Coast, had a profound impact on social change in the colonial city and on indigenous Ga readings of state, society, and history. Osu became the headquarters of the Mission's "Ga District," encompassing the Ga- and Dangme-speaking regions from Accra east to the Volta, from where indigenous catechists and teachers were gradually recruited.[10] Like their Twi-speaking brethren from Akuapem and elsewhere, this corps of young men was regarded by the missionaries to be essential not only for evangelism per se, but also for the program of vernacular education and the recording of organic folklore and history in which Württemburg pietism was grounded.[11] Despite the emphasis on African agency and the vernacular, the strictly hierarchical Basel Mission, with its greater numbers of European missionaries, was somewhat slower than the Methodists in ordaining its African catechists. This state of affairs clearly frustrated such long-serving evangelists as the independent-minded Carl Reindorf. It was Reindorf, finally ordained in 1872, whose *History of the Gold Coast and Asante* was to represent the most remarkable indigenous contribution to the Mission's extensive scholarly program.[12]

Carl Reindorf: Ga Pastor and Historian

Carl Reindorf's biography not only sheds light on his key role in the production of knowledge of the Ga past, it also provides an intimate case study with which to chart the dynamics of the Christian encounter in Accra. Born in 1834 at the Dangme trading town of Gbugbla (Prampram), he was the son of Christian Reindorf (1806–1865), a Euro-African of Danish-Ga ancestry, and Anoa Ama (a.k.a. Hannah, 1811–1902), a Ga woman of Kinka.[13] Carl Reindorf was recognized as a "mulatto" member of the Sanshishiwe lineage of Osu's Asante Blohum *akutso*, yet also had links to centers of political and ritual power in Kinka.[14] It was sitting at the feet of his paternal grandmother, Okaiko, Reindorf tells his readers, that as a child he was introduced to Ga traditions, and it was she who inspired him to begin the systematic collection of oral material eventually published in the *History*.[15] The young Reindorf was also close to his maternal grandmother, Amarkai, who like Okaiko was a member of the powerful Onamokowe of the Gbese *akutso*.

Although Reindorf's father was regarded as a Christian, it was his mother Anoa Ama who reportedly "had the say in religious affairs."[16]

This balance of religious influence between a devout Ga mother and a somewhat indifferent mulatto father appears to have been the norm among the young scholars of Reindorf's generation.[17] A devotee of Ligble, the principal civic deity at Gbugbla, she offered her infant son to the *jemawon* as a *wonbi* ("child of the *won*"), a status that often led to a vocation as a ritual specialist.[18] "I should have become a priest either of Nai at Akra or Klote at Christiansborg," Reindorf muses, "if I had not been born a mulatto and become a Christian."[19] In 1842, Reindorf was enrolled in the Danish school at Osu and two years later was baptized. In 1847, he recalled in a robust ordination speech, "I felt no more relish for the Danish language," and he switched to the new Basel Mission school, where classes were conducted in English.[20] It was about this time that Reindorf conducted his first experiment in Christian worship, appealing to God to prevent his threatened enlistment as a Danish soldier, "an office I never liked."[21] When, in 1850, Rev. Johannes Zimmermann arrived at Osu and initiated the policy of teaching in the Ga vernacular rather than in English, most of the scholars abandoned the school, Reindorf heading down the Dangme coast as a trading agent for an uncle. At this time his mother attempted to renew his attachment to the Ligble cult. However, a dramatic incident in which a *woyo* when possessed by the *jemawon* Ligble failed to recognize him—a *wonbi*, the god's own "child"—sowed seeds of doubt in his mind as to the veracity of indigenous deities. In 1852, Christian, now seemingly imposing his will in religious matters over the strong-minded Anoa Ama, recalled his son to Accra, enrolling him as a trainee catechist under Zimmermann. Although confirmed into the church, his belief in a Christian God, he later admitted, was as yet nominal, his process of personal conversion continuing fitfully for a number of years.

Reindorf's personal conversion narrative raises a number of issues. The first concerns the religious affiliation, and wider social identity, of Euro-Africans. Adherence to Christianity was certainly one of a range of cultural attributes that contributed to a distinct "mulatto" identity in nineteenth-century Accra. The nature and boundaries of that identity were so fluid, however, that the terms "Euro-African" and "mulatto" are of limited analytical value without individual contextualization. Reindorf readily identified himself—and was seen by others—as a mulatto. Had he continued to be attached to the *gbatsu* of Ligble at Gbugbla and become a traditional religious practitioner, he would still have been considered in some ways a mulatto, yet in other ways his identity within the community would have been quite different. Moreover, it would be mistaken to assume that the shift away from established Ga cultural practices on the part of the largely Euro-African merchant elite necessarily implied a concomitant move toward practicing Chris-

Figure 5.1   Rev. Carl Reindorf with a group of Osu Christians, c. 1900. (Photograph by Max Schultz [at left of photo], Basel Mission. Copyright Basel Mission Archive, Basel, Switzerland. Ref. No. D-30.03.058. Reproduced with permission.)

tianity. As we have seen, much of the hostility between the missionaries and Euro-African merchants was generated by the robustly secular life-styles of the latter. When in 1883 C. J. Bannerman, a scion of Accra's most famous Euro-African family, was confirmed into the Basel church, Reindorf reflected that "of all the youngmen from Accra who have studied at Sierra Leone, and also of all the Bannermans . . . he only . . . has desired to lead a Christian life. May he really become a light for the Bannermans!"[22]

A second and related issue is that of the social impact of western education. If many nineteenth-century Euro-African merchants were little more than nominal Christians, then formal education represented a more definitive requisite of elite status. Education (*wolonkwemo*) and, more specifically, literacy (*wolon nilee*) were central to the social identity of the *owula*, the wealthy and influential "gentleman."[23] With the expansion of the mercantile economy and the apparatus of colonial rule, literacy had important occupational consequences for the growing numbers of "scholars" in Accra. The emphasis placed by Reindorf and other catechists on the role of schooling in their conversion suggests the importance of the missions' provision of formal education and the attainment of literacy in the perception of the social power of Christianity. The equation of the power of literacy with Christianity, however, was a slow and complex process, as Reindorf's scholastic career indicates. The so-called "language question" continued to be a contentious issue, the Basel Mission's emphasis on vernacular primary education attracting protests from those who had identified proficiency in English as a vital resource in colonial Accra. "Why should we trouble ourselves about Ga, our own language we hear already?" Reindorf was repeatedly asked. "We prefer English, for we shall have advantage by that!"[24] These sentiments accorded with the requirements of the colonial state, the Education Ordinance of 1882 stipulating that mission schools could receive financial assistance only if English was the medium of learning.[25]

Conversion in Ga Town and Country

Despite the growing importance of literacy in the colonial town, many early conversions took place outside the context of the link between Christianity and Western education. A large proportion of those initially drawn to the new religion, particularly in the farming villages of the Accra plains, appear to have been slaves, pawns, outcasts, and others whose position in the Ga community was liminal and ambiguous.[26] In common with other African societies, part of the attraction of Christianity for those of low status was that the Church represented a body of potential social allies. Membership provided a range of resources—spiritual and otherwise—which could alleviate a lack of social power. It was these individuals who traditionally would have been among those most inclined to become *agbamei*, devotees, or *wonwebii*, "shrine slaves," of indigenous cults. Reindorf's first ten years as an ordained pastor were spent at Mayera, a village on the Accra plains near the main Basel Mission outstation of Abokobi. His report of a pastoral visit to a hamlet headed by a Christian convert neatly captures the position of a slave community at the very margins of the Ga social formation and on the cusp of self-generated conversion: "When I was there, one of them told me, 'We do not know to what party we belong; because we never go to Homowo . . . neither have we . . . observed Christmas since a very long time, therefore we celebrated last Christmas'. But how they . . . celebrated it is plain: without God and without Christ, a new invented Homowo!"[27]

If the open spaces of Accra's rural hinterland continued to provide a certain freedom for groups of slaves and other marginalized people to experiment with new modes of belief, the crowded ritual space of the coastal towns was altogether more contested. The most volatile conflict between established authorities and Christian converts arose in the early 1870s in La, the populous *man* to the immediate east of Osu and locus of the cult of the powerful oracular *jemawon* Lakpa. In 1870, the Basel Mission leapt at an offer made by La *mantse* Male Atsem of a piece of land in the town for a church and school, employing Reindorf and the renowned Ga lay preacher Paulo Mohenu as intermediaries in the transaction.[28] The authority of the La *mantse* to alienate land and thereby provide an opening for Christianity was challenged by Lakpa *wulomo* Boi Fio and the local devotees (*agbamei*) of the cult, who mobilized forcefully against the Mission by repeatedly breaking down the building works.[29] The Mission responded by turning to the British courts, successfully suing Boi Fio and his followers.[30] Resistance faltered, allowing the chapel and school to be completed. Shortly afterward an outbreak of smallpox swept through La, an event widely believed to be connected with the religious conflict. A number of alarmed *Labii* began tentatively to approach the newly established church, membership rising from 7 to 57 between 1873 and 1875.[31] Local tension remained high, again escalating when Christian converts broke with custom by fishing on Tuesdays, the day consecrated to the sea god Nai. Led by Abraham Odamete, who had been forbidden from even approaching the sacred precincts of the Kpeshi lagoon or the seashore, the action of the La Christians was considered an act of desecration that further "fanned the flames of persecution."[32]

The contours of Christian conversion were also determined by gender relations, and in particular by the institution of marriage. Accra was little different from elsewhere in Africa insofar as the missionaries viewed polygynous marriage as one of the greatest obstacles to the inculcation of Christian values and the creation of a self-sustaining Christian community.[33] It was largely in response to representations from the Basel and Methodist missions that the colonial government, albeit with some reluctance, enacted a Marriage Ordinance in 1884. The new law recognized monogamous marriage as legally distinct from "country" or "native" marriage, and both Missions made unions under the provisions of the Ordinance a condition of church membership.[34] However, European and indigenous churchmen, as well as secular educated African opinion, subsequently began to express serious misgivings regarding the 1884 legislation.[35] In common with other towns on the West African coast such as Lagos, the tension between Christian and country marriage emerged as a complex social issue.[36] Although the missionaries had favored legislation in order to curtail polygyny and divorce within their congregations, it became apparent that the near impossibility of obtaining the latter when married under the Ordinance was losing the churches both potential and existing converts.[37] Victorian Christian notions of domesticity clearly conflicted with the fiercely guarded independence of many Ga women. Secular African opinion was more concerned with problems of inheritance, and with the fact that the greater social status of Christian marriage was leading to escalating and socially corrosive monetary costs.[38] A general complaint, as noted by the report of the Enquiry commissioned

Figure 5.2 "King of Christiansborg and his [unnamed] bride," c. 1890. Wedding portrait of Gottfried Alema Dowuona (c. 1840–1897), a Basel Mission catechist and teacher enstooled as Osu *mantse* in 1887. (Copyright Basel Mission Archive, Basel, Switzerland. Ref. No. QW-30.11.30. Reproduced with permission.)

in 1905 to reform the Marriage Ordinance, was that "the wife is apt to become 'wild,' that she 'behaves proudly against her husband,' and is 'not so submissive as a woman married by native law.'"[39] As we shall see, rising patriarchal concern in Accra over the moral dangers posed by excessive female autonomy was not confined to the ranks of the Christian community.

As in other parts of Africa, the advance in the fortunes of Christianity in Accra was linked to the expansion of colonial rule. After ploughing stony ground for many decades, by the end of the nineteenth century the churches were an established part of town life, the Basel and Methodist missions being joined by the Roman Catholics in 1893 and the Anglicans in 1905.[40] In the political arena, the enstoolment of a Christian or the conversion of an existing officeholder—as in the early case of Osu *mantse* Frederick Noi Dowuona—rarely led to a complete rupture with custom. Rather, a series of negotiations tended to ensue, whereby the *manbii* agreed to excuse the convert from certain sacral duties associated with the stool.[41] As J. R. Myers, who became the caretaker of the Akanmaji stool in 1894, explained: "As I am a Wesleyan I did not wish to perform the customary ceremonies. The Wesleyan elders allowed me to look after the stool but not to sacrifice. Aikai used to do the ceremonial part."[42] These compromises seem to have accelerated the ongoing separation of sacred and secular authority in Accra. A. B. Quartey-Papafio described this process occurring within his own Kpakpatsewe in the 1880s. The head of the lineage, he writes, traditionally served as both *akwashontse* and *wulomo* of the *jemawon* Gua, the god of thunder, lightning, and blacksmithing. During the tenure of his father William Quartey-Papafio and then mission-educated uncle William Quartey, the office of Gua *wulomo* was hived off to a separate branch of the *we*.[43] Both pagan and Christian hierarchies were ready to compromise over the issue of conversion. The perceived benefits of enstooling literate scholars, men whose command of new skills enabled them better to deal with the demands of colonial power, made often staunchly traditionalist Ga elders more willing to tolerate the intimate connection between literacy and Christianity.[44]

MUSLIMS, CHIEFS, AND PRIESTS:
THE "BRAIMAH THE BUTCHER AFFAIR"

Although religious change in early colonial Accra must primarily be seen in terms of the encounter between indigenous structures of belief and Christianity, the latter was not the only world religion to have an impact on the town. Few Ga actually converted to Islam, although some Muslims, most notably members of the Brazilian Tabon community, effectively "became" Ga. Many Ga, however, readily utilized selective elements of the Islamic faith, Reindorf noting in 1876 how peripatetic Muslim diviners made a healthy living manufacturing the amulets used in obtaining the goals of war and peace.[45] Yet from the perspective of the late nineteenth century, with the Methodist and Basel missions making laboriously slow inroads into the Ga community and the immigrant Muslim population rising steadily, the dominance of Christianity over Islam in Accra was far from certain. In terms of Ga politics, relations with the Muslim community was, if anything, a more salient issue than those with the Christian missions.[46] Indeed, an attempt to incorporate the Muslim community into the established Ga order following the death of Taki Tawia in 1902 had widespread political repurcussions. Popularly dubbed the "Braimah the Butcher Affair," the ensuing dispute tells us much about religious and social change in turn-of-the-century Accra.

The arrival of the Tabons from Brazil in 1836 represented the first influx of Muslims into Accra. Incorporated into the Otublohum *akutso* under the patronage of Ankra of Dadebanwe, these ex-slaves and their descendants, while retaining a distinct identity based largely on their continuing adherence to Islam, became recognized as very much a part of the Ga community.[47] In the following decades a trickle of Hausa traders settled in Accra, one of whom, Malam Idris Naino from Katsina, was recognized as the first Muslim headman (*sarkin zongo*) and Friday Imam.[48] Numbers of Muslim migrants increased from the 1870s, the Hausa pioneers being joined by Yoruba, Fulani, and other ethnic groups. Ga leaders granted the expanding community permission to reside in their own quarter, or *zongo*, to the immediate north of Kinka, and in villages on the Accra plains.[49] In contrast with the Tabon returnees, these later Muslim settlers remained aloof from indigenous affairs, a separation that reflected both the strength of their regional trading diasporas and the changing power structure of colonial Accra. Even further removed from established norms of patron-clientage were the police of the "Hausa" Constabulary, who from 1888 were headquartered at the colonial capital in a new cantonment located between Kinka and Osu.[50] Although not all practiced Islam and most spoke a vehicular variety of Hausa, the troops developed a close relationship with the civilian Muslim community, illustrated most graphically by the willingness of the Muslims to mobilize in aid of colonial law and order in the conflicts of the 1880s and 1890s. Individual soldiers also forged a role in civilian affairs, most notably the famous Native Officer Ali (d. 1908), who by the 1890s had emerged as a leader of Accra's Hausa community and a broker with the colonial state.[51] All this served to exacerbate the social distance between the two communities, many Ga leaders regarding the growing autonomy and power of Islam with some anxiety.[52]

Cultural tensions between Muslim and Ga surfaced again in 1891, when it emerged that the former were fishing, hunting crocodiles, and cutting firewood at the sacred Sakumo River, in ways that contravened customary practice. Asere *mantse* Akrama explained the gravity of the situation to the government: "It is . . . our rule (or the fetish's) that no-one is to fish in the River Sakumo with baskets, . . . a thing never done before in this country since the World was made. This is a serious offence . . . and if we all are not depended on the Government, this is a case that Accra people will not care to lose . . . their lives. This River Sakumo we look upon as our greatest support."[53] When Sakumo *wulomo* Ogbame and the chiefs demanded that the Hausa refrain from violating the *jemawon*, they simply refused to comply.[54] The sudden death of a kinsman of Taki Tawia was widely believed in Accra to be a result of the continuing desecration. The *Ga mantse*, who voiced the fear that he would be the next to incur the wrath of Sakumo, finally succeeded in halting basket fishing through an injunction in the High Court.[55] Despite this legal intervention, disputes between Muslim settlers and Ga office-holders over access to the Sakumo would continue into the first decades of the twentieth century.[56]

Although the Ga tended to identify Muslim migrants simply as "Hausas," what was in reality an increasingly heterogeneous community was itself becoming prone to factional dispute. When Malam Idris Naino died in 1893, he was succeeded as Friday Imam by his brother Abu Bakr and as *sarkin zongo* by his son Muhammad Baako.[57] By the end of the decade, the authority of these Hausas to speak for all Muslims was challenged by the Yoruba under the leadership of Braimah, a butcher from Ilorin who had made his fortune rearing cattle on the Accra plains for the urban market. In 1899, Braimah charged Abu Bakr with adultery and declared one Malam Osumanu to be Imam, a claim supported by a third ethnic faction, the Fulani community. With conflict over the Sakumo River continuing, Taki Tawia appears to have grasped an opportunity to assert Ga influence over the divided Muslims. In the final months of his life he began to make preparations for the recognition of Braimah as a chief and *anobulo*, "councillor." This action was perceived to be more than merely extending recognition to the leader of a "stranger" community. Rather, it was seen as a step toward the full incorporation of Braimah and his followers into the town, as groups of "*gboi*" had been assimilated throughout Accra's history.

Taki Tawia died before he could put his plan into action. After forty years as "father of the town," his demise triggered a period of dissonance and discord in Accra. The ambiguity surrounding the line of descent through which Taki had secured the stool in 1862 raised a question mark over which of the three "royal" *wei* in Abola the succession should pass.[58] Problems were compounded by uncertainty regarding exactly who was entitled to manage the stool while a suitable successor was chosen. Gbese *mantse* Okaija, who many thought should assume the position of acting

Ga mantse, had withdrawn from politics and left Accra. A forceful and energetic character, Okaija (1892–1910) had been in dispute with both Taki and the "youngmen" of the Gbese *asafo* companies some years earlier, and had repaired to Krobo to trade.[59] Moreover, the influential Asere *mantse* Akrama had died in 1896, and his stool remained vacant until late in 1902. In the power vacuum it was Taki's close associates from the Abola *akutso* who attempted to stamp their authority on town affairs: Kojo, an *asafoatse* and famous *tabilo* (warrior) who had presided over the late *mantse*'s funeral; J. E. Mettle, a scholar and well-known traditional doctor; and Okai Mensah, a son of *Ga mantse* Yaote (1859–1862) acting as stool caretaker. In November, they decided to go ahead with the formal installation of Braimah, presenting the Yoruba butcher with the regalia of office that Taki had ordered to be made. Braimah sent calabashes of kola nuts to leading Muslims with messages declaring that "he had been elected a chief by the people of Accra," and for nights afterward the *zongo* echoed with the celebratory drumming of his Yoruba followers.[60]

The right of the Abola elders to take such a step was immediately contested by the other quarters. In early December, the installation of Braimah was considered by the *akwashon* court. The *akwashon* ruled that the installation was null and void, that Kojo and Okai Mensah were guilty of "vainly swearing the King's oath," and that the Gbese *mantse* was indeed the correct person to manage the Ga stool.[61] Messengers were sent to Krobo to pacify Okaija, who after some persuasion returned to Accra with his personal prestige considerably enhanced. Defying the *akwashon*, Abola leaders continued to maintain that Okai Mensah was stool caretaker. Invoking urban perceptions of the moral topography of town and country, they argued that Okaija's prolonged absence in the "bush" rendered him unfit to manage town affairs.[62]

The "Braimah the Butcher Affair" had escalated to the point where the central issue had become the balance of Ga political power, between Abola and the other *akutsei*, and between the secular and sacral components of the office-holding hierarchy. Requesting more information on the historical antecedents of the status of the Gbese *mantse*, the colonial government received a detailed account dating back to the mid-eighteenth century by P. C. Randolf, an articulate spokesman for the Gbese *akutso*. The Gbese *mantse*, Randolf explained, customarily took charge of political affairs when the Ga stool was vacant, while sacral duties were retained by functionaries of the Abola *akutso*.[63] A key element in this distribution of power was the office of Sakumo *wulomo*, the holder of which came from the Sakumowe of Gbese but was at the same time closely associated with the ritual aspects of the *Ga mantse*'s Okaikoi stool.

This most powerful of sacral offices had not been invulnerable to the forces of religious change. In 1894, Sakumo *wulomo* Ogbame had converted to Christianity, his baptism and public "confession" being reported by the Methodist missionaries as a spectacular breakthrough in their evangelizing efforts.[64] Few details exist of the public reaction to this dramatic event. What is clear is that Ogbame, who took the name Paul Mensah, quit Accra soon after. He was reported as returning eight years later, a month before the death of Taki Tawia, having renounced Christianity and seeking to reestablish himself as *wulomo*.[65] By early 1903, he was again exercising his right to collect the revenue from the ferry over the Sakumofio lagoon, dividing the money with *asafoatse* Kojo and supporting the Abola *akutso* in the interregnum dispute. This proved too much for Okaija and the Gbese leaders. On May 4 they attempted to depose Ogbame and to physically evict him from the sacred precincts of Sakumotsoshishi (lit. "under Sakumo's tree").[66] Despite the assistance of the colonial police, this operation proved unsuccessful, and it was a further three weeks before Okaija managed to dislodge the controversial *wulomo*. The incident forced the British to clarify their policy on the role of the police in Accra, officials being more than a little surprised to learn that Okaija had simply requested the men from the police station and then used them to pursue his own political ends.

What had enabled the Gbese faction to isolate and remove *wulomo* Ogbame was that *mantse* Okaija struck a deal with Okai Mensah and the Abolas. On May 28, after a meeting brokered by Legislative Council member Chief John Vanderpuye, Okaija "beat gong-gong" through the streets of Kinka to the effect that the dispute was over.[67] Okai Mensah agreed to accept the ruling of the *akwashon* court that political authority following the death of a *Ga mantse* passes to Gbese, and in return appears to have been assured that his choice as successor would be accepted by the other quarters. On January 25, 1904, the Abola elders enstooled one Kwaku Otsire, a twenty-year-old tradesman and the maternal grandson of *Ga mantse* Ofori Kpakpo of Teiko Tsuruwe (1856–1859), under the name Taki Obili.[68] Meanwhile, the parallel dispute within the Muslim community was largely settled by the intervention of the British government, which requested Muhammad Fulata Bornu, a respected cleric resident at Cape Coast, to take over as Imam at Accra.[69] With the exception of Muhammad Baako and a small group of followers, this solution was accepted by all the parties. Braimah retained recognition as the *de facto* head of Accra's Muslim Yorubas, the one-time butcher from Ilorin consolidating his position as a local notable.[70]

The political conflict over the status of Braimah and the succession to the Ga stool is illustrative of the ways in which Accra was changing by the turn

Figure 5.3 The Accra Central Mosque, c. 1920s. (Photograph by F. D. Walker, Wesleyan Methodist Missionary Society Archives, File 1195. Copyright The Methodist Church. Reproduced with the permission of the School of Oriental and African Studies Library, London.)

of the century. Incoming migrants were no longer required to secure the patronage of Ga officeholders, Hausa notables instead establishing themselves as urban patrons, *mai gida*, in their own right. Fortified by mercantile wealth and a religion entirely removed from local sources of spiritual power, Muslim settlers forged a new brokering role and an independent cultural niche in the colonial city. This self-confidence was physically symbolized by the construction of a Friday mosque in the *zongo* in the 1890s. A bitter, seven-year factional dispute over the control of the mosque following the death of Braimah in 1915 underlines the continuing importance of the building in the cultural identity of Accra's Muslims.[71]

Accra's function as a locus of sacred sites is further suggested by the struggle for physical control over the Sakumo *gbatsu*. The importance of the Sakumo cult center was graphically demonstrated with the rise to power of Taki Kome in 1826, and the shrine would remain a highly contested political resource into the twentieth century. Political action in Accra was historically focused on three sacred meeting places: Sakumotsoshishi, Mojawe, the site of the *mantsemei*'s appeal court, and Amugina, ancient site of the *gbatsu* of the god Amugi. In the early colonial period these were joined by two purely secular spaces: Akoto-Lamptey Square, and from the 1910s Bukom Square, in the heart of the Asere quarter.[72]

THE POLITICS OF THE SACRED AND SECULAR, 1904–1910

Visions of the Colonial Town

On two consecutive days in February 1904, a large party of Ga dignitaries and their followers gathered at Christiansborg Castle to present the newly enstooled *Ga mantse* Taki Obili to the British authorities and to bid farewell to the departing Governor Nathan. A month later, the chiefs reconvened at the seat of colonial power to welcome Nathan's successor, John Rodger. These meetings, the transcripts of which are preserved in the official "Palaver Books," provide a revealing glimpse at the general state of affairs in Accra at the start of the new century as perceived by the participants, both African and European.[73] "You are not illiterate . . . [so] will therefore understand European ideas as to the value of healthy towns, of sound education, of intelligent agriculture and of honest trade," Nathan counseled the young *Ga mantse*, summing up the colonial view of good government. "You must avoid borrowing money," he cautioned, "this means you must avoid litigation."[74] The *mantsemei* were indeed concerned about litigation: not with avoiding it, but with the old problem of exercising their legal jurisdiction without coercive power and in the face of competition from the colonial courts. "Now-a-days," Gbese *mantse* Okaija explained to Nathan, "we have no power to force people to attend our courts and . . . we scarcely get our living. . . . The only thing we wish you to do . . . before you go is to give us the power over our people we have asked for."[75] Nathan reiterated colonial policy: that the NJO of 1883, which gave official recognition to chiefs' tribunals and prisons, would continue to be selectively applied only to rural districts without immediate access to colonial courts.[76] He noted with satisfaction, however, that after years of sullen resistance the people of Accra were finally beginning to pay the municipal house tax and to recognize the value of the Town Council, a development acknowledged by Okaija.

The town leaders also voiced considerable pessimism regarding the outlook for agriculture and trade, and there is some evidence to suggest that the assessment of their own chronic financial insecurity and of more general economic difficulties in Accra was not without foundation. The census of 1901 had recorded the urban population as 17,892, a fall of over 2,000 from the 1891 figure.[77] Both push and pull factors probably accounted for this decline: the dislocation of patron-client trading networks in the 1890s, the continuing importance of labor migration to the Bights, and, it might be posited, the beginnings of Ga involvement in the nascent cocoa economy in the forests of southern Akyem Abuakwa. An increase in male outmigration is indicated by gender ratios in Kinka and Nleshi, where 1,060 more women than men were enumerated in 1901 compared with only 433 more women ten years earlier.[78] In 1904, moreover, the Accra region was in the grip of a severe drought that had already lasted several years, forcing farmers to abandon plots in the vicinity of the town and causing severe hardship for both urban and rural dwellers.[79] As in the past, drought served to exacerbate religious conflicts over competing claims to ecological management, trouble flaring again at La when the Christian *mantse* Tagoe Asuman (1901– destooled 1905) was blamed for the lack of rain by the *agbamei* of the Lakpa cult.[80]

The desire voiced by the departing Governor Nathan for "healthy towns," so often official shorthand for a more thoroughgoing control of urban space, reemerged at the center of Accra politics in the months following Taki Obili's enstoolment. As we have seen, the wish to rid the city of the more visible manifestations of African "custom" was not confined to the British administration; it had long been part of the modernizing discourse of the literate— and increasingly Christian—local elite. The outrage in the 1870s over the powers of the Naa Dede Oyeadu *wulomo* was an early indication of how religion and belief lay at the heart of this contested vision of Accra. As Cape Coast's *Gold Coast Leader* fulminated in 1903: "It is a great pity that public demonstration of Fetish dances is so much encouraged at Accra the headquarters of the Gold Coast Colony than other places. Fetish Priests and Priestesses can be seen . . . disturbing the peace of the town with their drums and noise and no Constable goes to . . . stop them. On Sundays . . . dances take place regularly. Dances which ought not to be entertained by any civilized and Christian Government."[81] Here, the *Leader* betrays not only a Christian vision of "traditional" Africa, but a stereotypical Fante view of Accra, whose elevation to colonial capital continued to rankle with the Cape Coast elite.

The ideal of a "civilized and Christian" capital city was, of course, one shared to a large extent by the colonial regime. This official vision of Accra stood in contrast to an alternative reading of urban civilization, that defined by the cosmology and ritual topography of the Ga world. Neither of these visions was monolithic, nor were they immune from change. Their fundamental antagonism, however, can be expressed quite simply: whereas Accra represented the political, cultural, and sacral epicenter of the Ga world, British officials viewed the colonial capital as an essentially European domain, unfit for a "proper" African state. African affairs, it was repeatedly opined, were best conducted in the bush, not in the envisaged urban showcase of expatriate enterprise and ordered modernity.

Figure 5.4 *Ga mantse* Taki Obili and his household, c. 1904. This portrait was probably taken at the time of Taki Obili's enstoolment in 1904. The *Ga mantse* and the unnamed women on his right wear luxury *kente* cloth from Asante. (Photograph by F. A. Ramseyer, Basel Mission. Copyright Basel Mission Archive, Basel, Switzerland. Ref. No. QV-30.071.0471. Reproduced with permission.)

In 1904, the government moved to further restrict ritual practice in Accra, following alarm at the "pandemonium" that reigned in the streets of the capital during the month-long *yalafemo* ("Great Lamentation") for the late Taki Tawia.[82] The initial target of official opprobrium was the *Homowo* festival, in particular the sexually explicit *oshi* dance. After complaints of a particularly graphic *oshi* in August, the dance was banned. The newly enstooled Taki Obili was fined the hefty sum of fifty pounds and had his permit to celebrate the remaining *Homowo* festivities canceled.[83]

Less than a year later, Taki Obili again fell foul of the British authorities, following an accidental drowning in the Sakumofio lagoon eight miles west of Accra. The coastal lagoons (*fajii*; sing. *fa*) occupied a prominent place in Ga ritual topography. They were regarded as physical manifestations of powerful deities, and continued to have considerable economic value in terms of saltmaking, fishing, and—in the case of the Sakumofio—ferry tolls. The violation of Sakumo by Muslim settlers remained a volatile political issue, yet control over the lagoon was also contested within the Ga hierarchy. Following his enstoolment, Taki Obili complained that certain chiefs were refusing to hand over ferry tolls cus-

Figure 5.5   The funeral procession for a departed *mantse* passes through the streets of Accra, c. 1917. (Copyright Basel Mission Archive, Basel, Switzerland. Ref. No. D-30.01.045. Reproduced with permission.)

tomarily divided between the *Ga mantse* and the Sakumo *wulomo*.[84] Despite some decline in the status of the great war deity, the lagoon itself together with the coastline at its mouth, known as *fa na*, remained a highly sacred and spiritually hazardous zone, intricate rites governing the seasonal opening and closing of the Sakumofio waters to the sea.[85] A drowning in the lagoon was potentially catastrophic. It necessitated the temporary abandonment of the *fa na* fishing villages and of canoe traffic while the *wulomo* orchestrated purification rites, services for which the family of the deceased were required to pay.[86] In August 1905 Taki Obili, the reinstated Sakumo *wulomo* Ogbame, and Amartey Kwao, headman of the *fa na* village of Fayemo, pleaded guilty in the DC's court to charges of illicitly burying the body of a young girl who had drowned in Sakumofio, "with intent to prevent the holding of an inquest."[87]

Death and burial had long been a contested political issue in Accra. The conviction of Taki Obili and his codefendants and the subsequent proscription of the custom of exacting payments from the family of drowned persons marked a further encroachment by British authority into Ga funerary ritual. This process had earlier been signposted by the out-

lawing of mortuary slaying in the mid-nineteenth century and of intramural sepulture in 1888. The 1888 legislation lay at the center of the
campaign to improve the sanitary condition of the new colonial capital,
yet government attempts to cajole the townspeople to abandon the burial
of their dead beneath Accra's ancestral houses met with widespread resistance until the first years of the 1900s.[88] Reindorf reported in 1889
that the horror with which the Ga viewed interment in the new public
cemeteries was akin to that of being cast unburied into the bush. Fear of
being caught out by the new law was actually encouraging the return to
the fold of elderly backsliders. Many had left the Church specifically to
be laid to rest in their own houses, but when push came to shove pre-
ferred the sanctified mission cemetery to being consigned to a common
burial ground.[89] At the same time, the desire to be buried at least within
the confines of one's own town if not one's house continued to shape
attitudes to conversion. Thus, catechist Isaac Odoi wrote in 1897 that the
fear of being interred in the Basel Mission cemetery at Osu was one of
the main problems he faced in attracting adherents from the more stubbornly "pagan" *man* of Kinka.[90] The response of leading officeholders,
beginning with Sempe *mantse* Allotei in 1895 and followed by *Ga mantse*
Taki in 1902 and Gbese *mantse* Okaija in 1910, was to be buried instead
in Akan-style mausoleums constructed at sacred spots immediately outside the town boundaries. Given the ambiguous and potentially hazardous supernatural environment of these zones, this represented a major
innovation in Ga mortuary practice. As we will see in the next chapter, it
also led to the increasing politicization of burial in 1920s Accra.

Three months after the drowning at the Sakumofio lagoon, the British
mounted a third intervention into Ga ritual affairs. On November 10,
1905, in circumstances that presumably stemmed from fresh allegations
of priestly expropriation, the police raided the *gbatsu* in Asere of Naa
Dede Oyeadu, the *jemawon* who presided over childbirth.[91] The *wulomo*
Kofi Quaye and two assistants were arrested and later imprisoned, sacred objects removed, and the "Oyeadu fetish" suppressed, "to the joy of
Christians but to the Heathens sorrow."[92] The combined effect of this
succession of incidents in 1904–1905 was to confirm the impression
shared by colonial officers, sections of the educated indigenous elite, and
European and African churchmen that Accra—and Kinka in particular—
continued to represent a bastion of paganism and unsavory African tradition. Indeed, things appeared to be getting worse. "Since Tackie Obilie
has been placed on the . . . stool there has been a tendency on the part of
the natives to disregard more openly than formerly educated opinion,"
opined the Accra DC, citing as evidence "the 'Oshie Custom' parade in
the streets of Accra last year, the Otufu Custom at Christiansborg this

year, and now the publicity, almost impertinent, given to the Sekum [i.e., Sakumo] custom."[93] Despite colonial power, the steady advance of Christianity, and the weight of "educated opinion," Accra's urban identity continued to be shaped by its role as the sacral epicenter of the Ga world.

Towns, "Custom," and "Tribal Organization"

Recurring struggles over ritual space in the colonial capital must be located within the context of the evolution of the policy of indirect rule in the Gold Coast. While officials entertained hopes that the Ga townspeople would follow the "progressive" lead of the educated elite, by the turn of the century it was becoming clear that old political and social forms were not about to wither away in Accra. Despite Nathan's pronouncement on the distinctiveness of the coastal towns, 1904 saw the opening of a debate within the administration over whether or not to extend the provisions of the NJO to all parts of the old Colony.[94] This debate soon widened beyond the corridors of the Secretariat to the Ga quarters, as *mantsemei*, *wulomei*, lineage elders, and private big men—and occasionally "big women"—advanced conflicting claims to be the legitimate custodians of Ga custom.

A key public arena for dialogue and debate over the meanings of custom was Accra's Supreme Court. In a series of large-scale and often dramatic legal battles, control over economic resources became intertwined with the reformulation of political and ritual power. The spatial growth of the colonial capital and the rising value of urban land acted as catalysts for conflict. For successful litigants, the immediate spoils often came in the form of government compensation for urban land compulsorily acquired under the Public Lands Ordinance of 1876. However, escalating political conflict transcended the ostensible bone of contention—control over land—to encompass deeper questions of culture, belief, identity, and power: who was and who was not *ganyo kron*, a "true Ga"?; by what processes were strangers incorporated into the town?; which lineages, officeholders, and quarters held authority over which estates?[95] Rising tensions deepened two historic political fault lines within Accra: that between the authority of sacred and secular officeholders; and that between rival town quarters.

The first of these famous court actions was the so-called "Harbour Blockyard Case" of 1907. It was triggered when Alata *mantse* Kojo Ababio on the one hand and the Koole *wulomo* and people of the Sempe quarter on the other filed opposing claims over land required for extensions to Accra's port facilities.[96] At issue was the status of the Alata quarter and the ritual authority of the *wulomei* of Accra's great civic cults.

Koole *wulomo* Anan Bibio claimed that despite the accumulation of secular power by chiefs, the lagoon goddess Koole remained the sacred guardian and "owner" of Accra and all Ga lands.[97] The 1907 case set the tone for a succession of legal disputes in which the remaking of Accra was fought out over the following decade. As in subsequent actions, Kojo Ababio was represented by Thomas Hutton Mills, a barrister intimately associated with the Alata stool who was emerging as a successor to his late uncle Edmund Bannerman as the leading figure of the literate Ga elite.[98] Barrister for the Koole *wulomo* and the Sempe *akutso* was A. B. Quartey-Papafio, an equally articulate advocate of the historical rights of the Asere quarter and its allies in general, and his own family, Kpakpatsewe, in particular.[99] Kojo Ababio and Hutton Mills built their case around the contention that the land in question had been occupied by Alata people since the seventeenth century, when Wetse Kojo and his followers arrived with the English in Accra. Their adversaries sought to emphasize the alien identity of the Alatas, whose rights of occupation ultimately rested on the sanction of the Sempes, the original custodians of the land.

Much of the evidence turned on the meanings of Alata royal regalia, particularly the famous palanquin (*akpakai*) of Wetse Kojo. The *akpakai* had huge cultural significance in Accra, symbolizing the wealth and virtue of powerful strangers and—according to the Alata reading—their incorporation into the moral community of the town.[100] "The use of palanquins is not a Ga custom," Quartey-Papafio countered, Wetse Kojo and his successors being allowed to be borne in an *akpakai* only after paying customary fees to the Sempe *mantse*.[101] The importance of the palanquin in town affairs would have been plain enough to all Ga in court that day. A year earlier, Kojo Ababio had observed the funeral rites of his predecessors Kojo Ababio III and Kofi Oku, four weeks of ceremonies culminating in an ostentatious "second enstoolment" on January 29, 1906.[102] Kojo, surrounded by his chiefs, people, and the educated elite of James Town, was paraded aloft through the streets of Accra in the *akpakai* said to be that of Wetse Kojo.[103] Quartey-Papafio's point was that despite this recent display, Kojo Ababio was not a true Ga and that his authority derived, not from ritually sanctioned sources, but through the occupation of a stool created and maintained by wealth alone. The British judge, however, was convinced of the seniority of the Alata stool, awarding two-fifths of the compensation to Kojo Ababio and one-fifth each to the Sempe *akutso*, Akanmaji *akutso*, and Koole *wulomo*. The total sum of £110 would have been swallowed up by legal fees. What was really at stake was the balance of political power within James Town, the decision representing a legal benchmark in the struggle on the part of the Alata *akutso* to assert both its authority over Sempe and Akanmaji and its autonomy from Kinka and the *Ga mantse*.

These issues were being simultaneously contested outside of the colonial courts following the election of a new Sempe *mantse*, Anege Akwei, in September 1906. In a move aimed at countering Kojo Ababio's calculated show of power, the Sempe elders and Taki Obili announced that Anege Akwei was the senior *mantse* of Nleshi.[104] Faced with two office-holders claiming to be "James Town *mantse*," and in the process of formulating a new Native Jurisdiction Bill that would finally be applied to Accra, the government launched its inquiry into the workings of the Ga constitution. The Commission of Enquiry into Ga "tribal organization" of October 1907 was also prompted by claims emanating from the Asere *akutso*.[105] Asere leaders were anxious that recognition be extended to the *akwashon* court, and in 1906 barrister-journalist A. B. Quartey-Papafio took up the cudgel on behalf of the Ga military tribunal in the *Gold Coast Advocate*.

Quartey-Papafio's columns reveal the lengths to which rival Ga hierarchies struggled to maintain legal jurisdiction in the face of competition from colonial courts. It was not only the colonial government that was attempting to curtail the clout of ritual specialists in Accra. Between 1904 and 1905, the *Advocate* reported, the *mantsemei* had moved against the judicial prerogatives of the *wulomei*: "All the Fetish priests . . . were forbidden to hear cases or take fees for going into matters. A gong-gong was beaten throughout the Town proclaiming these . . . customary laws."[106] This represented a clear break with established practise in Accra. *Wulomei* had long been recognized as possessing the essential esoteric knowledge to "go into matters" regarding the divine and supernatural realms. Although Koole *wulomo* Anan Bibio was allied with prominent chiefs in the Harbour Blockyard Case against the threatening autonomy of Alata *mantse* Kojo Ababio, the *mantsemei* were wary of the claims of the *wulomo* and the Onamokowe to be the ultimate guardians of Ga lands. The efficacy of the proclamation terminating the adjudicatory powers of priests is unclear, but in 1914 Taki Obili and his fellow chiefs moved again. In an effort to stem "illicit" land sales, they announced that the Koole *wulomo* was prohibited from "having anything whatever to do with the stool lands of Accra of which he was caretaker," and that "we as Native Rulers . . . have . . . resumed the control and care of the said lands."[107]

The reformulation of "customary" law was further influenced by the 1907 Enquiry and the 1910 Amendment to the NJO. With regard to the status of the Sempe quarter, the commissioners concluded that Anege Akwei had been correctly enstooled as *mantse*, while Kojo Ababio was recognized to be strictly the leader of Alata rather than the whole of Nleshi.[108] Nevertheless,

British officialdom continued to regard the resourceful and modernizing figure of Kojo Ababio as the *de facto* "James Town *mantse*." Likewise, the Osu *mantse* was recognized as holding clear historical precedence in military and legal terms over the *nshonamajii* of La, Teshi, Nungwa, and Tema. While a general consensus among the Ga witnesses supported these views, that part of the Report dealing with the *akwashon* was based on altogether flimsier evidence. Judged to be an innovation that "does not appear to fill a place in the judicial system usual to native communities," it was refused official recognition as a native tribunal under the terms of the new NJO.[109]

The recognition that Accra's indigenous political order was different from that "usual to native [i.e., Akan] communities" led to further doubts as to whether the NJO should in fact be applied to the colonial capital at all. The fragmented nature of the Ga state was seen by some officials as having been exacerbated by the pace of recent social change, making it undesirable that "an old authority which the community is outgrowing be reimposed even in a modified form."[110] The hybrid urban environment of Accra was seen to be singularly unsuited to any form of indirect rule. Chief Justice W. B. Griffith, Jr. was adamantly opposed to the universal application of the amended NJO. He argued that the increasingly heterogeneous and educated population of Accra would be compelled to seek justice in "illiterate tribunals" rather than the readily accessible DC's court, in a situation where "the feeling between James Town and Ussher Town is . . . so strained that no James Town man expects justice from an Ussher Town Court."[111] However, despite both official and unofficial African opposition in the Legislative Council, the bill was finally passed at the end of 1910.[112]

It is telling that the first action of the *Ga mantse* under the terms of the new Ordinance was to bow to pressure from the administration and pass a series of bylaws prohibiting the performance of two "immoral" dances, *osibisaba* and *ashiko*, recently developed by the "youngmen" of Accra.[113] The evolution of new forms of popular culture in early-twentieth-century Accra will be discussed in the next chapter. It can simply be noted here that, despite repeated attempts at legislation, neither colonial officials nor indigenous authorities succeeded in securing effective control over the reformulation of Accra's cultural space. The appearance of these innovative dances and their accompanying musical styles—secular in nature but emerging both in form and in spirit from the proscribed *oshi* dance of the *Homowo* festival—indicates how old cultural motifs were transformed and reappropriated by subaltern groups. By the second decade of the new century, the ire of the established guardians of town morality was also directed toward the role of women—especially young women—as *woyei*, spirit mediums. The ensuing struggle emerged at the center of the process of Ga religious change in the colonial city.

GENDER, BELIEF, AND RITUAL POWER

The Rise of the *Woyei*

In October 1916, Christopher Brandford Nettey, a prominent "scholar" and *asafoatse* of the Gbese *akutso*, addressed a letter to Secretary for Native Affairs F. G. Crowther in which he outlined what he considered to be the main social and economic problems facing Accra. Nettey, who over the years had acquired a reputation as a critic of the established order—both colonial and indigenous—was far from happy with the "very deplorable condition of things" in the capital.[114] He directed the SNA's attention first to the rising price of food in Accra's markets: "Time was when foodstuff in general and fish in particular was very cheap, but now even those in the Government Service who are First Class Officers drawing the highest salary that a black-man can possibly earn . . . are complaining of the heavy bill." Dismissing the popular belief that inflation was due to the growing numbers of "strangers" migrating to Accra on the new railway, Nettey identified the cause as an alliance between unscrupulous chiefs, fishermen, and women traders dedicated to pushing up the price of fish.[115] "The women . . . can never deal fairly and justly with us; they buy fish on credit from the fishermen . . . and retail to the people at 100% so that the price is now fabulous."[116]

What is of relevance here is not the soundness or otherwise of this economic analysis (although the war years were indeed characterized by sharp fluctuations in the supply and price of food),[117] but the connection Nettey draws between the commercial shrewdness of Ga women and what he describes as the "increase of Fetich [sic] and Heathenism in Accra." Governor Griffith (1885–1895), he recalled, "gave an order that all . . . Fetich women dancers [i.e., *woyei*] were to be turned out of . . . Accra, and that under no circumstance were they to . . . dance in the Town," a move carried out following representations from Edmund Bannerman and Taki Tawia.[118] "It was a fact as it is today," he went on,

> that these Fetich women . . . scatter. . . poisonous liquids . . . to make people sick [then] . . . inform the friends and relatives . . . that it is such and such fetich that has taken hold of the individual. They are then . . . called in and . . . having the antidote ready . . . effect a cure . . . and the pocket of the fetich people is usually filled. If the individual dies, then the fetich people claim all the belongings of the dead which their friends and relatives readily hand over.[119]

During the years when the *woyei* were barred from dancing openly in Accra, Nettey believed, the rate of mortality fell markedly. However, owing to *Ga*

Figure 5.6 A *woyo*, with face and chest whitened with clay, draws an evening crowd in the streets of Osu, c. 1904. The steeple of the new Basel Mission chapel rises in the background. This photograph calls into question the efficacy of the ban on *woyei* practicing in Accra decreed by Governor Griffith and *Ga mantse* Taki Tawia in the 1890s, a ban not lifted until 1916. (Photograph by Max Schultz, Basel Mission. Copyright Basel Mission Archive, Basel, Switzerland. Ref. No. QD-32.032.0162. Reproduced with permission.)

mantse Taki Obili having recently married a *woyo*, "the old privileges have been granted with the result that the death rate is rising fearfully especially among women who are pregnant."[120] What he found particularly alarming was that the old *woyei* had not only returned to town but were openly training a new generation of young Ga women in their esoteric crafts.

Concern over the prominent role of women in the stubborn persistence of so-called "fetishism" in Accra continued to be voiced by male members of the largely Christian Ga elite. The fears expressed by Nettey in 1916 were taken up six years later by the *Gold Coast Independent* in a series of articles under the title "Akon fetish dance must be abolished." The *Independent*'s reportage confirmed that the activities of traditional religious practitioners had undergone a marked resurgence in Accra over the previous decade.[121] Most visible were the female mediums, *woyei*, of deities of the *akon* (Twi: *akom*) cult, "yam-eating" war gods reckoned to be of Akuapem origin whose rites were conducted, and who spoke through their *woyei*, in the Twi language.[122] "Women are more easily hypnotised and influenced by the practice than men," cautioned the *Independent*, citing cases of young girls who after watching *akon* performances in the street and noting the "awe and admiration which the onlookers demonstrate" had subsequently become possessed by the particular *jemawon*.[123] Families unable to pay the fees for the propitiation of the *jemawon* were forced to hand over the young woman to become an acolyte of the cult, an option that still entailed considerable expense:

> What happens is that the parents faced with such a financial crisis have to pawn . . . every valuable article they possess to raise the money to keep the daughters in servitude and drudgery for three years. The term of apprenticeship can be shortened according to the paying capacity. . . if the parents are able to pay cash down the whole affair may be gone through in three months! Very often other children . . . are given away as peons [i.e., pawns] in the way of domestic slavery to raise the . . . funds. . . . The writer was told of the case of a young girl who had been baptised into the Christian faith, who recently renounced her vows, having become possessed. The poor mother who was a Christian could not do otherwise than give up her . . . faith and adopt the fetish of her daughter. . . . The last account . . . was that she had gone stark mad. This condition . . . must have been brought about by worry and anxiety.[124]

It is instructive to compare these alarmist tones with Field's ethnographic observations on the issue. Arriving in the Ga towns in the early 1930s, Field too noted the prominence of female *woyei*, both those who acted as the mouthpiece of civic *jemawojii* and growing numbers of "private" or "freelance" mediums who usually offered their spiritual services in conjunction with a male herbalist.[125] In contrast with elite African opinion, Field did not regard such women as a threat to indigenous Christian civilization, but literacy and Christianity as dual threats to the virtues of the old Ga order. Field neatly encapsulated the tension between what she viewed as two opposed and irreconcilable systems of belief in the person of a *woyo* of Sakumo, who when first possessed by the god was a practicing Christian. "She was several times possessed, and eventually yielded and became an official *woyo*. To-day there is no *woyo*. . . more jealously conscious of the prestige of her calling then she."[126] "There are no stouter pillars of the ancient order," Field adds approvingly, "than those who have been Christians and deliberately come back."

The perception in Accra by the 1920s was that the influence of "freelance" ritual specialists was increasing at the expense of that of established religious and secular officeholders. This led to calls for the restoration of the *wulomei*'s ancient authority to manage the ritual topography of the Ga towns. One correspondent to the *Independent* regarded this rehabilitation as "essential for the protection of the Ga Nation":

> In the olden days whenever an okonfo (fetish man or woman) was in possession of idols or fetishes with the intent of destroying . . . people's lives, the priests who are our ministers and doctors had power to order the arrest of such an individual, and to give instructions that all of her idols . . . be seized. . . . And after the matter was gone into . . . the culprit was fined, and all the idols or fetish were burnt in public. . . . I therefore . . . appeal to all our Mantsemei and Priests . . . for the immediate resuscitation of the custom.[127]

The public incineration of ritual objects is a stereotypical image of the collision between Christian evangelism and paganism throughout sub-Saharan Africa. The demand voiced here provides a striking reminder that contests over religious authority continued to occur within the structures of indigenous belief.

The Case of Akoshia Sawyerr

It is a criminal prosecution in the Police Court that offers the most richly detailed insights into the gendered politics of indigenous religious belief in early colonial Accra. The case was something of a sensation in the capital. Reported verbatim in the *Gold Coast Independent* throughout the last three months of 1926, it served to provide further graphic evidence for those elite voices that had long warned of the intimate connection between the horrors of "fetishism," debt, servitude, and the machinations of dangerous women.[128] A similar language of moral crisis shaped by shifting gender relationships has also been identified in interwar Asante.[129] Whereas Allman locates an emerging climate of "gender chaos" firmly in Asante's rapidly commercializing cocoa economy, the emphasis in Accra seems to have been on the ritual rather than the economic power of Ga women. This difference may reflect the greater autonomy historically exercised by many Ga women in Accra's urban trading economy relative to the Akan forest kingdoms. In common with Asante, however, efforts by Ga women to secure economic and religious independence as "freelance" *woyei* posed a threat to the balance of conjugal and ritual power.

Historians and anthropologists have tended to offer two standard interpretations of the prominence of women in spirit possession cults in

Africa.[130] One focuses on the physiological basis of women's desire for spiritual healing, in particular problems associated with reproduction. The other emphasizes a context of gender conflict, stressing that cult membership offered women compensation for low social status. Although both these aspects appear to have played a role in the rise of the *woyei* in early colonial Accra, the case of Akoshia Sawyerr provides evidence for more recent and less instumentalist readings. As Strobel points out, these interpretations view both the cult and the act of possession as "cultural texts" embodying a range of ambivalent meanings, in particular meanings about gender. Rather than simply triggering the standard denunciations of the enemies of Christian civilization and patriarchal order, the events of 1926 also embody the ambivalent meanings of Accra as a sacred urban space.

The events leading to the prosecution and eventual conviction of the *woyo* Akoshia Sawyerr on charges of pawning and coercion, as reconstructed from testimony dispersed throughout the *Independent*'s reportage, can be adumbrated as follows. Early in 1926, Naa Aku Quartey, an Accra businesswoman, dispatched her niece Dede to the Akuapem town of Mampon to trade. Returning home on the Aburi Road, Dede's parcel fell off the back of the lorry as it passed through Oyamfa, a large *aklowa* on the Accra plains attached to the seaside town of La. Inquiries made by Aku revealed that the parcel, a bundle of textiles containing a tin full of money, had been found by Atchoi Afia, daughter of the Oyamfa farmer Botchway Kojo. When Atchoi denied having found the parcel, Aku swore a curse, invoking the destructive aid of three *jemawojii*, Afram, Fofie, and Odumantey. Some months later, an unusual number of deaths began to occur at Oyamfa. In the space of three months, eight people—including Atchoi's husband—had died. Amid growing alarm, Atchoi finally returned the parcel to Aku. The termination of the curse required the "pacification" (*dai*) of the three *jemawojii*, and in August Botchway Kojo contracted the *woyo* Akoshia Sawyerr to perform the necessary *daiamo* ceremony.

In common with many *woyei*, Akoshia was a well-known and respected figure in Accra. As a young girl she had earned her living by selling rum, until one day she was "embraced" by the *jemawon* Afram at the village of Mayera. Despite the resistance of her husband, Akoshia was apprenticed to the *akon* cult leader Bribri Kwadjo, under whom she completed her training in about 1919. Akoshia's success in her new calling can be gauged by the fact that by 1926, although she cannot have been more than thirty years old, she too had trained some ten *woyei*. She was accompanied to Oyamfa by an impressive entourage of twenty-four personal assistants (*sapati*) and musicians (*dadefoi*).[131] On August 19, the

Figure 5.7 A Ga *woyo*, c. 1890. The *woyo* wears prestigious *adinkra* cloth from Asante, bracelets and anklets of sacred white beads (*adobi*) and black seeds (*ayiblibi*), and carries her ritual sword. (Courtesy of the Foreign and Commonwealth Office Library, London.)

party set out from Accra to Oyamfa, where Akoshia performed the *daiamo*, during which she became possessed by Afram. The exercise was an acknowledged success. The deaths stopped, and as Akoshia herself testified: "When the fetishes [*jemawojii*] were in the village it became hot, but since the pacification it is cool."[132]

The alleged offense occurred with regard to the payment for the pacification. The bill amounted to over £55, an enormous sum in the 1920s and an indication of just how lucrative the vocation of *woyo* could be.[133] After

Botchway Kojo failed to raise the money in Accra, it was alleged that Akoshia accepted Atchoi Afia and her sister Kai as pawns to secure the debt. Akoshia denied this, claiming that she accepted Atchoi only as an apprentice *woyo* and Kai as a *sapati* to her sister. While possessed by Afram, who was speaking through her in Twi—a language she insisted she could not herself speak—Akoshia had by all accounts struck Atchoi on the head with her ritual sword. That night, according to some as a result of the blow, Atchoi too was violently seized by the *jemawon*. The charge of coercion arose from Akoshia allegedly having offered Atchoi a choice between becoming a *woyo*, or certain death at the hands of the god Afram.

What emerges from the courtroom testimony is the extent to which Ga leaders competed not only with the colonial state but also with female religious specialists for control over ritual space in Accra. When the *woyei* disregarded an attempt by Taki Tawia some three decades earlier to limit their powers of appropriation, the chiefs enlisted the aid of Edmund Bannerman and Governor Griffith in proscribing their activities within the town.[134] Banned from the arena of urban civilization, the *woyei* were allowed to dance in the "bush" only. In 1916, *Ga mantse* Taki Obili summoned a meeting of the banned religious practitioners, at which it was decided that they would be allowed to resume practice in Accra. Their fees were to be strictly limited to thirty-two shillings, one sheep, and stipulated amounts of cloth and utensils, bringing them into line with those charged for the uttering of oaths in *mantse*'s tribunals. The leading *akonfoi* agreed to this condition, paving the way for the widely reported expansion of the occupation of *woyo* in the streets of the capital.

More difficult to contextualize in a process of historical change is that evidence that directly addresses the issue of belief. Important here are Field's observations on the tension between the need of the *woyo* to "perform" in a set style, and the underlying belief in the power of the *jemawon* to possess her mind and body.[135] This tension was addressed by Akoshia in the witness-box of the colonial courtroom.[136] Her *jemawon*, she explained, was the river Afram, a tributary of the Volta running through Akwamu country. Each year, Akwamu associates delivered a quantity of water from the river, which when placed in her sacred pot and stared into to the hypnotic drumming of her *dadefoi* "brought on" Afram. Akoshia attempted to describe the moment she would lose consciousness with the arrival of the *jemawon*: "When you look in the pot . . . you see the fetish and talk to it, when you see it it looks like the river. You will see it white—like His Worship—the whole water appears white. . . . I have not seen a river speak, but when it embraces a person it speaks."[137] This testimony was followed by an extraordinary scene when Akoshia was conducted to the yard behind the courthouse with her full entourage in order to demonstrate the veracity of her claims. There she was duly possessed by Afram, the excitement among the onlookers being such that the police had to be called to disperse the crowd. Despite this display, the unfortunate Akoshia was found guilty on both charges and sentenced to one year's hard labor. In this case at least, the forces of colonial law and order together with those of indigenous patriarchy had won the day. Nevertheless, despite the lurid accusations of C. B. Nettey and others, many town notables who testified in the trial of Akoshia Sawyerr clearly regarded *woyei* with deep ambivalence. The acknowledged proximity of *woyei* to the supernatural realm served to place real limits on the willingness of traditionalist officeholders to support those elite voices that cast such women as little more that shrewd confidence tricksters.

CONCLUSION: RELIGIOUS CONTINUITY AND CHANGE IN THE COLONIAL TOWN

What does the prominent role of *woyei* like Akoshia Sawyerr in the religious landscape of 1920s Accra tell us about religious change in the early colonial city? First, contests over the activities of female mediums must be located in the context of conflicting visions of urban civilization. In this case, established chiefs, the scholarly elite, and the colonial state found themselves united in the face of a perceived threat to urban order from women branded as dangerous "fetish priestesses." Second, despite the growing importance of Christianity, indigenous religion continued to offer innovative solutions to religious needs and social anxieties in the colonial town. In her study of Ga religion and belief, Field draws a sharp contrast between the leeward towns from La down to Tema on the one hand, and the three *majii* of Accra on the other. Whereas religious life in the former remained dominated by the great civic cults, in the latter the tutelary *jemawojii* competed not only with the Christian churches but with a plethora of private ritual specialists, imported yam-eating Akan deities, exotic "medicines," Islam, and new cults.[138] By the 1920s, this religious panoply included four newly formed independent African churches, and, by the early 1930s if not earlier, an Akan healer regarded as the "greatest witch-doctor-medicine-man in the Gold Coast."[139] The latter entered the thriving urban market in religious services as an intermediary of the deity of the renowned Tongnaab shrine of the Tale people of the Northern Territories, which in Accra and elsewhere became known as the cult of "Nana Tongo." Religious inspiration in Accra did not just come from across the sea—it also continued to flow from the forests and savannas of the north.

In the face of these changes, the cults of the *jemawojii* in Accra demonstrated a stubborn resilience. C. E. Clerk of Akuapem spoke for many, both Ga and non-Ga, when he observed in 1926 that "although Christianity is spreading . . . there is no hesitation in stating that the Ga-Adangme tribes are more addicted to fetish worship than the Akan tribes; this could easily be witnessed during the Homowo season."[140] The pessimistic tone of missionary reports from Accra continued into the early twentieth century, an outlook borne out by the low levels of church membership compared to other early centers of evangelical endeavor such as Cape Coast and Akuropon. After a century of labor the Presbyterian Church, under the auspices of the United Free Church of Scotland following the expulsion of the Basel Mission during World War I, could boast of only 758 communicant members in Accra in 1918, a figure rising to 974 by the end of our period in 1929.[141] For the majority of Ga townspeople, the ancestors and the civic "gods of the world" remained the focus of religious belief and practice.

Why was this? Field's emphasis on the importance of "family gods" and Clerk's reference to the vitality of *Homowo* are both suggestive. The answer must lie in the continuing strength of established institutions, both sacred and secular, in defining the idea of moral community in Accra. The close identification of local communities with the intricate ritual topography of the old urban neighborhoods created an intimacy with the ancestors and the *jemawojii* that the nineteenth-century missionary churches and later denominations found difficult to interrupt. The most visible manifestation of this identity was the *Homowo* festival, the reaffirmation of Accra as a moral community. In short, *Homowo* defined what it meant to be Ga, and most Christian converts continued to participate to varying degrees in the annual rites. Indeed, attempts by the Scottish Mission to prevent its members from participating in *Homowo* in the mid-1920s were met with considerable resistance, including the departure of some to the more liberal Anglican Church.[142] Just as the domestic cults of ancestors and the civic cults of the *jemawojii* were arenas of quotidian reaffirmation and reflection, so *Homowo* served as a great annual moral renewal. As we shall see in the final chapter, by the 1920s *Homowo* was also an arena of recurring political conflict, its ideology of cultural unity overwhelmed by factional struggle and popular discontent.

NOTES

1. BMA D-1, 31/37, Jeremias Engmann to Committee, 1 Jan. 1880, reporting a common response to Basel Mission preachers in the streets of Osu.

2. BMA D-1, 31/51, Daniel Saba to Committee, dd. Agbowodo, 31 Dec. 1879, quoting two young men who wished to become Christians.

3. J.D.Y. Peel, "The pastor and the *babalawo*: The interaction of religions in nineteenth-century Yorubaland," *Africa*, 60 (1990). For the debate over African conversion, see Emefie Ikenga-Metuh, "The shattered microcosm: a critical survey of explanations of conversion in Africa" in K. Holst-Peterson (ed.), *Religion, develop-*

ment, and African identity (Uppsala, 1987); Robert W. Hefner (ed.), *Conversion to Christianity: Historical and anthropological perspectives on a great tradition* (Berkeley, 1993), 20–25; see too Adrian Hastings, *The Church in Africa 1450–1950* (Oxford, 1994), 325–337.

4. WMMS GCC, Box 262, File 1857, No. 18, J. A. Solomon to GS, 25 June 1857; *Gold Coast Free Press*, 19 Sept. 1899, "Obituary—Rev. John Plange"; the family background of France (1824–1885) is obscure, but see the brief autobiography in WMMS GCC Box 263, File 1859-67, No. 1, F. France to GS, 11 Feb. 1859.

5. F. L. Bartels, *The roots of Ghana Methodism* (Cambridge, 1965); Anne Hugon, "L'implantation du méthodisme en Côte de l'Or au XIXe siècle: Stratégies d'évangélisation et modalités de diffusion (1835–1874)," Ph.D. thesis, University of Paris, 1995.

6. WMMS GCC, Box 261, File 1849, No. 27, Wharton to Beecham, 20 Sept. 1849.

7. WMMS GCC, Box 264, File 5, Penrose to Boyce, 23 Jan. 1875, and Penrose to Parks, 18 Feb. 1875; see also Synod Minutes, Box 268, Report of Accra and Aburi Circuit, 1884, by T. B. Freeman.

8. Noel Smith, *The Presbyterian Church of Ghana, 1835–1960* (Accra, 1966), 45–64; for the same attitude displayed by the Basel Mission toward Douala, see Austen and Derrick, *Middlemen*, 67.

9. NAG EC 6/19, "The Church of Christ at Accra before 1917," by H. Debrunner, dd. Akropong, Sept. 1954.

10. A useful source for the African personnel of the mission at Osu in the 1850s is the *Gold Coast Independent*, 22 Sept. 1928, "1928: The centenary year of the Basel Evangelical Mission," by W.J.A. Staud. Richly detailed material on Euro-African identity and the conflicts of conversion is found in the autobiographical essays by fourteen trainee catechists enclosed in BMA D-1, 6, Steinhauser and Zimmermann to Committee, dd. Abokobi, Jan. 1856.

11. A crucial vehicle for this project was the *Christian Messenger/Sika-nsona Kristofoia Sanegbalo/Sika-mpoano Kristofo Senkekafo*, appearing from 1883 to 1888 as a bimonthly containing articles in English, Ga, and Twi, 1893–1895 in separate Ga and Twi editions, and from 1905 in Twi only: see Fred Agyemang, *Christian Messenger centenary 1883–1983* (Accra, 1983).

12. See Jenkins, "Gold Coast historians," 296–358; idem, "Intellectuals, publication outlets and 'past relationships': Some observations on the emergence of early Gold Coast-Ghanaian historiography in the Cape Coast, Accra and Akropong 'triangle': c. 1880–1917" in P. F. de Moraes Farias and Karin Barber (eds.), *Self-assertion and brokerage: Early cultural nationalism in West Africa* (Birmingham, 1990); and for further insights, T. C. McCaskie, "Komfo Anokye of Asante: meaning, history and philosophy in an African society," *JAH*, 27 (1986), 323–329; Kwame Bediako, *Christianity in Africa: The renewal of a non-western religion* (Edinburgh, 1995), 39–58.

13. Biographical data are found in BMA D-1, 6, Steinhauser and Zimmermann to Committee, dd. Abokobi, Jan. 1856, enclosed: "Biography of Carl Chr. Reindorf," 21 Sept. 1855; BMA D-1, 24/50, "Carl Reindorf, Catechist," by Elias Schrenk, 21 Jan. 1872; D-1, 24/95, "Biography of Carl Chr. Reindorf. As delivered at the Ordination on 13th October 1872"; Reindorf, *History* (2nd ed., 1966), 3–16; Carl D. Reindorf (ed.), *Remembering Rev. Carl Christian Reindorf* (Accra, n.d. [1984]).

14. On Reindorf's contested paternal genealogy and "mulatto" identity in Osu, see Parker, "*Mankraloi*, merchants and mulattos."

15. Reindorf, *History*, iv.

16. BMA D-1, 24/50, "Carl Reindorf, Catechist," by Elias Schrenk, 21 Jan. 1872.

17. See BMA, D-1,6, Steinhauser and Zimmermann to Committee, dd. Abokobi, Jan. 1856, esp. "Biography of Adolf Briand," n.d.

18. On *wonbii*, see Field, *Religion and medicine*, 179.

19. Reindorf, *History*, iv.

20. BMA D-1, 24/95, "Biography of Carl Chr. Reindorf."

21. Ibid.

22. BMA D-1, 36/42, Reindorf to Committee, 4 Sept. 1883; for Edmund Bannerman's lack of interest in churchgoing, see NAG ADM 11/1/1086, E. Bannerman to Hodgson, 14 Feb. 1897.

23. The concept *wolonkwemo*, lit. "the art of looking inside a book," was distinct from *niikasemo*, "learning." For a discussion of these terms, see *Gold Coast Independent*, 17 Aug. 1918.

24. BMA D-1, 27/135, Reindorf to Committee, 10 Feb. 1876.

25. Dakubu, *Korle meets the sea*, 153.

26. BMA D-1, 27/125, Reindorf to Committee, 17 Nov. 1875 and 25/1, Reindorf to Committee, 14 Jan. 1873.

27. Ibid.

28. On Mohenu (1809–1886), a religious practitioner and healer from Teshi who converted in 1857, see E. M. Lartey-Odjidja, *Paulo Mohenu: The converted fetish-priest* (Accra, 1965).

29. NAG SCT 2/6/2 Accra Judgement Book Vol. 2 Part 1, *Labadi v. Christiansborg*, 1902.

30. NAG SCT 2/4/9 Div. Court Vol. 3B, *Elias Schrenk v. Ashong Lomotey, Buoy Feo*, 1872.

31. Presbyterian Church of Ghana Archives, La Baptism Register, 1853–1889; Debrunner, *History of Christianity*, 187.

32. NAG ADM 11/1/1457, testimony of J. J. Arkrong, dd. Labadi, 21 June 1905; see too BMA D-5, 32 Letter Book, Schrenk to Commandant, 7 Nov. 1871, and Schrenk to Male Atshem, King of Labadai, 2 Nov. 1871.

33. Cf. Hastings, *The Church in Africa*, 317–325; Margaret Strobel, "Women in religious and secular ideology" in Hay and Stichter, *African women*, 106–108.

34. PRO CO 879/20, African No. 253, *Correspondence respecting the law of marriage in the Gold Coast Colony, June 1885.*

35. See *Gold Coast Chronicle*, 9 July 1896; *Gold Coast Express*, 12 July 1897; NAG ADM 11/1/1457 Marriage, J. M. Sarbah to CS, dd. Cape Coast, 20 Jan. 1905.

36. Cf. Mann, *Marrying well.*

37. WMMS GCC, Box 766, File 2, D. Kemp and J. Muller to CS, 22 July 1895; NAG ADM 11/1/1457, A. Mohr, G. Zurcher, and others to CJ, dd. Christiansborg, 29 Apr. 1905, and A. Bartrop, Wesleyan Mission, to CJ, 26 Apr. 1905.

38. For some discussion, see Roger Gocking, "Competing systems of inheritance before the British courts of the Gold Coast," *International Journal of African Historical Studies*, 23 (1990).

39. NAG ADM 11/1/1457, Report of Enquiry into the Marriage Ordinance, 1884, n.d. [1905].

40. See Paul Jenkins, "The Anglican Church in Ghana, 1905–1924," *THSG*, 15 (1974).

41. See BMA D-1, 42/68, Johannes Anum to Committee, dd. Teshie, 31 Oct. 1885, on the refusal by the Christian Teshi *mantse* Nii Kote to serve each year as a drummer at the Lakpa shrine at La; NAG ADM 11/1/1118 Labadi Native Affairs Vol. 1, *passim*, on intensive ongoing negotiations between Christian converts in La and devotees of Lakpa; D-1, 48/62, Reindorf to Committee, 16 Jan. 1889, on the baptism of a number of respected elders of Reindorf's own Asante Blohum *akutso* of Osu.

42. NAG ADM 11/1/1087, interview between SNA and Okai, Akrong, J. R. Myers, and others, Dec. 1910.

43. Quartey-Papafio, "Native tribunals," 326–327.

44. See NAG ADM 11/1/1139, Tettey to CS, 20 Oct. 1887, on the enstoolment of Basel Mission catechist and teacher G. A. Dowuona as Osu *mantse*; NAG ADM 11/1/498 Chiefs—literate and illiterate, minute by SNA, 4 Feb. 1913: of the eleven gazetted Ga *mantsemei* in 1913, six were listed as literate, a figure representing 50 percent of literate Head Chiefs in the Eastern Province and 37 percent of literate Head Chiefs in all three provinces of the Colony.

45. BMA D-1, 28/135, Reindorf to Committee, dd. Mayera, 27 Dec. 1876.

46. See Quartey-Papafio, "Native tribunals," 438–440. The 1891 census recorded religious affiliation in Accra as Christians: 2,434; Muslims: 1,617; Pagans: 15,948. While only 12 percent of Accra's population were enumerated as Christians, the figures for Cape Coast and Elmina were 30 percent and 22 percent, respectively.

47. See NAG SCT 2/4/59 Div. Court Vol. 46, *Jemima Nassu v. Basel Mission Factory and Victoria Van Hein*, 1915; Quartey-Papafio, "Native tribunals," 439.

48. An important source for the early history of the Muslim community in Accra is an Arabic manuscript, *al-hamiyatu'l-Sughra*, written in 1938 on the death of Naino's son Muhammad Baako: see K. O. Odoom, "A document on pioneers of the Muslim community in Accra," IAS *Research Review*, 7 (1971).

49. LTR Conveyances and Leases 1897–1900 Vol. 5, 305–306.

50. Gillespie, *Gold Coast police*, 24.

51. On Ali's military career, see Marion Johnson, "The slaves of Salaga," *JAH*, 27 (1986), 358.

52. See Dakubu, *Korle meets the sea*, 129–138; and for a comparable situation in late nineteenth-century Lagos, see Robin Law, "Local amateur scholarship in the construction of Yoruba ethnicity, 1880–1914" in Louise de la Gorgendière, Kenneth King, and Sarah Vaughan (eds.), *Ethnicity in Africa: Roots, meanings and implications* (Edinburgh, 1996), 81.

53. NAG ADM 11/1/1086, Chief Akramah to DC, 23 Nov. 1891.

54. Ibid., King Tacki and others to CS, 9 Apr. 1892.

55. NAG ADM 11/1/1087, minute by A. Reinhold, Government Interpreter, 27 Jan. 1893, and DC to CS, minute, 4 Feb. 1893.

56. NAG SCT 2/4/31 Div. Court Vol. 20, *King Taki v. Bokobli*, 1900; NAG ADM 11/1/1502, Tackie Obili to DC, 15 Sept. 1904; NAG ADM 11/1/581 Appeal from the Native Tribunal of the Ga Mantse, DC to Commissioner for the Eastern Province [CEP], 26 Apr. 1915.

57. Odoom, "A document," 3; ADM 11/1/1502, Crowther to Governor, 16 June 1909.

58. NAG ADM 11/1/1086, Hull to Governor, 23 Jan. 1903; and see Chapter 2.

59. NAG ADM 11/1/1775, interview between Nathan and P. C. Randolf, n.d. [May 1903]; ADM 11/1/1088, Ayi Bonte, Gbese *mantse*, to DC, 8 Oct. 1924; ADM 11/1/1756, 1925 Notes of Evidence, evidence of Kojo Ababio, 78-85.

60. NAG ADM 11/1/1502, interview between Acting Governor Arthur and Native Officer Ali and others, 28 Nov. 1902.

61. NAG ADM 11/1/1086, John Vanderpuye to CS, 7 Jan. 1903, enclosed: "Notes of a meeting of Chiefs of Quarters and the Chief and Captains of Akuashon," by E. W. Quartey Papafio.

62. Ibid., Captain Kojo to Nathan, 10 Jan. 1903, and Chief Kofi Nunoo to SNA, 12 Jan. 1903.

63. Ibid., P. C. Randolf to SNA, 18 Jan. 1903. Philip Carl Randolf (or Reindorf) (1845–1933) was a paternal cousin of Rev. Carl Reindorf. His extensive knowledge of Gbese oral tradition was earlier demonstrated by an account of the emergence of the *akutso* included by Reindorf in the *History*, 103–111.

64. Bartels, *Roots of Ghana Methodism*, 137.

65. NAG ADM 11/1/1775, interview between Nathan and P. C. Randolf, n.d. [May 1903].

66. NAG ADM 11/1/1086, minute by T. E. Fell, 5 May 1903; ADM 11/1/1775, interview between Nathan, Okaija, and others, 16 May 1903.

67. Ibid., interview between Nathan, Captain Kojo, and Okai Mensah, 14 May 1903; ADM 11/1/1086, Okaija to SNA, 29 May 1903.

68. NAG ADM 11/1/1087, Interview between Nathan and Okai Mensah and others, 26 Jan. 1904.

69. NAG ADM 11/1/1502, Crowther to Governor, 16 June 1909.

70. By 1907 Braimah was reported to be the largest cattle owner in Accra: NAG ADM 11/1/9, interview between Rodger and Accra chiefs, 3 Aug. 1907.

71. See file NAG ADM 11/1/1448 Death of Chief Alhaji Braimah [1915–1926].

72. For discussion, see NAG ADM 11/1/1088, T. R. Quartey to SNA, 18 Feb. 1921.

73. NAG ADM 11/1/1773, meetings dd. 2 Feb., 3 Feb. and 10 Mar. 1904.

74. Ibid., meeting dd. 2 Feb. 1904.

75. Ibid., meeting dd. 3 Feb. 1904.

76. See further PRO CO 96/417, Rodger to Lyttleton, No. 203, 27 Apr. 1904, enclosed: Report on Native Affairs 1903, by H. M. Hull, SNA, the first report of the new Native Affairs Department, created in March 1902.

77. NAG ADM 5/2/2, Report on the census for the year 1901. The number of Europeans resident in the colonial capital was still only 96, up from 68 in 1891.

78. The figures are: 1891: 7,917 males, 8,350 females; 1901: 6,891 males, 7,951 females.

79. NAG ADM 11/1/1773, meeting dd. 10 Mar. 1904; Decima Moore and F. G. Guggisberg, *We two in West Africa* (London, 1909), 61.

80. NAG ADM 11/1/1118, "Memo as to stool of Labadi," n.d. [1905].

81. *Gold Coast Leader*, 18 July 1903.

82. On Taki's *yalafemo*, see NAG ADM 11/1/1087, Chapman to CS, 13 Mar. 1904, DC to SNA, 15 Apr. 1904, and Tackie Obile to SNA, 7 May 1904; Kilson, *The diary of Kwaku Niri*, 23–24; see also Adjei, "Mortuary usages," 95.

83. NAG ADM 11/1/1087, minute by Hull, 18 Aug. 1904, M'Carthy to SNA, 26 Aug. 1904; *Gold Coast Advocate*, 27 Aug. 1904; ADM 11/1/1437, "Suppression of objectionable customs," by S. D. Codjoe, n.d. [c.1930].

84. NAG ADM 11/1/1481 Ferries, Tackie Obile to DC, 25 July 1904; on the Sakumo ferry see ADM 11/1/9, interview between Rodger and Accra chiefs, 3 Aug. 1907.

85. See Field, *Social organization*, 163–165.

86. NAG ADM 11/1/1087, T. Hutton Mills to Curling, 9 Sept. 1905, Taki Obili to Curling, 11 Jan. 1906.

87. Ibid., DC to SNA, 15 Aug. 1905.

88. See Parker, "The cultural politics of death and burial."

89. BMA D-1, 48/62, Reindorf to Committee, dd. Christiansborg, 16 Jan. 1889.

90. BMA D-1, 66/147, I. Odoi Philipps to Committee, 31 Dec. 1897.

91. Kilson, *The diary of Kwaku Niri*, 30.

92. Ibid.; see also NAG ADM 11/1/1437, "Suppression of objectionable customs."

93. NAG ADM 11/1/1087, DC to SNA, 15 Aug. 1905. The *otofu*, or *dipo*, custom was a female puberty rite practiced by those sections of the Osu community who worshipped gods of the Dangme *me* cult: Field, *Religion and medicine*, 185–189.

94. PRO CO 96/420, Rodger to Lyttleton, Conf., 28 Nov. 1904; Kimble, *Political history*, 467–469.

95. For similar struggles over the definition and redefinition of identities in the Akan state of Akyem Abuakwa, see Richard Rathbone, "Defining Akyemfo: The construction of citizenship in Akyem Abuakwa, Ghana, 1700–1939," *Africa*, 66 (1996).

96. NAG SCT 2/4/41 Div. Court Vol. 30, *Land at Accra re Public Lands Ordinance 1876*, 1907.

97. Koole was closely associated with the Sempe *akutso*, which maintained historic links with Onamokowe of Gbese, the family that provided the *wulomo*: Quartey-Papafio, "Native tribunals," 436–437.

98. Son of Emma Bannerman and James Town merchant John Hutton Mills, Thomas Hutton Mills (1865–1931) turned to law after being dismissed as a government clerk for his outspoken role in the disturbances of September 1886. Returning to practice in Accra in 1894, he rose to prominence during the debate over the Town Council and Compulsory Labour Ordinances in 1897 and the following year became the first African barrister appointed to the Legislative Council. A prominent Anglican and member of the Accra Town Council (1905–1911), Hutton Mills (later Hutton-Mills) was the leading advisor to Kojo Ababio and a robust champion of the rights of the Alata *akutso*.

99. Arthur Boi Quartey-Papafio (1869–1927), popularly known as "Lawyer Papafio," was the younger of the three prominent sons of the late *akwashontse* Chief William Quartey-Papafio and the wealthy Gbese businesswoman Momo Omedru. He and his brothers Emmanuel William, a wealthy merchant-farmer and advisor to various Kinka *mantsemei*, and Benjamin William, who in 1886 qualified as the Gold Coast's first indigenous doctor, represented a new, Western-educated form of the established sociopolitical clout of the Kpakpatsewe. Besides editing the *Gold Coast Advocate* (1904–c. 1914), Quartey-Papafio also wrote a series of scholarly papers for the *Journal of the African Society*, using both media to advance the claims of the *akwashon* court and the Asere *akutso*.

100. The significance of the palanquin is enshrined in the maxim *Beni oda ka akpakai mli, bele tsunye mibo—Awo!*, lit. "When the [large] *oda* lizard lies in the *akpakai*, the [small] *tsunye* lizard cries—Awo!" [a cry of exaltation]: for a brief exegesis, see Zimmermann, *Grammatical sketch*, Vol. 1, 162.

101. NAG SCT 2/4/41 Div. Court Vol. 30, *Land at Accra re Public Lands Ordinance*, 1907, opening statement by A. B. Quartey-Papafio.

102. NAG ADM 11/1/1087, Kojo Ababio to DC, 30 Nov. 1905, Hull to Governor, 19 Mar. 1906.

103. Ibid., Mantse Kodso Ababio IV to SNA, 2 Feb. 1906.

104. Ibid., Taki Obili to SNA, 15 Sep. 1906, Kojo Ababio to DC, 17 Oct. 1906, and Curling to SNA, 21 Dec. 1906.

105. Ibid., Osborne to SNA, 31 Dec. 1906.

106. NAG ADM 11/1/1138, *Gold Coast Advocate*, 8 Dec. 1906, "The native courts and the customary law."

107. NAG ADM 11/1/1088, Tackie Obile to SNA, 11 July 1914.

108. NAG ADM 11/1/1756, 1907 Report.

109. For the Kpakpatsewe response, a carefully prepared petition from *akwashontse* T. R. Quartey to London, see CO 96/507, Bryan to Harcourt, No. 233, 11 May 1911, enclosed: Quartey to Secretary of State, 27 Apr. 1911.

110. NAG ADM 11/1/1138, DC to CEP, 21 Apr. 1908.

111. Ibid., Report on the Native Jurisdiction Bill by a Committee of the Legislative Council, Minority Report by Sir W. B. Griffith, 29 Oct. 1908. Under the Ordinance, personal suits involving debt or damages under £25 if both parties were "natives" were transferred from the DC's court to African courts.

112. Kimble, *Political history*, 467–469.

113. NAG ADM 11/1/884 Indecent Dances, SNA to Takki Obiri, Conf., 19 Jan. 1909; ADM 11/1/316 Bylaws made by the Ga Manche re suppression of certain dances, 1911.

114. NAG ADM 11/1/620, Nettey to SNA, 5 Oct. 1916.

115. Construction of the Accra-Kumase railway began in 1909. Services as far as the cocoa-marketing town of Nsawam were inaugurated the following year, although the line, held up by World War I, did not reach Kumase until 1923.

116. NAG ADM 11/1/620, Nettey to SNA, 5 Oct. 1916.

117. See *Gold Coast Independent*, 8 June 1918.

118. NAG ADM 11/1/620, Nettey to SNA, 5 Oct. 1916.

119. Ibid. On the extreme gravity of accusing an individual of being a "poisoner," *sulo*, see NAG ADM 37/4/1 District Record, Accra, *J. A. Annan v. N. J. Nunoo*, 31 May 1916.

120. NAG ADM 11/1/620, Nettey to SNA, 5 Oct. 1916.

121. *Gold Coast Independent*, 23 Sept., 30 Sept., and 14 Oct. 1922. The weekly *Independent* was founded in 1918 by Dr. Frederick Victor Nanka Bruce (1879–1951), and throughout the inter-war years represented the voice of "respectable" elite opinion in opposition to a range of more populist, radical newspapers beginning with the *Voice of the People* (later *Vox Populi*).

122. *Gold Coast Independent*, 23 Sept. 1922; Field, *Religion and medicine*, 6.

123. *Gold Coast Independent*, 30 Sept. 1922.

124. Ibid. For a report of a similar moral crisis down the coast in Prampram, see ibid., 1 Dec. 1928, Awuley Surupu Oshiahene to editor, 15 Nov. 1928.

125. Field, *Religion and medicine*, 100–109. Ga healers or "medicine men" were known either as *tsofatse*, lit. "father of tree roots," or *wontse*, "father of the *won*," the terminology depending on the emphasis placed by the individual on herbal or spiritual medicine. The Twi word *akomfo*, broadly synonymous with *wulomo*, was also used by the Ga to describe a "private" ritual specialist.

126. Field, *Social organization*, 53.

127. *Gold Coast Independent*, 3 May 1924.

128. Ibid., 18 Sept. 1926–18 Dec. 1926, passim, reporting *IGP v. Akoshia alias Fetish Priestess*, 1926.

129. Jean Allman, "Of 'spinsters,' 'concubines' and 'wicked women': reflections on gender and social change in colonial Asante," *Gender and History*, 3 (1991); idem, "Rounding up spinsters: Gender chaos and unmarried women in colonial Asante," *JAH*, 37 (1996); see too Dorothy L. Hodgson and Sheryl McCurdey, "Wayward wives, misfit mothers, and disobedient daughters: 'Wicked' women and the reconfiguration of gender in Africa," *Canadian Journal of African Studies*, 30 (1996).

130. Strobel, "Women in religious and secular identity," 104.

131. On *dadefoi* and *sapati*, see Field, *Religion and medicine*, 67, 105–106; *Gold Coast Independent*, 14 Oct. 1922.

132. *Gold Coast Independent*, 11 Dec. 1926. As in Akan culture, the Ga used the terms cool ("it is cool": *e he ejo*) and hot to contrast the protective civilization of the town with the dangerous nature of the surrounding bush: Dakubu, "Creating unity," 516.

133. In the early 1920s, tradesmen in Accra could expect to earn £6–7 a month, male laborers £2 a month plus provisions, and female hawkers £2 a month. The salary of a female schoolteacher was £96 per annum, and that of a shorthand-typist, £85.

134. *Gold Coast Independent*, 13 Nov. 1926, evidence of Gbese *otsiami* Aikai Teiko.

135. Field, *Religion and medicine*, 100–109; idem, "Spirit possession in Ghana."

136. *Gold Coast Independent*, 11 Dec. 1926; see too the testimony of the acolyte Atchoi: ibid., 9 Oct. 1926.

137. Ibid., 11 Dec. 1926.

138. Field, *Religion and medicine*, esp. 65, 133.

139. Ibid., 135; see too Acquah, *Accra survey*, 148.

140. *Gold Coast Independent*, 26 June 1926, "Fetishism," by C. E. Clerk.

141. Smith, *Presbyterian Church*, 207–208. The Church became the autonomous Presbyterian Church of the Gold Coast in 1926.

142. *Gold Coast Independent*, 15 Aug. and 29 Aug. 1925; Jenkins, "The Anglican Church," 185.

6

Remaking the Town: Struggles for the Colonial City

"Ga Mashie! Why do feuds abound
Within thy walls so deeply laid?
The envy once of states around
And near; among those states a blade.

"Behold! Look how low she declines
Recurrent with internal strife
Her peoples' cries doth show the signs
How desperately her leaders rife

"A town now no more you are
The others proudly laugh to scorn;
They ask when gazing from afar:
'Is this the town in oneness born?'"[1]

Blomo jee nma ni ayeo.
(Quarrel is not food which is eaten.)[2]

This chapter examines the final stages of Accra's long transition from Ga city-state to fully-fledged colonial port city. It looks at the relationship between urban growth and town politics in the 1910s and 1920s, and argues that although the process of urbanization was fueled by the influx of migrant "strangers," struggles for control over the expanding city remained focused on the old Ga quarters. Indeed, the strains of urban change fueled rising levels of conflict within Ga state and society, culminating in the destoolment of *Ga mantse* Taki Yaoboi in 1929. By the end of the 1920s, not only had Accra been physically and demographically transformed, but the focus of town politics had begun to shift away from purely local concerns. The early colonial period in Accra was drawing to a close, giving way to a brief "High Colonial" interlude before the city emerged as the center stage of the anticolonial struggle in the late 1940s.

The formalization of British rule on the Gold Coast in the 1870s, followed by the extension of that rule over an enlarged colonial hinterland in the 1890s, were important landmarks in Accra's urban history. By the turn of the century, Accra had consolidated its position as the leading entrepôt port on the Gold Coast. Nevertheless, the pace of urban change was slow. It remained for the rapid expansion of the economy of the southern Gold Coast in the 1910s and 1920s, fueled by the boom in cocoa exports, to accelerate the transformation of the capital. The census of 1911 recorded the population of the municipality as 18,574, still less than that enumerated in 1891 and a figure similar to estimates from the mid-nineteenth century. Ten years later, the population—now spreading beyond the established boundaries of the three Ga townships—had doubled to 38,049 and by 1931 had reached 61,558.[3] Despite economic fluctuations and commercial competition from both expatriate firms and newly arriving migrants, many Ga townsmen and women were well placed to benefit from the growth of the colonial economy. Others experienced a deepening poverty in the dilapidated old quarters in the heart of the city. The indigenous core communities clung tenaciously to the vision of their ancient *nshonamajii*, "seaside towns," as the civilized heart of the Ga world, yet found themselves increasingly marginalized by opposing perceptions of the colonial capital.

FROM GA *MAJII* TO COLONIAL CITY

The Expansion of Accra

The first quarter of the twentieth century witnessed a fundamental shift in the nature of urban space in Accra, as the old Ga *majii* of Kinka, Nleshi, and Osu were subsumed into an expanding and increasingly heterogeneous city. As the commercial and administrative capital of the Gold Coast, Accra in this period acquired the attributes of a characteristically colonial port city.[4] The imperative of capital formation through the extraction of a surplus from the colonial hinterland was central to the shaping of the built environment, fueling the development of port and railway infrastructure, warehouse facilities, banks, and expatriate trading enterprises.[5] So too was the perceived requirement on the part of the British regime to intervene more actively in order to regulate this urban growth. As elsewhere in the colonial world, advances in Western medicine interacted with imperial ideologies to create a new emphasis on sanitation, order, and racial segregation, which conditioned

Figure 6.1 Loading cocoa into surfboats on Accra's waterfront, c. 1920. Photograph by J.A.C. Holm. Holm began working in his father's photographic business in 1908 at age eighteen, and established his own studio in 1919. (Reprinted by permission from Allister Macmillan [ed.], *The Red Book of West Africa* [1968] published by Frank Cass & Company, 900 Eastern Avenue, Ilford, Essex, England. Copyright Frank Cass & Co. Ltd.)

the reformulation of urban space and of social relations in the growing city. Reinforcing Accra's status as the urban showpiece of what the colonial mind had begun to perceive as a "model colony" were two institutions seen to symbolize the beneficence of imperial trusteeship in British tropical Africa: the Gold Coast Hospital at Korle Bu and the Prince of Wales College at Achimota.[6]

Yet the description of Accra as a typical colonial port city shaped by the requirements of capital presents only part of the picture. As Leeds has cautioned, the prolonged debate surrounding the nature of "the urban" has been overly dependent on the impact of Western capitalism on the historical experience of cities.[7] Accra was indeed the colonial capital and, until the opening of the harbor at Sekondi-Takoradi in 1928, the Gold Coast's principal port and link with the international economy. But it remained very much an African town in character. Much of this was due to the continuing vigor of Ga urban culture—to the resilience of Kinka, Nleshi, and Osu in preserving their spatial, social, and institutional integrity. Despite a flight to the new suburbs by some of their wealthier inhabitants, the three townships remained the focus of Ga political action and social life in the city. In common with the old hearts of port cities like Lagos, Douala, and Mombasa, downtown Accra—"*Ga*"—survived as an overcrowded, vibrant hothouse of indigenous culture and political intrigue.

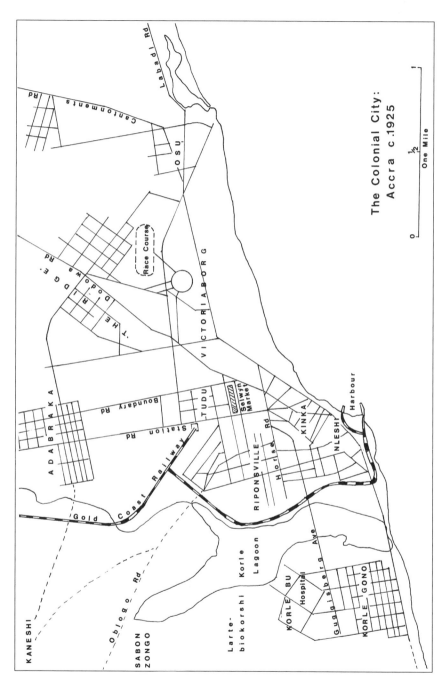

Map 6.1 The Colonial City: Accra, c. 1925

The initial creation of new residential areas beyond the boundaries of the three old settlements was a response to issues of disease and sanitation. Since the 1870s, the British had made a number of ad hoc attempts to improve the sanitation and order of the colonial capital, yet possessed neither the will nor the authority to stamp the desired degree of social control on the densely populated Ga quarters. A fire that in April 1894 destroyed much of Kinka was considered by some officials as a blessing in disguise. Although the disaster facilitated the widening of Otu Street, Accra's main commercial thoroughfare, the systematic "laying out" of the town remained on the drawing board.[8] The catalyst for change was British West Africa's first outbreak of plague in Accra between January and August 1908.[9] To combat the spread of the disease, the administration directed the *mantsemei* to order the temporary evacuation of the poorer and most crowded quarters of Nleshi and Kinka. Kojo Ababio responded by leading many of the *manbii* of the Alata and Akanmaji *akutsei* to the west bank of the Korle lagoon. Considerably fewer inhabitants of Kinka moved, and then with much reluctance, to a location on the main Kibi Road to the north of the town.[10] Following a request by Kojo Ababio for financial assistance for those Alatas who wished to remain to the west of the lagoon, the government began to lay plans for the creation of permanent settlements on these sites. Herein lies the origins of Accra's inner ring of twentieth-century suburbs: Korle Gonno, Adabraka, Korle Woko (or Riponsville), and Kaneshi.[11]

Four main points can be noted with regard to the spatial growth of Accra following the catalytic 1908 plague epidemic. First, urban and suburban land became an increasingly valuable economic and political commodity. The imperative for officeholders, lineage heads, and private individuals to establish control or outright ownership over land generated a kaleidoscope of legal struggles, which shaped local politics. This will be examined in more detail below, but it can be emphasized here that control over the expanding city was hotly contested from the outset. One well-documented example involves the dispersal of the Muslim community from the old *zongo* on the northern boundary of Kinka. Eager in the aftermath of the plague to relocate the inhabitants of the *zongo* and their large herds of livestock, the administration earmarked the site of Adabraka as a new Muslim township.[12] Due to a realignment of ethnic factions in 1907, however, the Hausa leader Muhammad Baako had already entered into negotiations with Kojo Ababio for a grant of land near the Alata village of Lartebiokorshi on which to resettle his followers.[13] Rejecting the government scheme at Adabraka, Muhammad Baako instead founded the new Hausa settlement under the patronage of the Alata *mantse* that became known as the *sabon zongo*. Kojo Ababio's right of alienation was subsequently challenged in the colonial courts by Asere leaders, who claimed that the area had originally been farmed by slaves attached to the Kpakpatsewe lineage. This pattern of conflict occurred repeatedly as Accra's urban frontier spread into the surrounding *kose*.

Second, although officially sponsored residential schemes on land purchased by the government molded the outward expansion of Accra, the colonial regime never succeeded in its aim of redeveloping the old *majii*. This objective was articulated in 1908 by a committee of the Accra Town Council that included rival barristers Thomas Hutton Mills and A. B. Quartey-Papafio. The Committee recommended the acquisition of designated "congested areas" and the abolition of the *agbonaa*, the traditional Ga compound house. "These congested blocks are on sites most suitable for building good stores and business premises," it reported, "being adjacent to the new Harbour Works, the Customs Office and sea front."[14] Agreeing with these leading representatives of the Ga elite, Governor Rodger informed Kojo Ababio that "when Accra is laid out afresh . . . the result will be that only the richer natives will be able to build within the town itself and the poorer ones will settle outside the municipal area."[15] A Town Improvement Committee comprising ex-officio plus African members was established to direct compulsory acquisition, demolition, and compensation, together with the carving of streets through the old quarters. Despite bursts of action, such as in the aftermath of an outbreak of yellow fever in 1911, the fear of overt resistance in the heart of the colonial capital nevertheless prevented the systematic demolition of the old towns. Many Ga relocated—and some were certainly forced to relocate—to the new suburbs, but these were often the wealthier rather than the poorer members of the community. The latter, many of whom were fishermen, fish sellers, and petty traders, remained crowded in Kinka, Nleshi, and Osu.[16] For many, the most immediate day-to-day contact with colonial power took the form of a running battle with sanitary inspectors hunting for mosquito larvae. Such was the stream of prosecutions that by the 1920s the Police Court was known by the women of Accra as the "Loloi [larva] Court."[17]

Third, the 1910s saw the emergence of racial segregation as an issue in the reordering of urban space. Europeans had historically lived side by side with Africans in Accra, often residing in rented storey houses scattered throughout the town quarters. Although some officials had removed to the "New Site" of Victoriaborg, this established residential pattern had largely survived the late nineteenth-century hardening of imperial racial ideology. It was challenged by the newly discovered mosquito theory of malaria and by the influence of Dr. W. J. Simpson of the London School of Hygiene and Tropical Medicine, who was rushed to Accra in 1908 to combat the plague epidemic. Simpson's report, effectively a blueprint for racial segregation,

strengthened the hands of the Sanitary and Medical Departments in determining the shape of the colonial city. Despite the opposition of the liberal-
minded Governor Sir Hugh Clifford (1912–1919), a belt of higher ground
running northeast of Victoriaborg through Osu farmland—dubbed "The
Ridge"—was acquired as a segregated zone for all European residents.[18]
However, the administration remained deeply divided over the issue. Ultimately unwilling to compel missionaries and private businessmen to abandon their downtown residences, it never rigorously implemented Simpson's
racial and sanitary policies. The Ridge was developed as an exclusively
European residential zone, but in this respect too, colonial authority was less
than fully successful in stamping its control on the old townships.

Fourth, the spatial and demographic expansion of Accra, as of other African cities, was fueled largely by migration. To reiterate, Ga state and society
throughout the eighteenth and nineteenth centuries was characterized by a
willingness to incorporate "strangers" into the institutions centered on the
coastal towns. As we have seen with regard to the Muslim community, the
expansion of colonial rule coupled with the growth of Accra beyond the
established *akutsei* meant that by the early twentieth century, officeholders
were losing their historic ability to mediate the terms of settlement. Diverse
groups of migrants from throughout the Gold Coast and beyond continued
to settle under the patronage of particular *mantsemei*, yet no longer sought,
or were required to seek, a more complete incorporation into Ga society.[19]
Not only do census returns register the steady decrease in the proportion of
Ga in the total urban population, but the colonial city grew beyond the effective control of established Ga hierarchies. Few of the earliest residents of
the new suburbs to the north of the old Horse Road boundary were Ga. The
area known as Katamanto, for example, was settled by Hausa blacksmiths,
Kwawu wood sellers, washermen from Togo and Dahomey, Lebanese traders, plus Akan, Dangme, Ewe, and Igbo.[20] One manifestation of this growing cultural pluralism was the formation by migrants of mutual support
groups, or "voluntary associations." Employing ethnicity, district of origin,
or hometown—or a combination of these identities—as a basis for membership, voluntary associations have long attracted the attention of social scientists concerned with the emergence of new institutional forms as a result of
adaptation to urban life.[21]

None of this is to suggest that Kinka, Nleshi, and Osu remained islands of entrenched tradition, insulated against those transformative
forces of the colonial city regarded by the early urban sociologists as
dynamic motors of modernization. Urban change was neither unambiguously "modern," nor did it bypass what has often been caricatured as a
staunchly traditionalist Ga political order, isolated both spatially and
ideologically in the old town quarters. That urbanization resulted in the

creation of new identities and social forms by migrants has long been a central tenet of African urban studies. However, little attention has been paid to the reconfiguration of established urban identities and institutions. At the same time as incoming migrants were transforming Accra, Ga townspeople were also formulating new responses to changing city life. By the 1910s and 1920s, the old *majii* were locked in debate over the past, present, and future of Ga state and society in Accra.

New Forms of Political Expression

The first quarter of the twentieth century also saw the emergence of new forms of political expression in Accra. Founded in Cape Coast in 1897 in response to the Lands Bill of that year, the Aborigines' Rights Protection Society (ARPS) is generally regarded as the Gold Coast's first "protonationalist" elite political organization. The threat of the Lands Bill made little impact in Accra, where in 1897–1898 Ga leaders were preoccupied with the protests against the creation of the Town Council, and the ARPS remained a vehicle of the literate Fante elite centered on Cape Coast.[22] Despite the affinal and cultural connections linking the elites of Accra and Cape Coast, the relationship between the two towns historically had been characterized by a degree of mutual antipathy fueled by commercial and political rivalry. The transfer of the British headquarters in 1877 marked a decisive shift in this long rivalry, signaling the start of a slow decline in the fortunes of Cape Coast. The antipathy of the Fante toward their old Ga middleman rivals emerges in the columns of the Cape Coast press, which tended to regard Accra as a town mired in "fetishism" and tradition, unsuited to its status as colonial capital. The *Gold Coast Nation*, mouthpiece of the ARPS, was particularly scathing about the lack of "national" consciousness of the Ga elite, which unlike that of Cape Coast was seen to be permanently locked in local political affairs.[23]

It was not until 1913 that ARPS leader E.J.P. Brown led a delegation to Accra to inaugurate an Eastern Districts branch. Brown found support limited exclusively to James Town, and in particular to the group of literate advisors to Alata *mantse* Kojo Ababio led by Thomas Hutton Mills and C. J. Bannerman.[24] Hoping the branch would "not be a Nine-Days Wonder like all things Accra," the delegation called on Taki Obili in Kinka. After protracted negotiations, "at which both sides displayed a highly developed and advanced stage in aboriginal statecraft, the Delegates succeeded in partially . . . convincing the Manche and his Councillors as to the likely good results . . . for the Ga community."[25] ARPS statecraft was not sufficient, however, to prevent the *Ga mantse* from dispatching messengers to the chiefs of the Western and Central Provinces to protest against the intrusion into Ga af-

fairs, or from decreeing that the Accra *manbii* were not to join the organization.[26] This merely confirmed, the *Nation* railed, the "insularity of the [Ga]
tribe, which some think persists in regarding itself as superior to and separate from the Twis and Fantis, the numerically important sections of the Gold
Coast Nation."[27] From the outset, the ARPS in Accra was largely subsumed
into local Ga politics. The Society's early association with James Town was
strengthened by the fact that its Secretary, Rev. S.R.B. Attoh Ahuma, son of
the Wesleyan pastor J. A. Solomon, was a close kinsman of Kojo Ababio. In
his capacity as editor of the *Nation*, Attoh Ahuma consistently supported the
interests of the Alata *akutso* in town politics.

The belated appearance of the ARPS can be contrasted with the formation of the National Congress of British West Africa (NCBWA) in Accra in
1920. Although the NCBWA's leading light was the Fante intellectual J. E.
Casely Hayford, by 1920 the colonial capital had clearly supplanted Cape
Coast as the focus of new forms of political organization and action. One
striking reflection of the shift in the Gold Coast's urban hierarchy in favor
of Accra is the location of barristers, the leading profession of the increasingly self-conscious and self-styled "intelligentsia." On the eve of the formation of the NCBWA, a total of 28 African barristers were practicing at
Accra. This compared with only 7 at Cape Coast and 8 at Sekondi, the growing rail terminus and port town in the colony's Western Districts.[28]

Social and Cultural Change

If the emergence of new types of political expression was one indication
of Accra's transition from Ga *majii* to twentieth-century colonial city, then
so too was the growing diversity of social forms—and problems—associated with modern urban life. Inequality, historically structured by the institution of slavery and deepened by the forces of the Atlantic economy, had
long been a characteristic of Accra's Ga townships. Despite the ending of
slavery, the growing visibility of urban poverty suggests a widening of socioeconomic differentiation in the colonial city. In 1920, attention was drawn
to the alarming numbers of "destitute and homeless" migrants sleeping rough
in Salaga Market, and when in 1923 relapsing fever hit Accra, 139 out of
161 cases were reported to be poverty-stricken Zabarima migrant laborers.[29]
As early as 1921, assistant SNA J. C. de Graft Johnson wrote a memorandum positing a link between rising levels of crime in Accra and unemployment—a good decade before the concept of urban unemployment began to
be recognized by the colonial mind of British tropical Africa.[30]

As growing numbers of young men from the Gold Coast and beyond
migrated to Accra in search of work, new forms of leisure and popular culture catered to the increasingly diverse urban crowd.[31] Drinking bars, social

Figure 6.2 Thomas and Florence Hutton Mills and their carriage men pose at the gateway of Temple House, Mills Road, James Town, c. 1920. (Reprinted by permission from Allister Macmillan [ed.], *The Red Book of West Africa* [1968] published by Frank Cass & Company, 900 Eastern Avenue, Ilford, Essex, England. Copyright Frank Cass & Co. Ltd.)

clubs, dance halls, and cinemas attracted both migrants and a new generation of indigenous Ga eager to create their own cultural life in the colonial city. The early twentieth century was a time of growing assertiveness on the part of young men and women in the urban centers of the Gold Coast, new avenues of wealth creation allowing a greater freedom from the control of patriarchal elders.[32] Many women sought to reshape gender relations and, as we have seen with the rise of freelance *woyei*, adopted new strategies to create an independent niche in the urban economy. One such strategy was prostitution. Centered on the drinking bars of the old quarters, prostitution was visibly on the increase in Accra by the 1920s, although associated more with migrant women than with indigenous Ga. An influx of so-called "*tutu*" prostitutes from Calabar in Nigeria in 1924 prompted calls for their repatriation, while growing numbers of Hausa courtesans (*karuwai*) in the *zongo* led to a demand from Chief Kadri English for the removal of "all unattached Hausa women" the following year.[33]

Despite some evidence for a widening gap between rich and poor, changes in urban culture began to erode the sharp distinction in Victorian Accra between the "cloth portion" of society on the one hand and the "frock" and "frock coat portion" on the other. The evolution of a distinctive popular culture and its interaction with Accra's elite social milieu is particularly apparent in the field of music and dance. By the turn of the century, Ga and Fante drum rhythms had begun to fuse with a range of outside influences, including regimental brass bands, church

Figure 6.3 "Saturday beach boxing," c. 1917. An indigenous form of boxing called *asafo atwere* was a popular leisure activity among Ga "youngmen" (*oblahii*) by the first decades of the twentieth century. (Copyright Basel Mission Archive, Basel, Switzerland. Ref. No. D-30.01.015. Reproduced with permission.)

music, and sea shanteys, to form a variety of new popular styles: *osibisaba*, *ashiko*, and *gome*.[34] The latter was the Ga version of the peripatetic *gombe*, which traversed the nineteenth-century Atlantic world from Jamaica to Freetown to Equatorial Africa, arriving in Accra about 1900 via Ga workers returning from the Congo and the Bights. Despite the attempt by the *mantsemei* to prohibit these "indecent" dances in 1911, the new syncopated styles flourished, and during World War I began to be orchestrated for dance bands catering to Accra's "high society."[35] By the 1920s, the new music had become known as "highlife." The ballroom version drew crowds in full evening dress to elite venues like the Rodger Club or to private parties such as those held by Thomas Hutton-Mills on the tennis courts behind his imposing James Town residence, Temple House.[36] Meanwhile, popular street styles utilizing African percussion and the guitar—that distinctly "lower-class" instrument popularized by Kru sailors and boatmen—continued to evolve. Drawing on the satirical traditions of the songs of the *asafo* companies, innovations such as the irreverent *osofoiajo*, the "dance of the clergy," continued to outrage elite commentators for whom the piano represented a more respectable enter-tainment option.[37] By 1923 the parlors of Accra's storey houses contained enough keyboards to allow one Henry K. Schultz to establish the town's first piano repair and tuning business.[38]

Cultural change is also apparent in the diversification of sporting activi-ties. Shooting and riding were already popular pastimes among African and Euro-African gentlemen in the mid-nineteenth century. By the 1860s, an Accra "native" eleven regularly engaged a team of European residents at cricket, a "mixed" eleven also taking on the officers of passing Royal Navy warships.[39] Horse racing emerged at the center of the elite sporting calender in 1889, with the inaugural meeting of the Accra Race Club. Race meetings remained important social events throughout the colonial period, attracting both "high" and "low" society, the Muslim community and European expa-triates.[40] "It was a curious sight," two visitors wrote of a government-spon-sored "gymkhana" at Accra's race course in 1905, "that mixture of black and white; in the enclosure, the native band in their khaki uniforms; the black lawyers and doctors in their immaculate English clothes; the native women, some in European dress, others in native kit with gold ornaments in their . . . hair; and the well-dressed English people; on the other side of the course, the crowd of natives."[41] Great popular excitement was also generated by an annual regatta, which from the early 1890s drew teams of canoemen from the length of the Gold Coast.[42] New participatory sports began to emerge by World War I, boxing proving especially popular among the young men of the old Ga quarters. As elsewhere in Africa, football also became hugely popular, organized by the early 1920s into an Accra Native Football League. All teams initially had Ga names, but in 1923, in a highly suggestive reflec-tion of the growing ethnic diversity of urban Accra, English names were adopted, the fifteen-strong league featuring teams such as Hearts of Oak, Queen's Park Royalists, Africs, Never Miss, and Rule Britannia.[43]

ALATA AND ASERE: POWER, IDENTITY, AND HISTORY

Despite urbanization, social change, and the emergence of new forms of elite political organization, politics in Accra in the first quarter of the twen-tieth century remained firmly focused on the Ga towns.[44] The urban economy may have undergone a dramatic expansion, but by the 1920s, Accra's indig-enous order was widely perceived to be in a state of crisis. To outside ob-servers, most articulately the anthropologist M. J. Field, Ga state and soci-ety appeared to have degenerated into a morass of internecine conflict be-tween self-serving, cynical political factions. "The native politics of Accra, like those of Lagos, are in an unholy mess," wrote one official in 1930.[45] As the stanzas from the poem "Lamentation for Ga" indicate, this dismal prognosis was not confined to the ranks of a British officialdom removed from and often mystified by the inner workings of the town. The historical record is replete with Ga voices equally alarmed by the seemingly endless cycle of "stool disputes," a disquiet manifested in an increasingly nostalgic view of the town in the second half of the nineteenth century under the benign guardianship of Taki Tawia.[46]

In common with central Lagos, downtown Accra maintained a reputation among both colonial officials and Africans as a cauldron of political intrigue. However, the nature of political dispute in the Nigerian and Gold Coast capitals was somewhat different. Whereas Lagos politics throughout the 1920s was dominated by the suspension, deposition, and deportation of the *Oba*, *Eleko* Eshugbayi, by the colonial regime, the major political struggles in Accra were fought out by Ga factions with only limited intervention by the British.[47] By the 1920s, disputes centered on the possession of chiefly office in Accra had reached internecine levels. Why this was so is somewhat puzzling. The usual explanation—shared by contemporary observers and historians alike—is that the primary motive was the financial benefits of chieftaincy.[48] However, although cupidity certainly fueled some conflicts, the historical record is replete with the complaints of long-suffering *mantsemei* that the benefits of office holding in colonial Accra had long been offset by its escalating costs and perils. Nevertheless, as in many of the Akan states of the Gold Coast Colony and Asante, it was the ubiquitous stool dispute that defined Ga political action. As contestants forged alliances and mobilized followers in support of claims to office, increasing numbers of townsmen and women were drawn into "stool affairs."

Little purpose would be served by recounting these often bewilderingly complex contests in any detail. Some stool disputes, such as those that gripped the Akanmaji *akutso* from 1910, the Asere *akutso* from the 1920s, and the Otublohum *akutso* from the 1930s, continued sporadically for decades and even for generations. What is important is locating rising political tensions in a context of continuity and change in patterns of economy and culture in Accra. Chieftaincy affairs within individual town quarters became entangled with two great conflicts that dominated politics in Accra throughout the 1910s and 1920s. The first was centered on the historical status of the Alata *akutso* of James Town, and the second was the campaign to destool *Ga mantse* Taki Yaoboi. Both can be seen as struggles over the past, present, and future of Ga state and society in Accra.

We return first to the sequence of confrontations between James Town (Nleshi) and Ussher Town (Kinka), which began with the action *Solomon v. Noy* in 1880, erupted violently with the *Agbuntsota* of 1884, and continued fitfully until reemerging in the colonial courtroom in 1907. The fundamental issue underlying the mutual hostility of the two townships was the status of the Alata *akutso*. By the early twentieth century, the efforts on the part of the Alata leadership to assert Nleshi's autonomy from the *Ga mantse* in Kinka began to be counterbalanced by an equally vigorous campaign within Kinka itself on the part of the Asere *akutso*. The contrast between these two poles of Ga political power is striking. On the one hand, the identity of the Alata quarter had been forged by a range of historical processes suggesting innovation and the acquisition of civic virtue: the incorporation of strangers, the accumulation of mercantile wealth, and the allegiance with European power. The Asere quarter, on the other hand, embodied ascribed status derived from original settlement, ritual authority, and *Gamei kron* ("true Ga") identity. The tension between these distinct sources of power had been at the heart of Ga politics since the formation of the coastal city-state. With the coming of colonial rule, the need to establish "constitutional" legitimacy in order to control economic resources—at first people but increasingly land—heightened this historic tension. As a self-styled bastion of Ga custom, the Asere *akutso* was inevitably drawn to the center of the alliance activated to challenge what was perceived as the illegitimate authority of Alata *mantse* Kojo Ababio. A succession of bitter legal actions beginning in 1910 also indicates how the reassertion of Asere influence began to reshape the balance of power within Kinka itself.

The suit *Tetteh Kwaku v. Kpakpo Brown* of 1910 provides a further example of how political action was fueled by the strains of urban growth.[49] The plaintiff, Tetteh Kwaku, was a prominent elder of the Abola *jase* and the leading councillor to his nephew, *Ga mantse* Taki Obili.[50] The proximate cause of the action lay in the plague epidemic of 1908, during which Tetteh Kwaku and other Kinka fishermen strongly objected to the inconvenience of being evacuated inland. With the blessing of the Kinka chiefs, Tetteh instead erected a dwelling at Chorkor (or Tsoco), a village on the western bank of the Korle lagoon. Kojo Ababio subsequently demanded that he remove himself from what was Nleshi land. When this call was ignored, a crowd of Alata men and women led by William Kpakpo Brown, an elderly and respected councillor to *mantse* Ababio, summarily razed the building.

Although Tetteh Kwaku was an elder of the Abola *akutso*, the courtroom encounter developed into a contest between Asere and Alata mediated by barristers A. B. Quartey-Papafio and Thomas Hutton Mills. Quartey-Papafio again orchestrated his case around an attack on the historic rights of the office of Alata *mantse*, stressing that the purchase of *oblempon* status by Wetse Kojo in the eighteenth century did not include control over town land. This was contrasted with the rights of first settlement of the *Ga mashi* migrants and the sacral authority of the Koole and Sakumo *wulomei* in Kinka. Hutton

Mills stuck with his 1907 strategy of demonstrating uninterrupted Alata occupation and the moral legitimacy of acquired wealth. The Chorkor land may contain sacred groves inhabited by *jemawojii* worshipped exclusively in Kinka, it was conceded, but also visible were potent traces of mercantile power: the ruins of a slave barracoon constructed by Wetse Kojo's son, Sackey. Hutton Mills also introduced dramatic evidence challenging the Asere claim that Wetse Kojo and his descendants had few cultural or kinship links with the *Ga mashi* people of Kinka. Tracing a line of decent through six generations, he demonstrated that the great *akwashontse* Kwatei Kojo and his progeny—including prosecution lawyer A. B. Quartey-Papafio—were themselves descended from the house of the "stranger," Wetse Kojo.

On February 21, 1910, Chief Justice W. B. Griffith, Jr. gave judgment for the defendants with costs. News of the decision spread swiftly from the courthouse. As was often the case in moments of political tension, the Ga women were the first to mobilize, those of Alata having already prepared white flags of victory.[51] The women of Sempe, meanwhile, gathered outside the *mantse we* and "sang songs conveying that their grandfather had no right to give away the land and that he had never done so."[52] Fighting later broke out when the victorious Kojo Ababio paraded in full state through the streets of James Town, Hutton Mills and C. J. Bannerman finding immediate reemployment representing those Alatas charged with riot. Shortly afterward, Asere *mantse* D. P. Hammond filed trespass charges against Hutton Mills, Bannerman, and *mantse* Ababio. Although the actions against the two lawyers were settled swiftly, they again defended Kojo Ababio against Hammond's charges when the suit finally went to court in 1912.

Mantse Hammond's action continued to raise the profile of the Asere *akutso* in the campaign against the Alata stool. At stake was control over the land at Lartebiokorshi granted by Kojo Ababio to Muhammad Baako's Hausa followers in 1907. This was claimed by Hammond on the grounds that "all the lands which belonged to the Gas were formerly attached to the Asere stool."[53] Daniel Philip Hammond was an ex-carpenter who had worked in the Bights throughout the 1880s before settling down in Accra as an independent trader. A literate Christian, he had already begun to make extensive land purchases on the cocoa frontier of Akyem Abuakwa when in 1902 he was chosen to succeed the late Akrama as *mantse*.[54] Like many rising businessmen for whom the obligations of public office conflicted with entrepreneurship, Hammond was reluctant to accept the position, claiming that he had never had any interest in stool affairs.[55] Despite some disquiet within Asere over his ongoing accumulation of private land, ten years on the stool had not prevented Hammond from emerging as one of the largest cocoa farmers in Accra.[56] This background had considerable relevance to the 1912 court action, when it emerged that the prime mover of the case was not *mantse* Hammond himself but E. W. Quartey-Papafio, elder brother of prosecution lawyer A. B. Quartey-Papafio and the most influential member of Kpakpatsewe of Asere. Lartebiokorshi, E. W. Quartey-Papafio testified, had long been farmed by slaves owned by his father "Old Papafio," and through prolonged occupation had effectively passed from being "stool land" to private property.

Kojo Ababio's articulate testimony was again central to the success of the Alatas in fending off these claims. His informed recitation of the founding of the *akutso* dwelt on the historic links between wealth, warfare, and political power: "the Mantse of Alata was made mantse by the Sempes and Akumajis as he had power and he had money and in going to war he always went in front."[57] Urban society, the Alatas strove to demonstrate, had fundamentally been reshaped by the wealth and authority derived from the European forts. As Kojo Ababio emphasized: "The English, Dutch and Danes used to interfere with the ownership of land . . . [and] with our native affairs."[58] This version of the town's past was vehemently challenged by Asere witnesses, who argued that European patronage had had little impact on relations of power in Accra. However, testimony that invoked the ritually derived authority of the original Asere migrants held little weight with a British judge who based his ruling on "title by occupation as distinct from the alleged historical title."[59] Again, the decision went the way of the Alata *akutso*.

Five months after his victory against the Aseres, Kojo Ababio struck directly at Kpakpatsewe by bringing charges of trespass against *akwashontse* T. R. Quartey, initiating an action that would reach the Privy Council in London.[60] At stake was control over farming land on the Sakumo River frontier, which had increasingly important implications for the balance of power within the urban center. Following a convoluted series of appeals, the results of each stage of the legal process being greeted by exuberant celebrations in the successful quarters, Kojo Ababio finally won the action in 1916.[61] Two years later he went on to consolidate his legal supremacy in the last great suit of the sequence, the famous *Land for Accra Water Works* of 1918.

Like the 1907 "Harbour Blockyard Case," the "Water Works Case" was triggered by the development of a piece of infrastructure aimed at eliminating an historical constraint to Accra's urban development: the construction of a water treatment plant on the Sakumo river for the capital's newly inaugurated pipe-borne water supply. The legal contest was characterized by the increasingly extreme claims advanced by the anti-Alata coalition in Accra, led in this case by Sempe *mantse* Anege

Akwei.[62] Anege Akwei sought to portray the people of Alata as servile strangers: "They were the whiteman's people—his slaves . . . from down the coast—Lagos men . . . they were all prisoners. No senior or junior among them."[63] Kojo Ababio countered with a quite different picture of the making of urban Accra: "I am a Ga. My grandfathers and grandmothers lived in Accra. I am also living in Accra, and all the people who are living in Accra came from somewhere else."[64]

The language of superordination and subordination, of origins rooted in either original migration or servitude, provides some indication as to why this fiercely contested political conflict transcended the complex machinations and material concerns of individual legal actions. The financial benefits derived from the village at stake in the 1913 case, for example, would have been far outstripped by the £20,000 Kojo Ababio allegedly spent contesting its control, a sum raised only by mortgaging the Alata *mantse we* to the Bank of British West Africa.[65] Unable to pay the costs of the 1918 case, the unfortunate Sempe *mantse* was imprisoned for debt for much of 1921, causing further financial problems for his small *akutso* due to the enforced closure of his tribunal.[66] Faced with soaring legal costs and unable to reverse the trajectory of favorable judgments accumulated by Kojo Ababio, the long campaign against the Alata *akutso* faltered following the Water Works Case. The 1920s saw a shift in the focus of Ga politics away from the rights and status of the Alata stool toward those of the paramount Ga stool of Abola.

THE POLITICS OF DESTOOLMENT

The escalation of stool disputes over the meaning of public office and the conduct of chiefs in the early-twentieth-century Gold Coast was in no way peculiar to Accra. In 1914, the Secretary for Native Affairs noted with alarm that destoolments by "popular movements" were on the increase throughout the old Colony, and between that year and 1924 a total of seventy-nine chiefs were forcibly removed from office.[67] Tensions between Ga "youngmen" (*oblahii*) and chiefs were being reported from Accra by 1913, fueled, according to the *Gold Coast Nation*, by the unconstitutional disposal of stool land by *mantsemei*.[68] The more "establishment" Accra weekly, Nanka-Bruce's *Independent*, also reflected upon rising intergenerational discord, pointing the finger of blame instead at the "spread of education" combined with "the fact that the cocoa industry made many insignificant persons . . . rich . . . and . . . disposed to pay less respect to their natural rulers."[69] Most observers were agreed that the *asafo* companies together with new "scholars' unions" were the organizational vehicles through which rising grievances—whether justified or not—were mobilized.

A number of historians have paused to consider the role of popular pro-test in the rash of chieftaincy disputes that swept much of the Gold Coast and Asante in the early colonial period. De Graft Johnson's early treatment of *asafo* companies as representing the rising aspirations of "commoners" or "youngmen" has been reworked in a variety of nationalist and class con-texts analyzing the unrest as a manifestation of nonelite anticolonial protest or incipient class consciousness.[70] There are problems with the tendency to reduce stool disputes to conflict between popular forces led by independently wealthy and literate youngmen on the one hand, and a traditionalist office-holding elite bolstered by colonial authority on the other. Although most work has focused on rural Akan areas, where the cocoa revolution effected more sudden change than in the coastal towns, evidence from Accra sug-gests that chieftaincy disputes were prosecuted by complex coalitions. Ga alliances were strongly influenced by the intricate political topography of the town quarters, cutting across incipient generational, class, and ideologi-cal divisions.[71]

The deposition of *Ga mantse* Taki Obili in August 1918 pushed the issue of destoolment to the center of town affairs. In what would become standard practice, a long list of charges was carefully drawn up by the "destooling party" for the benefit of the colonial government, which was required under the terms of the 1904 Chiefs Ordinance to establish that both election and deposition were carried out "in accordance with native custom."[72] The weight of the charges rested on the dual allegation that Taki Obili had mortgaged the Ga stool in order to trade in cocoa and had illegally taken possession of the sacred stools of his predecessors.

The economic background to the allegations was the contraction of inter-national trade due to wartime shipping shortages, which in February 1917 led the government to place strict limits on the issue of cocoa export li-cences.[73] Following the expulsion of the Basel Mission for alleged pro-Ger-man sympathies and the closure of their Trading Company in December of that year, Governor Clifford—to the displeasure of expatriate business—of-fered the available export licenses to the three paramount chiefs of Accra, Akuapem, and Akyem Abuakwa. In March 1918, the chiefs approached the Colonial Bank and agreed to pledge their stools as security for the sum of £20,000 to be used to charter a steamer. Although an increase in shipping space meant that the loan agreement was never acted upon, the chiefs made good use of their export licenses, Taki Obili dividing his share between the *mantsemei* and a number of private Accra merchants.[74] Protests over what was seen as a unilateral allocation coincided with the belated public discov-ery of the loan agreement.

The perception that Taki Obili had literally "pawned" the Okaikoi stool—the most potent material symbol of the collective identity of the Ga people—

was reinforced by the fact that a dispute was already simmering over his removal from the Taki Kome *we* of the ritually blackened stools of past *Ga mantsemei*.[75] On August 8, the *manbii* of Accra gathered at the sacred meeting place of Sakumotsoshishi where the chiefs demanded an explanation. The assembly was broken up by the police and when the *Ga mantse* refused to attend a second meeting two days later, the Abola *jase* "went before the Asafoatsemei and swore the big oaths of 'Momotse Tong,' 'Awuna So' and 'Taki Dina' that . . . they would serve him no longer."[76]

To what extent did the destoolment result from the mobilization of Accra's *asafo* companies as the vehicles for the grievances of commoners against chiefly power? A group of Kinka *asafoatsemei* certainly claimed a leading role in organizing opposition to Taki Obili, arguing that they were "the only sect of people by customary law entitled to bring a Mantse to trial."[77] In addition to *asafo* leaders, however, the *mantsemei*, the Abola *jase*, and the Nai, Sakumo, and Koole *wulomei* all came forward to press established "customary" rights with regard to the Ga stool. The most outspoken of the *asafo* leaders was C. B. Nettey. Despite being aged fifty-two in 1918, Nettey was in many ways the archetypal Gold Coast youngman. Literate, articulate, and politically motivated, he would emerge over the following decade as Accra's most implacable opponent of chiefly prerogative. He was also involved in some dubious business activities at the height of the concessions boom at the turn of the century, when as the self-styled "Chief Nettey of the Gbesies" he traveled to London in an attempt to sell land concessions in Akyem Abuakwa.[78] His controversial connection with Akyem continued when as a cocoa buyer at the market town of Pakro he allegedly set up a private tribunal, later attempting to collect tolls from Ga farmers in the Asamankese district. These efforts to establish himself as a local broker among the Ga settlers on the Akyem cocoa frontier brought Nettey into conflict with the Ga stool. His hostility toward Taki Obili was apparent in 1916, the accusation that the *Ga mantse* had fallen under the pernicious influence of "fetish women" being recycled in support of destoolment two years later.

Opinion in Accra was deeply divided over the deposition of the *Ga mantse*. Many notables argued that the Ga had no history of constitutional destoolment, agreeing with Anum Nunoo of Abola that "to apply the customs and usages of the Twis and Fantees to . . . the Ga Tribe and Peoples would be detrimental to the latter."[79] Taki Obili received further support from the *amanhene* of Akuapem and Akyem Abuakwa, the latter also fighting off an attempted destoolment arising from the cocoa export deal.[80] In contrast with the charismatic *okyenhene* Ofori Atta, who survived the challenge with the aid of the Gold Coast police, Taki Obili lacked the political capital necessary to gain the sympathy of the colonial regime.[81] Due to recurring complaints over the operation of his tribunal and prison—since 1910 officially recognized under the NJO—the *Ga mantse* was already out of favor with the administration.[82] Indeed, criminal charges relating to a series of illegal detentions were already being considered when the issue was overtaken by the events of August 1918. This was almost certainly a factor in the decision to confirm the destoolment. Reciting what would become the mantra of indirect rule in British tropical Africa, the SNA judged that the removal of Taki Obili had indeed been carried out "in accordance with native custom."

Ga Mantse Taki Yaoboi (1919–1929)

The elders of Abola moved swiftly in the selection of a new *Ga mantse*. On March 9, 1919, the *jase* enstooled Yaoboi, son of Okai Mensa of Amugiwe, who had acted as stool caretaker during the 1903 interregnum.[83] Aged forty in 1919, Taki Yaoboi was the latest in a long line of Ga officeholders who had earned their fame and fortune as migrant tradesmen before returning to Accra to trade on their enhanced monetary and social capital. Educated at the Wesleyan school, Yaoboi trained as a blacksmith, journeying to Cameroon and Leopold's Congo before serving as an engineer on freighters and working for eight years as a mechanic in Germany.[84] On returning to Accra he was employed by F. & A. Swanzy's new motor transport department and in 1912 was a founding member of a scholars' union comprising the younger members of the Abola *jase*, the "Abola Djasefoi Abii Asafo."[85] Literate, enterprising, and with progressive ideas, Yaoboi had just established his own motor garage when selected as a candidate for the Ga stool.

Despite these credentials, the political divisions over the fall of his predecessor ensured that Taki Yaoboi's legitimacy was questioned from the outset. Opposition first arose from the Abola Kpatashi house, led by Taki Obili's kinsman and advisor Tetteh Kwaku.[86] Failing to veto the succession, Tetteh Kwaku proceeded to take out a series of court injunctions in an effort to prevent the new *mantse* from reopening his tribunal.[87] The confirmation by the colonial regime of Taki Yaoboi's enstoolment discouraged his Kpatashi rivals. By the time of the arrival of the new Governor, F. G. Guggisberg, in October 1919, he was exercising his chiefly prerogatives without open opposition. Nevertheless, the vigilance with which the townspeople historically had monitored the actions of their officeholders was stepped up by Yaoboi's opponents, whose simmering resentment would remain a constant threat to his authority. Growing anxiety over the *Ga mantse*'s efforts to play a progressive role in elite constitutional politics would lead to a succession of attempts to remove him from office, until he too was finally destooled in 1929. His failure to reach an accommodation between "stool affairs" on the one hand and "modern" political action on the other was a reflection of the widening gulf between the two sides of Accra's urban identity, that of African city-state and colonial capital.

URBAN CHANGE AND GA POLITICS

Urban Development and Constitutional Politics

Guggisberg's robust governorship (1919–1927) had a lasting impact on the development of Accra and the evolution of colonial rule in the Gold Coast. Arriving at the height of a postwar boom in cocoa prices, he immediately unveiled an ambitious program of infrastructural development, to be followed by a more cautious series of constitutional reforms.[88] The new Governor shared with both expatriate and African business interests a sense of optimism with regard to continuing economic growth, and was willing to reward the achievements of the Gold Coast with limited political reform. As the main urban center and entrepôt port servicing the cocoa-producing forest region, Accra stood to benefit from tropical Africa's most spectacular peasant-led agricultural revolution.[89] As the colonial capital, it also consolidated its function as the center stage of "constitutional" political action.

In 1919, Accra was changing fast. Since the end of the war, a rash of new import-export ventures had been founded by local businessmen, such as J. Addo-Vanderpuye's Dawa and Anyiman Corporation (with a capital of £100,000), E. A. Manyo-Plange's Tropical Traders, and T. P. Allotey's Ga Trading Company.[90] Meanwhile, established merchants with roots in the declining port towns, notably A. J. Ocansey of Ada, were relocating their operations to the capital. With new trading stores rising from the High Street and rows of European bungalows marching along the Ridge, Accra was in the midst of an unprecedented construction boom. The railway together with a growing network of motor roads linked the capital with its growing agricultural hinterland, and by 1921 a total of 586 lorries and 214 cars were registered in Accra.[91]

Despite this economic expansion, the boom had created strains in urban society. Following a grand durbar on November 28, 1919, at which Guggisberg outlined his plans to the people of Accra, the Governor and the Ga chiefs engaged in a vigorous dialogue on the issues facing the town. The most pressing concern for both ruler and subjects was labor.[92] Disturbed that in the face of an acute local labor shortage, Ga artisans continued to travel in large numbers to the Bights, Guggisberg demanded whether "the French or the Belgian or any other foreign nation treat the black races better than the English." The answer from the *mantsemei* was quite simple: "the French and the Belgians pay higher wages." By early 1920, labor in Accra was reported to be in a "ferment," the newly-formed Artisan's and Labourer's Union threatening stoppages in support of pay claims.[93] Discontent over rising prices and racially determined pay policy also surfaced from the ranks of the African salariat, whose organized protests began in 1919 over the issue of war bonuses.[94]

The boom ended abruptly in mid-1920 with a slump in cocoa prices. The Gold Coast economy was pushed into several years of relative depression, which exacerbated existing hardships for many urban dwellers.[95] Guggisberg nevertheless pushed ahead with his development program. Korle Bu Hospital, situated above Korle Gonno on the western fringe of the expanding city, opened its doors in 1923. The Prince of Wales College, located in a rural setting near the old *aklowa* of Achimota, six miles to the north of downtown Accra, followed suit in 1927. Despite these triumphs, the economic downturn was to spell trouble for the Governor's envisaged constitutional reforms. The first stage of a gradual widening of electoral representation was to be the granting of an African majority on the Accra Town Council, a move that in 1924 provoked fierce popular resistance from the Ga townspeople.

The politics of Gold Coast constitutional reform in the 1920s is one of the few aspects of Accra's history to have received any sustained scrutiny. In his monumental history of the antecedents of Gold Coast nationalism, Kimble draws a lively picture of Accra as the setting for the emergence of modern anticolonial politics in West Africa. In *Lawyers in Gold Coast Politics*, Edsman builds on Kimble's pioneering study, carefully reconstructing the alliances between the two elite organizations, the ARPS and NCBWA on the one hand, and local Ga factions on the other.[96] Edsman identifies a subtle yet fundamental cleavage in elite urban politics in the early colonial Gold Coast. On the one hand stood the reformist modernization of J. E. Casely Hayford's National Congress, supported in Accra by the majority of the established wealthy elite and by the two "progressive" *mantsemei* Taki Yaoboi and Kojo Ababio. With the decline of the Congress in the late 1920s, the political aspirations of the old Accra elite became focused on the Accra Ratepayers Association (ARA). Led by such respectable establishment figures as Thomas Hutton Mills, John Glover Addo, Dr. F. V. Nanka Bruce, and Akilagpa Sawyerr, the ARA was formed in 1927 as a vehicle with which to contest municipal elections. On the other hand was the ARPS, dominated in the 1920s by the younger and more populist lawyers A. W. Kojo Thompson of Accra and

Kobina Sekyi of Cape Coast. In opposition to the Congress, which advocated a greater role for the urban intelligentsia through elective bodies such as town councils, the ARPS clung to John Mensah Sarbah's old "legal-constitutionalist" position that African political advance must occur through the reform of chiefly institutions. In 1920s Accra, the ARPS became closely associated with the coalition of forces seeking the destoolment of *Ga mantse* Taki Yaoboi, Kojo Thompson forming the populist Manbii Party in opposition to the establishment Ratepayers Association.

While Edsman demonstrates the intimate connection between "modern" and "traditional" politics in Accra, his emphasis—as the title of his work suggests—is firmly on the former, to the extent of regarding local Ga politics as a rather obscure, customary backdrop to the real action. He is right in stressing that the repeated efforts to destool Taki Yaoboi invariably "coincided with acute grievances conditioned by government policies."[97] Yet politics in the colonial capital continued to be conditioned by the interior architecture of Ga state and society. Fierce political debate over the remaking of Accra certainly interacted with, but was not solely created by, colonial rule.

Homowo: Continuity and Innovation

As we have seen with the struggle over the status of the Alata stool, by the 1910s the strains of urban growth fueled political debate that turned on conflicting versions of the Ga past. The need to (re)define the past in order to control the present and shape the future became increasingly apparent throughout the 1920s, as a coalition of disgruntled chiefs mounted a sustained challenge to prerogatives of the *Ga mantse*. As with the legal assault on the Alata *mantse* in the previous decade, it was the Asere quarter that led the opposition to the established political order in Accra.

The dramatic opening move of the Asere challenge came in August 1920, at a key moment of the annual *Homowo* festival. On *Homowo So*, the Thursday on which the rural *kosebii*—called that day "*sobii*"—flood into Accra for the main celebrations, Asere *mantse* D. P. Hammond and an entourage of elders and *wulomei* traveled north to Ayawaso hill. The site of the ancient capital overrun by the Akwamu in 1677, Ayawaso remained a key reference point in Ga perceptions of the past.[98] In an unprecedented action resonating with cultural meaning and political threat, the Aseres proceeded to the *aklabatsa* of Okaikoi. There they attended to the spiritual needs of the dead king—rites hitherto performed within Accra by the *Ga mantse*—before parading back to town the following day in full state.[99] The Ga quarters were plunged into immediate turmoil.

Figure 6.4   *Sobii* ("Thursday people") arrive in the city by train for the annual *Homowo* festival, Station Road, Accra, c. 1917. (Copyright Basel Mission Archive, Basel, Switzerland. Ref. No. D-30.01.038. Reproduced with permission.)

The implication of the Asere action, fully articulated in the subsequent government enquiry, was that they, and not the Abolas, were the true heirs of Okaikoi. The original stool of Okaikoi, the Aseres maintained, had been removed to the Slave Coast town of Little Popo after the catastrophe of 1677. The *Ga mantse* merely sat on a lesser "war stool" created for Taki Kome in the 1820s by the *jemawon* Sakumo, the authority of Okaikoi having passed directly to Asere through his "captain" and successor Nikoilai.[100] Refuting this reading of Accra's history, Hammond's opponents charged that the aging *mantse* was being cynically manipulated by others: "Nii Asere has never worshipped any of the fetishes [*jemawojii*] brought from Okai Kwei. He is a Christian!"[101]

The Asere's calculated pilgrimage to the *aklabatsa* of Okaikoi signaled the increasing politicization of the *Homowo* festival and of death and burial in 1920s Accra.[102] The two were inextricably linked, remembrance of the ancestors and lamentations for the more recent dead being at the heart of the ritual affirmation of the social order. Indeed, *mantse* Hammond cited the processions to the new mausoleums on the outskirts of Accra each *Homowo* as justification for his action in 1920: "Every

Mantse has a right to perform a new custom. After Mantse Tackie Tawia's death they introduced a new custom . . . of going to his burial place Mamprobi every year."[103] As political tension within Accra mounted, so the annual processions became more elaborate and defiant, symbolizing not cultural unity but the strident particularism of individual town quarters.[104] Hammond himself, who was to die in March 1922 and be interred in a mausoleum at Kaneshi, became the object of veneration for the Asere people, who marched out *en masse* each *Homowo* with *asafo* flags flying, muskets firing, and drums and gong-gongs beating in competition with rival quarters.[105]

Unlike the great Asante *odwira* festival, which entered a period of abeyance under colonial rule following the exile of the *Asantehene* in 1896, Ga *Homowo* not only retained its ritual vigor but became the scene of new forms of political mobilization.[106] The mass arrival of the "*sobii*" in Accra continued as the great symbolic bridging of the rural-urban cultural divide, despite the *Independent*'s lament that "much of the glamour and the impressive nature of this yearly invasion have been shorn off, owing to the people resorting more and more to the . . . lorry and the train to come into the capital."[107] Innovation was also apparent in the conscious borrowing of Akan forms, particularly in Alata, where by the 1920s the so-called "James Town *odwira*" had become a focal point of Accra's *Homowo* season. The climax of James Town *odwira* was a great durbar held in Ababio Square before the Alata *mantse we* and regularly attended by the Governor and other officials, a potent display of Kojo Ababio's carefully nurtured relationship with colonial power.[108]

Destoolment, Poison, and Murder: The Politics of Anxiety

The 1920 *Homowo* signaled the growing alienation of the Asere *akutso* and its allies that would lead to the first of four attempts to destool the *Ga mantse* in January 1921. The proximate cause of the destoolment was a collision between the guardians of Accra's sacred space and the forces of urban change. At stake was another issue at the heart of Ga belief: the ritual management of lagoons. As we have seen with the struggles of the 1890s and 1900s over the sanctity of the Sakumofio lagoon, control over the bodies of water that defined the Ga world remained a volatile issue in early colonial Accra. Urban redevelopment clashed with Ga notions of ritual space in 1919, when the government attempted to intervene on sanitary grounds in the natural opening and closing of the Korle and Klote lagoons to the sea.[109] In June 1920, a British business consortium approached Taki Yaoboi requesting a lease of the Korle lagoon with a view to converting it into a harbor.[110] It appears that town leaders were initially in favor, and an agreement was drawn up granting the businessmen an option on a lease. However, the political climate deteriorated as a result of the Okaikoi incident, the District Commissioner ruling that the Asere *mantse* had effectively usurped the customary rights of the *Ga mantse*. The response of the Aseres and their allies the Sempes was to reverse their attitude to the Korle agreement, loudly accusing Taki Yaoboi of "selling" the sacred lagoon—the physical manifestation of the tutelar *jemawon* Koole—to the Europeans. The culmination of a complex series of machinations was the declared destoolment of Taki Yaoboi by *akwashontse* T R. Quartey and the *asafo* companies of the two hostile quarters on January 22, 1921.[111]

The attempt to topple Taki Yaoboi in 1920–1921 was a failure. Following an exhaustive three-month inquiry, assistant SNA C. W. Welman concluded that the deposition had not been conducted in accordance with native custom. Welman would emerge as a key actor in town affairs in the 1920s. Despite his apparent reliance on the sanctity of custom, he was quite aware of the realities of change and innovation in Accra resulting from the impact of colonial rule. Secretary for Native Affairs from 1923 to 1928, he had a keen interest in the African past and in indigenous systems of belief, personifying a shift away from the often stereotypical attitude toward custom and "fetish" displayed by an earlier generation of officials.[112] Welman found little evidence to suggest that the campaign against Taki Yaoboi was a genuine popular movement by the townspeople of Accra.[113] Opposition to the *Ga mantse*, he concluded, was concentrated in two bitterly disaffected quarters, Asere in Kinka and Sempe in Nleshi, the prime movers in the destoolment clearly being the Kpakpatsewe family under *akwashontse* T. R. Quartey.

The political mobilization of this most powerful of Asere lineages was one of the most salient aspects of politics in early twentieth-century Accra. Imprisoned for debt at the time of the 1918 destoolment, T. R. Quartey reemerged to orchestrate the Asere case at the Okaikoi Enquiry and went on to lead the opposition to Taki Yaoboi and his ally Kojo Ababio throughout the 1920s.[114] The political struggle was not simply one between the forces of Ga tradition on the one hand and progressive modernity on the other. Quartey was closely supported by his highly educated kinsmen, the three Quartey-Papafio brothers, especially Arthur Boi, a founding member of the NCBWA. Yet within Asere, the perception was growing that what was the oldest and largest quarter of original *Ga mashi* migrants was in danger of being marginalized by a coalition of less hallowed stools, upstart "strangers," and colonial power. First activated by the official refusal to recognize the *akwashon* court under the NJO of 1910, this fear was exacerbated by the emerging idiom of indirect rule, in particular the British emphasis on the role of the *Ga mantse* as "paramount chief."

The atmosphere of growing anxiety within the Asere *akutso* was heightened by the death after twenty years on the stool of D. P. Hammond in March 1922. Hammond suffered a long, agonizing final illness, during which he was reported to have been "completely under the sway of T. R. Quartey."[115] Three days before his final demise, a group of *asafobii* led by Quartey launched an extraordinary physical assault on the *Ga mantse* and the elderly Osu *mantse* William Notei Dowuona (1916–1931) as they passed through Bukom Square in the heart of the Asere quarter, tearing away their cloths and state umbrellas and forcing them to seek shelter in their underclothes in the nearby residence of the Sakumo *wulomo*.[116] The conflict had reached a point where the streets of the old downtown neighborhoods were virtually off-limits to protagonists from adjacent *akutsei*. Field's Asere informants in the 1930s offer valuable insights into this escalating tension at the time of Hammond's impending death.[117] The distressed Aseres, they intimated, consulted an Islamic diviner (*klamo*) in order to ascertain the cause of the illness. Approaching an oracle through the use of cowries and the Koran, the *klamo* discovered that the dying *mantse* was the victim of an "unusually powerful bad medicine" activated by the deliberate starving to death of a crocodile, "which would not only kill him, but his successors to the number of three."[118] On March 28, a small crocodile was indeed discovered trussed up in a cemetery, and on that day the Asere *mantse* died. Field does not elaborate the point, but there is no doubt that the popular assumption in Asere was that Hammond had been "poisoned" by his enemies.

The political ramifications of D. P. Hammond's death affected Asere throughout the 1920s. In view of the menacing threat revealed by the *klamo*, it appears that Agbonwe, the lineage due to supply the next *mantse*, was unwilling to offer a candidate. In desperation, the elders finally prevailed upon Ayi Ansa, "a middle-aged man of courage, character and great intelligence" and a member of Hammond's own Frimponwe, to act as stool caretaker (*sei kwelo*).[119] A wealthy ex-carpenter who during the postwar boom had made extensive investments in real estate, Ayi Ansa progressively sold off houses in Accra and in the cocoa-trading towns of Mangoase and Koforidua in order to maintain his position as *sei kwelo*. Much of the money was reputedly expended on efforts to purchase "the strongest medicine obtainable . . . to counteract the effect of the medicine that threatened him and his successors."[120]

Despite Ayi Ansa's efforts, Asere anxieties were compounded by a second traumatic death only six months after that of D. P. Hammond. In August 1922, the horribly mutilated body of Boi Hammond, a young schoolteacher and close kinsman of the late *mantse*, was found on the outskirts of Accra.[121] The murder was never solved, and the extent to which it was linked to the alleged poisoning of D. P. Hammond, to the Asere succession, or to the wider political conflict in Accra can only be speculated upon.[122] What is certain is that it further fueled Asere hostility toward its rival quarters. "From the time Ayi Ansa was made Acting Mantse," one elder testified in 1931, "the state of affairs in Asere might be described to be worse than even the Awuna War . . . because at that time all Accra were against Asere."[123] The crime served to confirm Asere suspicions that its enemies were resorting to "bad medicine," although the almost stereotypically ritual nature of the murder suggests the work of *agents provocateurs* rather than the former.[124] "Poisoning" was again suspected when a number of leading elders later died in quick succession, as recalled by an elderly Asere resident in the 1970s: "according to the western belief [they got ill and died], we may say so, but according to our belief . . . it was terrible . . . and everybody was afraid."[125]

Despite the belief that "all Accra were against Asere," the unity of the Asere *akutso* itself began to crack under the strains of the deepening crisis. Tinkering with traditions of origin in order to strengthen contemporary political claims was a risky business, as a number of *akutsei* riven by internal stool disputes would discover to their cost. In the case of Asere, it was *mantse* Hammond's assertion that his stool had belonged to Nikoilai, first deployed in the colonial courtroom in the course of *Hammond v. Ababio* in 1912 and restated at the 1920 Okaikoi Enquiry, which was considered by others in the quarter to be an illegitimate reshaping of tradition. The aggrieved party was the powerful Joshishiwe lineage, which angrily claimed that its own stool had always been recognized as that of the ancient war leader Nikoilai.[126] Under the leadership of the occupant of that stool, Nii Amasa, Joshishi split from the rest of Asere, aligning itself with the embattled *Ga mantse* Taki Yaoboi.

Although such tangled claims and counterclaims were of dubious historicity, identities rooted in traditions of origin took on a heightened importance in the face of the new uncertainties and anxieties of the colonial dispensation. The letter columns of the local press give some indication of the passions aroused, the *Independent* publishing an ongoing debate on the history of Asere entitled "The Man in the Palanquin."[127] As this evocative heading suggests, the argument again turned on the historic balance of power between original migrants and later "accumulators," each camp accusing the other of founding a usurpatory "palanquin stool." The point here is that these issues were of greater moment to the mass of Ga townspeople than the constitutional concerns of the elite ARPS and NCBWA. Far from being obscure atavisms, cultural accretions from the precolonial past continued to determine the nature of Ga politics at a time of accelerating urban change.

NATIVE *OMAN* AND BIG TOWN, 1924–1929

Revolt Against Town Council Reform

Popular protest against efforts to reform the Accra Town Council was linked with a renewed attempt to destool the *Ga mantse* in 1924–1925. As in 1897–1898, it was the issue of municipal taxation that galvanized the townspeople of Accra into open opposition to the colonial regime and those perceived as its collaborators. Soon after his arrival, Guggisberg expressed dissatisfaction with the working of the Gold Coast's three town councils in Accra, Cape Coast, and Sekondi. In 1921, he appointed a committee to formulate plans for reform. The committee, comprising colonial official John Maxwell together with NCBWA leaders J. E. Casely Hayford and E.J.P. Brown of Cape Coast and Thomas Hutton Mills and John Glover Addo of Accra, recommended that the official control of councils be replaced by an elected majority headed by an African mayor. The new bodies were to be self-financing through an increase in rates. By endorsing these proposals, Guggisberg was effectively meeting one of the central reformist demands of the Congress, which supported the passage of the resulting bill through the Legislative Council. Both the Governor and the African urban elite held high hopes for the Municipal Corporations Ordinance (MCO), which would initially be applied only to Accra. "The Native Oman administer and look after their people, and the Town Councils look after the big towns," Guggisberg declared at the official opening of the capital's new Selwyn Market in 1923, restating the established colonial vision of town and country. "There is no necessity for clashing between the two."[128]

However, notions of urban improvement shared by the government and indigenous intelligentsia were not necessarily endorsed by the townspeople of Accra. Just weeks before the Governor announced his plans, a huge body of angry market women marched on Christiansborg Castle to protest their forced removal from the old Salaga Market.[129] Subsequent events would force the official mind to confront the deep ambiguity of Accra's urban identity. Despite Guggisberg's dualistic vision of indirect rule, Accra was both "native *(o)man*" and "big town."

Shortly after it had been passed by the Legislative Council in July 1924, a copy of the MCO was obtained by C. B. Nettey and other *asafoatsemei*, who decided to mobilize against the measure.[130] The "youngmen" succeeded in raising popular fears that an oppressive new measure was about to be imposed on the town with the connivance of the *Ga mantse* and the elite ARPS/NCBWA leadership. Fueling popular hostility was the perception that Taki Yaoboi was circumventing customary processes of communication and consultation, a fear symbolized by the newly installed telephone in the *Ga mantse we*. "He has been in the habit of telephoning to the Police," an indignant *asafoatse* complained to Welman. "We are his soldiers!"[131] These suspicions were compounded by the unwillingness of NCBWA member Taki Yaoboi to condemn what he considered to be an overdue reform that he had already pledged to support. By September, Welman reported that while the MCO had the backing of the "progressive" *mantsemei* and the African elite, "the people of Accra, the masses, the Third Estate, in their Tribal organization under their Asafoatsemei . . . are arrayed against the application of the new law."[132] Following the breakdown of protracted negotiations between the parties in October, the hostile *asafoatsemei* announced to the town that the *Ga mantse* was destooled.

The disappointed Guggisberg appointed separate commissions to inquire into the hostility toward the MCO and the alleged destoolment. The former found that the strength of popular opposition was grounded in real economic hardship and genuine anxiety that the appointment of an African mayor would undermine the old Ga order. The resulting report provides a revealing glimpse into the changing nature of the colonial city.[133] Many witnesses testified that the competitive commercial climate coupled with the downturn after the boom of 1919–1920 had resulted in widespread hardship in Accra. The extension of European firms into the interior was particularly damaging to the long-established middleman role of Ga traders, both male and female. Meanwhile, the tradition of skilled labor migration was waning, as locally trained artisans had begun to push the Ga out of the Bights. The result was rising unemployment, also an acute problem for the growing numbers of literate school leavers. "What the parents have spent comes to nothing," protested Osu *mantse* Dowuona, registering elderly disquiet with the new urban popular culture. "We do not like the boys to play football and sing 'asafo'; they should be trained to build Achimota."[134] With many rate payers already in arrears and houses all over town heavily mortgaged, the proposed increases in local taxation and various licenses were widely resisted. The annual fee of twenty pounds for operating a drinking club over and above the thirty-pound spirit license was considered by Maxwell to be heavy, while permits for cinemas and theatrical entertainments also drew protests. The fiercest condemnation was reserved for the proposed increase in hawking licences from 12 to 18 shillings per annum, a move regarded as intolerable by the large numbers of poorer women who relied on petty trading to survive. The levy was also criticized by the educated elite of James Town on the grounds that it was the main weapon used by the *asafoatsemei* in whipping up the hostility of women of "the hawking class."[135] Dowuona summed up the situation with a Ga maxim: "It is very hard for a man carrying a load to be compelled to carry another." "What would you do?" the old chief demanded, "Go and leave town?"

At a time of growing economic difficulties, Nettey and his fellow *asafoatsemei* succeeded in mobilizing popular support against a measure widely regarded as an unjust imposition. However, after careful consideration Welman again refused to endorse the destoolment of the *Ga mantse*. The considered support of Alata *mantse* Kojo Ababio again proved crucial to Taki Yaoboi's political survival.[136] While the *Ga mantse* weathered the storm with support from Kojo Ababio and the colonial regime, the unrest wrecked the attempt to create an African-run town council in Accra. Guggisberg had hoped that municipal self-government would act as a "stepping-stone" to elective representation on the Legislative Council, and held out the latter as a carrot to the educated elite in a last-ditch attempt to implement the MCO. He underestimated the entrenched hostility toward the imposition of direct taxation among the townspeople of Accra. Rumors of a rates revision in early 1926 brought a further howl of protest, expediently led this time by Taki Yaoboi, forcing the Governor finally to abandon the Ordinance and to revise his new constitution.[137] Six of the nine Africans on a reformed Legislative Council were to be representatives of three new Provincial Councils of Chiefs, but the remaining three, instead of being elected by the ratepayers of Accra, Cape Coast, and Sekondi as originally envisaged, were now to be appointed by the government. As in the 1890s, the attempt to reshape Accra's town government was met by sustained popular resistance. The failure of Guggisberg's reforms reflected both the weakness of the colonial state in the face of urban protest and the difficulty in reconciling Accra's dual identity as native oman and big town.

Manbii, Ratepayers, and "Political Sanitation"

The second half of the 1920s saw the beginnings of a change in the nature of political action in Accra. The elaboration of the system of indirect rule and the reinstatement of municipal elections for the Legislative Council meant that for the first time, the politics of Gold Coast constitutional reform began to dominate local Ga politics. That something fundamental changed on the Gold Coast in the late 1920s has long been recognized by the established historiography. Kimble, whose unfolding narrative focuses increasingly on the political arena of the colonial capital, ends his long account of the antecedents of Ghanaian nationalism with the constitutional reforms of 1928. Changes within Accra interacted with wider forces in complex ways. The emergence of a new kind of urban politics was a reflection of the reformulation of urban space, as Accra grew beyond the nucleus of the old *majii*. Together, these two changes can be seen to mark the end of Accra's sixty-year transition from Ga city-state to colonial city. Accra remained the sacred epicenter of Ga state and society, but by 1930 its urban identity was shifting toward a new role as center stage of an emergent "national" politics.

Disappointed that only three seats on the Legislative Council were earmarked for nonchiefs, the ARPS/NCBWA decided to boycott Guggisberg's new constitution, mounting a campaign to convince the chiefs that the proposed Provincial Councils were contrary to "native custom."[138] NCBWA member Taki Yaoboi towed the Congress line, and was the only head chief not to attend the inaugural meeting of the Eastern Provincial Council at Nsawam in May 1926.[139] Taki's opponents in Accra continued to charge that he had "deserted his people and gone over to the Intelligentsia," yet responded by cementing their own alliance with the more populist faction of the urban elite.[140] Following the refusal of leading elite figures to accept nomination for Accra's vacant Legislative Council seat, the *Ga mantse*'s enemies surprised the administration by submitting their own candidate, the barrister A. W. Kojo Thompson.[141]

Like his political ally C. B. Nettey, Kojo Thompson (1880–1950) was a vocal champion of the rights of the youngman. His avowedly populist stance was reflected in the appropriation of the term *manbii* (townspeople or citizens) for his political vehicle, the Manbii Party. When, in 1927, Guggisberg reinstated direct elections for the three municipal Legislative Council seats, elite opposition to the constitution began to wane. Two parties emerged in Accra, Kojo Thompson's populist Manbii Party and the Accra Ratepayers' Association, the latter representing the established property-owning "high society." Kojo Thompson lost the inaugural contest to the Ratepayers' candidate, fellow barrister John Glover Addo, 780 of the city's 1,816 registered electors tuning out to vote.[142] Son of James Town merchant William Addo, John Glover Addo (1873–1933) joined J. E. Casely-Hayford of Sekondi and K. A. Korsah of Cape Coast as the Gold Coast's first elected Legislative Council members.

Intertwined with the tentative emergence of electoral politics in Accra was the ongoing struggle over the Ga stool. Encouraged by their alliance with Kojo Thompson, the anti-Taki Yaoboi town "opposition" made a third abortive attempt to effect a destoolment in October 1926.[143] The charges carried little weight with colonial officials, who were inclined to agree with Taki's supporters that the instigators were merely embittered "malcontents." "They are all 'small boys,'" Gbese elder Tete Tsuru retorted, employing a term broadly synonymous with "youngmen" but carrying greater pejorative intent. "Not one pays a tax equal to £30."[144] Nanka Bruce's weekly *Independent*, firmly behind the *Ga mantse*/Congress/Ratepayers axis, betrayed its own patrician leanings on the same theme: "The bastard term 'Manbii' is very misleading . . . for it denotes the whole people of a town including women, children [and] strangers and . . . is being conveniently employed as a cover for nonentities and irresponsibles."[145] This establishment view of Accra's urban crowd is revealing of the changing nature of the city, and is a striking anticipation of the language of nationalist politics in the 1940s and 1950s.

In March 1927, the political terrain of the Ga quarters shifted dramatically when a peace treaty was concluded between Asere and Alata. Relations between the two rival *akutsei* had sunk to a new nadir during the 1925 *Homowo*, when the Alata *asafo* companies had barred the Aseres from passing through James Town *en route* to the grave of *mantse* Hammond.[146] When the annual pilgrimage was again blocked in 1926, Ayi Ansa took Kojo Ababio to court. Yet what looked like a resumption of the cycle of litigation instead became a process of reconciliation, and the two chiefs ceremoniously agreed to bury the hatchet.[147] The reason for this historic rapprochement was the subject of intense speculation in Accra. Reports reached the SNA that the Aseres were elated by their recognition as a "Divisional Stool" under the new Native Administration Bill and "tired of maintaining an intransigence which has brought them nothing but worry and expense."[148] The British held high hopes that Ayi Ansa would now move to heal the rift with the *Ga mantse* in Abola. But peace with Alata had quite the opposite effect. It opened the way for Kojo Ababio to withdraw support from Taki Yaoboi, as the latter was engulfed by the final crisis of his troubled tenure, the Native Administration Ordinance (NAO) of 1927.

The NAO was an attempt to bolster the power of chieftaincy within a framework of colonial rule. Introduced into the legislature by the Colony's most authoritative "natural ruler," *okyenhene* Ofori Atta, it represented a formalization of the ideology of indirect rule that had long shaped the relationship between British power and African states on the Gold Coast. As such, it provoked the hostility of the urban intelligentsia, who united in opposition to the widening of chiefly power at the expense of their own political claims.[149] The strengthening of the judicial powers of newly designated Paramount and Divisional Chiefs also caused widespread disquiet within the lower echelons of chiefly hierarchies. In the politically fragmented environment of urban Accra, there were clear winners and losers. The *akutsei* of Alata and Asere, together with the towns from Osu down to Tema, were officially recognized as Divisional Stools and empowered to operate courts. The tribunals of the Gbese, Otublohum, Sempe, and Akanmaji quarters were closed, while all appeals were now automatically to be heard by that of the *Ga mantse* in his role as Paramount Chief.

The reformulation of "native administration" in Accra at the end of the 1920s can be interpreted as an attempt by the colonial state to finally impose its own vision of urban order on Ga state and society. The desire to rid the city of its multiplicity of African courts and overlapping political jurisdictions had been harbored by British officialdom since the 1870s.[150] The imperative to clean up Accra was made explicit by the SNA, who in a telling phrase hoped that the NAO reforms would result in the "political sanitation" of the colonial capital.[151] British hopes were soon dashed. The NAO served only to isolate the *Ga mantse*, undermining the very policy of indirect rule that it was designed to further. The judicial machinery of indirect rule in Accra was barely in place before it had ground to a halt. Unrest broke out when Taki Yaoboi's efforts to transfer cases from the officially defunct tribunals were fiercely resisted, the chiefs declaring that no cases involving parties from outside the Abola quarter should be taken to the *Ga mantse*.[152] As at the start of our period in the 1870s, law was at the very center of contested visions of town government.

The conflict culminated in the final destoolment of Taki Yaoboi in 1929. What is particularly striking about the end of the affair was the refusal on the part of the colonial government to intervene on behalf of the NAO and the beleaguered *Ga mantse*. One factor in this decision was the role of the influential Kojo Ababio, who broke the political deadlock by abandoning the erstwhile ally and going over to the destoolment camp.[153] More importantly, British officials continued to regard the urbanized Ga state as something of a special case among the native polities of the Gold Coast. The turmoil triggered by what were seen as progressive constitutional concessions served to underline the peculiar nature of the Ga social formation at the heart of the colonial capital. As in the 1900s, the official mind had serious doubts as to whether legislation governing the jurisdiction of indigenous rulers should be applied to Accra at all. The elaboration of indirect rule would come increasingly to dominate town affairs in the 1930s, a process that continued to be shaped by Accra's dual urban identity as colonial city and African polity.

CONCLUSION: ACCRA IN 1930 AND BEYOND

A central theoretical assumption underlying this study is that a town's specific urban character is derived from its function as a site of specialized institutions and of political action. The importance of politics in defining the town has particular relevance for the periodization of Accra's colonial history. Historians have often separated the initial phase of colonial rule in Africa from the period of "high" colonialism with World War I, and there are valid reasons to locate Accra within this conventional chronological framework. By 1918, Accra was beginning to undergo the transformations in urban life that would come to characterize the twentieth-century city in tropical Africa. However, it was the shift in the nature of the Ga political arena signaled by the events of the late 1920s that marks a more significant watershed in the evolution of the city. The destoolment of *Ga mantse* Taki Yaoboi in 1929 not only represented a rupture in the interior architecture of the Ga state, it also marked the point at which ongoing struggles to shape the town became inextricably linked to wider issues of Gold Coast constitutional politics.

The intensity with which Ga political factions contested the possession of traditional office continued into the 1930s and beyond, and indeed continues to this day. However, these conflicts unfolded within a changing city and an altered colonial framework. The NAO laid the legislative groundwork for the strengthening of indirect rule, a process pursued with greater urgency by hard-pressed officials with the onset of the Depression in the 1930s. Following the removal of Taki Yaoboi, his rivals succeeded in securing the reinstatement of Taki Obili in 1932. Obili remained on the stool until 1944, when he was deposed for a second time on the grounds of physical decline. Despite a return to partial stability with regard to the paramount stool, the British desire for the "political sanitation" of Accra was never realized. By the end of the 1930s, the capital afforded a picture of what one official described as a "crumbling fabric of Native Administration which is hastening towards complete disintegration."[154] Renewed attempts by the reformist Burns administration in the 1940s to prop up the edifice of indirect rule were overtaken by the transformations of the post–World War II world. Popular urban protest was a crucial catalyst for change, the Accra riots of 1948 underlining the pivotal importance of the capital city in the era of nationalism. The 1948 riots and the emergence the following year of Nkrumah's radical nationalism ushered in a new era in the history of Accra.

This takes us back to the trajectory of African urban studies outlined in the Introduction. To reiterate, the identification of the African city as a distinct entity had its origins in the problems posed by the changing urban environment of the 1930s and 1940s. Accelerating urbanization, the first manifestations of organized labor unrest, and the rise of a more explicit anticolonialism were indications that it was in the burgeoning cities that the colonial project in Africa first began to falter. What this social history of early colonial Accra has attempted to demonstrate is that the struggle for the control of African cities neither began in the 1930s, nor was simply contested between colonial rulers and newly urbanized townsmen. As the debates over the meanings of Ga identity in the 1920s show, contested visions of urban civilization shaped by the cultural accretions of the precolonial past predated and in many ways prefigured the contests of the nationalist and postcolonial periods.

NOTES

1. From "Lamentation for Ga," by E. A. Hammond, in the *Gold Coast Independent*, 30 Aug. 1924.

2. Ga maxim, from Zimmermann, *Grammatical sketch*, Vol. 1, 174.

3. Acquah, *Accra survey*, 30–31. Caution is needed with these figures, which are best regarded as an indication of the magnitude of change rather than exact population numbers.

4. See Ross and Telkamp, *Colonial cities*; O'Connor, *The African city*.

5. For the clearest vision of a rapidly modernizing "commercial Accra"—both expatriate and indigenous—see Allister Macmillan (ed.), *The red book of West Africa* (London, 1920, reprinted 1968), 172–212; also Richard R. Brand, "The role of cocoa in the growth and spatial organization of Accra (Ghana) prior to 1921," *African Studies Review*, 15 (1972); and cf. J. W. Brown, "Kumasi 1896–1923: Urban Africa during the early colonial period," Ph.D. thesis, University of Wisconsin, 1972.

6. For the official view of Gold Coast progress by the principal architect of reform, see Frederick Gordon Guggisberg, *The Gold Coast: A review of the events of 1920–1926 and the prospects of 1927–1928* (Accra, 1927).

7. Leeds, *Cities, classes and the social order*, 33.

8. PRO CO 96/244, Griffith to Ripon, No. 92, 3 Apr. 1894.

9. PRO CO 96 files contain extensive documentation, but see conveniently PP June 1909 LXI [Cd.4718] *Report by Professor W. J. Simpson on sanitary matters in various West African colonies and the outbreak of plague in the Gold Coast.*

10. PRO CO 96/470, Rodger to Crewe, No. 326, 1 July 1908, enclosed: Report of the Committee of Public Health. Requests became legally enforced orders in February 1908 with the passing of an Infectious Diseases Ordinance.

11. PRO CO 96/486, Rodger to Crewe, No. 511, 18 Oct. 1909.

12. Ibid.; NAG ADM 11/1/1502, interview between Rodger and Imam Fulata Boronu and others, 9 July 1908. Adabraka is a Hausa word derived from the Arabic *albarka*, "blessing."

13. For the shifting social and political configuration of the Muslim community, see NAG ADM 11/1/1502 [1901-13], ADM 11/1/1448 [1915-26], and ADM 11/1/1446 [1926-30]; also Deborah Pellow, "The power of space in the evolution of an Accra *zongo*," *Ethnohistory*, 38 (1991).

14. PRO CO 96/470, Rodger to Crewe, No. 326, 1 July 1908, enclosed: "Report of Committee of ATC on . . . the opening of Accra."

15. NAG ADM 11/1/1775, interview between Rodger and Kojo Ababio, 13 Aug. 1908.

16. Town planning and sanitation issues are voluminously documented, but see esp. PRO CO 96/571, Clifford to Bonar Law, No. 688, 26 Sept. 1916, enclosed: map of congested areas, and cf. Acquah, *Accra survey*, 41, fig. 6: Ussher Town, 1952. The failure of government aspirations is apparent: the most densely populated sections of Kinka were the same in 1952 as they had been in 1916, and remain so in the 1990s.

17. Patterson, "Health in urban Ghana," 256, see also Field, *Religion and medicine*, 132, on the complex negotiations over the redevelopment of sacred space.

18. For the acrimonious debate within the colonial regime over the issue of racial segregation, see esp. PRO CO 96/528, Clifford to Harcourt, Conf., 8 Mar. 1913, and memorandum by A. Fiddian, CO, 18 Apr. 1913; see also Curtin, "Medical knowledge."

19. See, for example, NAG ADM 11/1/1185, Grunshi elders to SNA, 14 Oct. 1922, on the challenge to the established authority of Gbese *mantse* Ayi Bonte from the Grushi community of Achimota.

20. Dakubu, *Korle meets the sea*, 63–64, citing Esther Akusia Aminarh, "The multi-lingual situation in the central Ashiedu Keteke area," Diploma Long Essay, Language Centre, University of Ghana, Legon, 1992.

21. See Little, *West African urbanization*; for the membership criteria of the ninety-four "tribal associations" in Accra in 1954, see Acquah, *Accra survey*, 104–107. Acquah notes that of those associations existing in 1954 the earliest dates to 1932, but on the formation of the Ewe Foreign Brotherhood Society in 1922, see the *Gold Coast Independent*, 14 Oct. 1922.

22. On the origins of the ARPS and its successful campaign against the Lands Bill, see Kimble, *Political history*, 330–357.

23. *Gold Coast Nation*, 30 May 1912; Kimble, *Political history*, 358–371.

24. *Gold Coast Nation*, 1 May 1913; NAG ADM 11/1/445, J. Blankson Mills to SNA, 30 Dec. 1912.

25. *Gold Coast Nation*, 15 May 1913.

26. Ibid., 29 May 1913 and 19 June 1913.

27. Ibid., 26 June 1913.

28. PRO CO 96/598, Clifford to Milner, Conf., 29 Mar. 1919.

29. NAG ADM 11/1/1089, meeting dd. 26 June 1920; Patterson, *Health in colonial Ghana*, 49; the nutritional disease kwashiorkor was first recognized by Western science in Accra, in 1931–1932: idem, "Health in urban Ghana," 265.

30. NAG ADM 11/1/1515, memorandum dd. 21 March 1921; on rising levels of burglary, PRO CO 96/590, Clifford to Long, No.254, 4 May 1918; and see generally John Iliffe, *The African poor* (Cambridge, 1987), 164–192.

31. Cf. Martin, *Leisure and society*, on Brazzaville.

32. For an analysis of the appropriation of alcohol use by young men as a manifestation of intergenerational struggle, see Akyeampong, *Drink, power and social change*, 47–69.

33. *Gold Coast Independent*, 21 June 1924, "Undesirable women and houses of ill-fame in James Town"; NAG ADM 11/1/1448, SNA to CS, 6 June 1925; see also Rouch, *Migrations au Ghana*, 123–124; cf. Iliffe, *The African poor*, 183–184; and on the *karuwai* of the Hausa *sabo* of Ibadan—often wealthy, independent women—see Cohen, *Custom and politics in urban Africa*, 54–59.

34. John Collins, *Musicmakers of West Africa* (Washington, 1985); idem, *Highlife time* (Accra, 1994); *Gold Coast Independent*, 10 Nov. 1928, "A short history of Gold Coast music."

35. Accra's first ballroom band, the Excelsior Orchestra, was formed in 1914, followed by the Jazz Kings and the Accra Orchestra in the early 1920s: Collins, *Musicmakers*, 2.

36. Collins, *Highlife time*, 42–46. The grandeur of the Hutton-Mills family in c. 1920 is captured in a striking set of portraits in Macmillan, *Red book of West Africa*, 156.

37. On the *osofoiajo*, the lyrics of which were in a Kru dialect, see the *Gold Coast Independent*, 29 Sept. 1928.

38. Ibid., 19 May 1923.

39. *African Times*, 23 Apr. 1869.

40. Ibid., 30 Nov. 1918, "Racing affairs in Accra," and A. W. Kojo Thompson and others to Secretary, Accra Race Committee.

41. Moore and Guggisberg, *We two in West Africa*, 51.

42. PRO CO 96/232, Griffith to Ripon, No. 85, 21 Mar. 1893.

43. *Gold Coast Independent*, 7 July 1923.

44. For an explicit comment on this contrast, see ibid., 3 Aug. 1918.

45. PRO CO 96/692/6581, minute by J. Flood, 10 June 1930.

46. See, for example, Rev. S.R.B. Attoh Ahuma, *The Gold Coast nation and national consciousness* (Liverpool, 1911, reprinted London, 1970), 48–59.

47. On Lagos, see Cole, *Traditional and modern elites*, 120–144; Mba, *Nigerian women mobilized*, 193–233.

48. Roger Gocking, "Indirect rule in the Gold Coast: Competition for office and the invention of tradition," *Canadian Journal of African Studies*, 28 (1994), 434; on this point, cf. Peel, *Ijeshas and Nigerians*, 210.

49. The verbatim transcription of this famous case could not be located. The opening statements and judgment only can be found in NAG ADM 11/1/641, *Tetteh Kwaku v. Kpakpo Brown and twenty-eight others*, 1910.

50. *Jase*, from the Twi *gyase*, was often used for the Ga term *sei he bii* and refers to the "household," or immediate family members and retainers, of an officeholder.

51. NAG ADM 11/1/1087, "Riot in Accra," 5 Mar. 1910.

52. Ibid.; see also NAG ADM 11/1/1088, Taki Obili to Rodger, 3 Mar. 1910.

53. NAG SCT 2/4/50 Div. Court Vol. 39, *Mantse D. P. Hammond v. Mantse Kojo Ababio and another*, 1912, evidence of D. P. Hammond; see further SCT 2/4/52 Vol. 40; SCT 2/6/3 Judgement Record Book Vol. 2, Part 2.

54. Field, *Social organization*, 132; Hill, *Migrant cocoa-farmers*, 225.

55. NAG SCT 2/4/50, *Hammond v. Ababio*, evidence of D. P. Hammond.

56. Field, *Social organization*, 162.

57. NAG SCT 2/4/50, *Hammond v. Ababio*, 1912, evidence of Kojo Ababio IV.

58. Ibid.

59. NAG SCT 2/6/3, *Hammond v. Ababio*, 1912, Judgment by P. Crampton Smyly.

60. NAG SCT 2/4/53 Div. Court Vol. 53, *Mantse Kojo Ababio IV v. T. R. Quartey and Quatie Kojo*, 1913.

61. For the eruptions of spontaneous celebration that greeted judgments, see, from a very pro-Alata perspective, the *Gold Coast Nation*, 13 June 1912, 23 Jan. 1913, and 12 June 1913.

62. NAG SCT 2/4/66 Div. Court Vol. 50; SCT 2/4/67 Vol. 51; SCT 2/4/68 Vol. 52; SCT 2/6/8 Judgement Record Book Vol. 4, *Land for Accra Water Works*, 1918.

63. NAG SCT 2/4/67 Vol. 51.

64. NAG SCT 2/4/68 Vol. 52.

65. See ibid., evidence of Kojo Ababio.

66. NAG ADM 11/1/667, SNA to DC, 19 May 1921.

67. PRO CO 96/543, Clifford to Harcourt, Conf., 24 Mar. 1914, enclosed: Report of Native Affairs Department, by F. Crowther, 27 Jan. 1914; Guggisberg, *The Gold Coast*, 244.

68. *Gold Coast Nation*, 4 Sept. 1913.

69. *Gold Coast Independent*, 13 July 1918; on the rise of the "youngmen," see esp. PRO CO 96/567, Clifford to Bonar Law, Conf., 26 May 1916.

70. Kimble, *Political history*, 469–473; Johnson, "Protest: Tradition and change"; Paul Jenkins (ed.), *Akyem Abuakwa and the politics of the inter-war period in Ghana* (Basel, 1975); Jarle Simensen, "Rural mass action in the context of anti-colonial protest: The *asafo* movement of Akim Abuakwa, Ghana," *Canadian Journal of African Studies*, 8 (1974); Dominic Fortescue, "The Accra crowd, the asafo, and the opposition to the Municipal Corporations Ordinance, 1924–1925," *Canadian Journal of African Studies*, 24 (1990); Beverley Grier, "Contradiction, crisis, and class conflict: The state and capitalist development in Ghana prior to 1948" in I. L. Markovitz (ed.), *Studies in power and class in Africa* (New York, 1987).

71. See Gocking, "Indirect rule," on the dominance of town factions in Cape Coast; and for an Asante case study, Sara Berry, "Unsettled accounts: Stool debts, chieftaincy disputes and the question of Asante constitutionalism," *JAH*, 39 (1998).

72. NAG ADM 11/1/1088, Report on Enquiry into destoolment of Tackie Obili, Ga Mantse, by J. T. Furley, SNA, 21 Oct. 1918 [hereafter 1918 Report].

73. PRO CO 96/593, Clifford to Long, Conf., 3 Oct. 1918.

74. See NAG ADM 11/1/1088, 1918 Report.

75. Parker, "Ga state and society," 316.

76. NAG ADM 11/1/1088, 1918 Report. The oath *Taki Dina* evoked the 1880–1883 exile of Taki Tawia in Elmina (Ga: *Dina*).

77. NAG ADM 11/1/1088, C. B. Nettey, Senior Gbese Asafoatse, Laryea Ayikai, Asere Asafoatse, and Thos. Otoo, Otublohum Asafoatse, to SNA, 12 Aug. 1918.

78. PRO CO 96/408, Nathan to Chamberlain, Conf., 10 June 1903; biographical data are also found in NAG SCT 2/6/13 Judgement Record Book Vol. 9, *Captain C. B. Nettey v. The Gold Coast Independent*, 1928.

79. NAG ADM 11/1/1088, Anum Nunoo to Clifford, 26 Aug. 1918.

80. Ibid., Nana Ofori Atta to Taki Obili, 15 Aug. 1918.

81. On Ofori Atta and Akyem Abuakwa, cf. Richard Rathbone, *Murder and politics in colonial Ghana* (New Haven, 1993), 63–65.

82. NAG ADM 11/1/1088, files "Ga mantse—Illegal imprisonment by" [1916], and "Tackie Obile, Ga mantse—Conduct of" [1918].

83. Ibid., David Quartey, Ga *jasetse*, to SNA, 8 Mar. 1919.

84. Macmillan, *Red book*, 223.

85. NAG ADM 11/1/1089, J. T. Hammond to SNA, 16 July 1923.

86. NAG ADM 11/1/1088, Tetteh Quarcoo to Clifford, 21 Mar. 1919, and Asere, Otublohum, and Sempe *mantsemei* to SNA, 27 June 1921.

87. NAG ADM 11/1/1088, Harper to Ayi Bonte, Gbese *mantse*, 22 Apr. 1919, and Akilagpa Sawyerr to SNA, 30 Apr. 1919, re *Tetteh Kwaku v. Tetteh Quaye*.

88. See Guggisberg, *The Gold Coast*, 120–124, 238–240.

89. On the expansion of cocoa, and Ga participation on the cocoa frontier as migrant farmers and brokers, see Hill, *Migrant-cocoa farmers*.

90. See Macmillan, *Red book of West Africa*, 194–212.

91. Hill, *Migrant cocoa-farmers*, 234–238.

92. NAG ADM 11/1/1778, interview between Guggisberg and *mantsemei*, 29 Nov. 1919.

93. NAG ADM 11/1/1088, Messrs. Thompson, Moir, and Galloway to SNA, 12 Jan. 1920; ADM 11/1/778 Artisans and Labourers, Secretary for Works to SNA, 18 May 1920; Kimble, *Political history*, 44.

94. See Kimble, *Political history*, 102–105.

95. See NAG ADM 11/1/1089, Monthly meeting of *mantsemei* with DC, Sept. 1920, on the hardship caused by high prices for imported foodstuffs.

96. Björn Edsman, *Lawyers in Gold Coast politics c.1900–1945: From Mensah Sarbah to J. B. Danquah* (Uppsala, 1979); see too Samuel S. Quarcoopome, "Political activities in Accra: 1924–1945," M.A. thesis, University of Ghana, 1980; idem, "The politics and nationalism of A. W. Kojo Thompson: 1924–1944," IAS *Research Review*, New Series, 7 (1991); Fortescue, "The Accra crowd."

97. Edsman, *Lawyers*, 97.

98. NAG ADM 11/1/1088, Enquiry into the Action of the Asere Mantse in going to Okai Kwei, by B. Crabbe, DC, n.d. [Sept. 1920] [hereafter Okaikoi Enquiry, 1920]; see too Chapter 1.

99. For a description of the Asere rites at Ayawaso (or Okaikoi) in the 1930s, see Field, *Social organization*, 180. Field, seemingly unaware of the innovation and conflict of 1920, treats the rites as a timeless custom. For an indigenous Asere reading, see NAG CSO 21/10/13 Homowo, "Okaikoi celebration," by E. C. Nunoofio, Secretary of Asere Division, Ga State, n.d. [1950]; and for further descriptive material from the 1960s, Marion Kilson, "Ritual portrait of a Ga medium" in Benetta Jules-Rosette (ed.), *The new religions of Africa* (Norwood, NJ, 1979).

100. NAG ADM 11/1/1088, Okaikoi Enquiry, 1920, evidence of Asere *mantse*; on the creation of the Taki Komewe "stool house," see Chapter 2.

101. Ibid., evidence of Gbese *mantse* Ayi Bonte. Hammond's faith and, more generally, whether practicing Christians should be accepted as *mantsemei*, continued to be issues of considerable weight in Accra: see esp. NAG SCT 2/4/59 Div. Court Vol. 46, *J. R. Meyers v. Abossey Okai*, 1915.

102. Parker, "Cultural politics of death and burial."

103. NAG ADM 11/1/1088, Okaikoi Enquiry, 1920.

104. For vivid descriptions of the processions, see the *Gold Coast Independent*, 30 Aug. 1924, 29 Aug. 1925, and 28 Aug. 1926.

105. See NAG ADM 11/1/923 Asere Yearly Custom.

106. For the cultural and political significance of the precolonial Asante *odwira* and for comparative insights into the historical treatment of ritual festival, see McCaskie, *State and society*, 144–242.

107. *Gold Coast Independent*, 15 Aug 1925, "Homowo So."

108. See esp. ibid., 24 Aug. 1929.

109. NAG ADM 11/1/1054 Lagoons, DC to SNA, 14 Apr. 1920; ADM 11/1/1088, M. Inglis, Public Works Department, to ATC, 18 Aug. 1920.

110. NAG ADM 11/1/1756, Report on enquiry into the alleged destoolment of Tackie Yaoboi, Ga mantse, 1921 [hereafter 1921 Report], 10.

111. For a detailed narrative, see ibid., 10–18.

112. Welman's historical and ethnographic interests were displayed in his founding and editorship of the *Gold Coast Review* in 1925; see esp. C. W. Welman, "James Fort, Accra and the Oyeni fetish," *Gold Coast Review*, 3 (1927).

113. NAG ADM 11/1/1756, 1921 Report, 31; NAG ADM 11/1/1089, Welman to CS, 9 Sept. 1921.

114. See NAG ADM 11/1/1088, D. P. Hammond, T. R. Quartey, and others to SNA, 28 May 1921, protesting *Ga mantse* Taki Yaoboi's membership of the NCBWA.

115. NAG ADM 11/1/1089, DC to SNA, 14 Mar. 1922.

116. NAG ADM 11/1/1089, Taki Yaoboi to SNA, 25 Mar. 1922, and interview between Gbese *mantse* and SNA, 28 Mar. 1922, when Ayi Bonte demanded that steps be taken to recover the *Ga mantse*'s cloth from his assailants to prevent pieces being sewn into Asere *asafo* flags.

117. Field, *Social organization*, 173–175.

118. Ibid., 174.

119. Ibid. Succession to the Asere stool rotated between two houses: Frimponwe (or Teiko Akotia Awosikawe) and Agbonwe (or Teiko Dinwe). Field, ibid., 178–179, adds a third house, which she argues provided Akrama's immediate predecessor Teiko Ansa (c. 1860–1868), but there is strong evidence to suggest that this was manufactured by her Frimponwe informants to facilitate their formal enstoolment of Ayi Ansa in 1930: see esp. file NAG SNA 1166/31 Asere Stool Succession Dispute.

120. Field, *Social organization*, 174; see too NAG SNA 1166/31/7, Judgement of the Ga State Council in the matter of the Asere Stool Dispute, 21 July 1931, evidence of Amos Quartey, 16.

121. Parker, "Ga state and society," 330–332.

122. Circumlocutious hints are found in NAG ADM 11/1/1088, Samuel Addy and others of Atukpai subdivision of Gbese to DC, 3 Feb. 1925.

123. NAG SNA 1166/31/7, Judgement of . . . 21 July 1931, evidence of Amos Quartey, 15.

124. For valuable comparative insights, see Rathbone, *Murder and politics*.

125. NAG ADM 5/3/221 Ga Traditional Council Commission of Enquiry, testimony of Alfred Awuley Clottey, n.d. [1975–1976].

126. On Asere, see *Proceedings of the Government Enquiry on the relative position of the Nikoi Olai Stool of the Djorshie We and the Frempong and Agbon Stool of the Asere Division of the Ga State, 1958*.

127. *Gold Coast Independent*, 26 Jan. 1924, 21 June 1924, and 4 Dec. 1926.

128. PRO CO 96/637, Guggisberg to Devonshire, No. 175, 23 Feb. 1923, enclosure 1.

129. *Gold Coast Independent*, 13 Jan. 1923.

130. For a detailed account of events, see NAG ADM 11/1/1756, Report of the Commission of Enquiry into the alleged destoolment of Ga Mantse Tackie Yaoboi, April 1925; also Fortescue, "The Accra crowd"; Edsman, *Lawyers*, 71–81.

131. NAG ADM 11/1/889, interview dd. 5 Sept. 1924.

132. PRO CO 96/649, Guggisberg to Thomas, No. 746, 12 Sept. 1924.

133. PRO CO 96/656, Maxwell to Amery, No. 611, 28 Aug. 1925, enclosed: *Report on the objections lodged with the Colonial Secretary against the application of the Municipal Corporations Ordinance, 1924, to the Town of Accra*, Sessional Paper No. 1 1925–1926, by H. S. Newlands.

134. Ibid., 15.

135. Ibid., 21, evidence of Akilagpa Sawyerr.

136. See NAG ADM 11/1/1756, 1925 Report, esp. 28–30.

137. NAG ADM 11/1/889, interview between SNA and Committee representing the Mantsemei and Manbii of Accra and Osu, 2 Mar. 1926.

138. For an outline of constitutional reform in the late 1920s, see Kimble, *Political history*, 441–455; Edsman, *Lawyers*, 82–123.

139. See NAG ADM 11/1/925, Tackie Yaoboi to CEP, 14 May 1926.

140. NAG ADM 11/1/1088, DC to SNA, 20 Sept. 1926, quoting Gbese *mantse*.

141. NAG ADM 11/1/925, DC to SNA, 28 Aug. 1926.

142. Kimble, *Political history*, 452.

143. NAG ADM 11/1/1088, "A brief report of the proceedings of the destoolment of Tackie Yaoboi," by C. B. Nettey, 26 Oct. 1926.

144. Ibid., DC to SNA, 28 Oct. 1926.

145. *Gold Coast Independent*, 6 Nov. 1926. Accra's other newspaper, the fortnightly *Vox Populi*, supported the rival camp, but it is unfortunate that the archives contain no copies before 1930.

146. Ibid., 29 Aug. 1925; NAG ADM 11/1/923, Memorandum concerning events in Hansen Road, by H. Newlands, 16 Sept. 1925.

147. *Gold Coast Independent*, 26 Mar. 1927; NAG SCT 2/6/12 Judgement Record Book Vol. 8, *Ayi Ansa and Kojo Ababio*, Mar. 1927.

148. NAG ADM 11/1/1089, SNA to CS, 9 Apr. 1927.

149. Kimble, *Political history*, 490–500.

150. See NAG ADM 11/1/704, "Report on Native Jurisdiction Bill—Accra tribunals," by B. Crabbe, DC, 28 Feb. 1922.

151. NAG ADM 11/1/1089, SNA to CS, 10 Aug. 1928.

152. Ibid., DC to SNA, 7 May 1928.

153. Ibid., "Charges served on Tackie Yaoboi . . . at Kpeshina," 17 Nov. 1928; *Gold Coast Independent*, 23 Feb. 1929 and 11 May 1929.

154. PRO CO 96/757/31165/A, London to MacDonald, No. 747, 13 Nov. 1939, enclosed: Report on the Eastern Province for 1938–39, 23.

CONCLUSION

Jen tamo ka, eya hiehie ni eba sese.
(The world is like a crab, it goes backwards and forwards.)

By the end of the 1920s, Accra was a very different town from that at the beginning of our period in the 1860s. Its built environment had been transformed, its population had tripled from roughly 20,000 to 60,000, and its urban frontier had grown beyond the confines of the old Ga quarters. The three original townships, Kinka, Nleshi, and Osu, had been subsumed into a rapidly expanding colonial port city and administrative capital. The strains of urban growth together with the proximity of the central organs of the colonial state had created challenges for Ga state and society quite different from those facing other African polities on the Gold Coast. In terms of political relationships, the authority of Ga notables had been eroded to a far greater extent than had that of indigenous rulers in the forest states of the interior. As the city grew, the *mantsemei*, the "fathers of the town," lost control of their ability to mediate the terms of settlement for incoming migrants. The indigenous Ga still formed a clear majority of the urban population in 1930, but their predominance was in decline in the face of accelerating migration from the Gold Coast and beyond. "Strangers" were no longer incorporated into the institutions of Ga state and society as in the past. Instead, they sought a new independent niche in the freedom of the town. In short, the precolonial city-state had become a colonial city.

Despite these transformations, much had also endured. What makes Accra so distinctive among the port cities of the West African littoral is that, far from being marginalized by the forces of urban change, indigenous Ga state and society retained much of its institutional integrity and cultural vigor. Accra remained very much an "African" town in character, closer to

Mombasa than to Nairobi or to Lagos than Dakar in terms of urban typology. The aim of this conclusion is to sum up the dynamics of continuity and change in Accra, and to suggest how the story of the making of the town in the early colonial period might contribute to a better understanding of Africa's urban past.

The first point to make concerns the nature of precolonial state and society in Accra—the baseline from which this study begins. Contrary to Field's protofunctionalist vision of the precolonial Ga towns as harmonious, organic communities, I have argued that from the very outset, Accra was a highly contested site of political power. It was also very much a state, albeit of a segmentary nature. In the 1860s, the Ga could look back on nearly two centuries of painstaking demographic and institutional reconstruction after the disaster of the Akwamu conquest. Following the rupture of 1677–1681, centralized political power in Accra emerged only intermittently, as rival local factions, Akan suzerains, and European forts competed for access to mercantile wealth and for control over the urban arena. Nevertheless, Ga notables proved remarkably adept in retaining a stake in the lucrative middleman economy and in the power structures of the Gold Coast. Despite political fragmentation and a compromised sovereignty, the three Accra seaside towns consolidated their position as sites of exchange, wealth, and power. The very things that made Accra a state—organized political, military, legal, and religious institutions—are also the things that made Accra distinctively "urban."

The first half of the nineteenth century saw an evolution in the nature of Accra's middleman role, as Asante overrule gave way to the vague jurisdiction of the three European forts and the slave trade was replaced by "legitimate" commerce. In the entrepôt ports of the Gold Coast, the forces of the Atlantic economy gradually began to dominate those of the African interior. The pace of change accelerated dramatically in the late 1860s and early 1870s, with the formalization of British colonial rule on the Gold Coast. The elevation of Accra to the status of colonial capital marked a major turning point in the town's history. The new colonial dispensation brought a complex mixture of opportunity and threat to the Ga. By the turn of the century, the urban hierarchy of Gold Coast trading towns had shifted decisively in favor of Accra. However, colonial rulers possessed a quite different vision of urban space than the Ga townspeople, and sought to remake Accra in their own fashion.

Change occurred both in Accra's relationship with its hinterland and in the detailed fabric of urban life. For much of the nineteenth century, town leaders had requested a greater commitment from their European trading partners in order to protect and extend commerce. Yet *mantsemei* soon found their roles as political, economic, and legal brokers eroded by an increasingly assertive colonial state. British rulers were particularly eager to "cut out the middleman" in the colonial capital, which was perceived by the colonial mind as a European rather than African domain. The loss of the ability to wage war undermined the position of Ga officeholders, as well as established notions of male civic virtue. The abolition of slavery represented an assault on the concept of wealth in people, triggering a gradual unraveling of established social relations in Accra and its immediate agricultural hinterland. The desire on the part of the British to dispense with the services of local leaders brought an early crisis in 1880, when *Ga mantse* Taki Tawia was arrested and deported to Elmina.

Colonial state building also threatened the position of the literate merchant elite. In contrast with other West African port cities such as Freetown and Lagos, Accra's nineteenth-century elite emerged directly from the indigenous community rather than from groups of liberated "Creole" slaves. Although many were Euro-Africans of Danish, English, and Dutch descent, local affiliations meant that they tended to identify themselves very much as Ga. For a moment in the turbulent transitional period of the late 1860s, the merchant elite did attempt to forge a distinct political identity in the form of the putative Accra Confederacy. This aspiration soon foundered on the new British colonial project and, more importantly, on the strength of established Ga institutions. In other coastal cities, Creoles, Krios, or Saros would come to form a nonindigenous elite that would largely eclipse local notables in political affairs in the early colonial period. In contrast, Euro-African "scholars" remained part of local society and key actors in indigenous town politics.

The expansion of expatriate commerce and rising European racism of the new imperial age spelled the end of the mid-nineteenth-century "age of African merchants" on the West African coast. By the 1890s, local elites were no longer indispensable for the operation of colonial commerce and had been excluded from the upper echelons of the British administration. At the same time, the growth of educational facilities and a widening of employment opportunities began to swell the ranks of Accra's literate community. As an increasingly diverse "petite bourgeoisie" joined the old Victorian merchant class, growing numbers of young men—and some women—sought to carve out a new niche in the colonial town by utilizing literacy and other "modern" skills. Leading scions of established Euro-African and Ga trading families also began to abandon commerce for new professions, in particular law. Local barristers, men such as Thomas Hutton Mills and A. B. Quartey-Papafio, became key mediating figures in Accra's political life, moving with ease between the elite milieu and the Ga quarters.

The way in which Ga society effectively reabsorbed the Euro-African elite points to a fundamental conclusion about the nature of Accra. Despite the urban transformations of the early colonial period, "traditional" social and political relations continued to predominate in the city. The historical literature has tended to view Africa's Atlantic port cities from Dakar to Lagos and on to Luanda and Cape Town essentially as westernized enclaves. In terms of politics, these urban centers are seen as the location of emergent modernizing elites, with rural hinterlands remaining the preserve of more traditionalist indigenous rulers. The picture that emerges of Accra is far more complex. Ga state and society demonstrated a striking resilience in the face of the forces of colonial change. Despite Accra's function as the site of the central mechanisms of imperial order, the British were neither willing nor able to impose the desired degree of control over the old Ga townships that formed the core of the colonial capital. Accra was a colonial city, yet its social history continued to be fashioned largely by its African inhabitants rather than its European overlords. "Town affairs" remained by definition "African affairs."

The emphasis on the resilience of indigenous state and society is not simply to suggest an unchanging continuity of precolonial cultural forms. Urban change reshaped old idioms and gave rise to new social and political voices within the Ga community. For example, the termination of interstate warfare effectively ended Accra's role as a fulcrum of political and military exchanges on the eastern Gold Coast. Nevertheless, the Ga military organization survived, the *asafo* companies continuing to act as vehicles for the mobilization of rising "commoner" or "youngman" aspirations in town affairs. British interventions into the arenas of law, slavery, and ritual affairs had a similar outcome. Old relationships and roles were renegotiated, enabling *mantsemei* and other town notables to retain a significant degree of moral legitimacy. Christianity gradually formed a new moral community, offering an alternative vision of the future. However, rather than effecting a revolutionary overthrow of Ga belief, the new religion joined the mosaic of deities and cult complexes in Accra's competitive sacred space. For the majority of Ga, it was far from clear that the old gods had failed. Indigenous belief continued to dominate the religious life of the early colonial city.

If Ga chiefs and the literate elite alike struggled to maintain a political voice under the new colonial dispensation, the voice of the common townspeople also fought to be heard in the informal settings of Accra's town quarters. It was here that Ga women, "youngmen," and other anonymous faces in the urban crowd struggled to make their own claim in the making of the town. Just as incoming migrants sought freedom and opportunity in urban life, the first decades of the twentieth century was a time of growing assertiveness on the part of a new generation of Ga townsfolk. Yet in this respect too, Ga institutions largely withstood the pressures of social change. Newly literate and aspirant "youngmen" certainly made themselves heard in town affairs, but lines of political tension tended to run down the fissures between established town quarters rather than between those of generation or class.

As colonial rule and urban change generated new anxieties and conflicts, the Ga past itself became a contested political resource. Rising tensions within Accra came to a head in the 1920s, in a series of internecine disputes focused on the possession of traditional public office. Although our sources tend to emphasize outbursts of overt conflict rather than quotidian struggles, it is clear that this was a time of feverish political intrigue in the old town quarters. The centrifugal tendencies that had long characterized the Ga social formation came to the fore, as increasingly bitter chieftaincy contests were prosecuted in the idiom of past relationships. At a time of rapid social change and economic insecurity, political factions sought to utilize history in order to advance contemporary claims to Accra's physical and cultural space.

What is particularly striking about Accra politics in the early colonial period is the salience of contrasting visions of what made the town and how the town had been made. In many ways, these debates within the Ga community prefigure later academic discussions on the nature of the urban and the impact of urbanization in Africa. By the early twentieth century, a fundamental political division had emerged in Ga readings of the making of Accra. Ascribed status based on a combination of original occupation, "true Ga" identity, and sacral knowledge competed with acquired status derived from innovation, outside connections, and the accumulation of wealth and prestige. Town politics—or perhaps better, "the politics of the town"—were shaped by the nuances of an indigenous urban culture stretching back to the seventeenth century. Like the crab, Ga visions of the town looked backward to the past and forward to an uncertain future.

BIBLIOGRAPHY

ARCHIVAL SOURCES

National Archives of Ghana, Accra

ACC 1969/67-75 Ga Native Tribunal, Civil Record Books.

ADM 1/9/1-4 Original Correspondence. Letters from Governor, Gold Coast, to Officials etc. (local).

ADM 1/10 Original Correspondence. Letters (Miscellaneous) from Officials etc. to Governor, Gold Coast.

ADM 1/12/3 Letters from Civil Commandant, Accra, to Colonial Secretary, Cape Coast.

ADM 5/2/1-17 Census Returns.

ADM 5/3 Commissions, Committees, Missions etc.

ADM 8/1 Civil Service Lists.

ADM 11/1 Secretary for Native Affairs Papers.

CSO Papers [unclassified administrative papers from the 1930s].

EC/6/1-20 Basel Mission Papers, Accra.

EC/7/1-48 Papers of Christiansborg Presbyterian Middle Boarding School 1867–1935.

SC 2 Bannerman Papers.

SCT 2/4 Divisional Court, Accra, Civil Record Books.

SCT 2/5 Divisional Court, Accra, Criminal Record Books.

SCT 5/1/46 Letter Book (William Addo) 8.2.1866–15.6.1867.

SCT 17/4 District Court, Accra, Civil Record Books.

SCT 17/5 District Court, Accra, Criminal Record Books.

SCT 2/6 District Court, Accra, Judgement Books.

Land Title Registry, Accra

Registers of Documents, Conveyances and Leases, and Mortgages.

Presbyterian Church of Ghana Archives, Accra

La Baptism Register, Burial Register, and Family Register.

Furley Collection, Balme Library, University of Ghana, Legon

FC N75-84 Dutch Diaries and Correspondence.

Public Record Office, London

CO 96 Gold Coast Original Correspondence.
CO 97 Gold Coast Acts.
CO 98 Gold Coast Sessional Papers.
CO 99 Gold Coast Government Gazettes.
CO 100 Gold Coast Blue Books.
CO 879 Confidential Print: Africa.
PRO 30 Carnarvon Papers.

Royal Commonwealth Society Collection, Cambridge

Papers of Sir John Glover, Files 6–17.

Basel Mission Archive, Basel, Switzerland

D-1 Incoming Correspondence, Gold Coast, 1828–1914.
D-5, 32 Letter Book.
D-10 Miscellaneous manuscripts.
D-31, 3/1-2 Indentures Books.
Paul Jenkins's Abstracts from the Gold Coast Correspondence of the Basel Mission.

Wesleyan Methodist Missionary Archives, School of Oriental and African Studies, London

Synod Minutes, Gold Coast 1842–1910.
Correspondence, Gold Coast 1835–1944.

PUBLISHED GOVERNMENT SOURCES

Great Britain Parliamentary Papers

Ghana

Proceedings of the Government Enquiry on the relative position of the Nikoi Olai Stool of the Djorshie We and the Frempong and Agbon Stool in the Asere Division of the Ga State, 1958, n.d. [1959].

NEWSPAPERS

Accra

West African Herald (Accra, Freetown, and Cape Coast, 1859–1873)
Christian Messenger/SikaNsona Kristofoia Sanegbalo (Accra, 1883–)
Gold Coast Chronicle (Accra, 1890–1902)
Gold Coast Independent (Accra, 1895–1898)
West African Gazette (Accra, 1896)
Gold Coast Free Press (Accra, 1899)
Gold Coast Express (Accra, 1897 and 1899–1900)
Gold Coast Advocate (Accra, 1904–1914)
Gold Coast Independent (Accra, 1918–1948)

Cape Coast

Gold Coast Times (Cape Coast, 1874–1885)
Gold Coast Assize (Cape Coast, 1883–1884)
Gold Coast News (Cape Coast, 1885)
Western Echo (Cape Coast, 1885–1887)
Gold Coast Echo (Cape Coast, 1888)
Gold Coast Methodist/ Times (Cape Coast, 1884–1885 and 1894–1897)
Gold Coast Aborigines (Cape Coast, 1898–1902)
Gold Coast Leader (Cape Coast, 1902–1929)
Gold Coast Nation (Cape Coast, 1912–1920)

London

African Times (London, 1862–1902)

SELECT BIBLIOGRAPHY

Abbreviations used:
JAH: *Journal of African History*
JAS: *Journal of the African Society*
THSG: *Transactions of the Historical Society of Ghana*
IAS: Institute of African Studies, University of Ghana, Legon

Abrams, Philip. "Towns and economic growth: Some theories and problems" in P. Abrams and E. A. Wrigley, eds. *Towns in societies: Essays in economic history and historical sociology*. Cambridge, 1978, 9–33.
Acquah, Ioné. *Accra survey*. London, 1958.
Addo-Aryee Brown, A. "Signs and omens." *Gold Coast Review*, 2 (1926), 285–289.
———. "Historical account of Mohammedanism in the Gold Coast." *Gold Coast Review*, 3 (1927), 195–197.
Addo-Fening, R. "The background to the deportation of King Asafo Agyei and the formation of New Dwaben." *THSG*, 14 (1973), 213–228.

Adjei, Ako. "Mortuary usages of the Ga people of the Gold Coast." *American Anthropologist*, 45 (1943), 84–98.

Agbodeka, F. "The Fanti Confederacy 1865–69: An enquiry into the origins, nature and extent of an early West African protest movement." *THSG*, 7 (1964), 82–123.

Agyemang, Fred. *Christian Messenger centenary 1883–1983*. Accra, n.d. [1983].

Akrong, Abraham. "Integration and adaptation: A case study of La and Osu asafo religious culture." *THSG*, New Series, 2, (1998), 57–70.

Akyeampong, Emmanuel Kwaku. *Drink, power, and cultural change: A social history of alcohol in Ghana, c. 1800 to recent times*. Portsmouth, NH, 1996.

Allman, Jean. "Of 'spinsters,' 'concubines' and 'wicked women': Reflections on gender and social change in colonial Asante." *Gender and History*, 3 (1991), 176–189.

———. "Rounding up spinsters: Gender chaos and unmarried women in colonial Asante." *JAH*, 37 (1996), 195–214.

Allott, A. N. "A note on the Ga law of succession." *Bulletin of the School of Oriental and African Studies*, 15 (1953), 164–169.

———. "Native tribunals in the Gold Coast 1844-1927." *Journal of African Law*, 1 (1957), 163–171.

Amartey, A. A. *Omanye aba*. Accra, 1969.

Ammah, Charles. *Ga Homowo and other Ga-Adangme festivals*. Accra, 1982.

Amenumey, Divine. "Geraldo de Lima: A reappraisal." *THSG*, 9 (1968), 60-72.

Anquandah, J. *Rediscovering Ghana's past*. London and Accra, 1982.

Arhin, Kwame. "Diffuse authority among the coastal Fanti." *Ghana Notes and Queries*, 9 (1966), 66–70.

———. "Peasants in 19th-century Asante." *Current Anthropology*, 24 (1983), 471–480.

———. "The political and military role of Akan women" in Christine Oppong, ed. *Female and male in West Africa*. London, 1983, 91–98.

———. "Rank and class among the Asante and Fante in the nineteenth century." *Africa*, 53 (1983), 2–22.

———. "The Asante praise poems: The ideology of patrimonialism." *Paideuma*, 32 (1986), 163–198.

Attoh Ahuma, Rev. S.R.B. *The Gold Coast nation and national consciousness*. Liverpool, 1911, reprinted London, 1971.

Austen, Ralph A., and Jonathan Derrick. *Middlemen of the Cameroons Rivers: The Duala and their hinterland c. 1600–c. 1960*. Cambridge, 1999.

Austin, Gareth. "Indigenous credit institutions in West Africa, c. 1750–c. 1960" in Gareth Austin and Kaoru Sugihara, eds. *Local suppliers of credit in the Third World, 1750–1960*. London, 1993, 93–159.

———. "Human pawning in Asante, 1800–1950: Markets and coercion, gender and cocoa" in Toyin Falola and Paul E. Lovejoy, eds. *Pawnship in Africa: Debt bondage in historical perspective*. Boulder, 1994, 119–159.

Azu, D. Gladys. *The Ga family and social change*. Leiden, 1974.

Azu, Noa Akunor Aguae. "Adangbe (Adangme) history." *Gold Coast Review*, 2 (1926), 239–270; 3 (1927), 89–116; 4 (1928), 3–30.

Baesjou, R. "Dutch 'irregular' jurisdiction on the nineteenth century Gold Coast." *African Perspectives*, 2 (1979), 21–66.

Banton, Michael. *West African city: A study of tribal life in Freetown*. London, 1957.

Barbot, Jean. *Barbot on Guinea: The writings of Jean Barbot on West Africa 1678–1712*. 2 Vols. ed. by P.E.H. Hair, Adam Jones, and Robin Law. London, 1992.

Barnor, M. A. *A brief explanation of Ga Homowo*. Accra, 1923.

Bartels, F. L. *The roots of Ghana Methodism*. Cambridge, 1965.

Bevin, H. J. "The Gold Coast economy about 1880." *Transactions of the Gold Coast and Togoland Historical Society*, 2 (1956), 73–86.

Bruce-Meyers, J. M. "The origins of the Gãs." *JAS*, 27 (Oct. 1927), 69–76 and (Jan. 1928), 167–173.

———. "The connubial institutions of the Gãs." *JAS*, 30 (Oct. 1931), 399–407.

Christaller, Rev. J. G. *A dictionary of the Asante and Fante language called Tshi (Chwee, Twi)*. Basel, 1881.

Christaller, Rev. J. G., Rev. Ch. W. Locher, and Rev. J. Zimmermann. *A dictionary, English, Tshi (Asante), Akra*. Basel, 1874.

Cohen, Abner. *Custom and politics in urban Africa: A study of Hausa migrants in Yoruba towns*. London, 1969.

Cole, P. D. *Traditional and modern elites in the politics of Lagos*. Cambridge, 1975.

Collins, John. *Musicmakers of West Africa*. Washington, 1985.

———. *Highlife time*. Accra, 1994.

Cooper, Frederick. "The problem of slavery in African culture." *JAH*, 20 (1979), 103–125.

———. "Urban space, industrial time and wage labor in Africa" in F. Cooper, ed. *Struggle for the city: Migrant labor, capital and the state in urban Africa*. Beverly Hills, 1983, 7–50.

Coquery-Vidrovitch, Catherine. "The process of urbanization in Africa (from the origins to the beginning of independence)." *African Studies Review*, 34 (1991), 1–98.

Curtin, Philip D. "Medical knowledge and urban planning in tropical Africa." *American Historical Review*, 90 (1985), 594–613.

Daaku, Kwame Yeboa. *Trade and politics on the Gold Coast 1600–1720*. London, 1970.

Dakubu, M. E. Kropp. "Linguistic prehistory and historical reconstruction: The Ga-Adangme migrations." *THSG*, 13 (1972), 87–111.

———. *Ga-English dictionary*. IAS, Legon, 1973.

———. *One voice: The linguistic culture of an Accra lineage*. Leiden, 1981.

———. "Creating unity: The context of speaking prose and poetry in Ga." *Anthropos*, 82 (1987), 502–527.

———. *Korle meets the sea: A sociolinguistic history of Accra*. New York, 1997.

Daniell, William F. "On the ethnography of Akkrah and Adampé, Gold Coast, Western Africa." *Journal of the Ethnological Society*, 4 (1856), 1–32.

Datta, Ansu. "The Fante *asafo*: A reexamination." *Africa*, 42 (1972), 305–315.

Datta, Ansu K., and R. Porter, "The *asafo* system in historical perspective." *JAH*, 12 (1971), 279–297.

Debrunner, Hans W. *A history of Christianity in Ghana*. Accra, 1967.

Dickson, K. B. *A historical geography of Ghana*. Cambridge, 1969.

Dumett, Raymond E. "The campaign against malaria and the expansion of scientific, medical and sanitary services in British West Africa, 1898–1910." *African Historical Studies*, 1 (1968), 153–197.

———. "The rubber trade of the Gold Coast and Asante in the nineteenth century: African innovation and responsiveness." *JAH*, 12 (1971), 79–101.

———. "African merchants and trader's agents of the major towns of Ghana during the late nineteenth century." *THSG*, 13 (1972), 261–264.

———. "John Sarbah, the elder, and African mercantile entrepreneurship in the Gold Coast in the late nineteenth century." *JAH*, 14 (1973), 653–679.

———. "Pressure groups, bureaucracy and the decision making process: the case of slavery, abolition and colonial expansion in the Gold Coast, 1874." *Journal of Imperial and Commonwealth History*, (1981), 193–215.

———. "African merchants of the Gold Coast, 1860-1905: Dynamics of indigenous entrepreneurship." *Comparative Studies in Society and History*, 25 (1983), 661–693.

——— "Traditional slavery in the Akan region in the nineteenth century: Sources, issues and interpretations" in David Henige and T. C. McCaskie, eds. *West African economic and social history: Studies in memory of Marion Johnson*. Madison, 1990, 7–22.

Dumett, Raymond E., and Marion Johnson. "Britain and the suppression of slavery in the Gold Coast Colony, Ashanti and the Northern Territories" in Suzanne Miers and Richard Roberts, eds. *The end of slavery in Africa*. Madison, 1988, 71–116.

Duncan, John. *Travels in western Africa in 1845 and 1846* 2 Vols. London, 1847.

Edsman, Björn M. *Lawyers in Gold Coast politics c. 1900–1945: From Mensah Sarbah to J. B. Danquah*. Uppsala, 1979.

Ellis, A. B. *The land of fetish*. London, 1883.

———. *The Tshi-speaking peoples of the Gold Coast of West Africa*. London, 1887.

———. *The Ewe-speaking peoples of the Slave Coast of West Africa*. London, 1890.

———. *A history of the Gold Coast of West Africa*. London, 1895.

Engmann, Joyce. "Immortality and the nature of man in Ga thought" in Kwasi Wiredu and Kwame Gyeke, eds. *Person and community: Ghanaian philosophical studies I*. Washington, 1992, 153–190.

Ephson, I. S. *Gallery of Gold Coast celebrities*. Accra, 1969.

Falola, Toyin, and Paul E. Lovejoy, eds. *Pawnship in Africa: Debt bondage in historical perspective*. Boulder, 1994.

Field, M.J. "Gold Coast food." *Petits Propos Culinaires*, 42 (1993 [1931]), 7–21.

———. "The asamanukpai of the Gold Coast." *Man*, 34 (Dec. 1934), 186–189.

———. *Religion and medicine of the Gã people*. London, 1937.

———. *Social organization of the Gã people*. London, 1940.

———. "Some new shrines of the Gold Coast and their significance." *Africa*, 13 (1940), 138–149.

———. "The otutu and hionte of West Africa." *Man*, 43 (1943), 36–37.

———. "Spirit possession in Ghana" in John Beattie and John Middleton, eds. *Spirit mediumship and society in Africa*. London, 1969, 3–13.

Firmin-Sellars, Kathryn. *The transformation of property rights in the Gold Coast: An empirical analysis applying rational choice theory*. Cambridge, 1996.

Fortes, Meyer. *Kinship and the social order: The legacy of Lewis Henry Morgan.* London, 1969.

———. *Oedipus and Job in West African religion.* Cambridge, 1983.

Fortescue, Dominic. "The Accra crowd, the asafo, and the opposition to the Municipal Corporations Ordinance, 1924–25." *Canadian Journal of African Studies*, 24 (1990), 348–375.

Fyfe, Christopher. "Africanus Horton as a constitution-maker." *Journal of Commonwealth and Comparative Politics*, 26 (1988), 173–184.

Gillespie, W. H. *The Gold Coast police 1844–1938.* Accra, 1955.

Gocking, Roger. "Competing systems of inheritance before the British courts of the Gold Coast Colony." *International Journal of African Historical Studies*, 23 (1990), 601–618.

———. "British justice and the Native Tribunals of the southern Gold Coast Colony." *JAH*, 34 (1993), 93–113.

———. "Indirect rule in the Gold Coast: Competition for office and the invention of tradition." *Canadian Journal of African Studies*, 28 (1994), 421–446.

Greene, Sandra E. *Gender, ethnicity, and social change on the Upper Slave Coast: A history of the Anlo-Ewe.* Portsmouth, NH, 1996.

Gugler, Josef. "Urbanization in Africa south of the Sahara: New identities in conflict" in J. Gugler, ed. *The urban transformation of the developing world.* Oxford, 1996, 211–251.

Hansen, Karen Tranberg, ed. *African encounters with domesticity.* New Brunswick, 1992.

Hanson, Rev. A. W. "On the grammatical principles of the Ghã (Accra) language." *Journal of the Ethnological Society*, 4 (1856), 84–97.

Hastings, Adrian. *The Church in Africa 1450–1950.* Oxford, 1994.

Hay, Margaret Jean. "Queens, prostitutes and peasants: Historical perspectives on African women, 1971–1986." *Canadian Journal of African Studies*, 23 (1988), 431–447.

Henty, G. A. *The march to Coomassie.* London, 1874.

Hill, Polly. *The migrant cocoa-farmers of southern Ghana: A study in rural capitalism.* Cambridge, 1963.

Hopkins, A. G. *An economic history of West Africa.* Harlow, 1973.

Horton, James Africanus B. *West African countries and peoples.* London, 1868, reprinted Edinburgh, 1969.

———. *Letters on the political condition of the Gold Coast.* London, 1870, reprinted 1970.

Hunt, Nancy Rose. Introduction to special issue on "Gendered colonialisms in African history." *Gender and History*, 8 (1996), 323–337.

Hutchinson, T. J. *Impressions of Western Africa.* London, 1858.

Hutchison, C. F. *The pen pictures of modern Africans and African celebrities.* London, n.d. [c. 1930].

Iliffe, John. *The African poor: A history.* Cambridge, 1987.

Isert, P. E. *Letters on West Africa and the slave trade: Paul Erdmann Isert's "Journey to Guinea and the Caribbean islands in Columbia" (1788),* trans. and ed. by Selena Axelrod Winsnes. Oxford, 1992.

Jenkins, Paul. "The Anglican Church in Ghana, 1905–1924." *THSG*, 15 (1974), 23–39 and 177–200.

——, ed. *Akyem Abuakwa and the politics of the inter-war period in Ghana.* Basel, 1975.

——, ed. *The recovery of the West African past: African pastors and African history in the nineteenth century: C. C. Reindorf and Samuel Johnson.* Basel, 1998.

Jenkins, Ray. "Impeachable source? On the use of the second edition of Reindorf's *History* as a primary source for the study of Ghanaian history." *History in Africa,* 4 (1977), 123–147 and 5 (1978), 8–99.

——. "Intellectuals, publication outlets and 'past relationships.' Some observations on the emergence of early Gold Coast/Ghanaian historiography in the Cape Coast-Accra-Akropong 'triangle' c. 1880–1917" in P. F. de Moraes Farias and Karin Barber, eds, *Self-assertion and brokerage: Early cultural nationalism in West Africa.* Birmingham, 1990, 68–77.

Johnson, Marion. "Ashanti east of the Volta." *THSG,* 8 (1965), 33–59.

——. "The cowrie currency in West Africa." *JAH,* 11 (1970), 17–49 and 331–353.

——. "Census, map and guesstimates: The past population of the Accra region" in *African Historical Demography.* Edinburgh, 1977, 272–294.

——. "The slaves of Salaga." *JAH,* 27 (1986), 341–362.

Johnson, T. J. "Protest: Tradition and change: An analysis of southern Gold Coast riots, 1890–1920." *Economy and Society,* 1 (1972), 164–193.

Jones, Adam. "'My arse for Akou': A wartime ritual of women on the nineteenth-century Gold Coast." *Cahiers d'Etudes Africaines,* 132, 33 (1993), 545–566.

Jones-Quartey, K.A.B. *History, politics, and early press in Ghana.* Accra, 1975.

Kaplow, Susan B. "The mudfish and the crocodile: Underdevelopment of a West African bourgeoisie." *Science and Society,* 41 (1977), 317–333.

——. "Primitive accumulation and traditional social relations on the nineteenth century Gold Coast." *Canadian Journal of African Studies,* 12 (1978), 19–36.

Kea, Ray A. "Akwamu-Anlo relations, c. 1750–1813." *THSG,* 10 (1969), 29–63.

——. "Firearms and warfare on the Gold and Slave Coasts from the sixteenth to the nineteenth centuries." *JAH,* 12 (1971), 185–213.

——. *Settlements, trade and polities in the seventeenth century Gold Coast.* Baltimore, 1982.

——. "'I am here to plunder on the general road': Bandits and banditry in the pre-nineteenth century Gold Coast" in D. Crummey, ed. *Banditry, rebellion and social protest in Africa.* London, 1986, 109–132.

——. "Plantations and labour in the south-east Gold Coast from the late eighteenth to the mid nineteenth century" in Robin Law, ed. *From slave trade to "legitimate" commerce: The commercial transition in nineteenth-century West Africa.* Cambridge, 1995.

Kilson, Marion, ed. *Excerpts from the diary of Kwaku Niri (alias J.Q. Hammond) 1884–1918.* IAS, Legon, 1967.

——. "The Ga naming rite." *Anthropos* 63/64 (1968–1969), 904–920.

——. *Kpele lala: Ga religious songs and symbols.* Cambridge, MA, 1971.

——. *African urban kinsmen: The Ga of central Accra.* London, 1974.

————. "Ritual portrait of a Ga medium" in Benetta Jules-Rosette, ed. *The new religions of Africa*. Norwood, NJ, 1979, 67–79.

Kimble, David. *A political history of Ghana: The rise of Gold Coast nationalism 1850–1928*. Oxford, 1963.

Klein, Martin A., and Paul E. Lovejoy. "Slavery in West Africa" in Henry A. Gemery and Jan S. Hogendorn, eds. *The uncommon market: Essays in the economic history of the Atlantic slave trade*. New York, 1979, 181–212.

Knight, Franklin W., and Peggy K. Liss, eds. *Atlantic port cities: Economy, culture, and society in the Atlantic world, 1650–1850*. Knoxville, 1991.

Kudadjie, Joshua N. "Aspects of religion and morality in Ghanaian traditional society with particular reference to the Ga-Adangme" in J. M. Assimeng, ed. *Traditional life, culture and literature in Ghana*. New York, 1976, 26–53.

Lartey-Odjidja, E. M. *Paulo Mohenu: The converted fetish-priest*. Accra, 1965.

Law, Robin. *The Slave Coast of West Africa 1550–1750: The impact of the Atlantic slave trade on an African society*. Oxford, 1991.

————. "The historiography of the commercial transition in nineteenth-century West Africa" in Toyin Falola, ed. *African historiography: Essays in honour of Jacob Ade Ajayi*. London, 1993, 91–115.

————, ed. *From slave trade to "legitimate" commerce: The commercial transition in nineteenth-century West Africa*. Cambridge, 1995.

————. "Local amateur scholarship in the construction of Yoruba ethnicity, 1880–1914" in Louise de la Gorgendière, Kenneth King, and Sarah Vaughan, eds. *Ethnicity in Africa: Roots, meanings and implications*. Edinburgh, 1996.

Leeds, Anthony. *Cities, classes and the social order*. Ed. by Roger Sanjek. Ithaca, 1994.

Lever, J. "Mulatto influence on the Gold Coast in the early nineteenth century: Jan Nieser of Elmina." *African Historical Studies*, 3 (1970), 253–261.

Little, Kenneth. *West African urbanization: A study of voluntary associations in social change*. Cambridge, 1965.

————. *African women in towns: An aspect of Africa's social revolution*. Cambridge, 1973.

Lonsdale, John. "European scramble and conquest in African history" in R. Oliver and G. N. Sanderson, eds. *The Cambridge history of Africa Vol.6*. Cambridge, 1985, 680–766.

————. "The moral economy of Mau Mau: Wealth, poverty and civic virtue in Kikuyu political thought" in Bruce Berman and John Lonsdale. *Unhappy valley. Conflict in Kenya and Africa*. London, 1992, 315–504.

Lovejoy, Paul E. *Caravans of kola: The Hausa kola trade, 1700–1900*. Zaria, 1980.

————. *Transformations in slavery: A history of slavery in Africa*. Cambridge, 1983.

————. "The impact of the Atlantic slave trade on Africa: A review of the literature." *JAH*, 30 (1989), 365–394.

Lovejoy, Paul E., and David Richardson. "The initial 'crisis of adaptation': The impact of British abolition on the Atlantic slave trade in West Africa, 1808–1820" in Robin Law, ed. *From slave trade to "legitimate" commerce: The commercial transition in nineteenth-century West Africa*. Cambridge, 1995, 32–56.

Lynn, Martin. *Commerce and economic change in West Africa: The palm oil trade in the nineteenth century.* Cambridge, 1997.

Mabogunje, Akin L. "Urban planning and the post-colonial state in Africa: A research overview." *African Studies Review,* 33 (1990), 121–203.

———. "Overview of research priorities in Africa" in Richard Stren, ed. *Urban research in the developing world. Vol. 2. Africa.* Toronto, 1994, 21–45.

Macmillan, Allister, ed. *The red book of West Africa.* London, 1920.

Maier, D.J.E. "Asante war aims in the 1869 invasion of Ewe" in Enid Schildkrout, ed. *The Golden Stool: Studies of the Asante centre and periphery.* New York, 1987, 232–244.

Mann, Kristin. *Marrying well: Marriage, status and social change among the educated elite in colonial Lagos.* Cambridge, 1985.

———. "The rise of Taiwo Olowo: Law, accumulation, and mobility in early colonial Lagos" in Kristin Mann and Richard Roberts, eds. *Law in colonial Africa.* Portsmouth, NH, 1991, 85–107.

Mann, Kristin, and Richard Roberts, eds. *Law in colonial Africa.* Portsmouth, NH, 1991.

Manning, Patrick. *Slavery and African life: Occidental, Oriental and African slave trades.* Cambridge, 1990.

Manoukian, Madeline. *Akan and Ga-Adangme peoples of the Gold Coast.* London, 1950.

Marshall, P. J. "Eighteenth-century Calcutta" in R. Ross and G. Telkamp, eds. *Colonial cities: Essays on urbanism in a colonial context.* Dordrecht, 1985.

Martin, Phyllis M. *Leisure and society in colonial Brazzaville.* Cambridge, 1995.

Mba, Nina Emma. *Nigerian women mobilized: Women's political activity in southern Nigeria, 1900–1965.* Berkeley, 1982.

McCarthy, M. *Social change and the growth of British power in the Gold Coast: The Fante states, 1807–74.* Lanham, 1983.

McCaskie, T. C. "Accumulation, wealth and belief in Asante history. I. To the close of the nineteenth century." *Africa,* 53 (1983), 23–43.

———. "R. S. Rattray and the construction of Asante history: an appraisal." *History in Africa,* 10 (1983), 187–206.

———. "Komfo Anokye of Asante: meaning, history and philosophy in an African society." *JAH,* 27 (1986), 315–339.

———. "*Konnurokusem*: Kinship and family in the history of the *Oyoko Kokoo* dynasty of Kumase." *JAH,* 36 (1995), 357–389.

———. *State and society in pre-colonial Asante.* Cambridge, 1995.

———. "Asante and Ga: The history of a relationship" in Paul Jenkins, ed. *The recovery of the West African past: African pastors and African history in the nineteenth century: C. C. Reindorf and Samuel Johnson.* Basel, 1998, 135–153.

McSheffrey, Gerald M. "Slavery, indentured servitude, legitimate trade and the impact of abolition in the Gold Coast, 1874–1901: A reappraisal." *JAH,* 24 (1983), 349–368.

Meredith, Henry. *An account of the Gold Coast of Africa with a brief history of the Africa Company.* London, 1812, reprinted 1967.

Metcalf, George. "A microcosm of why Africans sold slaves: Akan consumption patterns in the 1770s." *JAH,* 28 (1987), 377–394.

Metcalfe, G. E., ed. *Great Britain and Ghana: Documents of Ghana history 1807–1957.* London, 1964.

Miers, Suzanne, and Igor Kopytoff. "African 'slavery' as an institution of marginality" in S. Miers and I. Kopytoff, eds. *Slavery in Africa: Historical and anthropological perspectives.* Madison, 1977, 3–81.

Moore, Decima, and F. G. Guggisberg. *We two in West Africa.* London, 1909.

Nketia, J.H.K. "Historical evidence in Ga religious music" in J. Vansina, R. Mauny, and L. V. Thomas, eds. *The historian in tropical Africa.* London, 1964, 265–283.

O'Connor, Anthony. *The African city.* London, 1983.

Odoom, K. O. "A document on pioneers of the Muslim community in Accra." IAS *Research Review*, 7 (1971), 1–31.

Odotei, Irene. "The Ga-Danme" in J. O. Hunwick, ed. *Proceedings of the seminar on Ghanaian historiography and historical research, 20–22 May 1976.* Legon, 1977, 99–112.

———. "What is in a name? The social and historical significance of Ga names." IAS *Research Review*, New Series, 5 (1989), 34–51.

———. "External influences on Ga society and culture." IAS *Research Review*, New Series, 7 (1991), 61–71.

Ozanne, Paul. "Notes on the early historic archaeology of Accra." *THSG*, 6 (1962), 51–70.

———. "Notes on the later prehistory of Accra." *Journal of the Historical Society of Nigeria*, 3 (1964), 3–23.

Parker, John. "*Mankraloi*, merchants and mulattos: Carl Reindorf and the politics of 'race' in early colonial Accra" in Paul Jenkins, ed. *The recovery of the West African past: African pastors and African history in the nineteenth century: C. C. Reindorf and Samuel Johnson.* Basel, 1998, 31–47.

———. "The cultural politics of death and burial in early colonial Accra" in David M. Anderson and Richard Rathbone, eds. *Africa's urban past.* Oxford, 2000, 205–221.

Patterson, K. David. "Health in urban Ghana: The case of Accra 1900–1940." *Social Science and Medicine*, 13B (1979), 251–268.

———. *Health in colonial Ghana: Disease, medicine and socioeconomic change, 1900–1955.* Waltham, 1981.

Peel, J.D.Y. "Urbanization and urban history in West Africa." *JAH*, 21 (1980), 269–277.

———. *Ijeshas and Nigerians: The incorporation of a Yoruba kingdom.* Cambridge, 1983.

———. "History, culture and the comparative method: A West African puzzle" in L. Holy, ed. *Comparative anthropology.* Oxford, 1987, 88–118.

———. "The pastor and the *babalawo*: The interaction of religions in nineteenth-century Yorubaland." *Africa*, 60 (1990), 338–369.

Pellow, Deborah. *Women in Accra: Options for autonomy.* Algonac, MI, 1977.

———. "The power of space in the evolution of an Accra *zongo*." *Ethnohistory*, 28 (1991), 414–450.

Phillips, Anne. *The enigma of colonialism: British policy in West Africa.* London, 1989.

Pogucki, R.J.H. *Gold Coast land tenure. Vol. 3. Land tenure in Ga customary law.* Accra, 1955.

Priestly, Margaret. *West African trade and coast society: A family study.* London, 1969.

Quarcoo, A .K. "The Lakpa—Principal deity of Labadi." IAS *Research Review,* 5 (1967), 2–43.

Quarcoopome, S. S. "The politics and nationalism of A. W. Kojo Thompson: 1924–1944." IAS *Research Review,* New Series, 7 (1991), 11–21.

———. "Urbanisation, land alienation and politics in Accra." IAS *Research Review,* 8 (1992), 40–54.

Quartey-Papafio, A. B. "The law of succession among the Akras or the Gã tribes proper of the Gold Coast." *JAS,* 10 (Oct. 1910), 64–72.

———. "The native tribunals of the Akras of the Gold Coast." *JAS,* 10 (Apr. 1911), 320–330; 10 (July 1911), 434–446; 11 (Oct. 1911), 75–94.

———. "The use of names among the Gãs or Accra people of the Gold Coast." *JAS,* 13 (Jan. 1914), 167–182.

———. "Apprenticeship among the Gãs." *JAS,* 13 (July 1914), 415–422.

———. "The Gã Homowo festival." *JAS,* 19 (Jan. 1920), 126–134; 19 (Apr. 1920), 227–232.

Rathbone, Richard. *Murder and politics in colonial Ghana.* New Haven, 1993.

———. "Defining Akyemfo: The construction of citizenship in Akyem Abuakwa, Ghana, 1700–1939." *Africa,* 66 (1996), 506–525.

Reade, Winwood. *The African sketch-book.* 2 Vols. London, 1873.

Reindorf, Carl D., ed. *Remembering Rev. Carl Reindorf.* Accra, n.d. [1984].

Reindorf, Rev. Carl Christian. *History of the Gold Coast and Asante.* Basel, 1895.

Reynolds, Edward. "The rise and fall of an African merchant class on the Gold Coast 1830–1874." *Cahiers d'Etudes Africaines,* 54 (1974), 353–364.

———. *Trade and economic change on the Gold Coast, 1807–1874.* London, 1974.

Robertson, Claire C. "Post-proclamation slavery in Accra: A female affair?" in Claire C. Robertson and Martin Klein, eds. *Women and slavery in Africa.* Madison, 1983, 220–245.

———. *Sharing the same bowl: A socio-economic history of women and class in Accra, Ghana.* Bloomington, 1984.

———. "Women in the urban economy" in Margaret Jean Hay and Sharon Stichter, eds. *African women south of the Sahara.* 2nd ed. Harlow, 1995, 44–65.

Römer, L. F. *Tilforladelig efterrenning om Kysten Guinea.* Copenhagen, 1760.

———. *The coast of Guinea. Part IV. African history, customs and ways of life,* trans. Kirsten Bertelsen. IAS, Legon, 1965.

———. "On the Negroes' religion in general," trans. Irene Odotei. IAS *Research Review,* New Series, 3 (1987), 112–158.

———. *Le golfe de Guinée 1700–1750: Récit de L .F. Römer, marchand d'esclaves sur la côte ouest-africaine,* trans. Mette Dige-Hesse. Paris, 1989.

Ross, R., and G. Telkamp, eds. *Colonial cities: Essays on urbanism in a colonial context.* Dordrecht, 1985.

Rouch, J. *Migration au Ghana.* Paris, 1956.

Sarbah, J. M. "Maclean and the Gold Coast Judicial Assessors." *JAS,* 9 (Apr. 1910), 249–259.

Sheldon, Kathleen, ed. *Courtyards, markets, city streets: Urban women in Africa.* Boulder, 1996.

Simensen, J. "Rural mass action in the context of anti-colonial protest: The *asafo* movement of Akim Abuakwa, Ghana." *Canadian Journal of African Studies,* 8 (1974), 25–41.

Smith, Noel. *The Presbyterian Church of Ghana, 1835–1960.* Accra, 1966.

Smith, William. *A new voyage to Guinea.* London, 1744.

Southall, Aiden W., ed. *Social change in modern Africa.* London, 1961.

Stanley, Henry M. *Coomassie and Magdala: The story of two British campaigns in Africa.* London, 1874.

Strobel, Margaret. "Women in religious and secular ideology" in Margaret Jean Hay and Sharon Stichter, eds. *African women south of the Sahara.* 2nd ed. Harlow, 1995, 101–118.

Sutton, Inez. "The Volta river salt trade: The survival of an indigenous industry." *JAH,* 22 (1981), 43–61.

Szreszewski, R. *Structural changes in the economy of Ghana 1891–1911.* London, 1965.

Tenkorang, S. "The importance of firearms in the struggle between Ashanti and the coastal states, 1708–1807." *THSG,* 9 (1968), 1–16.

Tilleman, Eric. *En kort og enfoldig beretning om det landskab Guinea og dets beskaffenhed (1697): A short and simple account of the country Guinea and its nature,* trans. and ed. by Selena Axelrod Winsnes. Madison, 1994.

Van Dantzig, Albert, ed. *The Dutch and the Guinea coast 1674–1742: A collection of documents from the General State Archive at the Hague.* Accra, 1978.

Vogt, John. *Portuguese rule on the Gold Coast 1469–1682.* Athens, GA, 1979.

Welman, C. W. "James Fort, Accra and the Oyeni fetish." *Gold Coast Review,* 3 (1927), 73–88.

Wilks, Ivor. "The rise of the Akwamu empire 1650–1710." *THSG,* 3 (1957), 99–136.

———. "Akwamu and Otublohum: An eighteenth century Akan marriage arrangement." *Africa,* 29 (1959), 391–404.

———. *Asante in the nineteenth century: The structure and evolution of a political order.* Cambridge, 1975.

———. *Forests of gold: Essays on the Akan and the kingdom of Asante.* Athens, OH, 1993.

Wilson, Louis E. *The Krobo people of Ghana to 1892: A political and social history.* Athens, OH, 1991.

Yarak, Larry W. "West African coastal slavery in the nineteenth century: The case of the Afro-European slaveowners of Elmina." *Ethnohistory,* 36 (1989), 44–60.

———. *Asante and the Dutch 1744–1873.* Oxford, 1990.

Zimmermann, Rev. J. *A grammatical sketch of the Akra or Gã-language.* 2 Vols. Stuttgart, 1858.

UNPUBLISHED THESES AND PAPERS

Abbey, E.T.A. *Kedzei afo Yordan.* Accra, 1967, trans. by M. E. Kropp Dakubu, "When the river is crossed: Ga death and funeral celebration," typescript, 1971.

Clottey, Victor Mensah. "Music and dance of Oshie ceremony in the Homowo festival among the Gas." Thesis for Diploma in Dance, University of Ghana, 1968.

Gocking, Roger. "The historic Akoto: A social history of Cape Coast 1843–1948." Ph.D. thesis, Stanford University, 1981.

Hugon, Anne. "L'implantation du méthodisme en Côte de l'Or au XIXe siècle: Stratégies de'évangélisation et modalités de diffusion (1835–1874)." Ph.D. thesis, University of Paris, 1995.

Jenkins, Ray. "Gold Coast historians and their pursuit of the Gold Coast pasts, 1882–1917." Ph.D. thesis, University of Birmingham, 1985.

———. "'West Indian' and 'Brazilian' influences in the Gold Coast-Ghana, c. 1807–1914." Unpublished paper presented to the Conference of the Society of Caribbean Studies, 1988.

Kaplow, S. B. "African merchants of the nineteenth century Gold Coast." Ph.D. thesis, University of Columbia, 1971.

Kea, Ray A. "Trade, state formation and warfare on the Gold Coast, 1600–1826." Ph.D. thesis, University of London, 1974.

Parker, John. "Ga state and society in early colonial Accra, 1860s–1920s." Ph.D. thesis, University of London, 1995.

Quarcoopome, Samuel S. "Political activities in Accra 1924–1945." M.A. thesis, University of Ghana, Legon, 1980.

———. "The impact of urbanisation on the socio-political history of the Ga Mashie people of Accra: 1877–1957." Ph.D. thesis, University of Ghana, Legon, 1993.

Quaye, Irene. "The Ga and their neighbours 1600–1742." Ph.D. thesis, University of Ghana, Legon, 1972.

Rivière, Thierry. "Economie et politiques des peuples *ga* d'Accra (Ghana) au XVIIe siècle." Ph.D. thesis, University of Paris, 1994.

Wilks, Ivor. "Akwamu 1650–1750: A study of the rise and fall of a West African empire." M.A. thesis, University of Wales, 1958.

INDEX

Abokobi, 94, 160

Abola quarter, 10–12, 23, 53–54, 82, 156, 165–66, 207, 213

Accra Confederacy, 64–68

Accra plains, 2–9, 31, 143–44, 152 n.147; spread of Christianity to, 160

Accra Town Council, 35, 118, 141, 144–46, 169, 199; attempt to reform, 215, 222–24

Achimota College, 196, 215, 223

Ada, 57–61, 146, 214

Addo, John Glover, 215, 225

Addo, William, 63, 66–67, 75 nn.67, 70, 123, 125

Adultery, 23, 28, 85, 165

Agriculture: constraints of on Accra plains, 2–4, 170; role of slaves in, 7, 33, 91, 93–94, 119, 129, 209; stimulation of by urban growth, 30, 120–21, 165

Akan kingdoms, 2, 4, 128, 206; contrast with Ga, 7, 9, 16, 19, 48, 90, 132, 171, 177, 181, 185–86, 212; cultural influence of in Accra, 9, 16–17, 173, 218; historiography of, xxiv–xxvi; influence of *Ga mantse* over, 23, 56; rule of over Accra, 10, 28–31; use of ritual paraphernalia of in Accra, 12, 14, 18, 22, 175, 191 n.100. *See also* Akuapem; Akwamu; Akyem; Asante; Fante

Akanmaji quarter, 10–12, 18, 163, 175, 198, 206, 226

Akrama (Asere *mantse* c. 1869-1896), 85, 164–66

Akuapem, 2, 19, 31, 47, 56, 57, 69, 97, 157, 180, 182, 186, 211

Akutsei. See Town quarters

Akwamu, 19, 63–64, 68, 184; conquest of Accra by, 6, 9–10, 16–17, 28–29, 31, 38 n.26, 48–49, 216; and Otublohum quarter, 14, 48, 125

Akyem, 10, 29, 31, 69, 102–3, 170, 208, 211–12

Alata quarter (of Nleshi), 12–14, 18, 128–33, 174–77, 198, 205–10, 226

Alcohol: ritual importance of, 21; trade in, 69, 127; use and abuse of, 65, 73 n.18, 100, 130, 133, 202–3

Allotei (Sempe *mantse* 1891–1895), 140, 173

Anege Akwei (Sempe *mantse* 1906–1937), 176, 209–10

Anglican Church, 140, 163, 186

Ankra, Ajaben, 125–28

Ankra family. *See* Dadebanwe

Ankra, Kwaku, 14, 50, 93, 125–26, 164

Anlo Ewe, 58–61, 70

About the Author

JOHN PARKER is a lecturer in African History at the School of Oriental and African Studies, University of London. He is currently conducting research on the history of indigenous shrines in the Upper East Region of Ghana.